A

Lure of the Links

Lure of the Links

Great Golf Stories

AN ANTHOLOGY

EDITED BY

David Owen and Joan Bingham

With an Introduction by David Owen

The Atlantic Monthly Press
New York

Published simultaneously in Canada
Printed in the United States of America
FIRST EDITION

Library of Congress Cataloging-in-Publication Data

Lure of the links : great golf stories : an anthology / edited by
   David Owen and Joan Bingham ; with an introduction by David Owen.
      p.   cm.
   ISBN 0-87113-685-6
   1. Golf—History.   2. Golf stories.   I. Owen, David, 1955–   .
II. Bingham, Joan (Joan Stevens)
GV963.L87   1997
796.352—dc21   97-2979

DESIGN BY LAURA HAMMOND HOUGH

**GOLF
DIGEST**

The Atlantic Monthly Press
841 Broadway
New York NY 10003

10 9 8 7 6 5 4 3 2 1

Contents

II. The Idiosyncratic Nature of Golf

III. Fiction

IV. Covering the Game

Introduction

Many of golf's best moments occur off the course. There are the beers in the grill room when your round is over. There is the midnight inspiration that sends you tiptoeing into the backyard in your pajamas with a pitching wedge and a sleeve of balls. There are the equipment catalogs that make you feel like a kid with an inside track to Santa Claus. There is that first glimpse of Amen Corner on TV each April—official proof that winter is gone. And there is the pile of golf books and magazines that teeters next to your chair, ready to return you to your favorite frame of mind whenever it's too cold, too dark, or too wet to play.

For most of us, golf improves in retrospect. That triple-bogey on seventeen reveals itself, upon reflection, to have been a double-bogey derailed by a spike mark. And if your playing partner hadn't coughed at the top of your backswing on the tee, your drive most likely would have stayed to the left of the water: bogey. And if somebody's dog hadn't dug up the greenside bunker during the night, your sand shot surely would have landed on grass instead of sand, and you'd have had your par. In fact, you once sank a birdie putt from almost as far away. You can still remember every inch of that curling 40-footer, which broke left instead of right but, because you pushed it, tumbled in. And today, but for a handful of flukes, you damn near made birdie again.

Reading about golf provides similar opportunities for genial self-deception. The kinks in your game recede as you imagine the clashes of titans. As always, your enjoyment is heightened by the certainty that if *you* had come to the final nine holes with a lead that big, you wouldn't have let victory slip through your fingers, unlike Palmer. Then a remark of Hogan's reminds you of a grip change your pro recommended last year—a grip change that felt peculiar the one time you tried it, but that might be your ticket (you now see clearly) to the Senior Tour. Then a description of the sixteenth at Cypress Point transports you to the part of your mind where your children are grown, your spouse is merciful, and you have all the money in the world.

On the page, golf is a game you could almost get the hang of. As you read, your slice becomes a gentle draw, and your best shots swell in your memory until they have pushed aside everything else. Sometimes when I've been reading about golf, a feeling starts to build that's like a smoker's yearning for a cigarette. It's a physical longing that, as often as not, leads to anxious glances at the clock. Could I get to the driving range and back before the plumber arrives? Will my editor really care if that article is another day late? Isn't there maybe just enough daylight left for a quick nine holes, if I don't bother changing my shoes?

Best of all, reading about golf is less susceptible than golf itself to the depredations of age. When the yips have stolen our putting strokes, when we can no longer lift our drivers, when even driving a golf cart seems like too much effort, we will still have golf's huge and continually growing library to keep us in the game—even if we have to hire a caddie to read it to us.

In addition to having a literature, golf has a history. More than other sports, golf embodies its past. When fans debate whether Tiger Woods is the next Nicklaus, they do so with knowledge that Nicklaus was once the next Palmer, Palmer the next Hogan, Hogan the next Jones, and so on. Every second shot played on the fifteenth hole at Augusta National is a footnote to the four-wood Gene Sarazen holed in the 1935 Masters; every final-round collapse for the next fifty years will be measured against Greg Norman's in 1996. Each year's assortment of triumphs and disasters becomes a part of every golfer's permanent endowment—even yours and mine.

Golf's history is as powerful as myth. You don't have to play the Old Course at St. Andrews to feel part of an enterprise nine centuries older than Fenway Park. Every golf hole in the world is a tapestry of allusions to other golf holes, and those to others, all the way back to the first rabbit hole down which some bored shepherd knocked a stone with the end of his crook. Four-piece balls, graphite shafts, and melon-sized titanium clubheads may seem to a purist like desecrations, but they don't change anything important about the game. When the crucial moment arrives, you still have to play the shot, just as golfers always have.

Golf has endured and grown over most of a millennium because it goes too deep for us to screw it up. The game gets hold of us because it occasionally lets us visit unmapped regions of our characters without putting us in actual danger. It is a great game because in its best moments it scarcely seems like a game at all, yet it doesn't litter the ground with corpses.

So much has been written about golf that any sampling shorter than the Bible is likely to seem arbitrary. This anthology, like all anthologies, leaves out much more than it contains. Joan Bingham and I, in making our choices, have tried to include our favorite stories, articles, and essays while keeping in mind that *Lure of the Links* is unlikely to be the only golf collection on the reader's bookshelf. We've tried to favor the unfamiliar without entirely ignoring the already celebrated. Inevitably, readers will find stories missing that they wish had been included and stories included that they wish had been left out.

Among my personal favorites here are Henry Longhurst's essay on Jack Nicklaus's decision, in 1961, to turn pro—an essay that should interest anyone who has enjoyed watching Tiger Woods's seemingly instantaneous ascension to ruler of the golf universe; John Updike's short story "Farrell's Caddie," which would guarantee Updike the Nobel Prize if golfers were allowed to vote; Charles Price's intimate and haunting account of the final agony of Bobby Jones; Sarah Ballard's early profile of the young Nancy Lopez, who five years later would remake women's golf in her own image by winning nine tournaments, including five in a row, during her first full season as a pro; Herbert Warren Wind's stately account of one of golf's epochal showdowns, the "Duel in the Sun" between Jack Nicklaus and Tom Watson, at Turnberry in 1977; and Peter Dobereiner's funny, sad story about Joe Ezar.

What I like most about these stories and all the others in this book is that they enlarge the stage on which I imagine I wage my own struggle with this game. Golf is a deeply communal activity, even if you play it alone. As you reexperience it through the words of these writers, you realize that when you are on a golf course you are always in excellent company.

I.

The Players

Francis Ouimet—
Drama at Brookline

Will Grimsley

In the nineteenth century, it was the custom of Boston gentlemen to take weekend rides on horseback to the country. They usually stopped at a friend's estate or an inn for a respite before starting the long homeward trek.

A few of the riders decided it would be desirable to set up a private stopping place where sportsmen might relax, refresh themselves, and indulge in recreational activities. In 1860, seventy men proposed the establishment of a club. Outbreak of the Civil War thwarted the idea and the play was shelved until 1882, when The Country Club was organized.

The original invitation to prospective members was that the project should include a comfortable club house, restaurant, bowling alley, lawn tennis courts, and a track for race meetings. Golf was not mentioned by the founders. Nevertheless, a six-hole course was laid out in 1893. This layout, hewn out of a forest over a natural rolling terrain, ultimately was expanded to include twenty-seven holes divided into nines named Clyde, Squirrel, and Primrose.

From these rudimentary roots grew The Country Club of Brookline, Massachusetts—proudly retaining the capital "T," since it considered itself the first such club of its kind—destined to become an historic landmark in American golf.

If the Royal and Ancient Club of St. Andrews is the birthplace of British golf, then The Country Club at Brookline cannot be denied as the spot where the sport in the United States, while not actually born, got its great awakening.

Until 1913, when the annual U.S. Open Golf Championship was assigned to The Country Club, golf in America was considered a snobbish, panty-waist pastime indulged in only by the elderly and the idle rich. The best players were mainly English and Scottish. When the overseas stars consented to play in an American tournament, it was not a question of whether a Briton would win but rather which one.

So it was in September 1913. The dates of the U.S. Open were changed to permit the participation of the two great British professionals Harry Vardon and Ted Ray. The field included other notables, such as England's Wilfred Reid, France's Louis Tellier, and such rising American pros as Johnny McDermott, Mike Brady, and Tommy McNamara, but none figured to match strokes with Vardon and Ray.

Vardon was the stylist, a man of fluid grace and power—a picture golfer with the sensitive touch of a safe-cracker around the greens. Ray was a hulking two-hundred-pounder who cared little for form but who threw all his tremendous strength into his shots. He was the longest hitter of his day, the reigning British Open champion at the time. Vardon won five British Opens.

The least of American threats to this mighty one-two punch of British—a hundred-to-one shot by modern betting standards—was the frail, twenty-year-old gardener's son who lived across the road from The Country Club and who learned the game by toting clubs at twenty-eight cents a round. His name was Francis Ouimet. His father, an immigrant French-Canadian, did not understand golf and thought it a waste of time. His mother thought it was too strenuous for her thin, hollow-cheeked son.

After the first thirty-six holes of the seventy-two-hole medal play competition, it was no surprise to find Vardon and another Englishman, Reid, out front at 147. Ray, exploring the course's underbrush with his wild, booming drives, was two shots back, followed by MacDonald Smith and Jim Barnes, a pair of transplanted Scotsmen. Nobody paid much attention to Ouimet and another twenty-year-old youngster from Rochester, Walter Hagen, who were tied at 151.

At the end of the third round, Vardon and Ray were out front as expected but they had strange and unanticipated company. Young

Ouimet, the ex-caddie, had shot a creditable 74 over the rain-drenched course and had moved into a fifty-four-hole tie with the two British stars at 225. Excitement ran high at The Country Club but no one dared let hopes soar out of bounds. The neighborhood kid could not be expected to pull off such a miracle, Brookliners said.

Ray came slogging in with a final round 79 for 304. Shortly afterward, Vardon, his usually reliable putter gone sour, came home with a matching 79 for a two-way tie. The threats of Mac Smith, Barnes and Hagen drowned, one after another, on the soggy old course and only Ouimet was left with a chance—a faint one—to overtake the leaders.

Francis, showing no sign of tension although he acknowledged later that his nerves were strumming like guitar strings inside, came to the thirteenth hole needing two birdies on the final six holes to gain a tie. He was walking a tightrope. A bogey—a stroke over par—would certainly cook his goose.

A deafening roar went up when Ouimet chipped in from off the green to get a birdie at the thirteenth. Now he needed only one more birdie. He parred the long fourteenth and scrambled to stay even at the fifteenth and sixteenth. Two holes to play. At the dogleg seventeenth, Ouimet hit a good drive and put his approach twenty feet past the pin. It was a tough sidehill putt but Francis gave the ball a solid whack and the ball, as if guided by some unseen hand of destiny, rolled into the cup. The crowd's guarded optimism suddenly exploded into wild pandemonium. Ouimet needed only a par 4 on the final hole to tie.

A picture of cool determination, the Ouimet boy hit a good drive into the fairway, sent his approach to the front of the green and chipped five feet short of the cup. History was riding on the next stroke—a difficult putt surrounded by tones of pressure—but the reed-thin youngster in the checkered cap never wavered. He gave the line a quick, cursory look, strode up to the ball and knocked it into the back of the cup. He had tied Vardon and Ray for the Open championship.

It seems reasonable to assume that a young, fuzz-faced kid, going out the next day to face two of the world's greatest golfers, might spend the evening tossing in sleeplessness and munching nervously on his fingernails. Not Ouimet. He recalled that he went to bed early, slept well, and awoke the following morning to find rain beating against his window pane.

Although he may not have been gripped by tension, he nevertheless was not unaware of the importance of the occasion. "I realized I was just an amateur," he recalled later. "I played golf for fun. I considered professionals as something like magicians who had an answer for everything. I felt I was in the play-off by mistake."

Ouimet arrived at the first tee of The Country Club, accompanied by his ten-year-old caddy, Eddie Lowery, who played hooky from school to carry Francis' clubs. Lowery, later a successful San Francisco automobile dealer, sponsor of such well-known golfers as Ken Venturi and Harvie Ward and an official of the U.S. Golf Association, related years afterward that his principal duty, in addition to lugging Ouimet's cheap canvas bag, was to keep his client on a level psychological keel by reciting fixed lines. Before each of Ouimet's shots, the half-pint caddy in the white sailor hat was to mutter: "Take your time—you've got all day" and "Keep your eye on the ball."

Ouimet said he got himself into a perfect frame of mind. He decided to concentrate on each shot, play it for all it was worth, and then forget it—good, bad, or indifferent. "It was a wonderful mood to get into," he said. "I was numb."

The numbness appeared to be transferred to the tense, breathless crowd as the play-off match went to the nine-hole turn, still all square. The first important break came at the tenth, where Vardon and Ray both three-putted and Ouimet got down in par 3 on the 140-yard hole.

It was here that the intense pressure must have begun to seize the two visiting giants of the links, while falling off the bony shoulders of the former Brookline caddy. Both Vardon and Ray must have been haunted by the question: "What if I should lose to this strip of a youngster?"

At the fifteenth, the long, over-the-hill hole, the big, mustachioed Ray hit a spectator's derby with his drive, pitched into a bunker, took two blasts to get out and wound up with a double-bogey 6. This put him four shots back of Ouimet and three behind Vardon. At the dog-leg seventeenth, Vardon hooked his drive into the thick, knotty rough, played into the fairway and used his third shot to reach the green, two-putting for a 5. Ouimet, inspired by this opening, knocked in an eighteen-foot putt for a birdie 3. Now he had a three-stroke lead.

This disastrous turn shook the great Vardon. On the final hole, he blew a double bogey 6 and it did not matter that Ray, completely out of the picture, rallied with a birdie 3. Seemingly poised and unshakeable, young Ouimet laced his drive up the middle, hit his second to the green eighteen feet from the pin, and sent his approach putt to within four feet.

As Ouimet confidently measured the final putt, he looked a picture of tremendous calm to the tense gallery, but he recalled later: "For the first time, I thought about the championship. I couldn't get my breath. The green began heaving beneath me. I couldn't even see the hole."

He putted. The ball hit the back of the cup. Francis Ouimet was the new Open golf champion of the United States. He had fired an amazing 1-over-par 72 under the most trying of conditions and had won a play-off from two of the game's greatest stars. Vardon finished with a 77, Ray 78.

The hilarity at The Country Club over the neighborhood boy's historic triumph swept like wildfire throughout the rest of the country and abroad. The story was front-paged in the nation's newspapers and talked about on streetcorners, in clubs, in drugstores and in drawing rooms. Ouimet became an overnight national hero. Golf emerged as a game for the common man. Its popularity boomed.

An English journalist caught the spirit of the event when he wrote: "There will never be another like it. When we are old men, little golfing children will ask us to tell them again the romantic story of the twentieth of September in 1913."

There was nothing in Ouimet's modest beginning to indicate that he some day would be one of the immortals of American golf.

Francis was born May 8, 1893, in an outlying, thinly populated area of Brookline, a Boston suburb. While he was in grade school, his father moved the family to a house across the street from The Country Club, one of the most exclusive if not the poshest on the Eastern coast. He was eleven when he followed his older brother, Wilfred, into the club's caddy ranks. The rules strictly forbade caddies to play on the course, but Francis and Wilfred often sneaked in some stolen practice shots when the pro, Alex Campbell, was not looking.

The younger Ouimet quickly became infatuated with the sport. He acquired an old mashie and later a brassie in exchange for balls which he had found on the course. Frequently he would get up at five o'clock in the morning and sneak out on the course for some practice until he was chased by the greens-keepers. On weekends, he and friends would spend all day at a public nine-hole course at Franklin Park.

Francis worked in a dry-goods store to get enough money to pay entrance fees in tournaments. In 1910, at the age of seventeen, he tried to qualify for the National Amateur, scheduled at The Country Club, and failed. He tried the National Amateur again—without success—in 1911 and 1912, but he went to the finals in the Massachusetts State Amateur in 1912 and won it in 1913. In 1913 also, after winning the Open, he qualified for the first time for the National Amateur and went to the semifinals before losing to Jerry Travers.

Ouimet won the first of his two National Amateur crowns in 1914 at Manchester, Vermont, beating Jerry Travers in the final, 6 and 5, and that same year captured his first international title—the French Amateur. There was a seventeen-year victory drought before the tall, angular Bostonian crashed through to his second Amateur championship by defeating Jack Westland, 6 and 5, at Chicago in 1931.

During this long, lean period, Ouimet qualified for the U.S. Amateur tournament thirteen times. He reached the semifinals six times and finals once. In three of the semifinals—1924, 1926, and 1927—he bowed to Bob Jones, whom he called "the greatest golfer who ever lived." Chick Evans beat him in the last round of the 1920 Amateur at Roslyn, Long Island, 7 and 6.

He remained the true amateur, playing the game for fun and never letting it take a dominant role in his life. As a result, he never was able to add a second Open victory. After finishing fifth in 1914, he did not make another strong bid until 1925 when he finished in a second-place tie with Johnny Farrell, a stroke behind Jones and Willie MacFarlane.

Ouimet played in more Walker Cup matches than any other man. He served with the United States' international team as an active competitor from 1922 (when the series with Britain was launched) through 1934. In 1936, he took over the role as nonplaying captain and held this post until 1949, when he asked to be relieved.

On May 1, 1951, Ouimet was accorded the highest honor Britain can bestow upon a personality in connection with golf. He was elected captain of the Royal and Ancient Golf Club of St. Andrews in Scotland. Bedecked in a red coat, he played himself "in" by striking the ball off the first tee at the famous old links where the game is supposed to have been born.

He was the first non-Briton elected to the post. The Duke of Windsor in 1922 and the King of England in 1930 had been among the previous St. Andrews captains.

A scholarly, soft-spoken man, Ouimet epitomized the ideals of amateur golf set up by the U.S. Golf Association. Richard S. Tufts, former president of the U.S. Golf Association, said of him: "A thorough sportsman, modest, always considerate, a true amateur with the highest personal standards, he has always been devoted to the best interests of golf." One of his pet projects was the Francis Ouimet Caddy Scholarship Fund, providing caddies with funds for a college education.

Friends like to relate this story as an example of Francis Ouimet's extreme modesty:

After his victory in the National Open in 1913, Francis was approached by a seventy-year-old Brookline golf enthusiast, who said, "Well, Francis, now that you've won the championship, I don't suppose you'll find time to play with me any more."

"What are you doing next Tuesday afternoon?" young Ouimet asked.

—1966

My Favorite Caddy

Gene Sarazen

The story of the 1932 British Open actually begins in 1928 when I made a crossing to Europe with Walter Hagen. One evening during our voyage we were having a drink in the smoking room of the *Berengaria*, waiting for the auction pool to begin, when our conversation turned to the approaching British Open. "That is one title I want on my books, Walter," I confided to the man who had won that championship in 1922 and 1924. "I've invested thousands of dollars coming over and I'll probably go right on doing it until I win that title or get too old to play. If there's any one thing I want to accomplish in golf, it's to win the British Open."

Walter smiled at my earnestness. "Gene, you can never win the British Open," he replied, "unless you have a caddy like the ones I've had." He tested the new pinch of Scotch that the waiter had set before him. "Now, Gene, I'll tell you what I'll do. I've won the British Open a couple of times, so winning it doesn't mean as much to me as it obviously means to you. I'll loan you my caddy, Skip Daniels. He's an old fellow, caddies only in the county of Kent, just at Sandwich, Deal, and Prince's, no other courses. He's very particular about the men he caddies for. It's got to be someone special, like the Prince of Wales or Walter Hagen. Skip expects to caddy for me at Sandwich this year, but I think I can arrange it with him to caddy for you instead. One thing more. He's a very expensive caddy. He'll cost you at least thirty or forty pounds."

"The price, you know, Walter, is incidental," I said, "if he can bring me in a winner."

Hagen went into a few details on Daniels' personality and his infallible judgment in the 1922 Open. I felt great. I knew how important a caddy can be in winning any championship, especially on a foreign course.

I arrived at Sandwich early and asked the caddymaster for Daniels. "I'm afraid you can't have Skip," the caddymaster replied. "He's Walter Hagen's caddy." I told him that Hagen had agreed to loan me Skip for the Open, but no assignment was made until the caddymaster had checked with Hagen personally. Then he took me over and introduced me to Daniels near the pro shop. Daniels tipped his cap, and if he felt heartbroken at learning that he wouldn't be working with Hagen, he didn't show it. He was an old boy, all right, around sixty or sixty-one, old even for a professional British caddy. He wore a weather-beaten cap, an old celluloid collar, and a black oxford suit that had never been pressed in its lifetime. I think I fell in love with him at first sight.

Daniels had a wonderful effect on me during the ten days of intensive practice we put in. He had an enthusiasm I had rarely observed in caddies a third his age. He limped slightly, but after I had hit out a batch of balls, he would trot down the practice ground to retrieve them and then trot back. He knew instinctively how to inspire his man with confidence. "I've never seen Hagen hit the shots as well as you're hitting them, sir," he would say after an afternoon's workout. He did much more than carry his player's bag. He could just about tell you what you were doing wrong with a shot, and he'd tell it to you in a very nice way. In the evenings after dinner we would stroll out on the course with a putter and a dozen balls, and practice on the various greens. Daniels would point out the places he had patrolled against enemy invasion during the war. He knew every blade of grass along that stretch of the Kentish coast. He had lived in the bunkers and knew them like home.

Daniels and I had become very close friends by the eve of the championship. I made up my mind that I would follow his advice at all times. I knew I couldn't go wrong. He kept buoying my confidence with his own genuine confidence in my ability to win. I remember his final pep-talk: "I've watched Walter practicing, sir. He's recovering very well but he's not hitting the ball like you are. We should have no trouble beating him, and he's the man to beat."

Daniels and I played a heady first round of 72. We were moving at the same sanguine pace on the second day, when I pulled my drive on the fourteenth into the rough. This fourteenth hole, a par 5, is called Suez Canal because of the deep ditch that traverses the fairway some seventy yards or so before the green. I looked over my lie in the rough, took in the distance to the Canal, and concluded that I could carry it if I cracked a good wood out of the rough. Daniels shook his head. He tapped the blade of the mashie with his finger. "But, Dan, if I can get a birdie here," I explained, "I can beat Jurado and lead the field. I want to make those headlines." "This is no time to lead the field," Dan answered. "Tomorrow night is when you want to be in front, sir." "No, I'm going for it, Dan," I said stubbornly, and yanked my spoon out of the bag. I dug my spikes in and swatted the ball hard with my spoon. The tall, thick rough snuffed the ball out before it got started, and it squished only twenty yards nearer the hole, still in the rough. I tramped up to the ball. Giving Daniels no chance to cool me off, I lashed out quickly with my spoon again. I got the ball out this time, but that was about all. I finally ended up with a 7 on the hole. I could see from Dan's eyes that he was heartbroken. I had disregarded his advice to play a mashie from the rough safely short of the Canal, and follow it with an easy pitch to the green that would have given me a putt for my 4 and a sure 5. Dan tried to cheer me up as we started down the fifteenth—"We can make that up, Mr. Sarazen"—but I knew those were hollow words, and what he was really saying to himself was, "That's why Hagen beats this fellow."

Dan got me settled down and I finished the round in 76. He kept me going the following day. A 73 on the third round put me only one stroke behind the leader, Hagen. I felt confident at the luncheon interval between the third and final rounds that I was playing well enough to overtake Walter. In my room at the Guilford Hotel, I went over an acceptance speech with John Ford, the motion picture director, since the Prince of Wales was to present the cup to the winner, and I didn't know the proper etiquette for responding. Hagen went out on his final round about an hour and a half before I teed off. I made the turn in 36 and was walking down the twelfth when I saw a sleek limousine drive up with the Prince of Wales in the back seat. Hagen, wrapped in his polo coat with the huge mother-of-pearl buttons, lounged beside the Prince. They had come out to watch me finish. According to Daniels, whom I asked to get the dope, I was Hagen's last serious challenger. Walter had visited at least seven traps on his last round and had still scored a 72. I stayed with regulation figures until I reached the sixty-ninth, but when I slipped a stroke over par on that hole, Walter had his third British Open safely tucked away.

The difference between our totals, 292 and 294, was due to my boneheaded refusal to heed Daniels' advice on the Suez Canal. I admitted this to Dan in so many words as we said good-bye after the presentation ceremony. There were tears in Dan's eyes when he answered, "We'll try it again, sir, won't we? Before I die, I'm going to win an Open Championship for you."

In 1932 the British Open was scheduled to be held on the links of the Prince's Club in Sandwich, right next door to the Royal St. George course where I had lost and Hagen had won in 1928. Daniels would be available at Prince's if I decided to take another crack at the British Open, but I wasn't so certain I cared to knock my brains out any more trying to win that ornery championship. I had failed at Muirfield in 1929, and in 1931 at Carnoustie, where I had played pretty fair golf, I again trailed the winner, Tommy Armour, by two strokes. There were other considerations. Money was scarce in 1932 and getting scarcer, and I was in no mood to squander away the bank account I had slowly been able to build up through my labors on the winter circuit.

It was Mary who decided that I should go over for the British Open. One evening that spring, after I had returned from Lakeville— I had changed my club affiliation from Fresh Meadow to Lakeville in 1931—Mary sat me down in our living room and assumed her best I-am-talking-business-so-be-prepared-to-take-me-seriously voice. "Gene, I don't believe that I've ever seen you playing better than you are right now," she said, starting out on a very good foot. "I know how hard you've been working on keeping in condition, running up and down the fronthall steps, swinging that heavy club, morning, noon, and night, cutting yourself down to one cigar a day. Now don't interrupt me, Gene. Last week I was talking with Tom and Frances Meighan and they agree with me that your golf is better than it ever was and that you ought to play in the British Open."

"That's all very well and good," I answered "but what about the financial side of such a trip? This isn't any time to throw away a couple of thousand, Mary. It would cost me just about that to cover all my expenses. I don't see it."

"I've given that a lot of thought, too," Mary said. "I decided it would be a good investment, everything considered." She stopped for a moment and felt me out with a smile. "Now, Gene, I've got your tickets and your hotel reservations all taken care of. The only thing you have to do is get your passport fixed up. You're sailing a week from tomorrow on the *Bremen*."

I had a smooth crossing, and an enjoyable one, thanks to the lively company of Fred Astaire. In London the first man I ran into at the Savoy was Roxy, a crony from Lakeville and a fanatic golf fan. Roxy was going to play at Stoke Poges the next day and persuaded me to come along.

When we arrived at Stoke Poges, a young caddy—he was about twenty-seven, a stripling among British caddies—grabbed my bag. We whistled around the course in 67. "I'm going to caddy for you in the Open," the young man informed me when the round was over. "I know just the type of caddy you need, Mr. Sarazen."

My mind flashed back to Daniels. "You're a very smart caddie," I told the aggressive young man. "But I've already got a caddie for the Open. Skip Daniels."

"Oh, I know Daniels. He must be around sixty-five now."

"Just about," I replied.

"He's too old to carry this bag," the young caddy continued. "His eyesight is gone. On top of that I've heard that he's been ill. Why don't you let me caddy for you at Prince's? I don't want to run Daniels down, but you'd ruin your chances if you took him on. The way you played today, you can't miss."

He had something there. That 67 had been as solid a round as I had ever played in England. If I could keep that up, no one would touch me in the Open.

I told the young man to meet me at Prince's.

After a few days in London, I went down to Prince's to practice. The first person I met, right at the gate, was Daniels. He was overjoyed to see me. While we were exchanging news about each other, I could see that the last four years had taken a severe toll of him. He had become a very old man. His speech was slower. That shaggy mustache of his was much grayer, his limp was much more obvious. And his eyes, they didn't look good.

"Where's your bag, sir?" Daniels asked, hopping as spryly as he could toward the back seat of my auto.

"Dan," I said—I couldn't put it off any longer though I almost didn't have the heart to say it, "Dan, this bag is too heavy for you. I know you've been in bad health, and I wouldn't want you to try and go seventy-two holes with it."

Dan straightened up. "Righto, sir, if you feel that way about it." There was great dignity in the way he spoke, but you couldn't miss the threads of emotion in his voice.

"I'm sorry, Dan," I said, and walked away. I had dreaded the thought of having to turn old Dan down, but I had never imagined that the scene would leave me reproaching myself as the biggest heel in the world. I attempted to justify what I had done by reminding myself that business was business and I couldn't afford to let personal feelings interfere with my determination to win the British Open. It didn't help much.

I was a hot favorite to win. The American golf writers thought that I had a much better chance than Armour, the defending champion, and the veteran Mac Smith, the other name entry from the States. George Trevor of the *New York Sun*, for example, expressed the belief that "Prince's course, a seven-thousand-yard colossus, will suit

Sarazen to a tee, if you will pardon the pun. It flatters his strong
points—powerful driving and long iron second shots." The English
experts were likewise strong for me until, during the week of practice, they saw my game decline and fall apart. The young caddy from
Stoke Poges did not suit me at all. I was training for this championship like a prizefighter, swinging the heavy club, doing roadwork in
the morning, practicing in weather that drove the other contenders
indoors. My nerves were taut and I was in no mood to be condescended
to by my caddy. He would never talk a shot over with me, just pull a
club out of the bag as if he were above making a mistake. When I'd
find myself ten yards short of the green after playing the club he had
selected, he'd counter my criticism that he had underclubbed me by
declaring dogmatically, "I don't think you hit that shot well." I began
getting panicky as the tournament drew closer and my slump grew
deeper. I stayed on the practice fairway until my hands hurt.

Something was also hurting inside. I saw Daniels in the galleries
during the tune-up week. He had refused to caddy for any other golfer.
He'd switch his eyes away from mine whenever our glances met, and
shuffle off to watch Mac Smith or some other challenger. I continued, for my part, to play with increasing looseness and petulance. The
qualifying round was only two days off when Lord Innis-Kerr came
to my hotel room in the evening on a surprise visit. "Sarazen, I have
a message for you," Innis-Kerr said, with a certain nervous formality.
"I was talking with Skip Daniels today. He's heartbroken, you know.
It's clear to him, as it's clear to all your friends, that you're not getting along with your caddy. Daniels thinks he can straighten you out
before the bell rings."

I told his Lordship that I'd been thinking along the same lines
myself. Daniels could very well be the solution.

"If it's all right with you, Sarazen," Lord Innis-Kerr said as he
walked to the door, "I'll call Sam the caddymaster and instruct him
to have Daniels meet you here at the hotel tomorrow morning. What
time do you want him?"

"Have him here at seven o'clock. . . . And thanks, very much."

Dan was on the steps of the hotel waiting for me the next morning. We shook hands and smiled at each other. "I am so glad we're

going to be together," old Dan said. "I've been watching you ever since you arrived and I know you've been having a difficult time with that boy." We walked to the course, a mile away. Sam the caddy-master greeted me heartily and told me how pleased everybody was that I had taken Daniels back. "We were really worried about him, Mr. Sarazen," Sam said. "He's been mooning around for days. This morning he looks ten years younger."

Dan and I went to work. It was miraculous how my game responded to his handling. On our first round I began to hit the ball again, just like that. I broke par as Dan nursed me through our afternoon round. We spent the hour before dinner practicing. "My, but you've improved a lot since 1928!" Dan told me as he replaced my clubs in the bag. "You're much straighter, sir. You're always on line now. And I noticed this afternoon that you're much more confident than you used to be recovering from bunkers. You have that shot conquered now." After dinner I met Dan by the first tee and we went out for some putting practice.

The next day, the final day of preparation, we followed the same pattern of practice. I listened closely to Dan as he showed me how I should play certain holes. "You see this hole, sir," he said when we came to the eighth, "it can be the most tragic hole on the course." I could understand that. It was only 453 yards long, short as par 5s go, but the fairway sloped downhill out by the 200-yard mark, and 80 yards before the green, rising 25 to 35 feet high, straddling the fairway and hiding the green, loomed a massive chain of bunkers. "But you won't have any trouble on this hole," Dan resumed. "You won't have to worry about the downhill lie on your second shot. You have shallow-face woods. You'll get the ball up quick with them. I should warn you, however, that those bunkers have been the graveyard of many great players. If we're playing against the wind and you can't carry them, you must play safe. You cannot recover onto the green from those bunkers." Yes, I thought as Dan spoke, the eighth could be another Suez.

That evening when the gathering darkness forced us off the greens and we strolled back to my hotel, Dan and I held a final powwow. "We can win this championship, you and I," I said to Dan, "if we do just one thing."

"Oh, there's no doubt we can win it, sir."

"I know, but there's one thing in particular we must concentrate on. Do you remember that seven at the Suez Canal?" I asked.

"Do I!" Dan put his hand over his eyes. "Why, it's haunted me."

"In this tournament we've got to make sure that if we go over par on a hole, we go no more than one over par. If we can avoid taking another disastrous seven, Dan, I don't see how we can lose. You won't find me going against your advice this time. You'll be calling them and I'll be playing them."

Mac Smith and Tommy Armour were sitting on the front porch when we arrived at the hotel. "Hey, Skip," Armour shouted. "How's Eugene playing?"

"Mr. Sarazen is right on the stick," Dan answered, "right on the stick."

The qualifying field played one round on Royal St. George's and one on Prince's. There isn't much to say about my play on the first day at Prince's. I had a 73, 1 under par. However, I shall never forget the morning of the second qualifying round. A terrific gale was blowing off the North Sea. As I was shaving, I looked out of the window at the Royal St. George's links where I'd be playing that day. The wind was whipping the sand out of the bunkers and bending the flags. Then I saw this figure in black crouched over against the wind, pushing his way from green to green. It was Daniels. He was out diagramming the positions of the pins so that I would know exactly how to play my approaches. I qualified among the leaders. You have to play well when you're partnered with a champion.

The night before the Open, the odds on my winning, which had soared to twenty-five-to-one during my slump, dropped to six-to-one, and Bernard Darwin, the critic I respected most, had dispatched the following lines to *The Times*: "I watched Sarazen play eight or nine holes and he was mightily impressive. To see him in the wind, and there was a good fresh wind blowing, is to realize how strong he is. He just tears that ball through the wind as if it did not exist."

On the day the championship rounds began, the wind had died down to an agreeable breeze, and Daniels and I attacked from the very first hole. We were out in 35, 1 under par, with only one 5 on that nine. We played home in 35 against a par of 38, birdieing the seventeenth and the eighteenth. My 70 put me a shot in front of Percy Alliss, Mac Smith, and Charlie Whitcombe. On the second day, I tied the course record with a 69. I don't know how much Dan's old eyes could perceive at a distance, but he called the shots flawlessly by instinct. I went one stroke over on the ninth when I missed a curling five-footer, but that was the only hole on which we took a "buzzard." We made the turn in 35, then came sprinting home par, par, birdie, par, par, birdie, birdie, birdie, par. My halfway total, 139, gave me a three-shot margin over the nearest man, Alliss, four over Whitcombe, and five over Compston, who had come back with a 70 after opening with a 74. Armour had played a 70 for 145, but Tommy's tee-shots were giving him a lot of trouble—he had been forced to switch to his brassie—and I didn't figure on too much trouble from him. Mac Smith had started his second round with a 7 and finished it in 76. That was too much ground for even a golfer of Mac's skill and tenacity to make up.

The last day now, and the last two rounds. I teed off in the morning at nine o'clock. Three orthodox pars. A grand drive on the fourth, and then my first moment of anguish: I hit my approach on the socket. Daniels did not give me a second to brood. "I don't think we'll need that club again, sir," he said matter-of-factly. I was forced to settle for a 5, 1 over par, but with Daniels holding me down, I made my pars easily on the fifth and the sixth and birdied the seventh.

Now for the eighth, 453 yards of trouble. So far I had handled it well, parring it on both my first and second rounds. Daniels had given me the go-ahead on both my blind second shots over the ridge of bunkers, and each time I had carried the hazard with my brassie. On this third round, I cracked my drive down the middle of the billowy fairway. Daniels handed me my spoon, after he had looked the shot over and tested the wind, and pointed out the direction to the pin hidden behind the bunkers. I hit just the shot we wanted—high over the ridge and onto the green, about thirty feet from the cup. I stroked the putt up to the hole, it caught a corner and dropped. My momentum from that eagle 3 carried me to a birdie 3 on the ninth. Out in 33. Okay. Now to stay in there. After a nice start home, I wobbled on the 411-yard thirteenth, pulling my long iron to the left of the green and taking a 5. I slipped over par again on the 335-yard fifteenth, three-putting from fourteen feet when I went too boldly for my birdie putt and missed the short one coming back. I atoned for these lapses by birdieing the sixteenth and the eighteenth to complete that long second nine in 37, 1 under par, and the round in 70, 4 under. With eighteen more to go, the only man who had a chance to catch me was Arthur Havers. Havers, with 74–71–68, stood five strokes behind. Mac Smith, fighting back with a 71, was in third place, but eight shots away. Alliss had taken a 78 and was out of the hunt.

If the pressure and the pace of the tournament was telling on Dan, he didn't show it. I found him at the tee after lunch, raring to get back on the course and wrap up the championship. We got off to an auspicious start on that final round—par, birdie, par, par. On the fifth I went one over, shook it off with a par on the sixth, but when I missed my 4 on the seventh I began to worry about the possible errors I might make. This is the sure sign that a golfer is tiring. The eighth loomed ahead and I was wondering if that penalizing hole would catch up with me this time. I drove well, my ball finishing a few feet short of the spot from which I had played my spoon in the morning. Daniels took his time in weighing the situation, and then drew the spoon from the bag. I rode into the ball compactly and breathed a sigh of relief as I saw it get up quickly and clear the bunkers with yards to spare. "That's how to play golf, sir," Daniels said, winking an eye approvingly. "That's the finest shot you've played on this hole." He was correct, of course. We found out, after climbing up and over the ridge, that my ball lay only eight feet from the cup. I holed the putt for my second eagle in a row on the hole, and turned in 35, after a standard par on the ninth.

Only nine more now and I had it. One over on the tenth. Nothing to fret about. Par. Par. Par. A birdie on the fourteenth. Almost home now. One over on the fifteenth, three putts. One over on the sixteenth, a fluffed chip. Daniels slowed me down on the seventeenth tee. "We're going to win this championship, sir. I have no worries on that score. But let's make our pars on these last two holes. You always play them well." A par on the seventeenth. On the eighteenth, a good drive into the wind, a brassie right onto the green, down in 2 for a birdie. Thirty-five, 39—74, even par. There was no challenge to my total of 283. Mac Smith, the runner-up, was five shots higher, and Havers, who had needed a 76 on his last round, was a stroke behind Mac.

Feeling like a million pounds and a million dollars respectively, Daniels and I sat down on a bank near the first tee and congratulated each other on a job well done. Our score of 283—70, 69, 70, 74—was 13 under par on a truly championship course, and it clipped two strokes off the old record in the British Open, Bob Jones' 285 at St. Andrews in 1927. (Incidentally, 283 has never been bettered in the British Open, though Cotton equaled that mark at Sandwich in 1934, Perry at Muirfield in 1935, and Locke at Sandwich in 1949.) Much as I was thrilled by setting a new record for a tournament that had been my nemesis for a decade, I was even more elated over the method by which I had finally reached my goal. I had led all the way. I had encountered no really rocky passages because I had had the excellent sense to listen to Daniels at every puzzling juncture. Through his brilliant selection of clubs and his understanding of my volatile temperament, I had been able to keep my resolution to go no more than one over par on any hole. The eighth, which I had feared might be a second Suez, had turned out to be my best friend. I had two 3s and two 5s on a hole on which I would not have been unwilling, before the tournament, to settle for four 6s. In fact, there wasn't one 6 on my scorecard for the four rounds of the championship. It is a card of which I am very proud.

After a shower, I changed into my brown gabardine jacket and was going over the acceptance speech I had prepared four years earlier, when the officials told me they were ready to begin their presentation ceremonies on the porch of the clubhouse. I asked them if it would be all right if Daniels came up and stood beside me as I received the trophy, since it had really been a team victory. They regretted to have to turn down a request they could sympathize with, but it was against tradition. I scanned the crowd gathering before the clubhouse, looking for Dan so that I could at least take him down front. I couldn't find him. Then, just as the officials were getting impatient about delaying the ceremony any longer, I spotted Dan coming down the drive on his bicycle, carrying a grandson on each handlebar. On with the show.

After the ceremony the team of Daniels and Sarazen got together for a rather tearful good-bye. I gave Dan my polo coat, and told him I'd be looking for him the next year at St. Andrews. I waved to him as he pedaled happily down the drive, the coat flapping in the breeze, and there was a good-sized lump in my throat as I thought of how the old fellow had never flagged for a moment during the arduous grind of the tournament and how, pushing himself all the way, he had made good his vow to win a championship for me before he died.

It was the last time I saw Dan. A few months later some English friends, who kept me posted on Dan, wrote me that he had passed away after a short illness. They said that after the Open he had worn the polo coat continually, even inside the pubs, as he told the golf fans of three generations the story of how "Sarazen and I did it at Prince's." When old Dan died the world was the poorer by one champion.

—1950

Bouncing Back
from a National Bout

Robert T. Jones, Jr.

My début in national championship affairs at the Merion Cricket Club, Philadelphia, in 1916 has given rise to a deal of comment, due to my lack of years, and as the personal statistics have been somewhat mixed I may explain that I was fourteen years and six months old, five feet four inches tall, and weighed 165 pounds—a chunky, rather knock-kneed, tow-headed youngster playing in long pants; supremely innocent of the vicissitudes of major tournament golf and the keenness of northern greens—so different from our heavy Bermuda texture in the South; pretty cocky, I suppose, from having at last won a real title, if only a state championship; and simply pop-eyed with excitement and interest. I had two weeks of violet-ray treatment for the lumbago that had tormented me earlier in the season, and it left me, never to return. I never had seen any of the great players who were to compete at Merion—Bob Gardner, then amateur champion, and Chick Evans, who had lately won the open championship at Minneapolis, and the others; and so far as I recall, I was not in the least afraid of any of them. I hadn't sense or experience enough to be afraid. Mr. Adair and Perry and I stayed at the Bellevue-Stratford hotel in Philadelphia and traveled out to the club on suburban trains. It was my first big trip away from home and I was having a grand time.

We played our first practice round on the West Course—there were, and are, two fine courses at Merion—and I never had seen any such beautiful greens. They looked like billiard tables to me and I was crazy to putt on them. But their speed was bewildering. I remember the sixth hole, then a short pitch down to the green over a brook, the green faced slightly toward the shot. I was thirty feet beyond the hole, which was in the middle of the green. Forgetting all about the faster pace of these new greens, I socked the ball firmly with my little Travis putter and was horrified to see it roll on past the hole, apparently gathering momentum, and trickle into the brook, so that I was playing 4 from the other side of the stream—a most embarrassing *contretemps*.

When the qualifying rounds came on, the field was divided into sections, one playing the morning round on the East Course, the other on the West Course, and both sections changing for the second round. I played the West Course in the morning and turned in a 74 which led the entire field for that round. After luncheon, when I got over to the East Course, word had got about that the new kid from Dixie was breaking up the tournament, and almost the entire gallery assembled to follow me. Gosh—it scared me to death! I fancy I led the field the other way in the afternoon, taking an 89, for a total of 163, about ten strokes more than will get you in, these days, but safe enough then. Perry got in by a play-off at 167, won his first match, and lost the second. I was drawn with Eben Byers for my first match, a former national champion, and everybody in our party began to condole with me. Tough luck, they said, catching a big one in the first round. But Mr. Adair clapped me hard on the back and told me not to mind what they said.

"Remember what old Bob Fitzsimmons used to say," he advised. "'The bigger they are, the harder they fall!'"

I thought that was a corking line, but as a matter of fact the name of Eben Byers meant nothing to me. I was a fresh kid, and golf as yet didn't have me down—at least, I didn't know it.

Mr. Byers and I played terribly. He was a veteran and I was a youngster, but we expressed our feelings in exactly the same way—when we missed a shot, we threw the club away. This habit later got me no end of critical comment, some of which hurt my feelings deeply, as I continued reading references to my temper long after I had got it under control to where there was no outward evidence of it except my ears getting red, which they do to this day—for I still get as mad as ever, missing a simple shot.

These columns I've read about my temper—it seems I got off on the wrong foot, and it was a long time before I was anywhere near in step with the critics, in the matter of disposition and deportment. . . . Even now it strikes me as a bit unreasonable that so much type should have been employed on the gusty vagaries of one petulant youngster, when so little has been printed about the same unaffected displays by great golfers twice his age and more. There was only a whimsical reference to the club-throwing of Mr. Byers, I remember; and since then I have seen more than one national champion rival both of us. Two years ago at Oakmont, I saw a competitor in the national amateur championship heave his putter into an adjoining wood and forbid his caddy to go after it—and he has been a national title-holder more than once. But nothing was said about it in the papers.

I'm not saying I didn't need some lecturing, mind you. The golf writers have been only too good to me, all along. And I was a sort of bad boy of golf, I suppose, and required an occasional spanking, such as appeared in a Boston paper of 1918, when Alexa Sterling and Elaine Rosenthal and Perry Adair and I were playing a Red Cross benefit match at Brae Burn. I kept those spankings in my scrapbook, you see, along with the more pleasant clippings. This one was as follows:

"Some interesting golf was shown during the match, interspersed with some pranks by Jones, which will have to be corrected if this player expects to rank with the best in the country. Although Jones is only a boy, his display of temper when things went wrong did not appeal to the gallery."

That was two years after Merion. And I was a year or two more, getting my turbulent disposition in hand. It wasn't an easy matter. . . . It's sort of hard to explain, unless you play golf yourself, and have a temper. You see, I never lost my temper with an opponent. I was angry only with myself. It always seemed, and it seems today, such an utterly useless and idiotic thing to stand up to a perfectly simple shot, one that I *know* I can make a hundred times running without a miss—and then mess up the blamed thing, the one time I want to make it! And it's gone forever—an irrevocable crime, that stroke. . . . I think it was Stevenson who said that bad men and fools eventually got what was coming to them, but the fools first. And when you feel so extremely a fool, and a bad golfer to boot, what the deuce can you do, except throw the club away? . . . Well, well—Chick Evans, writing years later, said I had conquered my temper not wisely but too well; that a flare now and then would help me. I liked that of Chick. But I could have told him I get just as mad today. I stopped club-throwing in public, but the lectures didn't stop coincidently. A bad name sticks. Having quoted one well-merited spanking, let me give an example of how hard it is to live down a wicked reputation.

Four years after Merion, and two years after Brae Burn, when I had reached the mature age of eighteen years and the club-throwing penchant had been completely hammered out of me, I was playing in my first national open championship, at the Inverness Club, Toledo, qualifying with Harry Vardon. At the last hole I messed up a good round and took a villainous 6, finally missing a putt of about four feet. I was mad—thoroughly mad, certainly. But I didn't mean to show it. I holed out the ball, which lay at the edge of the cup, and tossed the putter to my caddy. He was not looking for it and the club fell on the green. Next day the newspapers said that I was throwing my clubs again, and had hacked up a slice of the eighteenth green in a rage after missing a short putt. . . . That hurt me a lot.

Well, well—I don't throw clubs any more, in public, though once in a while I let one fly, in a little friendly round with Dad and Chick Ridley and Tess Bradshaw—and get a deal of relief from it, too, if you want the truth.

Returning to my first match at Merion in 1916, after this bit of *apologia*—which may not be in the best of taste—I repeat that Mr. Byers and I played very wretchedly and I think the main reason I beat him was because he ran out of clubs first. Somebody playing behind us said later that we looked like a juggling act. At the twelfth hole Mr. Byers threw an iron out of bounds and wouldn't let his caddy go after it. I finally won, 3–1, and felt no elation whatever over my successful debut in a national championship. I knew I was lucky to win, the way I had played, and that I ought to have been well drubbed.

The second match I played better. This was with Frank Dyer, champion of several states and districts, and he started fast, putting me 5 down in the first six holes. I was getting dizzy. "So this is big league golf," I reflected. Then Frank made a few mistakes and I saw he was human, and I began to play better. At the turn I was 3 down and when we stood on the eighteenth tee I had a 4 left for a 32 coming in, and was 1 up. I was shooting some hot golf and was enjoying myself immensely.

We both hooked from this tee and one ball stopped in a fairly convenient position on top of a mound while the other was at the foot of the same mound, in a distinctly distressing situation. We were playing the same kind of ball, a Red Honor. Mine had gone on an excursion out of bounds at the second hole and was wearing a tar-stain from the roadway; I didn't change the ball every sixth hole, as I do now, figuring that the one in play may be knocked slightly off-center. I didn't stop to examine and identify the balls, but confidently whaled away at the one under the mound and missed the shot grievously, taking a 6 and losing the hole. After holing out I looked at the balls, and discovered I had played his ball and he mine. There was nothing to do about it then—we had played out each with the wrong ball, and the score stood. We started the second round even, and I won, 4–2.

By this time the golf writers were paying me a good deal of attention and some of the things they wrote made me feel extremely foolish. They wrote about my worn shoes and my dusty pants and my fresh young face and other embarrassing personal attributes. I never had considered my shoes or pants before, so long as they held together. Golf wasn't a dress-up game, to me, and it was a new and puzzling experience to be looked at closely by so many people. I never had thought much of my face, for example, and it seemed sort of indelicate thus to expose it in print, not to mention my pants. The galleries were the largest I had ever seen, of course, and only half a dozen familiar faces, but everybody was curiously friendly. . . . I remember thinking these Yankees must be pretty good folks, after all.

So I got through the second round and in the third round I met Robert A. Gardner, then champion, and the biggest gallery I had yet seen followed the match, which I will describe with some detail because of a certain significance it always has had, for me—it was in this match that I first got my fresh young head under the bludgeonings of chance, and, I must confess, wound up by bowing it.

Bob was playing with an infected finger, a handicap that rendered his game uncertain, and possibly cost him the championship in the end, as he lost to Chick Evans, who, however, was playing admirably in the finals.

I shot a 76 in the morning round and was 1 up. We were having a fine match, never far apart. In the afternoon we continued playing evenly and at the sixth tee we were square. When I planted my second shot on the green five yards from the pin I felt certain of going into the lead again, as Gardner's second was above the green and to the right, in a difficult place from which to approach. But he chipped stone dead and got a half.

At the next green my ball was fifteen feet below the cup and Bob's was off to the left. Again he chipped dead for a half.

I wasn't discouraged. He can't keep on doing it, I told myself. I'll get him yet!

Playing the eighth hole, my second shot was ten feet from the pin and Bob's was on the ninth tee—and this time he didn't chip dead. After his third shot he was still outside my position, and then I felt the break had come. He couldn't keep on doing it. The break had come. . . . But Gardner sank his twelve-foot putt, and I missed my ten-footer, and he had halved another. It seemed he *could* keep on doing it.

As for me, I couldn't. The break had come. But it was not my break. My fresh young head was bloody—and bowed. Frankly, I blew up. Bob won five of the next seven holes. He beat me, 5–3, holing a twenty-foot putt for a par of 4 at the fifteenth, after driving out of bounds.

They all told me it was a tough match to lose. But I've lost many a tough match since then, more than one by being clearly outplayed—and more than one because I simply blew up under pressure. And I've been out-finished in more than one medal-play championship. But I never have felt quite the same way again. In after years I began to reason the business out a bit; as I said early in these memoirs, I never learned anything from a match that I won; I got my golfing education from drubbings. And very lately I have come to a sort of Presbyterian attitude toward tournament golf; I can't get away from the idea of predestination.

The professionals, you know, have a way of saying of the winner in a competition, "It was *his* tournament." And step by step, and hole by hole, and shot by shot, you may trace it back and see that he was bound to win—after it is all over. . . . There's a tremendous lot to this game; and I fancied when I started this little story that maybe I could think a little of it out as I went along, and tell people about it. But it's a big assignment; too big for me. I may have reasoned out somewhat of the mechanical side; perhaps just a bit of the psychological side. But behind it all, and over it all, there is something I think nobody understands.

Anyway, as they said, this was a tough match to lose, because I had played very well up to the place where those continued recoveries of Bob's had broken my back, and next day one of the papers had a well-written account of the match which gave me a lot of credit and concluded with these lines:

"Carefree and unconcerned, save with the big dish of ice-cream awaiting him at the clubhouse, the Georgia schoolboy swung along from the fifteenth green in his worn shoes and dusty pants and sweat-streaked shirt, whistling an air from a recent musical comedy, as jaunty and complacent as if he had just won his first national championship instead of having just been beaten in the third round. He was thinking about the ice-cream."

But I wasn't. I was puzzled, and hurt, some way. Not with Bob Gardner, who had played so pluckily when his shots were not coming off, and had kept the pressure on, when I was hitting the ball better. Bob, as I recall it, was an abstract figure; he was in the picture only as an agent for something else, that I didn't understand. I had felt all along that I could beat Bob Gardner, but there was something besides him that was big and hard and invincible. . . . That was what kept the pressure on me; that was what beat me. Fatality wasn't even a word to me then; and it doesn't mean now what I want it to.

But as I walked back to the clubhouse—and I got the ice-cream, too—I kept wondering over and over again in a vague way what was on Bob Gardner's side, that had beat me, and made me blow up, when I was hitting the shots better than he was. Would it be on my side sometimes? I wondered. Or—with a queer little sinking sensation— would it always be on the other side?

You know, I never have made sure what it was, and is. I have found out this much: In the long run it seems to play no favorites— if the run is long enough. In my case it was a run of seven years.

—1927

Playing the Old Course
with Joyce Wethered

Robert T. Jones, Jr.

Ordinarily I would never take advantage of a friendly round of golf by making the play of a person, kind enough to go around with me, the subject of an article. I realize that everyone likes to play occasionally a round of golf when reputations can be forgotten, with nothing more at stake than the outcome of the match and a little friendly bantering afterwards.

Just before the British Amateur championship at St. Andrews, Miss Joyce Wethered allowed herself to be led away from her favorite trout stream in order to play eighteen holes of golf over the Old Course in company with her brother, Roger, Dale Bourne, then recently crowned English champion, and myself. At the time, I fully appreciated that Miss Wethered had not had a golf club in her hand for over a fortnight, and I certainly should have made no mention of the game had she not played so superbly.

We started out by arranging a four-ball match—Roger and Dale against Miss Wethered and myself—on a best and worst ball basis. I don't know why we didn't play an ordinary four-ball match, unless we fancied that the lady would be the weakest member of the four and that in a best-ball match her ball would not count for very much. If any of us had any such idea at the start of the match, it is now quite immaterial, for there is not the slightest chance that we should admit it.

We played the Old Course from the very back, or the championship tees, and with a slight breeze blowing off the sea. Miss

Wethered holed only one putt of more than five feet, took three putts rather half-heartedly from four yards at the seventeenth after the match was over, and yet she went round St. Andrews in 75. She did not miss one shot; she did not even half-miss one shot; and when we finished, I could not help saying that I had never played golf with anyone, man or woman, amateur or professional, who made me feel so utterly outclassed.

It was not so much the score she made as the way she made it. Diegel, Hagen, Smith, Von Elm and several other male experts would likely have made a better score, but one would all the while have been expecting them to miss shots. It was impossible to expect that Miss Wethered would never miss a shot—but she never did.

To describe her manner of playing is almost impossible. She stands quite close to the ball, she places the club once behind, takes one look toward the objective, and strikes. Her swing is not long— surprisingly short, indeed, when one considers the power she develops—but it is rhythmic to the last degree. She makes ample use of her wrists, and her left arm within the hitting area is firm and active. This, I think, distinguishes her swing from that of any other woman golfer, and it is the one thing that makes her the player she is.

Men are always interested in the distance which a first-class woman player can attain. Miss Wethered, of course, is not as long with any club as the good male player. Throughout the round, I found that when I hit a good one I was out in front by about twenty yards— by not so much when I failed to connect. It was surprising, though, how often on a fine championship course fine iron play by the lady could make up the difference. I kept no actual count, but I am certain that her ball was the nearest to the hole more often than any of the other three.

I have no hesitancy in saying that, accounting for the unavoidable handicap of a woman's lesser physical strength, she is the finest golfer I have ever seen.

—1930

The Last Days of Bobby Jones

Charles Price

By 1968 Bobby Jones' health had slipped from the terrible to the abysmal. His eyes were bloodshot from the spinal disease he had endured for twenty years, his arms atrophied to the size of a schoolgirl's, his ankles so swollen by body fluids they spilled over the edges of his shoes. This was a man who could once effortlessly drive a golf ball a sixth of a mile.

Still, he had not lost the humor with which he viewed so many things, often at his own expense. Confined to a wheelchair all day, he had to be put into and taken out of bed by a male nurse, who was the size of a linebacker. "He handles me like a flapjack," Bob said by way of complimenting the man when he introduced us. Then he chuckled. Bob laughed a lot, although never out loud, and he laughed during his last days mostly to put people at their ease, especially strangers. Meeting him then for the first time could be a shock, and Bob knew it. But he insisted on shaking hands with everybody, painful as it had to be, excruciating if his hand were squeezed. But it was part of the price he insisted on paying for having been Bobby Jones, the one and only.

Having covered the Masters for twenty years, I had become his companion during it by a choice that was as much his as mine. Those years became the most fulfilling of the forty-four I have been writing about golf. I've never written about them, and I don't know why. In looking back, that period in his life seems as towering as the Grand Slam.

For ten years we had been collaborating on a number of writing chores. Since I then covered the tournament for *Newsweek* and wrote a column elsewhere that appeared only monthly, I had the time to act as his legman. He had long been unable to watch the Masters even from a golf cart, and his son, Bob III, was on the course most of the day as an official. I became somebody who could bring younger players and foreign writers to him, someone with whom he could pass off a casual observation about the tournament on TV without fear of explaining himself, someone he could share lunch with now that he no longer would eat where people could watch him.

We would sit at a card table next to a window in his cottage that overlooked the tenth tee. A curtain prevented spectators from looking in but allowed Bob to peer out. He had the same thing for lunch almost every day. First there'd be a couple of dry martinis, which he drank with relish but scolded himself for. "I shouldn't be drinking these," he said to me one day. "They don't mix with my medicine." The martinis would be followed by a hamburger, in part because he liked hamburgers but mainly because he could no longer cut meat and disliked anyone cutting it for him, so gnarled had his fingers become.

Bob smoked more than two packs of cigarettes a day, sometimes in chain fashion, and they were lined on the card table in neat rows for him, each in a holder so he would not accidently burn himself. An elegant lighter, covered in leather, sat ready. All he had to do was push down a lever that any child could. But even that was becoming an effort. So, with as much nonchalance as I could devise, I'd pull out a cigarette of my own, thereby giving me the excuse to light his.

He had been a man who never looked as though he needed help, even when he was dying, and it was part of Bob's magnificence that his disablement evoked admiration more than pity. Those cigarettes were actually a token of his will to live, not the other way around. One day he left me speechless after I lighted one for him. "I've got to give these things up," he said. "They're bad for me."

I had long known what was wrong with Bob, and he asked me not to write about it while he was still alive. "People think I've got arthritis," he said. "Let's let it go at that."

Actually, he had what is known as syringomyelia—pronounced *sir-ring-go-my-ale-ee-ah*—an extremely rare disease of the central nervous system. It took eight years to diagnose. Researching it, I found neurosurgeons who had never even seen a case. "And I guess," one told me, "that I've treated 20 cases of amyotrophic lateral sclerosis, or Lou Gehrig's disease."

Syringomyelia is a disease you are born with, although it is not hereditary and does not manifest itself until much later in life. Bob had been forty-six when his symptoms first appeared. His right leg began to pain him, then the right arm. Eventually, he lost the use of both legs. For a while he got around on elbow crutches, then a "walker" and finally a wheelchair. Then his whole body began to waste away.

Even in that condition he went to his law offices in Atlanta every day he could, chiefly to keep from vegetating. The disease had no effect on his mind. Indeed, the complex nature of it is such that it doesn't kill you, as it didn't Bob. Clinically, he died from an aneurysm, but actually from the exhaustion of just trying to stay alive. "If I'd known it was going to be this easy," he told Jean Marshall, his secretary, days before he died, "I'd have gone a long time ago."

Bob and I first collaborated in 1959, when he agreed to rewrite some old instructional articles for *Golf* Magazine, of which I was the first editor. Three years later he wrote the introduction to a history I had written with his help, which by itself has been widely quoted, especially his line about golfers sometimes being "the dogged victims of inexorable fate."

A few years later another book of mine had been dedicated to him, and we had talked about golf at such length and in such detail that I suggested he put together a book from his old newspaper columns and magazine articles. He had written hundreds, not a word of them ghosted. Bob was reluctant, what with his flagging energies, but I convinced him it had to be done. People would be interested in what he had to say about golf a century after he was gone, or long after every other golfer's thoughts had left the public yawning. His ideas were so eloquent, so down to earth, so free of technicalisms. He agreed when I volunteered to collect them, cut out what was dated, and dovetail the rest into logical order. These were words Bob himself hadn't read for thirty years or more.

Like a lot of people who are good at it, Bob did not like to write, only to have written. Notwithstanding, he threw himself into the project. My manuscript was retyped by Mrs. Marshall into triple-spaced pages so Bob could mark between the lines any changes he wanted, which he did with a ballpoint pen inserted into a rubber ball he could grip with his crippled fingers.

Sitting with me across from his desk in Atlanta, he'd study every word, pushing each page aside only after he was sure of what he wanted to leave to posterity. I'd note the changes, all the while finding excuses to light his cigarettes. When he was finished, I'd take the changes back to New York, where I lived, while he pondered what was still to be done. The whole process took almost a year. Bob was the most honestly modest golf champion ever. But he was well aware of, and conscientious about, his unique role in the game's history.

The book became *Bobby Jones on Golf* (Doubleday & Co., 1966) and I was pleased to learn from Mrs. Marshall that work on it had given Bob a new purpose in life. For the first time in years he was doing something creative and constructive, something only he could do. That's what Bobby Jones was all about. He did things in golf only he could do, of which the Grand Slam is just a monument.

At this stage in our friendship, it had become apparent that Bob was passing some sort of torch to me. I was a writer and I represented the generation immediately after his. He wanted to leave somebody behind who could straighten out he facts of his life if they had to be, as O. B. Keeler did when Rob was at the peak of his career. There was no other explanation for all he told me about that career. Bob not only seldom reminisced, he disliked to.

We were joined once in his cottage by two former U.S. Open champions from his era. Bob did all the listening, and I could see he was getting restless. Finally, he made an announcement. "I wonder if you fellows would excuse us," he said. "Charley and I have something to discuss that can't wait." Minutes went by after they left. I had to come out and ask him what it was he wanted to discuss. "Oh, nothing," he said. "I just can't stand sitting around talking about ancient history."

Yet he would with me, all day long, with the Masters Tournament taking place just outside his window. Armed with his confidence in me, I approached him about doing a film on his life, concentrating on the Grand Slam, the drama of which had never been explained to my satisfaction. He was reluctant, as I knew he would be. But I pointed out the inevitable. If he didn't do the film, somebody else would eventually, disarticulating it with the sort of hyperbole he hated and which he made such an effort to avoid in his own accounts.

So he agreed. Somehow word got out before we had hardly begun and we were approached by potential producers, one of whom conferred with us in Atlanta. But the project never got much further. Bob became too exhausted to continue. He never came back to the Masters and died in December 1971.

I was abroad at the time. When I got home, there was a package from Bob's office for me. In it was that lighter with which I had lit so many of his cigarettes, trying to circumvent his pride. There was a note from him, typed by Mrs. Marshall but signed by Bob in his scrawl. "You weren't fooling me a bit," it said.

—1991

The Babe Comes Back

Al Laney

Peabody, Massachusetts, July 3, 1954—

Mildred Zaharias, she who is known to all as The Babe, won the second women's National Open golf championship at the Salem Country Club today by the overwhelming margin of twelve strokes and with the very fine seventy-two-hole score of 291.

Mrs. Zaharias, leading by seven strokes as the final day began, played two closing rounds in 73 and 75 and the mere figures of her four rounds—72, 71, 73, 75—speak eloquently of her quality as golfer, athlete and competitor. The total is three strokes above a really difficult course par and all three were dropped on the final few holes when she was very tired and so far ahead as to be practically out of sight.

The positions of those who were behind her in a field which included all of the best professional girls and many of the fine amateurs of the country, does not really matter, but here is the order in which they finished.

Betty Hicks, a former amateur champion, was second with a total of 303 and Louise Suggs was third at 307. Tied at 308 with Mary Wright, the low amateur, was Betsy Rawls, defending champion, and then came Jacqueline Pung who lost a play-off to Miss Rawls last year, at 309. The remainder of the forty who qualified for the last two rounds then were strung out, some with well-known names but very high scores.

It is impossible to praise too highly the play of the new champion for what we saw here probably was the finest consecutive four

rounds of golf on a championship course under championship conditions ever played by a woman.

Mrs. Zaharias was the only one of all the girls here who understood how the difficult Salem course should be played and had the
shots to do it. She alone negotiated the strenuous three-day journey
without once faltering until near the end when she was very tired and
had many strokes in hand, playing the same fine brand of golf in every
round, never once yielding to the pressure and tension that an Open
championship, under the banner of the U.S.G.A., must always bring.

She was tied with Claire Doran, the Cleveland amateur, at the
end of the first round for a two-stroke lead and she moved to a seven-
stroke lead at the halfway mark which would have enabled her to
coast home today. But by noon it had increased to ten strokes.

Other girls had fine single rounds though none so fine as her best
and none could put two such together. Four such as she achieved
seemed wholly out of the reach of any other. It is a score which any
male golfer in the land could be happy to have on his card.

So now The Babe's name will be engraved on the new U.S.G.A.
Open Trophy where it belongs, just below that of Miss Rawls, who
won the first Open at Rochester last year. The Babe did not play in
that one. Everyone will remember that she was then just recovering
from a cancer operation and the fact that she has come back in so
short a time to play such wonderful golf makes her victory the more
remarkable.

There is no doubt that The Babe's excellence took something
from the tournament in the way of tension and excitement but it
stands alone as a performance to be admired by all. After she had
fired her 71 on Friday, the tournament was over so far as the winner
was concerned, leaving only the battle for second money by way of a
contest.

But the struggle for second place in a big golf tournament is not
really very interesting and nobody bothered much about what the
other girls were doing on the last day. They were, in fact, having a
nice quiet little scramble for position which, if The Babe's score had
been removed from the top, could have developed into an exciting
event.

The champion's play, however, was most interesting from several points of view. With so big a lead to start the third round this morning she was in a position to play it safely and conservatively for a moderately good score. Even a 75 or a 76 would have made her position practically impregnable at lunch time.

She did play it this way for the most part but with the caution dictated by circumstances she mingled great boldness at times. First she made sure that on no hole would her score get out of control but she was forever seeking opportunities to save a stroke. Many times she went straight for the pin when everyone expected her to play safely to the middle of the green for par.

Sometimes this cost her strokes but at other points she got them back by the same methods. Going out this morning she was over par twice and under once and coming home she was over once and under once. She was in the happy position of being able to lose a stroke without the slightest worry, knowing she could probably get it back somewhere along the line and not caring much if she did or didn't.

This made every hole a little adventure for her and the crowd. The Babe thoroughly enjoyed the day and so did all of us who went with her. We all knew that we were seeing the best there is, a real champion giving an outstanding performance.

She acted the part of a champion to perfection and her progress twice around the course was a queenly procession with her nearest pursuers, already dimly seen in the far distance at the start, fading more and more out of the picture as the day wore on.

At the very end the champion's quality stood out most strongly. Over the last four or five holes The Babe had begun to fly the first faint distress signals. Her tee shots, which had been wonderfully accurate for three days, began to fade and hook badly, a sure sign of fatigue.

At the final hole, with all the people lining the course and waiting to escort her home, she sliced her drive badly into a wicked place among trees She could have used as many strokes as she pleased to finish and the sensible thing to do was to sacrifice a stroke and play back to the fairway. But The Babe took the position that this was no way to finish. She found a tiny opening and she took a long iron and went through it toward the distant green. A champion's shot and a great roar greeted it. It gave her a chance for a par 4. She missed it by an inch but she had finished in a champion's way.

For The Babe has now completely outclassed all her challengers. She has set the pattern by which a champion should act on the course and off it and in the future all women golfers must be judged as they measure up to the standard or fail to do so.

—1954

Nancy Lopez Lines Up a Big Future

Sarah Ballard

Since the oil companies began to move away and the government shut down Walker Air Force Base a few years ago, there has been relatively little to get excited about in Roswell, New Mexico. The town sits in the high dry plains, a pleasant place that because of its climate is now beginning to attract retired people from other parts of the country. Anglo-Americans and Mexican-Americans form the basic population, their lives intertwined, as they have been ever since the Anglos moved into the Southwest. Sixteen-year-old Nancy Lopez of East First Street is Mexican-American, and although she may be the best young girl golfer in the country, in Roswell East First Street is a long way in spirit from the country club.

By sheer force of her achievements Nancy has become an institution in Roswell, a kind of junior natural wonder. She won the New Mexico Women's Amateur Golf championship three straight years, starting when she was twelve, and a lot of other things besides. Last August she went to Jefferson City, Missouri, to try for the big time, the United States Girls' Junior championship. Nancy came away with her first national title and a ranking as the number-one girl golfer in the country. She did it the hard way. One hole down at match play with two holes to go, she sank a twenty-five-foot putt on the seventeenth to draw even and a six-foot downhiller on the eighteenth to win and become the youngest champion since Hollis Stacy in 1969. This week in Bernardsville, New Jersey, she is trying for a second junior title, and after that she will go after a bigger prize, the Women's Amateur in Montclair, New Jersey.

She got ready for both those events back in Roswell, basking in a warm celebrity glow. As she tees up on the first hole of the long flat course at New Mexico Military Institute, people honk cheerily at her from passing cars. Senior citizens cross fairways to shake her hands and ask how folks treated her when she was playing in Wisconsin or Illinois or Missouri, or wherever it was they used to live. High school kids wave to her and she honks back as she "drags Main" in her bright yellow Ford, a gift from her father.

Domingo Lopez has learned a lot of tricks for keeping a young girl's interest and competitive drive alive in the eight years since Nancy began trailing him around Roswell's nine-hole municipal course. The idea of rewards is one of them. "First I gave her one dollar for As at school. Then I gave her one dollar for birdies," he says. Now, many birdies and quite a few As later, the ante has been raised to things like a family trip to Los Angeles for the LA Open last January or mag rims for the wheels of her car. Lopez is a small, wiry, sunbaked man of fifty, known widely as "Sunday," an Anglo nickname he picked up playing city league baseball in his youth. He has worked hard all his life, first tenant-farming cotton just outside town and, since World War II, as a body and fender man. On his own he built the East Second Body Shop, at first large enough for only two cars but grown now to take ten or twelve. Working from 6 A.M. to 5 P.M. each day, he makes a comfortable living, owns a two-bedroom house a block from his shop, drives an eighteen-year-old pickup and an eleven-year-old Cadillac, and, through very careful planning and severe self-denial, has just enough left over to finance his daughter in the amateur style to which the USGA is accustomed. Nancy's car, he hastens to explain, was partly a reward for good grades, hard work and competitive success. But it was also a great boon to his wife Marina, who for years had spent her days shuttling Nancy back and forth to golf courses.

USGA rules allow junior players to accept financial help toward transportation, housing and caddie fees for junior tournaments from sources outside their immediate families. But until early this summer nobody in Roswell had ever thought to offer Nancy any aid. (The Roswell Country Club to this day has not made her a member, although it has declared that her family can join—for a fee that is obviously well beyond Domingo Lopez' means.) An organization called the Roswell Seniors and Retirees, which includes many newcomers with quite a few golfers among them, finally broke the ice. When Nancy returned from Jefferson City with the junior title, it gave a banquet for her and invited everybody who was anybody in Roswell's business community. The Seniors and Retirees used the occasion to let it be known that it was high time Roswell demonstrated a little gratitude. The Chamber of Commerce responded with five hundred dollars toward her expenses at the Women's Western Golf Association junior championships in Wisconsin this summer. Nancy won that event and reached the semifinals of the Western Women's Amateur as well. She was able to return one hundred dollars because an interested family named Lindell from Winfield, Iowa, not only housed her between the tournaments but drove her all the way home to New Mexico.

"I'd like to work, to have my own money," says Nancy, who understands about money pressures. "Sometimes I feel guilty. I think I could get a pretty good job. I can type sixty-five words a minute and I could learn bookkeeping from my mother. She does it for my dad. But my dad doesn't want me to work. He thinks it would tire me and take too much time away from my golf." There are other things Nancy would like to do, too, that are proscribed, such as swimming— "It uses the wrong muscles and softens my calluses"—and tennis—"I played it some, but once I sprained my ankle, and it scared me. My dad said then I should stick to golf." But there are compensations, too.

"My husband tells me, 'Don't let her do the dishes. It will hurt her hands,'" says Marina Lopez, chuckling. "She gets away with a lot."

Last January, as a sophomore, Nancy was allowed to join the Goddard High School boys' varsity golf team. Each Friday through the winter, in every kind of weather, the team traveled by car to such places as Clovis and Hobbs and Andrews and finally to the state championships in Las Cruces. The Goddard Rockets beat Albuquerque High by four shots for the team title, and Nancy placed fifth in individual scoring with 77, 82–159. The winner shot 150.

"When we were playing in March in Clovis," said Nancy shivering in July heat at the memory, "our hands were freezing before we even teed off, and by the ninth hole it had started to rain and we wanted to quit. By the fourteenth it had begun to hail and we went in, but the pro told us to go on back out. I told myself, 'I have to be a boy now. If I quit, the coach might not let me back on the team.' So I finished with a 41 on the back and then went inside, washed my pants to get the mud off—they were soaked anyway—and just put them back on ready to go home. Then they told us we had to go back out for a playoff. We won on the first hole, thank goodness."

Out of a deep-seated mistrust of motels, Marina Lopez—a short, plump realist who carries an umbrella as a sunshade on the golf course—chaperones her daughter to tournaments where there is no private housing. Domingo stays home in Roswell, hammering out dented fenders and thinking about Nancy's future.

"I want her to be happy if she wins and happy if she loses. I want her to be able to do whatever she decides to do. Maybe she will go to college if she can get a scholarship. But I am saving money now so if she goes on tour she can have three years to win. Some of them, you know, take a long time to get started. Right now I have maybe enough for the first year. I used to be a baseball player, a pitcher, and I believe I was good enough to get to the major leagues. But I never had a chance. That is why I want to give Nancy a chance."

Although he had only three years of school, Domingo Lopez is an instinctive teacher and the only golf instructor Nancy has ever had. "He knows my game better than anybody," says Nancy. "He can tell me what to do even though he can't do it himself." But more and more Nancy now makes her own adjustments. Just this summer she has worked a loop out of her swing, slowed her backswing, and she has shortened her putting stroke. When a friend sent her a snapshot he had taken at a tournament, she was surprised to see that she was up on her right toe at the top of her backswing. Now her heel is firmly planted. And, most important, she has slightly altered the unorthodox grip that was causing her to slice and costing her distance off the tee. Frank Hannigan of the USGA, who watched her play for the first time last summer in the Juniors, said, "Purists would say she needs a radical change, and it's not too late for that. But I think possibly her strength allows her to overpower her bad grip. It will be interesting to see how she develops. She has a superb touch on and around the greens and, wow, what a great instinct to win! She made *all* the important putts in match play."

When she was ten and had just competed in her first Roswell Ladies' golf tournament, Nancy told her father she wanted to be as good a golfer as Mrs. Jo Boswell, who was Roswell's leading female player at that time and had won the tournament. Her father told her, "Yes, you be as good as Mrs. Boswell—and maybe a little bit better." The next year, at eleven, Nancy was runner-up to Jo Boswell by three strokes, and at twelve she won. That was also the summer she won her first state women's championship. In those days her fingernails were chewed down to the quick and she threw up so often before her matches that she made it a habit to get dressed in a bathroom. Experience and accumulated success have given her poise and a pleasantly confident manner that is betrayed only in the nervous jiggling of her legs. The idea that she might have limits hasn't occurred to her.

"Development is unpredictable in junior girls," says Hannigan, who has seen a lot of them come and go. "They mature quicker than boys. I think a lot of girls at fifteen are playing the best golf they'll ever play. They find out, thank God, that there are other things in life beside golf."

For a Mexican-American girl in southern New Mexico, even one who can sink putts under pressure, the alternatives—the "other things in life"—are limited, and the chances are that before long Nancy Lopez will be taking her best shot and trying to make her living on the LPGA tour. And Domingo Lopez back home in Roswell will be hammering and hoping.

—1977

The Coming of the Bear

Henry Longhurst

I am very surprised that Jack Nicklaus has turned pro and I cannot help feeling that the last year or so represents the only period in the history of golf in which he would have done so. It was widely felt in America that neither he nor his fellow amateur, Deane Beman, could "afford to turn pro." They were doing so well as they were. Both were selling insurance, through contacts acquired on account of their prowess at golf.

Let me make myself absolutely plain about this. The above is not a thinly disguised "crack" at their amateur status. It is impossible, and unreasonable, to suggest that a man should not do business with people who are all the more glad to transact it with him on account of distinctions he has gained in other spheres. That applies as much to stockbrokers in this country as insurance men in the States.

Nevertheless the rewards to Nicklaus and Beman have already been outstanding. Nicklaus in his second year at the University at the age of twenty was already credited with $25,000 a year. Beman, a couple of years ahead of him, had already "turned pro" at insurance. He works at it like a beaver and he and his twenty-six-year-old partner hope next year to make $125,000. He draws $6000 a year in expenses from the firm to help to pay for the golf that brings him the business, but that, believe me, is little enough by American standards. Beman is now a dedicated insurance man who plays exceptional golf, not a golfer who sells insurance.

The rewards open to Nicklaus in the near future were, therefore, rosy indeed. It can only have been through the offer of even greater, and presumably guaranteed, rewards that he turned pro. Only in the last two or three years have such rewards been available to the three or four leading players in the world—mainly through television.

How will Nicklaus fare in direct competition with Palmer and such like? I think very well. Firstly, let me go on record as saying that, like Palmer, he is not only a fine golfer but a very fine fellow. He looks the world in the eye with a fearless sincerity and he has "guts." This to me was proved at Pebble Beach this year, when he was subjected to a series of eighteen-hole matches against opponents who had everything to gain and nothing to lose. It is easy to say "Anyone can beat anyone over eighteen holes"—though it isn't true, of course. It is a different thing to determine "No one is going to beat *me* over eighteen holes." I believe he would have won if the matches had been over six holes.

Last year Nicklaus declared that in golf his one ambition was to win the Open and the Masters. I see no reason why he should not. Over the past two years his aggregate in the two Open championships, though he won neither, was better than that of any other player. He has all the assets. He has terrific length—so much so that he recently won a 72-hole competition without taking anything bigger than a 6-iron for his second at a par-4 hole. Not only that, but he is straight. All through the week at Pebble Beach you could take his drives for granted. As Palmer says in his book, the old days of "you drive for fun and putt for money" are long since past.

With his awkward, rather cramped style, Nicklaus is an exceedingly good putter, too. If you can drive anything from 250 to 300 yards, straight, and then have anything from a 6-iron to a wedge to a watered green with a large ball, *and* are a fine holer-out, you are not often going to descend to taking 70! At Pebble Beach, Nicklaus was 20 under par for the week.

I hope that he will enjoy his life as a professional. One thing I am sure: the profession is fortunate to have got him.

—1961

Nicklaus and Watson at Turnberry

Herbert Warren Wind

In the opinion of most Scots and most golfers from other lands, the best course on the west coast of Scotland is not Troon (over which the British Open has periodically been played since 1923) but Turnberry, thirty miles or so to the south. It was finally added to the rota of the British Open in 1977, and though it was in far from its best condition, it produced what many people on both sides of the Atlantic consider the finest and most dramatic stretch of golf ever played in a major event. In the third round the two leaders, Jack Nicklaus and Tom Watson, pulled away from the rest of the field with a pair of sensational 65s. On the fourth round Nicklaus added a 66, but it wasn't good enough: Watson had a 65. Far ahead of the pack, the two leaders were engaged virtually in match play. Their duel was not decided until the last hole, which both of them birdied.

One of the many points of difference between the United States Open and the British Open—perhaps the two most important golf competitions in the world—is that the British championship, since its inception, in 1860, has been played on only fourteen courses, while ours, which was started thirty-five years later, has been played on nearly fifty courses. There are a lot of reasons for this disparity, such as the size of the United States and that of Great Britain and Northern Ireland (with a combined area smaller than Oregon); the unwritten law that the British Open is played exclusively on seaside courses; and the preference of the Royal & Ancient Golf Club of St. Andrews, which conducts the British Open, for limiting the number of courses

in the championship rotation (or "rota," as the British say), as opposed to the policy of the United States Golf Association, which
conducts our Open, of holding our championship in all sections of
the vast continental spread of our country. In respect to this last
matter, most golfers regard Baltusrol, in Springfield, New Jersey, and
Oakmont, outside Pittsburgh, as exemplifying the traditional U.S.
Open venue, because these two clubs have put on the most Opens.
However, when you come right down to it, each has held the championship only five times (Baltusrol in 1903, 1915, 1936, 1954, and
1967; Oakmont in 1927, 1935, 1953, 1962, and 1973), and in Baltusrol's case, it should be noted, three different courses have been used.
On the other hand, St. Andrews has been host to the British Open
twenty-one times, and Muirfield, some fifteen miles east of Edinburgh,
a good solid eleven. I mention all this because 1977 was a rather
unusual year in that neither championship was being played at a truly
familiar course. Southern Hills, that splendid course in Tulsa, where
our Open was won in mid-June by Hubert Green, was staging it for
only the second time, and the British Open, which Tom Watson won
in early July, was played for the first time ever on the Ailsa course,
in Turnberry, about fifty miles south of Glasgow. The Turnberry
Hotel, a long, low white stucco building with a pinky-brick-colored
slate roof, is perched atop a fairly high ridge and overlooks its two
courses: the Ailsa, the championship layout, and the Arran, a very
good one.

The wonder, I suppose, is that it took the R. and A. so long to
award the Open to Turnberry (which is how golfers refer to the
championship links), because for twenty years and more the course
has generally been acknowledged to be the best on the West Coast
of Scotland. However, the R. and A., as Wordsworth said of the
Thames, glideth at its own sweet will. In 1961, it gave Turnberry
a tryout by holding the British Amateur Championship there, and
two years later it used the course as the site of the Walker Cup
Match. Turnberry acquitted itself favorably both times, and this undoubtedly had a good deal to do with its receiving the ultimate
laurel, the Open. Tied in with this is a somewhat more complicated
story. Whenever you hold a golf event of some importance in Scot-

land—as a rule, the Open is played alternately in England and in Scotland—you must take pains to see that neither the East Coast nor the West is slighted. As far as championship courses are con-cerned, the East Coast has always been well endowed. To begin with, there is St. Andrews itself, which sits on a small bay off the North Sea. Then, there is Muirfield, undoubtedly the finest classic course in Britain. Muirfield, situated on the south shore of the Firth of Forth, first held the Open in 1892, shortly after succeeding grim, obsolete Musselburgh, on the outskirts of Edinburgh, as the home of the world's oldest golf club—the Honourable Company of Edinburgh Golfers, established in 1744. Add to this duo chill Carnoustie, on the north shore of the Tay estuary, which was admitted to the rota in 1931, and you have three excellent cham-pionship courses. What about the West Coast? Well, the Open was a West Coast monopoly during its first eleven years. The club that initiated the championship was Prestwick, which occupies a ram-bunctious stretch of duneland on the east shore of the Firth of Clyde, and from 1860 through 1870 the Open was played there. In 1871, the Open was temporarily suspended, and when it was resumed, the following year, a new pattern was introduced: Prestwick held it in 1872, St. Andrews in 1873, and Musselburgh in 1874, and it continued to be rotated over those three courses until 1892, when the championship underwent a number of revolutionary changes. Among other things, it was extended from a thirty-six-hole compe-tition to a seventy-two-hole competition, and several new courses, including some in England—Sandwich and Hoylake, in particular—became regular members of the cast. It wasn't until 1923, though, that a second course on Scotland's West Coast, Troon, just north of Prestwick—the two courses are actually contiguous—was cho-sen for the Open. Troon shortly became the only West Coast course on the rota, for after 1925 Prestwick was dropped. Its grounds were not commodious enough to accommodate the swelling galleries, provide adequate parking space, and meet the sundry other demands of a modern golf championship. Moreover, the course did not have the necessary length to test the top golfers in the world, and, ironi-cally, the very features of Prestwick's terrain which had caused the most excitement in the early years of the Open had become sadly outdated. For example, on the short fifth hole and the two-shot seventeenth, the greens were completely hidden from view by huge sand hills. The sand hill on the fifth was proudly called the Himalayas, and the one on the seventeenth the Alps, since in that period a blind approach shot was esteemed as the last word in golf-course *haute couture*, and other clubs envied Prestwick's good fortune in having been so generously endowed by nature. Today, the crusty old course serves as a fascinating museum of what golf was like in the days of the gutta-percha ball.

When a golfer thinks of Turnberry, the first thing that comes to mind, I suppose, is the glorious vista from the hotel on the ridge: the two courses below are spread out over the tumbling duneland along the Firth of Clyde; the Mull of Kintyre and the jagged hills of the island of Arran rise in the distance across the firth; and to the south Ailsa Craig, a colossal granite rock shaped like the top half of a Rugby football, thrusts itself out of the water.

Some two and a half weeks after the U.S. Open, a good many members of that band of gypsies that plays or follows international golf was gathered at Turnberry, and on the evening of the first day of the British Open a number of them were looking down from the Turnberry Hotel at the Ailsa course, on which the last threesomes were finishing their rounds. There has been a golf course on this strip of billowing duneland since before the turn of the century, when the owner of the property, the Marquis of Ailsa, had a private course constructed. In about 1909, shortly after the Marquis sold the land to the Glasgow & South Western Railway, two substantial courses were laid out over it by Willie Fernie, the professional of the Old Troon Golf Club, up the coast. The courses were converted into a training station for the Royal Flying Corps during the First World War. They recovered slowly but encouragingly in the 1920s. Then, in the Second World War, the land was requisitioned as a base by the Royal Air Force Coastal Command, and the two courses all but disappeared from sight as hangars, eighteen-inch-thick runways, and the rest were installed. In the early 1950s, the courses made a mira-culous recovery. Mackenzie Ross, the golf-course architect who had been called in, was not only able to remove just about all traces of the wartime airbase but had improved both the Ailsa and the Arran beyond all expectation. In the case of the Ailsa, he did this by mak-ing perceptive use of the heaving, eccentric terrain on many of the inland holes, the precipitous sand hills near the shore and the nar-row valleys they enclosed, and the handsome stretches of land di-rectly alongside the Firth of Clyde. In recent years, it has become standard practice to refer to the Ailsa course as the Scottish Pebble Beach, because seven holes in a row—the fourth through the tenth—follow the firth. In a way, this appellation is misleading, for the holes are not edged by steep cliffs, like the ones along Carmel Bay, nor are they elevated nearly as high above the water. There are two particu-lar beauties—the fourth and the ninth. The fourth is a par 3 of 167 yards on which the tee and the hard-to-hit green are separated by a thick growth of beach grass. The old custom, more common in Brit-ain than here, of giving golf holes names as well as numbers has all but disappeared, because only too often it fostered the same kind of cute, vapid clichés as the naming of beach houses. The fourth hole on the Ailsa, however, is an exception, it is called Woe-be-Tide, which is extremely appropriate when the tide is high and a stiff wind is coming off the water. On the ninth, a 455-yard par 4, possibly the best and fiercest hole on the course, the tee is straight out of a Gothic novel: it sits atop a small, high crag that sticks out into the firth. From the tee, the golfer must carry his drive about two hundred yards across an inlet to reach the nearest part of the curving fairway. How much of the inlet the tournament golfer chooses to bite off depends on the wind. On British seaside courses—and this applies to the holes that do not actually border on the sea as well as to the ones that do—the principal hazard is the heavy, moisture-laden wind. It follows that under ordinary conditions the key to playing the Ailsa well depends on correctly judging the effect that the wind will have on your shots, and making allowance for this. On the Ailsa, as on most seaside courses, the wind keeps shifting—blowing first out of one quarter and then out of another. For example, on the sixteenth, a 409-yard par

4, I have seen a golfer playing with a following wind get home easily in the morning with just a pitching wedge on his second shot, and then, in the afternoon, seen the same golfer playing into the wind fail to reach the green after a solid drive and a well-struck 3-wood. For the 1977 British Open, the Ailsa measured 6,875 yards—2 yards longer than Southern Hills. Par, as at Southern Hills, was 70—35 out and 35 in.

Before proceeding any farther, I should explain that for the Open the Ailsa did not look or play the way it normally does. To begin with, there was no rough to speak of. The last three years, Britain has been hit with uncommonly hot and parching summers, and the condition of many of the golf courses—those at Turnberry among them—has suffered severely. This year, the Turnberry area, like most of Britain, was also plagued with a long, wet winter, which prevented the grass on the golf courses from getting a proper start. In addition, the Ailsa, which sorely needed both water and sunshine as the Open drew near, went through a damaging stretch of five rainless weeks just prior to the championship. As a result, the fairways were edged by the wispiest kind of rough—a thin, random collection of fescue, buttercups, plantain shoreweed, Yorkshire fog, dandelions, and assorted other weeds, grasses, and wild flowers. As if this weren't disheartening enough, the weather was wrong for the Open. On the first day, the nice, light morning breeze shut down at noon. In the afternoon, the temperature climbed to about eighty-five degrees and there was seldom a breath of breeze. British linksland courses are designed to be played in a wind, and, inevitably, the scores on the first round ran rather low. John Schroeder, of California, led with a 66. Seven other players were in the 60s, and there would have been more had the pins not been placed in dangerous spots on the hard, kittle greens. Johnny Miller, the defending champion, who had brought in a 69, predicted that if there were more of these windless days on the roughless course the scores might run in the low 60s. Before leaving Turnberry that evening for Ayr, where I was billeted, I took a last look at the Firth of Clyde, silver with mist. It had been covered with mist throughout the day, and, while you could see Ailsa Craig, which is not far offshore, the island of Arran and the Mull of Kintyre had not been visible at any time.

Ayr is some twenty miles to the north of Turnberry, and the drive up the back road, which I took that evening, was the ideal anodyne for the long day in the sun. The road winds through Scottish country-side at its tranquil best. You drive past soft-green sloping fields, some of them thick with Ayrshire cows, others punctuated with hayricks, which in this part of Scotland have a sort of ziggurat shape. Ash, oak, and pine trees separate the fields and line sections of the road. Now and then, for a change of pace, you pass a well-kept ruin or slow down through a village where the gardens of the squat stone houses are aflame with roses, which bloom so brilliantly in Scotland. When you cross the Doon River, you know you are bearing down on Ayr and the heart of Robert Burns country. On this drive, two thoughts filled my mind: first, how wonderful it is that so much of Scotland's coun-tryside remains comparatively untouched, and, second, how disap-pointing it would be if we had a continuation of this Tulsa-like heat and still air, rather than typical British Open weather, which sends you striding out into a bracing breeze with a tweed cap on your head and a sweater under your tweed jacket, and carrying a raincoat just in case. Well, the way it turned out, we were in for three more hot, sticky, un-Caledonian days.

On Thursday, the day of the second round, Miller was one of the earliest finishers. He had taken a 74, and wore a mournful expres-sion. "I have thrown away any chance I had of winning the British Open," he said. "You can't shoot a 74 and expect to be in conten-tion. There are going to be a lot of very low scores today, the way the course is playing." Miller had hardly finished saying this when Mark Hayes, a young Oklahoman, brought in a 63—a new record low round for the championship. It could easily have been a 62, for Hayes had missed his par on the eighteenth. Then the word circu-lated that Hubert Green was burning up the course—7 under par for the round with five holes to play. I was one of the detachment that raced out to pick up Green, and saw him bogey three of the last five holes. He had to be satisfied with a 66. Just when it seemed that we were watching the old Tucson Open, things began to settle down, for no apparent reason. In any event, among the players in the running, the lowest round completed late in the day was a 66, by Roger Maltbie, the promising young Californian. This gave him the lead, at 137—a stroke ahead of Green, Nicklaus, Tom Watson, and Lee Trevino, in a tournament that from this point on was almost totally dominated by American golfers. In the end, eleven of the top twelve finishers were Americans.

Late that Thursday afternoon, I was on hand when Henry Cotton completed his second round. The winner of three British Opens (in 1934, 1937, and 1948), and undoubtedly the finest British golfer of modern times, Cotton is now seventy. The oldest of five former champions who received special invitations to play at Turnberry (he had played in his first Open exactly half a century before), Cotton had jumped at the chance. When he holed a short putt on the home green for an 82—since he did not make the thirty-six-hole cut, this putt undoubtedly represented his final stroke in a British Open—a round of applause erupted from the spectators in the stands. He doffed his cap in appreciation. This gesture evoked another round of applause. Visibly affected, Cotton tipped his cap again, and then, straightening his Lanvin sports shirt, slowly headed for the clubhouse.

In the years ahead, all that will probably be remembered about the final thirty-six holes of the 1977 British Open is the fantastic duel between Nicklaus and Watson, who were paired on both the third and the fourth day and threw some altogether stupendous golf at each other as they fought it out—neither of them ever taking a backward step—right down to the seventy-second green. In the high excitement provoked by their shot-making and their admirable combativeness, many experienced golf hands were, understandably, ready to proclaim this the greatest of all British Opens, and, for that matter, the greatest championship ever played anywhere. I don't know if I am prepared to go quite that far, but I do know that I cannot remember a head-to-head battle that can begin to compare with the one that Nicklaus and Watson waged two days running. On the third round, a 66 put Crenshaw only three strokes behind Nicklaus and Watson, and he managed to stay within possible striking distance of the two leaders on the fourth round until, after playing twenty-six consecutive holes without a bogey, he took 6, 2 over par, on the ninth. Then he collapsed, utterly. In retrospect, over the last two rounds the tournament was, in effect, a match between Watson and Nicklaus, although technically, of course, they were engaged in a stroke-play tournament. In the end, the man who finished in third place, Green, was a full ten strokes behind Nicklaus and eleven behind Watson.

When the Watson-Nicklaus duel began to assume epic dimensions, midway through the third round, it virtually erased interest in everything else that had occurred, or would occur, on the Ailsa course that day. Nevertheless, I should like to mention—much too briefly—a few noteworthy performances on that third day before returning to the leaders. I am thinking of the 67 by Peter Thomson, the Australian veteran who has won five British Opens, the first of them in 1954; also of the 67 by Arnold Palmer, in the course of which, exasperated after foozling several short putts, he decided on the seventh green to try putting cross-handed—the left hand lower on the shaft than the right—and came roaring down the last nine in thirty strokes, holing for one birdie from fifteen feet, for three birdies from thirty feet, and for still another birdie, on the home green, from thirty-five feet. It is years since Palmer, who in his prime sank more long putts than any champion in history, has had a day like this on the greens, and—not only because it is his manner to understate his feelings—I can't remember when I last saw him so honestly delighted with his golf. (On the final round, staying with the cross-handed grip and putting well, he had a 69 and finished in seventh place.) I feel compelled to add one more detail. On the third round, Green, only one stroke off the pace, gave us, on the very first hole, a short par 4, an all too painful reminder of his old penchant for wrecking his chances in a tournament by messing up one hole dreadfully. After pulling his approach into a bunker, he muffed his first explosion shot, hit his second over the green, played a mediocre chip and a poor putt, and wound up with a 7. He had a 74 that day, but maybe winning our Open is beginning to give Hubert Green something he never had before, for he came back on the last round to play a confident, steady 67.

Now to Watson and Nicklaus. No sooner had they teed off on Friday, the day of the third round, than the air began to bristle. Just about everyone in the immense gallery was thinking about their classic encounter on the final nine holes of this year's Masters, when Watson, playing right behind Nicklaus and completely aware of what he had to do to stay with this tremendous finisher, refused to be awed, and finally beat him by birdieing the seventy-first hole. Nicklaus, who is now thirty-seven, has been the best golfer in the world for the last twelve years, or possibly even longer, and he sees no reason to cede his throne to any young pup, since he believes that in many ways he is a better golfer today than he has ever been. Watson, who is ten years younger than Nicklaus, is patently an improved player this year. His left side controls his swing just the way it should, and his footwork is very good—not that these are the things you are most conscious of while watching him. What impresses you most is the quickness and decisiveness with which he plays his shots, the freedom of his hitting action, and the sharpness with which he strikes the ball. Much as Watson respects Nicklaus, you felt at Turnberry that he relished the challenge of facing him head-to-head. On both days, he played the better golf from tee to green, but Nicklaus came through with so many stunning recoveries and got down so many long and difficult putts in key situations that until the very end he was the man in command and Watson the hard-pressed pursuer.

Perhaps the most effective way to get across the furious attacks and counterattacks that made this protracted confrontation between Watson and Nicklaus so memorable is simply to set down, with a minimum of embellishment, what took place on the significant holes. On Friday, Nicklaus, off fast, birdied the first hole, a 355-yard par 4, when he played his sand-wedge approach three feet from the cup. Watson answered this with a birdie 3 on the third, a 462-yard par 4; his second shot, a 5-iron, left him only a six-foot putt. On Woe-be-

Tide, the par-3 fourth hole, both men hit 6-irons, Watson stopping his shot two feet from the pin. Nicklaus, however, holed from twenty feet. Two birdies. On the sixth, a 222-yard par 3 across a deep swale, Nicklaus moved out in front by two strokes. He smashed a 2-iron to twelve feet and made the putt. Watson, who was bunkered off the tee, missed his try for a par from eight feet. On the seventh, a 528-yard par 5 that moves uphill most of the way, Watson reached the green in two. Nicklaus, who was starting to pull his tee shots, was never on the fairway on this hole but curled in another good-sized putt—this one from twelve feet—to match Watson's birdie. Scores at the turn: Nicklaus, 31; Watson, 33.

Starting home, Nicklaus continued to pour it on, birdieing the tenth, a 452-yard par 4, with a twenty-five-foot putt. Watson then holed from ten feet for *his* birdie. The fourteenth is a 440-yard par 4 to an elusive green. Here Nicklaus made his first real error of the day, misreading the three-footer he had for his par. Watson, who had looked as if he might fall a stroke farther behind when his approach bounded over the green, got down in two from the rough with a per-fectly gauged chip and actually picked up a stroke. Only one behind now. He got that stroke back on the next hole, the 209-yard fifteenth, when he knocked in a twenty-footer for a birdie 2. On the seven-teenth, an eminently birdieable 500-yard par 5, both made their 4s. Nicklaus let a big chance slip away here: his second, a great 2-iron, finished three feet from the pin, but he pushed his putt for an eagle a shade off line. Scores for the round: Nicklaus, 65 (31, 34); Watson, 65 (33, 32). Each had made six birdies and one bogey. Nicklaus was never behind on this round, but the two short putts he failed to make on the in-nine had cost him the lead.

On Saturday, Nicklaus was again off fast. He jumped into a two-stroke lead with a birdie on the second, a 428-yard par 4, by playing a remarkable 7-iron from an awkward sidehill stance in the rough (the ball was well above his feet) ten feet from the pin. Watson bogeyed the hole, pulling his approach to the left of the green and taking three to get down. Nicklaus increased his lead to three strokes with another 2 on Woe-be-Tide, holing this time from thirty feet.

Watson then mounted a terrific rally. He cut away one stroke of Nicklaus's margin with a birdie 3 on the 411-yard fifth when he followed a lovely 5-iron with a sixteen-foot putt. He cut away another stroke on the long seventh when he reached the green in two, using a driver off the fairway, and two-putted for his birdie. On the eighth, a 427-yard par 4, Watson cut away the last stroke of Nicklaus's lead with yet another birdie: after a 5-iron approach to the heart of the green, he rapped in a twenty-footer. (I don't believe I have ever before seen two golfers hole so many long putts—and on fast, breaking, glossy greens. They were also doing such extraordinary things from tee to green that it was hard to believe what you were seeing.) Then, having come all the way back, Watson once again fell behind. On the ninth, the 455-yard par 4, where the tee is set on the isolated crag, he pushed his drive into the rough on the right, pulled a 1-iron across the fairway into the rough on the left, and needed three more shots to get down. Nicklaus saved his par when he eased a touchy downhill twelve-footer into the cup. Scores on the front nine: Nicklaus, 33; Watson, 34.

On the twelfth, a par 4 only 391 yards long, Nicklaus, after pitching with a wedge, rolled in still another long putt—a twenty-two-footer—for a 3. This birdie moved him out in front by two strokes, and many of us felt at that moment that we had perhaps watched the decisive blow of the struggle. After all, holes were running out fast now—only six were left—and how often does a golfer of Nicklaus's stature fail to hold on to a two-stroke lead as he drives down the stretch? Watson was not thinking in those terms. At this point, he rallied once again. He birdied the thirteenth, a shortish par 4, with a well-judged wedge shot twelve feet from the pin and a firm putt. Then he again birdied the fifteenth, the 209-yard par 3: using a putter from the left fringe of the green, he stroked a sixty-footer smack into the middle of the cup. Now Watson and Nicklaus were again tied. Everything to play for.

Two pars on the sixteenth. On the seventeenth, the 500-yard 5, Watson was down the fairway with his tee shot, a few yards shorter than Nicklaus, who was in the rough on the right. Considering the circumstances, Watson then played one of the finest shots of the day—a 3-iron that was dead on the pin all the way and finished twenty-five feet beyond it. Nicklaus went with a 4-iron. He hit it a trifle heavy, and the ball came down in the rough short of the green and to the right. Throughout these last two rounds, Nicklaus, on his frequent visits to the rough, had improvised a succession of astonishing shots to scramble out his pars and an occasional birdie, and here he punched a little running chip that climbed up and over two ridges in the green and came to rest three and a half feet past the cup. Watson was down in two safe putts for his birdie 4. Nicklaus, who hadn't missed a putt all day, missed his short one. The ball started left and stayed left and didn't touch the cup. A 5, not a 4, and at the worst time possible. Now, trailing Watson by a stroke, Nicklaus's only hope was to birdie the eighteenth, a 431-yard par 4 on which the fairway bends to the left. After Watson had played a prudent 1-iron down the middle of the fairway, Nicklaus, going with his driver, belted a long tee shot that kept sliding to the right—far to the right, and deep into the rough. He was faced with an almost unplayable lie: the ball had ended up two inches from the base of a gorse bush; and, to complicate matters, a branch of the bush, some two feet above the ground, was directly in the line of his backswing. He would be hard put to it to manufacture any kind of useful shot. Watson to play first, going with a 7-iron. He couldn't have hit it much better: the ball sat down two feet from the pin. Nicklaus now, playing an 8-iron. Still not giving up. With his great strength, he drove his club through the impeding gorse branch, managed to catch the ball squarely, and boosted it over the bunker on the right and onto the green thirty-five feet from the cup. He worked on the putt, studying the subtleties carefully, as if the championship depended on it. Then he rammed it in for his 3. Tremendous cheers. Watson chose not to give himself too much time to think about the two-footer he now had to hole to win. After checking the line, he stepped up to the ball and knocked it in. Another salvo of cheers—for Watson, and also for both Watson and Nicklaus and the inspired golf they had played over the last thirty-six holes of the Open. The scores for the concluding round: Watson,

65 (34, 31); Nicklaus, 66 (33, 33). (Nicklaus incidentally, had only one bogey over the last two rounds.) Their scores for the tournament: Watson 68, 70, 65, 65—268. Nicklaus, 68, 70, 65, 66—269. Both shattered to smithereens the old record total for the British Open of 276.

For some reason or other, Jack Nicklaus always moves one more in defeat than in victory. I don't know exactly why this is, for he is an excellent winner. Anyway, he is probably the best loser in the game. He was direct and honest in his assessment of why Watson had won: Tom, he said, had played better golf than he had on both rounds. He had no alibis. Nevertheless, for all his self-possession, it was observable that Nicklaus had been hit hard by losing a second major championship to Watson this year on the final holes after giving the pursuit of winning everything he had. That last phrase is important. No matter what the odds are, Nicklaus never stops fighting, and you never know when he will contrive some small miracle like that impossible 3 on the last hole. In a word, I should say that over the past dozen years, without any question, he had been far and away the best competitor in any sport in which it is one individual against other individuals, not team against team.

How was Watson able to play so superlatively, to keep coming back so valiantly time after time? Alfie Fyles, his gnarled little caddie from Southport, near Liverpool, who also caddied for Watson when he won the British Open at Carnoustie in 1975, put it this way: "His swing is better, more compact. His approach to the game has improved a great deal. He thinks better. He's a mature golfer now." What underlies the confidence that Watson exhibited throughout his extended duel with Nicklaus? For one thing, his triumph in the Masters undoubtedly convinced him that he had reached the point where he could stand up to a giant like Nicklaus. For another, he is able to get himself up very high when he faces Nicklaus, for he appreciates that this is essential. He also knows that he is a sound driver and a sound putter, and, though he doesn't make this kind of pronouncement, he believes he hits the ball as well as anyone. Despite a sensitive temperament and an active imagination, he is now able to relax under pressure. This, of course, helps him to execute his swing well, and when a golfer like Watson feels that he is swinging just the way he wants to, it affirms his feeling of confidence and imbues him with an extraordinary resilience.

The general feeling at Turnberry after the Open was that the R. and A. is almost certain to award the Ailsa course a regular place on its championship rota. After all, if the course produced such a thrilling Open when it was in relatively poor shape, it is only logical to think that it will provide a first-rate test when it is its real self—bearded with some good Scottish rough, and swept by good Scottish winds that will bring the bunkers into play and make ball control critical. (It is, I admit, something of a mystery how the almost defenseless course yielded so few low scores—other than those by Nicklaus and Watson—on the last two and a half days. Some players I talked with thought that the hard-surfaced, rolling greens had effected this, making it difficult to stop one's approaches close to the pins and also to putt consistently well. This suggests that the two leaders, locked deep in their duel, simply forced each other to rise above the conditions.) Everything being equal, the British Open should be back at Turnberry in about seven years. By that time, we should have a much better idea whether Tom Watson is just a very talented golfer or a great golfer. While he is different from Bobby Jones in many ways, there is in him more than a touch of Jones. In seven years, Jack Nicklaus will be forty-four, and yet I wouldn't be at all surprised if at that distant date this prodigious athlete still loomed as a serious contender for the championship.

—1985

The Once and Future Gary Player

Jaime Diaz

With 159 tournament victories around the world, including nine majors, the great South African Champion is indisputably the most successful international golfer of all time.

Gary Player has won so often over so long a period of time, it's difficult to pinpoint exactly when his prime occurred. In one of his more zealous moments, he might even argue that it hasn't ended. But it once had a beginning, and it wasn't long after that Player stamped his image on our collective memory: a gymnastic silhouette in all black (with just a dash of white in his wingtips), biceps stretching the sleeve openings of his Ban-Lon mock turtle, close-cropped pompadour glistening above a face both boyish and rugged, eyes innocent, intense and ruthless all at once.

At the same time, that ageless package—which stays so alive because even at sixty-one and draped in looser fitting earth tones, Player, right down to his thirty-two-inch waist, has hardly changed—conspires against his accomplishments' being appreciated. Player reminds people so much of Jack La Lanne they forget how often he beat Jack Nicklaus.

In golf's history, he's come as close as anyone else to the scope of the Golden Bear feats, making his selection as a Memorial Tournament honoree, which he is for 1997, inevitable. From 1959 to 1978, Player won nine professional majors, a figure exceeded only by Nicklaus and Walter Hagen. Before his thirtieth birthday, he became only the third man to win all four of the professional major championships, joining Gene Sarazen and Ben Hogan. Nicklaus soon became the fourth, and with one more U.S. Open title Player would have matched Nicklaus as the only person to achieve the professional Slam twice (Jack needs one more British Open to complete four cycles). In every season from 1955 to 1982, Player won at least one sanctioned international professional tournament, a remarkable twenty-seven-year victory streak which is ten years longer than anyone else ever achieved. Since competing on the Senior Tour, he has won eight of that tour's major championships (counting, as he does, two British Senior Opens), which is more than anyone else.

Besides being the first foreign winner of the Masters, Player has won the staggering total of 159 tournaments around the world, making him indisputably the most successful international golfer of all time. He did much of it in an era in which it took him fully forty-five hours to commute from his native South Africa to the United States in a propeller-driven aircraft (sometimes with all six of his children and more than thirty pieces of luggage in tow). He won the British Open three times (in an unprecedented three different decades), the Australian Open seven times, the World Match-play five times, the South African Open thirteen times. He is the only golfer to break 60 in a national championship, with a 59 in the 1974 Brazilian Open. His worldwide record dwarfs the efforts of subsequent globe-trotters, including Seve Ballesteros, Nick Faldo, Greg Norman and Nick Price, all of whom have had the assistance of private jets and appearance fees.

A Scrappy Style

Yet Gary Player, despite his permanent place in golf's pantheon of champions, has never quite been anointed with the majesty that the names of Nicklaus, Palmer, Hogan, Snead or Nelson carry. Part of it was his five-foot-seven-inch height, part of it was his scrappy style. He has been characterized as doing it with grit rather than genius, with industry more than artistry. Along with Palmer and Nicklaus he made up the "Big Three," but he was always the third member. About the only thing anyone was prepared to call Player the best at was bunker play, which implies a need to scramble, to compensate for a lack of tee-to-green excellence.

As much as he won, there never seemed to be an extended period when he was clearly the best golfer in the world. Instead, in the midst of the American domination of the game in the 1960s and 1970s, Player was the pesky little man from the other side of the world who interceded during the successive primes of Palmer, Nicklaus, Lee Trevino, Johnny Miller and Tom Watson. Player would pop up in bursts, but, at a time when the PGA Tour was truly the center of golf's universe, he rarely stayed on it long enough to be dominant. Although in 1961 he became the first foreign-born golfer to win the American tour's money list, he never did so again. His finest year was probably 1974, when he won both the Masters and the British Open, but his claim to being the best even that year was mitigated by Miller's eight PGA Tour victories.

Player reveres Gandhi as a model of humility, but if there is anything that taxes his own, it's his record. For one thing, in his mind, it's not over. By Player's count, he has seventeen professional majors including his senior career, while Nicklaus has twenty-two (Player does not consider The Tradition, which he has never won but Nicklaus has won four times, a major), and the chase is still on. "As great as people say Jack was, I played with him at his peak and he was even better," Player says in tribute. "But longevity is the ultimate criterion. All I'm saying is to wait until all the playing is over to judge the record." For another, he's convinced too few understand how much he sacrificed by choosing to make his home in his native South Africa. "If I had come to live in America in my prime, I would have won more majors," says Player, his voice low with earnestness. "I certainly would have won more than twenty-one U.S. tournaments. Now that more players are starting to play around the world, people are realizing the difficulty of what I accomplished. Half the time in the U.S., I was competing with one hand tied behind my back."

Passion versus Discretion

Strong words, but such statements burst out of Player. He is simply too confident, too honest, and too ambitious to keep it inside. Especially when the subject is golf, the man's passion overpowers his discretion.

"I like Corey Pavin—so gutsy," Player says, when asked to assess who he admires among modern players. "He reminds me of me, but I was stronger." To emphasize, he drops into a wide stance and brings his right forearm into position. "If we arm-wrestle, I guarantee you I would take him down (the arm snaps down) like that."

His friends and family have come to accept such crowing as the exhaust from one of the highest-revving engines ever seen. "We call them 'Gary Player statements,'" explains his eldest son, Marc, who administers his father's business empire. "My dad aspires to be the most and best of everything. It's what challenges him about life, and sometimes he gets carried away. He can exaggerate or be overly dramatic, but it's genuine. He sees life new all the time. Most people are bored. He never is."

It's also the quality that has always made Player, apart from his foreign passport, essentially an outsider. While he qualifies on many counts as a prototypical everyman—the working-class background, the self-taught swinger, the undersized underdog, and the outgoing nature that reached out to galleries and made him likable to his peers (Nicklaus calls him "the old South African charmer")—he's a tough guy to identify with. The fact is, adopting Gary Player as Everyman would have made being an average Joe way too much work.

A Human Dynamo

Whether he is pushing the benefits of high-fiber diets, weight-training, yoga, or the power of positive thinking—all areas in which as a golfer he was decades ahead of his time—Player is a human dynamo who tends to make normal people uncomfortable with what they haven't done with their own lives. The man even has a personal "Ten Commandments of Life," a distillation of the fervent codes by which he's striven to live. ("A promise made is a debt incurred" is his third commandment. "The fox fears not the man who boasts by night, but the man who rises early in the morning" is the sixth.)

Player would probably be easier to identify if all of his excesses were the manifestations of an unhappy, obsessive-compulsive control freak, a lonely Type A run amok. But the confounding thing is that he's quite the opposite. Player has been married to the same woman for forty years, is close to all of his six children, dotes on his six grandchildren, and has real friends on six continents. During and after apartheid in his native South Africa, he has been a hero to both black and white. On his thousand-acre estate near Johannesburg—Blair Atholl—he maintains a nursery school and a primary school serving four hundred black children that includes accommodations for teachers and their families. After winning the 1965 U.S. Open, he donated his twenty-five-thousand-dollar check to junior golf and cancer research. "I think the thing about Gary is that there is nothing bad you can really say about him," says Arnold Palmer.

In Pursuit of Greatness

It's a complex picture, one that's tended to blur Player's feats on the course. But in another way, it's easy. All the effort and all the extremes, all the passion, were for a simple aim—to be the greatest golfer who ever lived. So when Player did all those Gary Player things—practicing in bunkers until he had holed five times, convincing himself that the course he was playing that week was among the finest in the world, lugging sixty pounds of barbells with him on his transcontinental travels—it was all part of a grand design. His willingness to go to extremes, to do the unorthodox, to commit to uncharted waters ("there are no half measures," he is fond of saying), is a manifestation of his lifelong adherence to his eighth commandment, borrowed from Winston Churchill: "Trust instinct to the end, though you cannot render any reason." In his incredibly focused mind, Gary Player had no choice.

As the great British golf chronicler, Pat Ward-Thomas, wrote of Player: "No golfer that I have known, not even Hogan, Nicklaus or

Palmer, has been more lastingly consumed with the desire to conquer and prove himself the greatest of all golfers."

To those who saw Player early in his career, it seemed an absurd goal. His size, an unorthodox method that included an overly strong grip, a flat swing and a chronically off-balance finish, as well as a stabby putting stroke, all stacked the decks against him. "I remember being quite appalled at his method," said Peter Alliss, who first saw Player in the mid-1950s. "A few well-meaning older pros told him he'd be better off to go back home and get a nice club job." Even after he'd made himself a legend, there remained an unfinished quality to Player's golf that prompted the late golf writer Peter Dobereiner to quip, "No better than a two handicap, really."

But Player had a genius for winning of, in the words of Ward-Thomas, "the natural games player." It involved all the intangibles—courage, resourcefulness, an unerring sense of moment, and, above all, desire.

"There was nothing really exceptional about Gary's game," said Nicklaus of his good friend, "except one thing: his desire to win. I've seen him win tournaments you thought there was no way he could win, just do it on pure guts. I don't think Gary was a great driver of the golf ball. I don't think he was a great iron player. He was a good putter, not a great putter. But, when he really needed to be, he was a great driver, and a great iron player, and he made the putt when he needed to make it. Gary, as much as anyone I ever saw, has that thing inside him that champions have."

Fiercely Competitive

Whatever that thing is, those who played against him knew it was there. Arnold Palmer has called Player the fiercest competitor he ever encountered. Nicklaus has called Player's second-place finish by a stroke to Raymond Floyd at the 1969 PGA Championship—when Player was under death threats and antiapartheid demonstrators tried to disturb his rounds by, among other things, throwing cups of ice in his face—the greatest performance he has ever seen on a golf course.

"If I ever won a tournament in my life, I won that tournament," says Player. Seve Ballesteros said that being Player's playing partner in the final round of the 1978 Masters, when Player birdied seven of the final ten holes to win, was vital to making him a major championship winner. It's the stuff that allowed Player to defeat Tony Lema in the thirty-six-hole semifinal of the 1964 Piccadilly World Matchplay after falling 7 down with seventeen holes to play, a match he later said "contains my whole life story." Lee Trevino, who knows something about overcoming obstacles, understands the essence of Gary Player.

"Everything Gary's ever done in golf probably seemed impossible to most people," said Trevino, "but the man's got more belief in himself than anyone I've ever seen. He's always been David against Goliath. He was small but he was strong, and he worked tremendously hard. Biggest thing, he had—has—a gigantic heart."

Tough Beginnings

Player was born November 1, 1935, in Johannesburg, South Africa, the third of three children to Harry and Muriel Player. The family lived in a poor neighborhood built directly over a gold mine called Robinson Deep, where Harry Player was a mine captain who spent most of his working life twelve thousand feet underground. The elder Player was a big man, six feet one inch, more than two hundred pounds, with a gregarious disposition and booming laugh that earned him the nickname Laughing Harry. One of Gary's earliest memories is seeing his father emerge from the mine at the end of his shift, take off his boots, and empty liquid out of them. "I thought it was water," says Player. "It was sweat." By the time Harry Player died in 1977 at the age of seventy-eight, he had been all over the world to see his son win golf tournaments.

Muriel Player was a well-educated woman who mixed affection with an insistence on correct manners. The nurturing environment was one that, early on, made Player feel special. "My parents always encouraged us," he says. "I'm sure it gave me the belief that what I could conceive, I could achieve. It's the greatest gift you can give a child."

At the age of forty-four, Muriel Player succumbed to cancer after a long battle. Gary was eight years old, and he calls his mother's death the key event in his life. "That was the moment my case-hardening started," he wrote in his 1991 autobiography, *To Be the Best: Reflections of a Champion*. "That loss was to breed an independence, a toughness of spirit, and an awareness of adversity and discipline that have never left me. . . . All that I am and all that I have become is in some way a tribute to her. [Her loss] has been a means for me, as it were, to settle some unfathomable debt."

In his mind, Player has never paid it back. He still carries a "burning regret that she never saw what I made of myself." Throughout his life, he has had a recurring dream in which his mother appears before him and he tells her all that he has achieved, but she is unable to hear him.

There would be more toughening at the hands of his brother Ian, six years older than Gary, who, as the founder of Africa's International Wilderness Leadership foundation, has for several decades been one of the leading conservationists in the world. Shortly after their mother's death, Gary attempted to run a mile course with his brother, only to fall to the ground exhausted after less than a half mile, gasping, "Ian, I just can't make it." The older boy yanked Gary to his feet and dressed him down. "You can do anything you want to. Remember that. There's no room for 'can't' in this life." He punctuated his message with a swift kick to Gary's rear end. "Ever since," says Player, "if I've been tempted to say 'I can't,' I feel that kick again."

Golf Seemed a Sissy Game

Player was drawn to athletics, and, although he was small, he excelled in cricket, track, gymnastics and boxing. He also had an affinity for Hollywood westerns and celluloid heroes like Hopalong Cassidy, which spurred his love of horses and served as the inspiration for his all-black outfits. Golf seemed a "sissy game." But when Harry Player, a low handicapper, took his fourteen-year-old son to Virginia Park Golf Course for his first-ever round, Gary parred three holes in a row. "I always picked up sports quickly," says Player, who respectfully takes issue with Sam Snead's statement that "Gary Player did more with less than any golfer I've ever seen." "I had a great deal of talent. But talent alone will only take you so far."

He had more motivation to play golf because of Vivienne Verwey, the daughter of Virginia Park head pro Jock Verwey. One year younger than Gary, she worked in the golf shop and was an accomplished junior player. She beat Gary like a drum in their early matches, the only concession being that she played off the forward tees. "I'm going to marry that girl," he told a friend.

At fifteen, Player literally broke his neck showing off for friends by jumping headfirst into what he thought was a soft compost pit. For more than a year he had to remain physically inactive. Although he nearly went stir-crazy, he didn't waste the time.

"I would stand in front of a mirror and say to myself, 'You're the greatest golfer in the world' hundreds of times," he remembers. "You can call that vainglorious, but I wouldn't have accomplished a fraction of what I've done if I hadn't talked to myself this way."

The Travels Begin

In 1953, at the age of eighteen, he turned professional, taking an eighty-dollar-a-month assistant's job at Virginia Park. Two years later, he won his first tournament, the 1955 East Rand Open, near Johannesburg. Funded by a collection from friends and local golfers, plus his father's bank loan, Player took the equivalent of five hundred dollars to play his first foreign tour, which would include his first airplane ride (he's logged an estimated eight million miles since, entailing the equivalent of more than two years of his life in the air). His first stop was Cairo for the Egyptian Match-play Championship on the banks of the Nile. Player beat fellow South African Harold Henning for the title, and three hundred dollars.

Next he went to Great Britain for the first of what this year will be forty-three consecutive British Opens. Upon arriving at St. Andrews, he found the guest houses full and the hotels too expensive for his miserly budget. That first night, he slept in a sand dune off the Firth of Forth.

Early in 1956, Player won a tournament at famed Sunningdale near London by shooting 70, 64, 64, 68, 72—338 for five rounds. Afterward, the great Australian player and teacher, Norman Von Nida, told him, "Kid, you've really got it." Player was fascinated. "I asked him, 'What is *it*?' He responded, 'Well, nobody can define it, but you've got it.' I still don't know what 'it' is. I only know it when I see it. It's a way of moving, a way of carrying yourself. It's what a good thoroughbred horse has. Snead had it. Palmer had it. Nicklaus had it. Tiger Woods has it."

The next year, Player made his first trip to America, where the game's best players made it clear by example that he needed to improve his game. He was particularly struck by his inability to reach the par 5s at Augusta in two shots. So Player continued to strengthen his body, while weakening his hooker's grip and learning how to carry the ball through the air farther. The next year, he won his first American event, the 1958 Kentucky Derby Open.

If Player needed any reinforcement, he got it from his idol, Ben Hogan, in the Southern Hills locker room after finishing second in the 1958 U.S. Open. "Hogan got about an inch from my face and locked me with those cold eyes. I'll ever forget it. 'Son,' he said, 'you are going to be a great player.' Can you imagine hearing that from Hogan. Man alive!"

First Major

The next year, Player won the British Open at Muirfield. He started the final day, in which thirty-six holes were played, eight strokes behind the leader, Belgian Flory van Donck. But, partially fueled by van Donck's comment that Player would never make it because his swing was too flat, he played brilliantly. On the seventy-second tee, needing a par for 66 and certain victory, he drove into the rough and made a double-bogey 6. Believing he had blown the championship, he waited for the next two hours as contender after contender fell back. Finally, when van Donck and England's Fred Bullock failed to birdie the final hole, Player at twenty-three was the British Open champion.

Much has been made of Player getting early momentum in major championships from the failures of others, but he believes his ascension was inevitable. When asked if he believes losing because of that final double-bogey at Muirfield would have devastated him, Player chuckled at the absurdity. "Oh no," he said. "I was too determined."

The churning has never stopped. In his autobiography, Player offers an almost chilling insight. "What I have learned about myself," he wrote, "is that I am animal when it comes to achievement and wanting success. There is never enough success for me. I cannot attain enough."

Player's greatest attainments came in the 1960s, that magical decade in golf when he, Palmer and Nicklaus were at or near their peaks. His victory at the 1961 Masters is generally remembered as a championship Palmer threw away by making a double-bogey from the middle of the eighteenth fairway to lose to Player by a stroke. It's been forgotten that, down the stretch, Player made a double-bogey on the par-5 thirteenth hole and a bogey on the par-5 fifteenth. But, on the seventy-second hole, he saved par from the same greenside bunker that later victimized Palmer.

The next year, Player won the PGA Championship at Aronomink to give himself three legs of the modern Grand Slam. Palmer and Nicklaus also had three legs when the U.S. Open came to Bellerive in 1965, at that time the longest course ever to hold a U.S. Open, and they were duly made the favorites. But Player realized he had a trance-like concentration that week. A large scoreboard near Bellerive's first tee had the names of the previous winners on it, with a blank after the slot for 1965. The first time Player studied the scoreboard, he says he clearly saw the blank filled by the name Gary Player in gold letters. He went on to defeat Kel Nagle in a playoff. Attaining the career Grand Slam before the age of thirty remains Player's proudest achievement.

Believing You're the Best

"Competing against Jack and Arnold, at our peaks, those were the greatest days of my life," said Player. "We tried like hell to beat each other. Each of us would tell the other two how he was going to beat them. It was understood that our competition was all out, with no mercy. But we always stayed great friends, which is something I treasure. It doesn't embarrass me to say I have great love for both Arnold and Jack.

"I don't want to sound boastful, but I always thought I was going to win when I played them. That's how a superstar thinks. That's a large part of being a superstar. Believing you're the best."

He needed that mental edge, because Player's victories were rarely textbook examples of perfect ball-striking. Rather, they were models of course management, emotional control, and the sheer ability to get it done. Those were the qualities that made Player so tough in match-play.

Player produced the most solid golf of his career in 1974, when he won the Masters and the British Open with wonderfully controlled performances. It would effectively mark the end of his prime, but Player was saving his most improbable exhibition of eleventh-hour heroics as the final validation of his greatness.

Crowning Achievement

When he came to Augusta in 1978, Player was forty-two and hadn't won in the U.S. since his 1974 Masters victory. He began the final round seven strokes behind, and was still far back after a disappointing par on the par-5 eighth hole. But then he went on a tear in which he birdied seven of the final ten holes, dramatically holing an eighteen-footer on the seventy-second hole. He shot 64, playing the final nine in thirty strokes. When Tom Watson, Rod Funseth and, finally, Hubert Green, all faltered down the stretch, Player, incredibly, had won.

"That Masters is my crowning achievement," says Player. "I was out of the tournament—out of it—but I simply never gave up. My focus was so intense, it was as if I poured every lesson I ever learned into that final nine holes. Do you know, I had two lip-outs on fifteen-footers and missed another birdie from six feet on that back nine? I could have shot 27! I was absolutely possessed! To beat those young players on that course, to convert that opportunity into victory, that was the finest moment of my career."

It was Player's last major championship. Miraculously, he would win the next two regular events, the Tournament of Champions and the Houston Open, to become the last player to win three times consecutively on the PGA Tour. They were his last regular tour victories.

Since joining the Senior Tour in 1985, Player has won eighteen more times. His last victory occurred in the same state where he won his first U.S. tournament, Kentucky, at the 1995 Bank One Classic, by closing with a 64.

"Golf is a puzzle without an answer," he says, with a smile. "You end up knowing a lot about nothing. I've won so many different ways, with so many different theories and thoughts. Nothing works for very long. It's a constant search. I've learned there are no absolutes in golf. You name me a player that does it one way, I'll name you one just as successful who does the opposite."

The Ultimate Survivor

But it was in this pressurized cauldron of unknowns that Player thrived, the ultimate survivor. "I suppose my greatest physical skill was getting the ball in play, one way or another," he says. "There were many, many times in major championships when I was lost, hitting absolute rubbish, but I would find a way to get the ball on the green. From there, I had the ability to make putts from ten feet and in. The ones you simply have to make.

"A champion finds the way to make the shot come off. People who don't understand say it's luck. There is always some luck, but luck is the residue of design. It's practice, it's instinct, it's eyesight, it's energy, it's feel. Finally, you know, it's desire. I don't know why I've always had so much, but it made the difference."

But even Gary Player's desire is finite. He has vowed that his final appearance in the British Open will come at St. Andrews in the year 2000. He speaks of wanting to spend more time in South Africa, where he has three residences, the thousand-acre primary estate called Blair Atholl outside Johannesburg, a beach home in Pletenburg Bay near Capetown, and his eight-thousand-acre stud farm near Colesburg in the country's Karoo, bordered by the Orange River. Player has named it Mandiba, a term of affection and respect South Africans often use when addressing Nelson Mandella. All three homes are underused, and all beckon.

At the same time, Player remains too much a warrior to simply walk away from competition. He loves the challenge and the age-defying concept of the Senior Tour, where he is known among his peers by the forever-young nickname of "Laddie." And when he returns to Augusta each year, he competes with all his heart, convinced that, if a hot putter could somehow get him into contention on Sunday, he would still thrive on the opportunity.

"I just haven't sorted it out yet," he says. "My life, in a way, is too full."

It's the complaint of a protean force. Player's rewards have been great, but so has his sacrifice. From private struggles, like forcing himself to do his daily exercises and being apart from his family, to public ones like enduring close defeats or being unfairly branded a racist, Player has paid a price. "Those who aim at great deeds must also suffer greatly" is a quotation from Plutarch's *Lives* that could have been Player's eleventh commandment. Of course, he would gladly pay the price all over again.

"I have been so blessed, so lucky with golf, with my family, with my health, all I can be is thankful," he says. "When I was younger, to achieve what I wanted to achieve, I had to be selfish. It's a very self-ish game. But I had a wife who was selfless. Can you imagine what it must have been like being married to me? Vivienne is the greatest thing that ever happened to Gary Player.

"As I've gotten older, I've come to understand that fewer things matter. Love is the most important word in our lives. As much as I'm proud of my record in golf, people will forget."

—1997

The Ride of Greg Norman's Life

Chris Hodenfield

It is not anger, or resentment, or even amusement that he feels. It is something like astonishment. when Mark McCumber looks at Greg Norman, he does not know what to think.

His confusion was neatly encapsulated in an image he saw one night in San Francisco. It was Norman coming out of an elevator, resplendent in a white suit and a dark turtleneck, stepping into a limousine for a night on the town. What an *aura*, McCumber thought. What an entrance.

"He *is* larger than life," McCumber reflected one day recently. And it's not just Norman's physical luminance; it's the staggering fortune he has amassed. It's the way he arrives at a tournament by helicopter. It's the Ferrari, not to mention his friendships with grand-prix race drivers.

And then there is the matter of Norman's lust for danger. It's those hairsbreadth escapes when he goes scuba diving at night. Does this somehow relate to Norman's overly dramatic golf game? It sure might.

McCumber's parents taught him not be envious, and he's not. "I'm *happy* for Greg," he says at last. It's just that McCumber doesn't know if Greg has earned all the attention. He wonders why people talk up Norman over a Hale Irwin or a Larry Nelson. *Why*, in the name of Arnie and Jack, is Norman given such regard? *Why* is he so darned rich?

Along with a few dozen of his PGA Tour brethren, McCumber looks at Norman and wonders why.

Duty and Betrayal

Every year Greg Norman plays in fifteen tour events in the United States. One of these is generally the Carlsbad, California, event now called the Mercedes Championships. In January he flew in from Asia on a Sunday and checked into the La Costa Resort & Spa. His swing advisor, Butch Harmon, would meet him on the range Monday for some loosening up. The rest of the week seemed wallpapered from end to end with duties.

The previous six weeks had been a grind of explanations and accusations. In November he had announced his support of a proposed World Golf Tour. Some old friends felt he was betraying the existing tours, and he felt some of his friends were betraying him by not supporting the new venture. When he went back home to Australia for two tournaments, he found himself embroiled in endless interrogations. He knew it would be rough in America, so once back in California, he did what he does by habit: He took charge.

On the driving range, facing the same players who had just weeks ago been violently critical of him, he had a jaunty wave and a prompt hello. For the writers who had hammered him over the proposed tour, he conducted a charming press conference in which he gently disarmed them.

Was he, for instance, in league with media magnate Rupert Murdoch in a drive for world golf domination? Pshaw! No such thing! Met the man only once, boys. And it's not *my* new tour, anyway. A couple of fellows just had an idea, and I thought I'd give it my support.

It was a masterful performance.

He would also be meeting with PGA Tour Commissioner Tim Finchem for a private session. There was business to conduct. There were dinners to attend, promotional film clips to star in, charity requests to honor.

He was a month short of his fortieth birthday. Up close you could see the deepening lines in his forehead and the more sunken set of his eyes. His skin had an unreal, almost orangy glow, like that of an actor still in his stage makeup. The eyes were pale blue and there were more sharp angles to his face than a box of knives. In his pres-

ence I thought of something I had once heard said of Burt Lancaster—
he exudes physical power.

Just standing quietly in a coffee shop, Norman has the bearing
of a gymnast about to do handsprings across the ceiling. This intensity makes him a hard guy to nail down. You can spend the morning
talking, and while he loosens up over the course of it, he in no way
seems carefree. Eight years ago, for another magazine story, I spent a
week in his company at his Orlando home. Back then he seemed a
hearty glad-hander and backslapper in all public situations. He paid
for every beer in sight. The rocketing trajectory of the early 1980s
seemed to be all his, and he walked through them as if basking in a
sunlit ticker-tape parade.

The only time he seemed locked in any ferocity was out on the
practice range, alone with his thoughts. But this first meeting was in
the spring of 1987, and he had just been skunked in the Masters playoff by Larry Mize for his second major miracle-shot defeat in a row,
and when he practiced chip shots then, he was thinking about that
sonofabitching chip shot of Larry Mize's. He would say it out loud,
too: "Here's a Larry Mize." Then he would stare that eye-bulging stare
at the infidel range balls. Elsewhere, he was all charm. Playing golf
with high-handicap friends, he was remarkably patient.

These days, one has to wonder if he is a changed man. I was curious how time had left its mark on him. Certainly he is thinned down
and more purposeful looking. In public you wouldn't want to say he
is cold, but he has definitely become watchful. A thousand hands
have reached for him at every event, and so his eyes have developed
a thousand-yard stare. If you catch him at the wrong moment his gaze
sweeps past you like a lighthouse beam. I began to think of him as
Old Iron Eyes.

"You have to understand Australian people," says fellow Aussie
Steve Elkington. "They're different from U.S. people; they're very
loyal. Greg's an extremely loyal person. If you're on the right side of
him, fine. If you're on the wrong side, he won't give you the time of
day. That's the way a lot of people are in Australia. We don't buddy
up with everybody. And in his position, everybody wants to be his
friend."

During his doggiest days last November, while playing in the Australian Open, Norman made a startling confession: "When I left Australia I left all my real mates behind and I've never really developed any true friendships in America. There's no one I can have a beer with and just talk about nothing."

He has for years talked moonily of leaving America behind and settling down in some cattle station in the Australian outback—an idea his American wife and children have not embraced. But even back home the critics take strips off him.

Peter Thomson, the godfather and overseer of Australian golf, is typically acerbic: "As a player I think it's fair to say he did not reach the great heights we hoped for and dreamed of. What we didn't realize was that he didn't have a natural rhythm to his game, like a Boros, a Snead or Hogan. Norman is like a stretched bow: You draw back the string and, *foom*, let the arrow go.

"Everybody gets tense. You're not human if you don't. It's that tension in his body, and probably his thinking, that has caused errors that have cost him championships."

That fateful 1993 Tour Championship in San Francisco, where he had trouble hitting two of the last three greens, the unseemly finish at Doral in March, all those Winged Foots and Augustas where he lost it at the end—these events hang over Norman's head like the sword of Damocles.

Schopenhauer once said that the first forty years of a man's life furnish the text, while the remaining thirty provide the commentary. But Norman is not having any of that talk—already a very strong fellow, he's made himself into more of a strongman: His full-time trainer comes over for the big workout five days a week. Norman travels with a plane full of weights; he does everything but dare you to an arm-wrestling contest. For the next five years, he's going to be murder on spikes and finish up the seven-year plan he started a couple of years ago. Then, at age forty-five, he'll retire, give it all up and find something new. He says, he says.

He's like Gary Player in that he'll hit you with this vast, blustery energy that will either convert you or leave you winded. And since he's taken so many knocks for his wealth, for his game, for the very size of his personality, an unsettling defensiveness can be heard in his assertions. It's as if he's saying, *"Don't try to make me feel guilty for my life."*

Beginnings of a Good Life

Royal Queensland is probably the nicest course in Brisbane, Australia. It's known as the most British of the local clubs. Pleasant, nearly flat, lined with enormous fig trees, it started out in 1920 as an Alister Mackenzie design, but the years and other men have left their changes. The most serious alterations were necessitated by the building of a highway bridge over the twelfth hole.

Toini Norman, the mother of Greg Norman, pauses in the fairway to point up at the soaring bridge. "Greg once hit a ball over that bridge," she says with an embarrassed smile. I gaze up at it. This is a big bridge. The towers seem to be no taller than the World Trade Center.

"We were having a sort of opening-day celebration after the bridge was finished," Toini says, "and somebody dared him to do it. He tried and tried, and finally with a 7-iron he hit a crane that was parked on top. So, you see, it can be done."

Mrs. Norman is by no means given to fulsome braggadocio. The daughter of Finnish immigrants, she has a kind of Scandinavian reserve to go along with a blossoming and friendly energy. A petite woman, she is a robust golfer with a long, flowing swing. The swing is just as efficient as she is. Stepping quickly, she knows where she is going and doesn't waste time, pulling her clubs on a hand cart they call a trolley. In between shots, she tells, with a bit of prodding, the stories of how her teenaged son played here.

We get to the tenth tee and face a narrow, serpentine fairway with a huge tree crowding on the right. Mrs. Norman says: "Well, Greg, of course, just hit it over that tree."

Of course.

We get to the green. "In 1973 the Australian Open was held here and Greg got in as an amateur. He would have been about eighteen. He was doing quite well until he got here." She points to a greenside bunker. "A friend of his was caddieing for him and put the bag down on the other side of the green and walked over to talk to somebody. Greg's ball came out and rolled over and hit the bag. And Greg knew right away that meant a two-shot penalty." She sighs tenderly. "So he ended up taking an 8. He was, well, quite upset."

He, ahem, burst out crying, didn't he? Mother, reddening, says "Yes."

Her husband, Mervyn Norman, plays along with us, but he uses an old green golf cart. It is the only cart I see on the premises. Merv is more the strong, silent type. One can instantly see that he is responsible for the genes that produce tremendous shoulders. Like his son, he looks like he packs a linebacker's pads under his shirt. No neck at all is apparent. A broad powerful nose hooks down over a thin mouth. Even though his family is also Nordic, he resembles a mighty Italian industrialist. In his youth, he played on national teams in a rough, brawling sport called rugby league. Even now at the age of sixty-six he looks ready for anything. Gripping a club in big hands, he takes something of a half golf swing, like a power chop.

Engineering and the mining business were his trade, but even in retirement he is likely to take off for Chile on business. Says Greg, "Dad is very—dogmatic might be a strong word, but when he wants to do something, he doesn't procrastinate. He does it [bangs desk] NOW!"

When Greg so suddenly put his weight behind a new World Tour, and dared anybody not to like it, one could only think of Merv Norman pounding his fist on the table.

Greg has a sister named Janis Wedge, older by two years, who works in the Brisbane city government. (Her twenty-one-year-old son is an aspiring pro with a name that cries out for headlines: Kristian Wedge.) Janis has her brother's direct style. She, like most people, feels the young Greg was enormously influenced by his mum, the cheerful, go-ahead, physically fit dynamo. As Greg ages, she sees more of Dad in his thinking, especially in his developing, take-on-the-world business sense. "They're constantly thinking," she says, "they're constantly on the go. They really don't know how to sit down and properly relax. Even when Greg goes fishing, it's like work."

Early Power

Toini was the golfer of the family. As legend tells us, she played at or close to a 4–handicap through most of her pregnancy with son Greg. (The concept of amniotic golf instruction bears some study. Davis Love III and Paul Azinger also have mothers who played competitive golf deep into their pregnancies.) When Greg was almost sixteen, he caddied for her, then borrowed her clubs and played a fast round. He became fixated on the game and within two years was a scratch player, getting his name in the papers with fat headlines.

Those earliest rounds of his took place at a raunchy old course across town called Virginia Golf Club. Many of Australia's golf champions got their start at a working man's club like Virginia—wide-open, friendly places that do not penalize the exuberant. His first pro, John Klatt, told him to "hit it as hard as you got." Klatt's reasoning was this: You can learn control later on, but not power. If you hit it in the wrong fairway, just hit back over the trees to the green.

At Virginia, then later at Royal Queensland, the Norman family put their names on a whole raft of club championship boards.

When Greg graduated from high school and announced to them he wanted to be a golf professional, the parents were not amused. Merv had always hoped his son would follow him into the engineering business. But he saw that his son had absolutely no use for school books. Greg was not even up to fulfilling his own dream of being an air force pilot. All he wanted to be was outdoors.

Which is a nice place to be in the state of Queensland, a big sprawling state (three times the size of Texas) on the northeast coast of Australia. Brisbane has the feel of a very clean San Diego—a sunshine factory where every kid grows up sunburnt.

Peter Thomson explains Australia's legacy. "We have a sporting instinct," he says, "and it is impressed upon every kid by his parents that whatever you do in sports, 'You're going to have to do it well or otherwise I'll kick your ass.' It's in all of us. We are pugnacious, cheeky winners. Every kid gets it—it's from our origins as part of a pioneering mob that came to a strange land to eke out a living."

If the son seems always ready to level with you, it is because of Merv Norman's constant refrains on the subject: "Tell the truth and you can never be found out later. Tell the truth and you're never uncomfortable."

If his surfing galoot of a son needed a swift kick, Merv would recite from William Cowper's poem about Boadicea:

Then the progeny that springs from the forests of our land,
Armed with thunder, clad with wings, shall a wider world
    command.

Greg was known among his friends for his astounding hand-eye coordination. He was a crack shot with a rifle, a tiger on the tennis courts and a demon at the snooker table. He could cast a rod beautifully, right- or left-handed. He was a bareback horseman. He was an exceptional batsman at cricket. He was a dedicated surfer. They went sailing and diving all the time. Once he fell on the bridge and knocked his front teeth out. He liked to rough it up at rugby, too, and in one grueling match had his new capped front teeth pushed in. With the second accident, the dentist was worried about the future of his mouth.

"That's why he took up golf," says Toini later, as she shows a photograph of young Greg grinning with a mouthful of metal teeth. "The doctor said to stay away from sports. Greg had to channel that energy into something."

An Aggressive Guy

If there was one thing Greg was known for, it was energy. He just had too much of it. "His idea of practice was *practice*," recalled his boyhood friend Glen Cogill. "He didn't just go muck around and have a drink. His hands would nearly bleed." If a club job demanded that he open the golf-shop doors at 7:30 A.M., he was out of bed at 4 so he could start practice at first light. (To this day he likes to rise at 5 A.M.)

In those days, when he was just a rough surf punk with shoulder-length white hair, it was not unknown for Greg to smash his fist into a locker after a tough loss, or drive a ball over the heads of a slow-moving group up ahead, or chase some cats up the road in his Cortina.

"He had his wild moments," notes his old mate Jimmy Barden. "Once we were towing Merv's boat back of my car and we got stuck in a traffic jam. So Greg says turn here, now turn here, and soon we were pulling this boat over the back nine at Virginia. I had no idea where we were going. He just kept pushing me along."

"And he was very aggressive with the girls," remembers Cogill. "Aw, yeah. Very aggressive guy. He used to get in a few scraps with the blokes over the girls. And he would not back off from anybody. Tough as nails."

Barden and Cogill have now settled into club-pro jobs, and they are comfortable with admitting that they were mere organ grinders while Greg was apparently Beethoven.

"He was very well organized," Cogill says. "He knew where he was going, and he wanted it real bad. That's the kind of guy he was. You could nearly call him cocky. At the junior pennants he'd say, 'I'm going to beat this guy five and four.' He was cocky for an Australian: We're a pretty negative people."

The Australians have what's called the Tall Poppy Syndrome: If anyone gets too big, the verbal knife comes out to cut him down to size. When Norman was nineteen, he and his other amateur cohorts from Virginia were on a six-hour bus ride to play a match against Grafton. Over the usual game of euchre, Norman suddenly announced that he was going to be the best player in the world and, further, he was going to be a millionaire by the time he was thirty. His friends offered the only possible response for such a skyrocketing poppy: "Shut up. You've had too much beer."

What saved Norman was falling under the tutorial eye of Charlie Earp, the club pro at Royal Queensland. A wiry legend of Australian golf, Earp was very tough, very conservative, and taught his boys first that *everything has to be neat.* And you have to be dressed properly, too. Perhaps because he is built along the lines of a jockey, Earp never got to live out his tour aspirations. And so he took delight in pushing students like Norman and Wayne Grady into the limelight. One of his methods, oddly enough, was teaching them to adopt "the aura of a clown."

Charlie pauses in the living room of his Brisbane home to explain. The room is a monument to Norman, with photographs and statues of him everywhere. Prominently framed is a shot of Earp serving as Norman's caddie at the 1984 U.S. Open at Winged Foot, where they lost in a playoff to Fuzzy Zoeller.

"Golf pros are really clowns," Earp says soberly. "I don't mean as idiots, but wanting to perform. You want to show people how good you are. You get these good players," he says, waving his hand toward the street, "but they don't have that flamboyancy, that clown performance about them. The clown in the circus is making people happy. Gary Player is like that, and so are Seve and Greg."

When one practiced, one always pretended that the shot was occurring in the swarming midst of Open pressure. In Norman he had a student possessed. "Greg dug up the driving range, he practiced so hard," says Earp. "It bloody looked like pigs had been digging it up. The committee wanted to bar him from the course."

"Downright Insolence"

Greg Norman was just twenty-one years old when he first discovered that with victory comes resentment. It happened in October 1976, at the West Lakes Classic on the Australian PGA Tour. He was not a full member of the tour at the time, being just an invited trainee, a fellow who really belonged in back of the shop cleaning Mrs. Budgewhistle's clubs.

He had, in fact, been playing golf only a little more than five years. This was his fourth professional event. But as soon as he opened with a 64, lowering the course record by three shots, the bright lights spun on him like Satan's own wicked grin.

"He played very aggressively," recalls Cogill, who caddied for him that week. "The Grange course is fairly short, tricky and narrow, and the other guys like Bruce Crampton were hitting 2-irons off the tee. But Greg kept going at it with a driver and ending up with just a chip wedge to the green, where the other guys had 7-iron. These guys couldn't believe how far he was hitting the ball."

He was, in those days, what he later would call "John Daly long." (An Australian newspaper would brand his 350-yard drives "downright insolence.")

"I couldn't believe what I was watching on TV," Barden remembers. "One week we're traveling around to competitions in an old car, finding some place to bum up a bed, and all of a sudden there he is winning the tournament."

Barden saw Charlie Earps' teachings in full flight. "That's where the showmanship comes up," said Barden. "He wasn't daunted or scared by being in the lead. He goes to West Lakes, and whammo."

And then his life went whammo. The winnings were just seven thousand dollars, but along with the money he had won in high-stakes gambling at Royal Queensland, Norman now had money to travel around Asia. He could afford, finally, to get those snaggly front teeth fixed once and for all.

In the aftermath of West Lakes, there was rapturous praise from some wise elders like Peter Thomson, but there was also to be heard that first gargling sound of envy. Some of his old mates started calling him a snob or standoffish. (According to Cyril King, an older man who knew him from the club, Norman was really just extremely shy in those days.)

Some of the veteran tour players were also irritated.

"Well!" his mother says. "David Graham and the others were there, and to have this whippersnapper, this trainee, come and take the tournament away from them, and by a large amount, too?"

But Norman proved to be a tough poppy to cut down because he was soon in a plane and gone.

Wealth in the Bare Hills

On Thursday of this year's Mercedes Championships, rain damage to the course led to postponement of the first round. There suddenly appeared in Norman's schedule a hole big enough to allow a visit to his equipment company, Cobra. The factory was just up the road. He went to the parking lot and found the silver Mercedes that the sponsor had set aside for him, and he took off.

The factory is situated in the bare hills of San Diego County among hundreds of sleek new industries that line the new streets like overgrown glass garages. The lunchtime sidewalks fairly bounced with joggers.

The golf club company is about the size of an airplane hangar, and it is a clean, bustling place, with dozens of workstations spread around the vast interior. Norman's outfit was casual—jeans, a long-sleeved white golf shirt and a black vest, white running shoes—but on him it had the look of a striking ensemble. On his wrist a brightly polished gold watch glittered like a miniature chandelier. With his shoes and his thrusting chin, he had the general air of a lion tamer.

As he passed the line, a woman called out that nine thousand five hundred clubs were made yesterday, which was a record. A man in the hallway whispered that stock had just climbed two points. Norman, it should be said, owns a piece of the company.

In the rear quarters of the factory is a section set aside for the alchemists who do custom work for the tour players. Rod Hirsch, a Cobra vice president with a merry smile, handed Norman a bronze-colored putter. It was not dissimilar to the player's usual Ping. Norman eyeballed it closely and pointed out the back topline. "What about this?" he asked "How come that's not straight?"

Hirsch's smile fell, as if the warden just announced his execution date. "I spent the morning making it absolutely flat," he said. Hirsch then took it to the grinding wheel to make it absolutely, positively flat.

After every session at the grinder, Norman subjected the putter to close, diamond-merchant inspection, then handed it back. Finally, without goggles, he went himself to the wheel and buffered the questionable edge.

Hirsch gazed uneasily at Norman hunched over the wheel. "You're going to get us all fired if the safety inspector sees this," he groaned.

While this was going on, other people were at work trying to make a shiny new sand wedge set up identically to Norman's mauled and gnarled old wedge with the flange half ground off. The only way to make the new one resemble the old one, it seemed, would be to drive over it a few times with a tank.

Again, Norman wrested the operation away from the technicians. I turned to Hirsch and asked if all tour players were this meticulous. It seemed the polite choice of words.

"As far as intuitive abilities," he whispered, "he's head and shoulders above the rest. A few others like Hale Irwin are meticulous, but Greg can actually tell the difference between one or two grams here and there.

"It makes it very hard to fit him because he gives us hell when it's not absolutely right."

The back door of the Cobra shop was opened up to let the sunny day in, and the blue sky was shattered by the passing of a formation of jets from Miramar Naval Air Station. I recalled from somewhere that Norman had once flown in the back of a fighter jet and so I asked him about it.

"Oh yeah," he muttered. "F-fours. I did barrel rolls, stood it on its tail."

Maybe it was the fresh sound of those jets outside, but the idea of piloting a twenty-ton Phantom with fifteen thousand pounds of thrust through the stratosphere seemed utterly preposterous.

"Nah," he said, as if we were discussing Nintendo. He held his hands out on each side. "Throttle in one hand, control in the other, just pull 'em straight back."

Then he broke down and actually grinned. "I told you," he said. "I've got a good life."

Death Wish? Or a Life Wish?

Kim Doren, a Cobra marketing woman, watched Norman arrive back at La Costa. Before he was half out of the Mercedes he was yanked almost in half by people who needed five or ten minutes. He looked like the only medical orderly to be found on a huge battlefield.

"I don't know how he does it," she said. "I remember when we were filming the new commercials, we had the film crew out on his new Medalist Course [in Florida], and we were shooting print ads at the same time so those photographers were there. In the middle of all this, Australian TV wanted to bring out some children for the Make-A-Wish Foundation. They wanted to see him as a kind of dying wish. But the course wasn't finished and it was all muddy, so out comes this earthmover with these poor children to see him. I must say, he was very kind to them."

Talk to enough people and you begin to hear a certain story over and over about Norman. It's not just that he's this legendary soft touch for Florida hospitals who want him to visit the dying; it's that he's also something of a world-class lifeguard. The stories pile up:

• Little Jamie Hutton, a kid stricken with leukemia, asks to meet Norman. At the 1988 Heritage Classic, Hutton is made the star of the TV broadcast as Norman escorts him around while winning the tournament for him. The leukemia eventually goes into remission. Hutton is now an aspiring journalist living in New York.

• Ask Janis for her favorite memory of her brother and she recalls the day she was skin diving and found herself wrapped up in box jellyfish, which are lethal. Then Greg, "my knight in shining armor," dives in, pulls her out of the mess, gets her into a boat and rows for shore at top speed. "Well, he saved my life, anyway," she says.

• Friends recollect the time that teenage Greg was standing on the balcony of an apartment while a friend was showing everyone how he could swim eight laps underwater. Only the friend seems to be stuck at the deep and, and the bubbles have stopped. Norman dives in, clothes and all, to get the guy, haul him to the surface and give him mouth-to-mouth resuscitation.

"I remember that guy in the pool," Norman says, lighting up. He pauses in the middle of his La Costa health-plate breakfast of fruit bowl, English muffin, and English breakfast tea. "Everybody was either mesmerized or joking about the situation. Nobody wanted to take the responsibility of going in.

"So . . . ," he shrugs. "From that day I *never* heard from him again. Completely disappeared from the game of golf, from surfing, from life!

"I can tell you another story." A serious look now. "A friend and I played football at Aspley High School. We were training one morning, doing laps. We're going side by side, and he falls right over on his face and has a coronary. Seventeen years old, has a coronary right beside me. Now the rest of the team is running, they thought he had tripped or something, and I'm there giving him mouth-to-mouth, his tongue is blue, his eyes have rolled back in his head. We got the ambulance, they gave him the injections. But he died.

"He was my buddy, we were running together, and thirty-five minutes later I'm seeing his mother arrive at the hospital, and I'm saying, 'He didn't make it.' Those exact words.

"I didn't go out and change my whole lifestyle, but it had an impact. I strengthened my mind. I know how powerful it is right now. You never forget the face, the smell. Those are the things that build your stamina, your character, and all that stuff."

Has he perhaps had any serious brushes with his own mortality?

"Aaaaah," he says, exhaling and stirring his tea, "when I was diving a couple of years ago, I was in eighty to ninety feet of water. I speared a fish and went to get it out of a hole. I go in and whack the top of my tank, the regulator, so unbeknownst to me the air started leaking out. I'm very conscious of my gauges and I knew I had fifteen hundred pounds of air. Fifteen minutes later it's like this—*aaugh*— you can't breathe any air in. And I thought, Jeez, and I look at my gauge and it's zero. Holy s———.

"My dive buddy was probably thirty-five feet away from me. I look at the gauge and I'm thinking, eighty-eight feet of water, I've got the air in my lungs. Do I go to my dive buddy and run out of air if I don't get to him quick enough? Or do I start going for the surface?

"And you think about all this in one second, two seconds. I knew the air in my lungs was compressed. So as I was going to the surface it would expand. So I decided to go up. But I knew I couldn't beat my bubbles up, because you do that, you get nitrogen narcosis and you could die. I'm going up, looking at my gauge, forty feet, thirty feet, I'm dying. By the time I got to the water surface I was shot.

"I got a little narked, as the saying goes, in my joints, the back of my neck, my knees, my ankles. My hands were aching, just killing me."

He laughs a little laugh, as if it's nothing richly symbolic that we're talking about here.

Respect and Contempt

Norman's bravery is never called into question, of course. It's his natural, spurting, high-profile aggression that sometimes gets ridiculed. Some U.S. players grumble about Norman being a pretty big-headed guy for having won only twelve PGA Tour events, plus the two British Opens, but the record is about even with American stars of his general age group, such as Curtis Strange, Payne Stewart and Fred Couples. And as Norman will heatedly tell you, he also plays on his home tour and a few other tours as well. Add on his fifteen European tour victories, plus wins in Australasia, and you get about sixty or so around the world. He thinks: Why don't they respect me? "I've spread my wings a hell of a lot to help the game of golf," he grumps.

Golf history is littered with dark dramas of tour stars who were dealt a devastating loss in a major and never recovered. Remember Arnold Palmer at the 1966 U.S. Open, Tony Jacklin at the '72 British Open and Tom Weiskopf at the '75 Masters? Norman's list of last-moment losses is pretty remarkable: The 1984 U.S. Open, '89 British Open, '86 and '93 PGA, and the '86, '87 and '89 Masters. He keeps on staging comebacks, but finds that reporters would rather talk about the losses than his equally sensational victories at the 1986 and '93 British Opens.

To his mounting irritation, he has learned what football teams like the Denver Broncos and the Buffalo Bills discovered long ago, and what basketball's New York Knicks learned last June: Athletes who get *real close* to grabbing that trophy but come up short at the last minute are not going to get some friendly Grantland Rice pat on the back anymore; they're going to get contempt.

And if you are rich, God help you.

Recent golf history is also littered with stories of champions who could win big, and win majors, for a brief period, then lose all idea of how they did it. What makes Norman so noticeable is that he keeps coming back and getting in contention. But even this backfires on him, and Johnny Miller demands to know how Norman could maintain a superb 68.81 scoring average in 1994 and win only once?

Norman never really had a long, painful period of poverty and denial, in which to incubate a certain sense of decorum about money and success. Directly after his West Lakes win in 1976, he went to Japan and won the first event he teed it up in, the Kuzaha Open. He went to Britain and almost immediately won again, taking the Martini International with a course-record, final-round 66 at Blairgowrie, beating Simon Hobday by three. Says Hobday, "I've been trying to forget him ever since."

Through Peter Thomson and Guy Wolstenholme, Norman hooked up with a flashy British entrepreneur-manager named James Marshall, who lived in the grand manner in Gloucestershire's polo-playing country. Norman moved into the estate, and Marshall set about smoothing the very rough edges off his hot kid.

Based on Norman's stunning debuts, Marshall was able to quickly secure an endorsement contract worth one hundred thousand dollars to play Wilson clubs. Norman, remembering Earp's admonitions that a pro must always look sharp, immediately went on a clothes-shopping spree in which he dropped seven thousand dollars in one day.

Then came the red Ferrari. And because that was too conspicuous, he bought a more subtle, silver Ferrari.

In not too much time Norman had to buy his way out of Marshall's contract; some friends of Norman's have suggested that it was quite expensive.

Norman was soon providing a major hunk of commission money for the International Management Group. In the early 1980s he found he could get forty thousand dollars for a one-day exhibition. He could also get as much in appearance money from tournaments (except in the States, where it is officially disallowed).

Then he got seventy-five thousand dollars from tournaments, then one hundred thousand dollars. Finally, as his agent Hughes Norton once recalled, an Australian tournament said the magic words: "Blank check."

At the Dubai Desert Classic this year, it was widely reported that Norman, Nick Price and Fred Couples each received two hundred thousand dollars in appearance fees. But that was an oil-rich desert kingdom. At some of the old Australian tournaments, the total official prize money could have been only two hundred thousand dollars. Peter Thomson railed from his pulpit as a TV announcer and newspaper columnist and called them "secret, underhanded payments— an insidious thing." But the tournament promoters swore up and down that Norman's presence meant so much to the gate and the TV attention that the fee was worth it.

The 1980s became Norman's era of maximum endorsement involvement. He had deals with a club maker, a hatmaker, a sportswear company, a car-rental outfit, a fast-food giant, a soup maker, a luxury car company, an airline, a computer manufacturer, shoe companies, plus book, magazine and newspaper deals. And he had to keep them all happy. He confessed repeatedly that he felt guilty whenever he said no.

Talking about Money

Norman stays locked up tight about the Seven Year Plan he devised in 1993, other than to hint about his retirement at the end of it. Part of the plan may have been to separate himself from his hyperactive agency, IMG. When he did that, some of his profound glumness began to ease.

That, anyway, is the reasoning of his new manager, Frank Williams. "He wasn't in control of his life," says Williams. "IMG was in control. He didn't know the whole picture, the whole agenda. They would have him play the Dunhill or the Tryall event because they could use that as further leverage. Greg didn't know quite what was going on."

Williams is a large, good-humored Englishman-Australian who started out in the carpet business before taking over the Australian Masters. "Greg is happy now because he's in control, you see?" Williams says. "He doesn't want to do a lot of one-off ads. Somebody recently offered him a great deal of money just to drive out his front gate, go down the road and do a short something for the cameras. A great deal of money. But he said no, because it would interfere with his daughter Morgan's soccer practice. He only wants to be involved with things he has a stake in."

So in Williams, Norman has now an aide-de-camp who travels with him and lives just for him. Norman's wife, Laura, is also part of the brain trust. Because of her diminutive size and warm charm, one might underestimate her. (She was a flight attendant when they first met; Norman claims he took one look at her, turned to Marshall and said, "I'm going to marry that girl.") She oversees most of the business decisions.

Norman is building golf courses, including the Medalist in his Hobe Sound, Florida, backyard, which he designed with Pete Dye, along with twenty-five other courses. He's investing in things like a grass-seed company and pitch-and-putt courses for kids and seniors. Rather than get an endorsement deal with a club manufacturer, he invested two million dollars in Cobra and now sits astride a very pleasant cash cow. The real significance behind that move was that it instructed all other tour stars with any leverage to hold out for their own piece of a company.

Generally a straightforward fellow, there are occasions when Norman wants it both ways. He'll tell you that money doesn't mean that much to him, that he had no idea when he made his first million. Then later he tells the story about the day in his late twenties when he called up each of his old pals in Australia who were on that bus trip to Grafton and informed them that he finally made his million.

When I talked to him in late 1987, he was just getting set for the season-ending Nabisco Championships (which later became the Tour Championship). Only the top thirty players were invited, and he thought this was unfair. "With prize money of this magnitude, I think all the players should play for it," he said then. "I feel for the guys numbers thirty-one to one twenty-five on the money list because they're the ones who are being hard done by. They're the ones who create the tour just as much as the top thirty, anyway."

Seven years later he was putting his name behind a World Golf Tour that would be limited to the top thirty players in the world, along with ten invitees. It probably seemed like a good proposition when it came across the transom, but, like so many other major moments in his life, it went off in his face like an exploding cigar.

Armed with Thunder

Why can't he slow down? Janis is only one of many who complain that you can never really *see* the guy anymore. At his estate near West Palm Beach, the dinner-table scene is likely to include some business partner involving Greg in a contract discussion.

He is already gone from home 280 days of the year. Does he really need a World Golf Tour? His wife Laura knows her feelings on the matter: "I wasn't crazy about the idea. I'd naturally like to have him around the house more with his feet up and watching TV. But Greg wants to do it." She tosses off a twinkling, what-the-hell laugh, because what can you do? She sees the same fire in her children, especially Morgan Leigh, twelve, who is good at golf but prefers soccer's high-octane action. The Shark's daughter is known in school as The Terminator.

Norman gets defensive if you ask him to slow down. "I'd definitely rather be burning up my body than have my body be burning me up," he says of his roaring, unstoppable, fidgeting energy. "I've always been that way." And always will be that way.

". . . Armed with thunder, clad with wings, / shall a wider world command."

Norman got the surprise of his life a couple of years ago when he was practicing on his backyard putting green and tried to get his son, Gregory Jr., then eight, to play with him a little. Greg Jr. is a sports-mad kid, loves football, basketball and hockey, and once announced he'd never wash his hands again after he got to shake hands with Wayne Gretzky. So Dad persuades him to join him for an hour, but Greg Jr. doesn't feel like stroking in a few.

"I said, 'What do you mean, you don't want to play golf?' And he said, 'Nah, Dad, I don't want to play like you do—too seriously.' He said, 'I can see how much work you put in and how much time you spend away from home.'

"He had that profound insight into the life of sport. It just absolutely blew my mind. He said, 'Dad, I just want to play for fun.'"

Is golf fun anymore for Norman?

Not bloody likely. Obsessions are never fun.

—1995

A Zone of His Own: Tiger Woods

Peter de Jonge

On a mild morning in late fall, Tiger Woods, a tall, thin, impossibly elegant Stanford freshman, is standing at the edge of the seventeenth green of the notorious Shoal Creek golf club near Birmingham, Alabama, awaiting his turn to putt. For Woods, who is almost invariably the longest off the tee, and very often the closest to the flag, waiting may be his most characteristic mode, and as he plucks his shirt from his chest, nudges up the bill of his cap with one fingertip, leans on his putter and crosses his legs, each gesture is pared to the nub and full of portent.

What makes his magisterial focus so riveting is the array of reasons he has to feel uneasy. They include, in no particular order, that with just over one hole to play in the Jerry Pate National Intercollegiate, one of the most prestigious tournaments in college golf, he is tied for the lead; that two members of a black activist organization have set up shop outside the golf club's tall iron gates to protest Woods's refusal to boycott the tournament; and that standing just off the green, in jacket and tie and a floppy yellow hat shading a bulbous nose mapped with hundreds of exploded red capillaries, is Hall Thompson, Shoal Creek's seventy-one-year-old founder, who in 1990, just before the PGA Championship here, assured a reporter that his club "don't discriminate in every other area except the blacks."

None of this holds a fly's worth of distraction to Woods, as he calmly looks over the sixty feet of double-humped green. Then again, he is used to dealing with far more expectation and distraction than has ever been dropped upon a single athletic head. While Woods's renown got a big push in the summer, when he became the youngest U.S. Amateur champion (he turned nineteen in December), he has been winning world titles since he was eight. Stanford University, which recruited him vigorously and gave him a full scholarship, includes a two-page "Tiger Woods At-a-Glance" flier in its press kit, and the first heading is "Ages 2–5." No less a golfer than Tom Watson calls Woods "potentially the most important player to enter the game in fifty years."

Along the way, the cult has been tirelessly maintained by Tiger's sixty-two-year-old father, Earl Woods, who seems to have conceived of his son's golfing career even before he helped conceive his son. As Tiger left the clubhouse for the final eighteen holes of the U.S. Amateur, the last thing Earl whispered in his ear was, "Let the legend grow."

Through the first fifty-three holes at Shoal Creek, he has displayed every facet of his shimmering teen-age game, from his prodigious drives and world-class putting to the towering long irons that are often compared to Jack Nicklaus's. On the few par 5s where it was worth his while, the six-foot-two, 150-pound Woods hit drives that carried well over three hundred yards. The rest of the time, he relied on a new pet shot, which he calls a "bump driver." "What you do, is move close to the ball, and just turn through it, with almost no release or hands," Woods says. "It's a very dead, soft shot, like playing downwind, but it goes straight."

Even rarer than Woods's ability to shape golf shots is his ability to shape the input and output of his mind. Perhaps because there is such an absurd number of things Woods is better off not thinking about, he has developed the Zen-like skill of detaching his brain from his game. "You ever go up to a tee and say, 'Don't hit it left, don't hit it right'?" Woods quizzes me. "That's your conscious mind. My body knows how to play golf. I've trained it to do that. It's just a matter of keeping my conscious mind out of it."

To play the game one shot at a time, unhaunted by your mishaps and unexcited by your fears, is golf's impossible self-selflessness riddle.

At Shoal Creek, at least, Woods does an unnerving impression of someone who has cracked it. After the tournament, when he is asked by a local reporter to describe his three rounds, he replies, "I played exactly the same all three rounds." And, amazingly, he had.

Woods's mind control is at least in part a result of his precocious start. Earl Woods believed that if talented athletes were exposed to the game early enough, they would be able to avoid the self-consciousness so common to golfers and perform with the instinctive verve of great basketball and baseball players. In other words, golfers could learn to play like real athletes. "I used to tell people that the next generation of great golfers are going to be those who were introduced to the game between six months and a year," Earl says.

That's why Earl, who didn't take up the game until he was forty-two but was playing to a 1 handicap within five years, dragged his son's highchair into the garage where Tiger could watch him hit balls into a net. Earl claims that at six months, Tiger had an attention span of about two hours, and that when he finally crawled down to take his own turn at the practice mat, he had already absorbed the basic principles of the swing. "His first swing was a perfect imitation of mine," Earl says.

Over the years, Tiger's game has become so ingrained that even under great pressure he can operate on what Earl calls "automatic procedure." There have been times after a round, when Earl has asked Tiger how he executed a certain shot, and Tiger says he doesn't know, and others when he can't even recall making contact with the ball.

The depth of Woods's concentration is particularly striking on the greens, where Woods has gone through the same pre-putt routine since he was six. A few summers ago, Charlie Sifford, the first black regular on the PGA Tour, came out to watch Tiger at a tournament in Texas. At one green, Earl turned his back to Tiger and began a hushed play-by-play for Sifford: "He takes one practice stroke, he takes another. He looks at the target, he looks at the ball. He takes another look at the target, he looks at the ball." And when Earl said "impact" at the exact instant Tiger's putter met the ball, all Sifford could say was, "Goddamn."

This is not to suggest that Woods's play is robotic. His movement is graceful and athletic in the extreme. But his detachment brings an exceptional serenity and inevitability to the whole enterprise. Woods exudes the pure focus and purposefulness of a sleepwalker making his way through the dark to the refrigerator. It's as if he has already made the shot or sunk the key putt, and all that remains is the minor technicality of the present catching up with the reality.

Back on the par-5 seventeenth at Shoal Creek, Woods's sixty-foot putt goes up and over the second mound and, after describing a big left-to-right break, comes to rest less than three feet from the hole. Woods calmly knocks it in to go one stroke ahead of his teammate William Yanagisawa. With Thompson standing behind his shoulder, Woods bumps his drive down the eighteenth fairway and follows it with a short iron to the center of the green. From there, he will roll in a twenty-foot birdie for a two-shot victory.

As he makes his way up the final fairway, a man standing on a distant terrace silhouetted against Double Oak Mountain fills the basin with an enormous rebel yell of "Go Tiger!" Momentarily diverted from his thoughts—or the absence of them—Woods lets a shy, bucktoothed grin crease his small round face.

Two weeks after Shoal Creek, Earl Woods, an ex–Green Beret who survived several tours in Vietnam before retiring as a lieutenant colonel, and his wife, Kultida Woods, whom he met in Bangkok, are sitting in their living room in Cypress, California, forty miles south of Los Angeles. They are describing the point at which their personal project to raise the greatest golfer who ever lived took on the righteous fervor of a crusade.

When Eldrick Woods was born in 1975 (his much-preferred nickname is in honor of one of his father's Vietnamese war buddies), Earl and Tida agreed that Earl would keep his job as a contracts administrator at McDonnell Douglas and that Tida would stay home. And that when Tiger was old enough to begin playing national junior tournaments, Earl would retire and Tida would go back to work. When Earl and Tiger began their barnstorming six years ago, they flew in the morning of an event, stumbled out for the opening round without sleep or a practice round, then checked into a Motel 6.

"One day, Tiger said, 'Pop, do you think we could get to the site early enough so I could get in a practice round?'" Earl recalls. "I thought about it, and I said: 'Son, I apologize. I promise you from this day forward, you will have just as good of a chance as any of these country club kids, and if I have to go broke, that's what we're going to do.' From that point on, we went a day in advance, he stayed with his peers at the Marriotts and the Hiltons, and he kicked butt and took names."

For Earl Woods, the matter of separate accommodations had a particularly sour resonance. As the first black baseball player at Kansas State University, and, Woods says, in the entire Big Eight Conference, he often had to stay by himself at black hotels and eat in the parking lot while his teammates were inside a restaurant. "We didn't want Tiger to grow up with an inferiority complex," Tida says in her still-thick Thai accent. "So even if we have to take out second mortgage or home equity loan, we let him have it."

As Earl, sucking on Merit 100s, describes the time that the three-year-old Tiger shot a 48 for nine holes, or the evening four years later, when he sank eighty four-foot putts in a row, he can sound like every other father of an athletic prodigy, operating in the foggy zone between visionary and madman. What distinguishes Earl is his conviction that, simply by nurturing a young black golfer, he is subverting the racial order.

Until Tiger, black golfers who made a mark have been miracles of self-creation, thorny characters with caddyshack swings who somehow overcame every disadvantage in terms of instruction, facilities and competition. Sifford, who in the 1950s almost single-handedly challenged the PGA's whites-only clause, wasted a decade of his prime as the personal golf tutor for the band leader Billy Eckstine. Calvin Peete, who won eleven PGA events in the mid-'80s, didn't take up the game until he was twenty-three.

Woods, on the other hand, has been raised as a kind of single-case experiment in equal-opportunity indulgence. He has received all the excessive advantages that have routinely been bestowed on white prodigies from Nicklaus and Watson to Phil Mickelson and

Ernie Els, current pros whose fathers deemed it necessary to install backyard putting greens.

Woods has been burnished and refined and tweaked to the very limits of his father's credit rating. The care and feeding of his game and mind have been entrusted to a hierarchy of professionals called Team Tiger. It includes Butch Harmon, the distinguished Houston-based swing doctor, and Capt. Jay Brunza, a Navy doctor who has doubled as Woods's sport psychologist and caddy (for major tournaments) since Woods was thirteen.

On a Friday night in early December, Woods was grabbed from behind in the parking lot behind his Stanford dorm. The mugger held a knife to Woods's throat, called him by name, then turned the knife around and punched him in the face with the handle. When I spoke to Earl Woods the next day, he told me that he had already assigned the mental aspect of the incident to Brunza. "They were able to work through the crisis trauma structure that was already in place to relieve any anxiety he might have had," Earl said. "As a matter of fact, the next day he took a final exam and did very well. He was able to focus." (Woods was only slightly bruised by the blow; the mugger has not been arrested.)

Newspaper articles about Woods often imply that this preternaturally composed young man has benefited from a military-style upbringing, but Earl's parenting style is more Mr. Rogers than Great Santini. By the time Tiger was born, his father (who has three grown children from a previous marriage) was well into his forties and retired from the military; the two have the kind of unambivalent, unharried relationship more common between a grandfather and a grandson. "Tiger has never been disciplined, never even been told what to do," Earl says, and then refers to a period very early in their relationship, "when I earned Tiger's respect, and he earned mine." Asked what he respects so much about his father, Tiger says, "Everything." Asked if he can be a little more specific, he says: "I basically respect everything he does. We're best friends."

One of the few issues on which they diverge is race. For Tiger, golf is all that matters, and the news media's constant harping on his race is belittling. For Earl, golf and race cannot be separated. "I told him straight out when he was a little boy," Earl says, "that in America, if you have a drop of black blood in you, you're black." But Tiger, besides Thai, also has Chinese, white and American Indian blood, and doesn't identify himself with one race more than another.

It's a familiar pattern—the father determined to do everything he can to prevent his son from being tainted by the prejudice he has had to deal with, and doing such a good job that the son doesn't see what all the fuss is about.

One of Woods's Stanford teammates is a highly ranked golfer named Notah Begay III, who is half Pueblo and half Navajo and is as self-consciously infatuated with his racial heritage as Woods is unintrigued by his own. Before the team headed to Alabama, Begay spoke with Woods about the political significance of Shoal Creek (which, in Woods's honor, he rechristened "Soul Creek").

"I told him," says Begay, who wears a big gold hoop earring, two dabs of red clay on his cheeks and black Oakley shades when he plays, "what a great slap in the face it would be to those who think that minorities are inferior, if he went down and won."

Before the tournament, when I asked Woods if the racist policies at certain country clubs provide a special incentive, he answered no. His father insists otherwise. "Of course it does," he says. "It provides drive. It provides inspiration. It provides motivation. It provides toughness."

And so it appears that Earl Woods has nurtured an almost perfect competitive psyche—one that combines the insider's absolute sense of entitlement with an outsider's private smoldering edge.

The racial significance of what Woods may one day accomplish— the PGA has had precious few black golfers and not a single black superstar—was not lost on the many black employees working the grounds of the plantation-style Shoal Creek. As Woods and the workers crossed paths during his rounds, they would often approach him and quietly pass along their encouragement. And at the start of the final round, a group of caddies, all of them black, came out to see him off the first tee.

* * *

When I interview Woods a couple of weeks later in the clubhouse of the Stanford golf course, he is less forthcoming in an hour and a half than in the occasional momentary exchanges we had on the fairway at Shoal Creek. Arriving exactly on time in a black windbreaker and black shorts, his short hair gelled back, he carries himself with the same exaggerated deliberateness and detachment that he brings to the course. But without the game, the effect is the opposite. Woods flows over a golf course as naturally as water finding its level. Off it, he can be wary and chilly.

Like so many other aspects of his life, the important decisions about how Woods will be spending his time at Stanford—and he insists he will stay the full four years—were carefully plotted long in advance.

His college plans call for putting on some muscle and learning enough about accounting to monitor the people who will be watching the millions he will make in endorsement contracts the instant he turns pro. He doesn't have an agent yet, but the International Management Group, the sports marketing giant, had Earl Woods on its payroll as a consultant for several years.

Although an excellent student who graduated from public high school with a 3.79 grade-point average, Tiger shows little enthusiasm for anything he's been studying. He describes his Western civilization reading as "antiquity, stuff no one is ever going to need to know."

When Earl Woods sent his son off to France in September to compete in the World Amateur Championships in Versailles, he urged him "to smell the flowers and soak it all in." Tiger ate at McDonald's every night.

"I'm very blah," Tiger says. "It bothers my girlfriend sometimes, but that's just the way it is." (The only thing Woods would reveal about his girlfriend is that she is from his hometown and not particularly interested in golf.) When I ask his parents how they would react if their son came home sporting an earring, like his teammate Begay, Tida and Earl shake their heads as if I just don't get it. "Tiger very very conservative," Tida says.

At Stanford, Woods's narrow agenda does not call for getting too close to his teammates, four of whom are returning starters from last year's national championship team with their own legitimate pro ambitions. The day before I arrived in Palo Alto, Woods had skipped practice, and Wally Goodwin, Stanford's Reaganesque head coach, tells me that the players had asked him "to bend Tiger's ear about it." Woods calls the lapse a "miscommunication."

His teammates say they have no problem being overshadowed by a freshman. (Woods won two of the four collegiate tournaments he competed in this fall while posting the second-lowest scoring average in the country.) What hurts is that Woods shows no interest in befriending them. When asked what Woods is like as a person, they say they have no idea. Even Begay, who competed against Woods on the junior circuit, and says he has always felt an unspoken bond with him, says, "There's Tiger, and then there's the four of us."

Although his teammates hope a genuine relationship will develop, it's not likely to happen anytime soon. Asked to what extent a game like golf can ever be a team sport, Woods says, "It's a team sport in that you're competing for a team as well as an individual title. I don't know what the other guys are doing, but I'm competing for both."

It's not that Woods can't be a generous teammate. He freely offers swing and putting tips to anyone with the good sense to seek his advice. It's just that Woods, following a script that was laid out before he was born, has other things to worry about besides getting touchy-feely with four college golfers. And what comes through so forcefully when you sit down with Woods is that he is not going to be easily shoved off course by anyone, whether it's his teammates, his coach, the press, a mugger, Hall Thompson or even the frequently excessive enthusiasms of his beloved old man.

"I'm the one who is sort of creating all this," Woods says. "And I'm the one who has to handle it."

—1995

Tigermania

John Hawkins

There he was on the evening of April 4, the Tuesday night of Masters week, wolfing down a cheeseburger and fries in an otherwise empty Wendy's about a mile down the street from Augusta National. His father was smoking a cigarette. His caddie was reading the newspaper. Anybody could have walked in and experienced an up-close-and-personal brush with greatness, although it's fair to say Tiger Woods wasn't *totally* famous eight months ago.

Besides, nobody walked in. Nobody stuck a hand in his face or turned five shades of red or disguised their young son as some woeful piece of autograph bait. Tiger just sat there and ate his food like any twenty-year-old kid, a fast-food junkie in ground-beef heaven, his mind no more occupied than the row of booths against the window.

It would have been easy to walk out to the stoplight and inform the clot of motorists that Tiger Woods was inside having dinner. A lot of people probably would have diverted their own plans, pulled into Wendy's and ordered the salad bar, so they could stand and gawk at Tiger as he wiped ketchup off his mouth. The very next afternoon, Jack Nicklaus made an announcement no less suitable for public consumption, gushing, "Both Arnold [Palmer] and I agree that you could take my Masters [six] and his Masters [four] and add them together, and this kid should win more than that."

It was as if Moses had authorized some English Lit major to rewrite the Ten Commandments.

The question isn't whether Tiger Woods will win a green jacket, or if he'll win a dozen of them, but if he'll still be eating at Wendy's on Washington Road two nights before the 2015 Masters or—go ahead, laugh now—at his own fast-food chain where each Tiger Burger weighs approximately one pound before cooking. He'll be forty by then, and if our crystal ball is accurate, he'll have ended a highly publicized dalliance with the aging but glamorous Cindy Crawford to align himself with Consuela, a six-foot-one, nineteen-year-old Brazilian supermodel who happens to have won four U.S. Women's Opens herself.

Tiger and Consuela won't just fly to golf tournaments. They'll be flying to their own golf tour, which won't be called the World Tour but the Minolta Universe Tour because it features two events on Venus and the Lunar Open, which is played on a golf course quite similar to a Scottish links. Oh, yeah. Tiger owns the moon. He bought it from Greg Norman back in 2007, or more specifically, acquired it for three billion dollars and a green jacket to be named later.

That's right. Norman never did.

We'll remember 1996 as a milepost of historical resonance, when an African-Asian-American superhero took a blowtorch to the game's competitive boundaries, glacial stereotypes and aristocratic principles. It was a year when the game really did change, the point at which our pristine little pastime moved out of the cathedral and into the casino, bringing with it a legion of fresh faces and neglected races. Rarely is the line between generations so clearly drawn. Tiger Woods didn't just make 1996 memorable. He did it in the space of two months.

And so it occurred. *Tigermania,* the phenomenon caused when a young athlete's success actually matches the hyperbole, became a bigger story than the kid himself. In Orlando, the site of his second win (in only his seventh start as a pro), galleries swelled to ten times their normal size. No wonder tournament director Michael McPhillips had leaped into a swimming pool (fully clothed) when he learned that Tiger had committed to the Walt Disney World/ Oldsmobile Classic.

"We sold over thirty-one thousand pork chop sandwiches," reported Kym Hougham from the Quad City Classic, Woods' third tournament as a pro. "That's more *people* than we had last year. We couldn't get tickets out to the gate fast enough." Oprah Winfrey's staff called in October. So did the nice folks from *Regis and Kathie Lee*. Can you imagine Ben Hogan cleaning his spikes on Kathie Lee Gifford's carpet? Golf used to be this nice little cottage industry. Now Tiger was getting calls from *Good Morning America*, Nickelodeon, Larry King, Fox's *After Breakfast*, Tom Snyder. . . .

"The *Cosby* show wants to write an entire episode around him," said Woods' agent, Hughes Norton of IMG. "They said they'd do whatever it takes. I've got a stack of offers six inches high."

Twenty years from now, those offers will be nothing more than amusing footnotes. Tiger will have a four-year-old son, a handsome little tyke named Jaguar, who will be belting 290-yard drives as a guest on *Late Night with Macauley Culkin*. Jaguar's old man will be playing only in the majors, closing in on Nicklaus' all-time record of eighteen. The Internet media will be all over him, though, because he seems more concerned with his NBA career—he's player-owner of the CompuServ Los Angeles Lakers—than with winning a seventh Masters.

Well, maybe not.

"He's a terrible basketball player, probably the worst I've ever seen," says Jerry Chang, one of Woods' best friends and his former teammate at Stanford. "He can't shoot. He can't jump. He has a minimum of passing and dribbling skills. We used to have an intramural basketball team and I can assure you, he's no Grant Hill."

There he was on the morning of July 22, sitting in a snack bar at London's Heathrow Airport after finishing tied for twenty-second at the British Open, looking a lot more like some carbohydrate-deprived foreign exchange student than the harbinger of an era. Again, Tiger Woods couldn't be bothered, which is to say that the business of England was carrying on rather nicely despite his presence. Maybe he was thinking about turning pro. Or maybe he was thinking about a Big Mac during the layover in New York.

Tigermania is about turning a young man into a legend. In record time.

In a year when various acts of Olympic heroism borrowed our conscience for at least a few weeks of summer, in a year when two of the most storied and visible franchises in sports history—the Dallas Cowboys and New York Yankees—won championships, Tiger Woods was the only performer who really mattered. He shattered the baseball-football-basketball monotony with raw brilliance and an amazing threshold for drama, turning ordinary golf tournaments into *Sports-Center* leads and front-page headlines in the *New York Times*.

You expected the Bulls to win another NBA championship. You knew Michael Johnson would get his gold medals. The joy in watching those events was derived mainly from witnessing greatness, from knowing the best team or the best man won. Tiger was different. Tiger was new, a frog thrown into the punchbowl at just the right time, a player whose performance, which surpassed even the most outlandish appraisals of his potential, makes the hype surrounding guys like Andre Agassi, Deion Sanders and Shaquille O'Neal seem like a waste of good saliva.

Tigermania is about turning the legend into cash. Sooner or later.

"He doesn't have to do anything now," says Jeff Jensen, a sports-marketing reporter for *Advertising Age*. "What would be smart is for Tiger to cultivate his fame for a couple of years, then do a big-bucks, long-term, soft-drink and fast-food deal. . . . It's not like Tiger's going to quit at the age of thirty-three. He has to look at a long-term strategy, something that will run twenty to thirty years.

"Tiger is going to be appropriate for certain products at certain points of his life and other products at other times. He's not going to be pushing soft drinks and fast food at the age of forty. Here's the formula: Align yourself with powerful marketers like Coke and McDonald's, then spin yourself off as an entire industry. Restaurants, web sites, a virtual-reality game—Tiger Inc. with diversified holdings."

It was written in the August 30 issue of *Golf World* that Woods "instantly became the richest pro never to hit a green in regulation," which was a pseudo-clever way of suggesting that his forty-million-dollar, up-front contract with Nike would have an adverse effect on his playing career. The guy who wrote that column would now like to say that he thinks Woods is actually a *better* player when rich instead of poor because he can fire at flags and hit drivers when he might otherwise go with a 2-iron and charge putts that call for a lag. He can try to win every tournament he enters because eighth-place money means nothing.

He can go for broke because he's never going to know what it feels like again.

There he was on the evening of October 4, exactly six months to the day since eating at Wendy's, trapped inside a two-story penthouse suite at the MGM Grand in Las Vegas. Nike had sent him some dark glasses. A couple of banks had sent him some credit cards, but two days before the first victory of his professional career, Tiger Woods had yet to learn how to use either of fame's most constructive tools.

That's not to say he won't. Or won't have to.

"My Tiger is a showman," insists his mother, Kultida Woods.

"From my perspective, the only athlete I can compare him to is [Michael] Jordan," says John Krzynowek, vice president of marketing for Tommy Armour. "Having said that, everybody has to step back and realize this kid is twenty years old."

But there is no stepping back, not anymore, not after the third straight U.S. Amateur and the wins at Las Vegas and Orlando, not after the stack of offers six inches high and the invitation to appear on the ABC sitcom *Suddenly Susan*. Golf does not lend itself willingly to superheroes. The best player of this particular era, a dashing blond Australian with millions and millions of dollars, may be more famous for all the tournaments he's blown than for those he has not.

Tigermania is fun. Tigermania is beautiful. But Tigermania is silly and, if we're not careful, it will be hazardous to golf's health.

"The biggest thing for me is, if I don't get him [to play], all I'm going to hear is 'Why isn't he here?' He's worth a minimum of five thousand tickets every day," says Mike Milthorpe, tournament director for the Bob Hope Chrysler Classic. "I'm watching a promotion on The Golf Channel for the Australian Open and it's Norman vs. the Kid. We could have a situation where this is a one-man tour.

"Everywhere I go, all people ask is, 'Is Tiger coming?' I hate it. He's bigger than Norman ever was. I certainly know that if Tiger doesn't come, the media isn't going to be talking about how we've got twenty of the top thirty players."

(Milthorpe didn't know it, but his problem was about to get worse. Hope himself called Woods in late November, hoping to persuade Tiger to play. However, sources say Woods will not include the tournament on his 1997 schedule.)

Nobody is more responsible for the perpetuation of Tigermania, at least on a relative scale, than this magazine. *Golf World* put Tiger Woods on its cover six times in 1996—nobody else made it more than twice. Asked about the Q Ratings, a formula devised to determine how famous somebody is, IMG's Norton says, "It's too soon. I thought about checking out of curiosity, but he's too new a celebrity to show up on the radar screen yet. There's a lag time involved."

But, Norton adds, "All the years I managed Greg [Norman] in his prime, never did *Monday Night Football* want him on at halftime. Never did *GQ* want to run him on their cover. If you measure things by the requests we've received, the conventional and unconventional requests, he's the most popular client we've ever had."

How good is that? How bad is that? Will Oprah care if Tiger suddenly develops a closed clubface at the top? Does Larry King know that a great golfer wins only 15 percent of the tournaments he enters over the course of his career? Nicklaus has 70 victories in 550 starts. Even during his best nine-year stretch (1967–75), Nicklaus won just 22 percent of the time.

If there is the opposite of a sure thing in this world, it's golf. Golf is about failure. But Tiger is supposed to be bulletproof. We don't just see him rewriting the record book. We see him publishing his own record book with his face on the cover because he's been on the cover of everything else.

Tigermania is about appealing to the masses. Even if the game was never meant for mass appeal.

"I don't know if Hootie & the Blowfish made golf hot," says *Advertising Age*'s Jensen. "They made it mainstream. Hootie, the ultimate mainstream pop icon, and their passion for golf, helped the game pertain a little bit more to the Everyman. They haven't necessarily made it hip. Tiger can make it hip. It's no secret that fashion marketers like Nike tailor their communication to urban areas, targeting African-Americans, and you're going to see Nike do that with him. They're going to leverage his identity as an African-American to those audiences. Tiger is definitely a mass-market icon. Definitely more than Hootie & the Blowfish."

Norton points out that Nike is bombarding the network airwaves with its third Tiger Woods commercial, which features children of all races saying, "I'm Tiger Woods." Never has Nike's commitment to the future run so deep.

"It's going to be the only Nike ad to run through Christmas," Norton claims. "The first one ran thirty-three times on network TV. This one will have a 50 percent larger flight schedule. No Jordan ads, no nothing. That alone tells you something truly amazing. This is a company whose weakest division, for years, was golf."

Goodbye, Little Penny. Hello, Big Bucks. According to Tim Rosaforte's new book, *Tiger Woods: The Makings of a Champion*, Harmon took Woods shopping the Monday after the Vegas victory, saying, "You can't wear Nike twenty-four hours a day." Once Tiger picked out some new clothes, the men arrived at the sales counter. Tiger pulled out a credit card but it didn't go through the computer. Tiger pulled out a second credit card. That didn't work either.

"Well, you activated them, didn't you?" Harmon asked.

"What's that?" said Tiger.

Harmon shook his head and reached for his wallet.

"That just shows he's a kid."

There he was on the evening of November 30, purely in his element, working on his putting stroke in a Palm Springs resort suite after the first day of the Skins Game. A videotape of the 1993 Ryder Cup was playing on the TV. Tiger replaced it with a tape of his life story compiled by the USGA but pulled it out after a minute. No way was he going to watch all this crap for the millionth time, not with three of his best friends and a relative stranger in the room.

So he found a Steven Segal movie. When that got old, he went back to the '93 Ryder Cup.

"God, I *have* to make that team," he said, looking ahead to 1997.

There is absolutely nothing pretentious or unusual about him. If the truth be told, Tiger Woods is very funny, an excellent storyteller, extremely likable and bright for a young man whose twenty-first birthday is still a month away. A showman, as Tida Woods calls her son. In the comfort of good company, when the guard is down and the microphones are nowhere to be found, Woods strikes you as a very talented person with the same interests—girls and golf—as anybody else his age. There are no secrets. Only some things the rest of the world doesn't have to know.

He acknowledges Tigermania and fully understands it, doesn't feel claustrophobic about it, but his relaxed behavior suggests there is something rather preposterous about putting a twenty-year-old with a great golf swing on a pedestal. That afternoon, the Skins Game had recorded an 8.2 rating, the highest for a golf telecast since the 1990 Masters. Last year's Skins Game attendance of thirty-five hundred had just been blown away by the ninety-five hundred often unruly spectators who had gathered at Rancho La Quinta CC a few hours earlier, not to see the past (Tom Watson) or the present (Fred Couples), but to see the future of American golf.

More than anything, Tigermania is about the future. At any price.

"He would play for free," Tiger's father, Earl, had said at dinner.

"He might not play for free," countered family attorney John Merchant, "but he'd play if you paid his expenses."

During a report from the Tour Championship in October, ESPN's Jimmy Roberts compared Tiger's pro debut to Beatlemania, temporarily abandoning his perspective on a story that has a lot of people crossing the line between reality and fantasy. There is no mass hysteria here. Even with an 8.2 rating, the Skins Game wasn't seen by even half as many people who watch any given NFL game on Monday night. For goodness sake, *Suddenly Susan* does better ratings than the Skins Game. When Brooke Shields walks through a Las Vegas hotel with Andre Agassi, everybody knows who they are. Everybody wants to see them wipe the ketchup off their mouths.

Tiger is famous now, sure, but he's a golfer. He's not Paul McCartney. Maybe that's why the six-inch stack of offers will go unanswered. He doesn't belong on *Oprah* or *Cosby* because he's not some guy who married Elvis' alien daughter or even Malcolm-Jamal Warner. Hughes Norton knows that. Most important, Tiger Woods knows that.

"My best shot ever?" he says, repeating the question talked about over dinner, which he had to delay to attend some Skins Game banquet. "Probably the [birdie putt] on the thirty-fifth hole at Pumpkin Ridge [in the 1996 U.S. Amateur final]. When you think about everything involved, that has to be the best."

It was on that seventeenth green where Tiger Woods proved once and for all that he is a champion for the ages. No matter what he does over the next twenty years, whether he wins a dozen Masters or dates a supermodel, it may never be enough. In 1996 and beyond, the reaction will always be bigger than the action itself.

—1996

And Some of the Men
in My Life

Harvey Penick
with Bud Shrake

Ben Hogan

I was playing in a charity match in Austin with Ben Hogan, and I heard him ask his caddie, "Which way is due west?"

It was a surprise to hear Hogan ask a caddie a question. Ben thought he knew his own game better than a caddie ever could. Ben judged his own distances and pulled his own clubs.

I wondered all day why Ben had asked that question. After the round, I brought it up.

"All other things being equal, greens break to the west," Ben said.

He is right, of course. There are many reasons why, I later found out, but unless the architect has tricked up the green to fool you, your putt will break to the west.

As a young man, Ben had a very bad pull hook. He worked it out himself, getting a good grip with his right hand well on top, the V pointing to his chin.

Pronation is what he called his secret. In the hitting area, his left forearm, or possibly his entire left arm, uncoiled. This got him inside the ball and gave him a snap.

Ben practiced thousands of hours perfecting his swing. At first he felt his swing was too long. He changed his stance to shorten his swing a little by adopting what is now the famous Hogan Stance— the right foot square to the line and the left toe turned out a few inches. Each of these foot movements shortens the backswing.

I like a long swing if it is kept under control, and Ben certainly learned to do that.

Jimmy Demaret and Hogan became pals. Jimmy told me he called up Ben before the first Legends of Golf Senior Tournament and asked Hogan to be his partner.

Ben replied he wasn't playing often or well.

"Come on and let's have some old-time fun," Jimmy said.

Ben said, "No, I couldn't help you."

Jimmy said, "So what? You never did."

Bobby Jones

Bobby Jones hit the best golf shot I ever saw in a tournament. I was playing in the group 150 yards behind him at East Lake in Atlanta at the Southern Open and had a clear view.

On the seventh hole there is a big canyon on the right of the green with a grassy hollow at the bottom. The weather had been nasty, and suddenly hailstones as big as marbles began falling. The whole green was covered with hailstones. Jones had been down in the grassy hollow, but had pitched the ball just to the crown of the hill where he could hardly tell a golf ball from a hailstone. From there, he chipped the ball among the hailstones and it rolled right into the cup—for a par.

Jones had a way of doing whatever was necessary. Jack Burke, Sr., said that to win a tournament the Lord has to put His hand on your head. This happened to Jones over and over.

Bobby didn't even play golf all that much. He'd put his clubs away in the summer when it was hot and get them out just in time to practice for a major tournament, which he would frequently win. He seldom played in college.

I've always said the best golf teacher of all has to be Stewart Maiden of East Lake. He taught Jones and Glenna Collett Vare.

Stewart never gave Bobby a formal lesson. He would just come watch Jones on the practice tee and say something like. "You didn't hit it with your backswing, laddie."

Bobby and his daddy both had hot tempers. They were playing together one day when daddy hit a bad shot and slammed his club on the ground. Then dad took a good practice swing and said, "What's wrong with that?"

"Nothing," Bobby said. "Try it on the ball sometime."

Bobby's famous putter, Calamity Jane, had a lot of tape and glue on the shaft because he broke it from time to time. Calamity Jane had the loft of a 2–iron, which was needed for the furry greens of those class. His putting stroke was long and smooth, like Ben Crenshaw's, but Bobby rolled the blade of the putter open and closed it during his stroke.

Like many players of the time, Bobby saw to it that his iron clubs were all red and pitted with rust on the face. This kept the ball on the face longer for more control.

Because Bobby made a number of movie shorts, his swing has been preserved on videotape and is widely studied by golfers of all levels.

He played with his feet close together, even on the long shots. That made it easier to turn, but a windy day could blow most players off balance—but not Jones.

At the top of his swing, Jones looked like he was waving a flag. People thought he turned loose of the club at the top. But he didn't. He just had a loose grip that, he said, "helped me to put some snap in the swing."

Jones had a long, smooth swing with a little loop at the top that brought the club to the ball from the inside. He was up on his toes at impact, but he kept perfect balance. He had a picture-book follow-through, with his elbows out front of his body.

"You just turn back and turn through," he said. He made the game look awfully easy.

People talk about the "relaxed" swing of Bobby Jones. But look at a photograph of Bobby's face at impact. You can see the frown of intense effort and concentration.

Sam Snead

Sam hit that low, bullet-type shot. If you want distance—whether it's for a shot-put, a BB gun or a cannon—you would want to launch at about a 45-degree angle. That's what most of us try to do.

But Sam hit down on the ball a little bit to get that bullet flying. For this reason, he used a driver off the tee with the loft of a brassie.

People would say Sam looked like he was aimed to the right. Playing at the Masters one time, another pro told him, "Sam, you are aimed at my caddie." Sam said, "No, I'm aimed at my own caddie."

For Sam the aim was perfect. He aimed a little to the right and hooked it.

I was trying to get Darrell Royal to play in Snead's style, but Darrell told me he was aimed too far to the right. Darrell thought he was pulling the ball. He wasn't accepting what I was saying.

But in the pro-am before the first Legends of Golf Tournament, Darrell was paired with Sam. Darrell came to me later and said, "I want to apologize. I didn't believe Sam could possibly be aimed to the right, but I stood behind him all day—and he was."

Sam had amazing agility. From a flat-footed stance he could leap and kick the ceiling.

Jimmy Thompson told me he always outdrove Snead on a still day or with the wind helping. But into the wind, Sam was in front of him every time.

Since he's the player who convinced me to become a teacher, I have always been a big fan of Sam's.

Jack Nicklaus

I can't take the slightest bit of credit for Jack Nicklaus, but he is the greatest player in history, so I have watched him closely.

Most anybody would have said the young Nicklaus couldn't have played well with that right elbow flying up the way it does. But he moves it back to his side as he starts down. And they'd say you can't play well lifting your left heel as much as he does, but they would be wrong. He doesn't lift it any more than Bobby Jones did, I don't believe.

Lifting the heel gives him a good turn and a comfortable position at the top.

Even though he is the best player who ever lived, young Jack, like all young pros at the time, was required to come to a PGA school taught by Byron Nelson and me. Byron and I thought he stood out head and shoulders above the fifty players in the school. Jack has no weaknesses in any department of the game.

A swing like his will last the rest of his life.

Tom Kite

Tom was a very long practicer on all phases of his game as a boy. He is an analytical person and a perfectionist. One day he asked me to watch him hit iron shots to the green. They looked perfect to me. "What's wrong with them?" I asked.

"They're flying about a foot too high," Tommy said.

Another time while playing, Tommy hit a 7-iron to four feet short of the cup. He frowned.

"What was wrong with that one?" I asked.

"I misjudged either the wind or the moisture of the green," Tom said.

I would give Tommy games to play while he practiced. I'd ask him to aim at a canister out on the practice range and draw the ball into it one time and fade it in the next. The range at our old club on Riverside Drive was beside the cart path en route to the first tee. I would stop foursomes coming by and say, "Watch this. Hey, Tommy, fade the ball into that canister." It put the pressure on him, and most of the time he hit the target.

Boys who practice a lot but seldom play don't learn to score. I made sure Tommy got off the range and onto the course as much as he needed. With his sound, compact swing and good short game, Tommy quickly picked up the real secret of golf—get your ball into the hole in a minimum number ot strokes. He has a knack for scoring.

At an NCAA tournament, the University of Texas team was seven strokes behind going into the last day. Tommy started the first seven holes 6 under par, inspired the rest of the team and Texas won the title.

I was very happy for Tommy when he tied for the NCAA individual championship as a senior. In fact, I was doubly happy because the boy he tied with was Ben Crenshaw.

In all the years I taught them, I would never let Tommy watch me with Ben, nor Ben watch me with Tommy.

What applies to one of them does not apply to the other.

Ben Crenshaw

Ben came to me when he was about eight years old. We cut off a 7–iron for him. I showed him a good grip, and we went outside.

There was a green about seventy-five yards away. I asked Ben to tee up a ball and hit it onto the green. He did. Then I said, "Now, let's go to the green and putt the ball into the hole."

"If you wanted it in the hole, why didn't you tell me the first time?" little Ben asked.

Ben's mother was a fine piano player. He may have inherited his extraodinary sense of touch from her. His father, Charles, was a very good athlete.

His natural swing is long and smooth, using mostly the shoulders. I encouraged him to play golf to his heart's content and to practice only when guidance was needed.

Ben is such an excellent athlete. One day he was playing with three other good golfers at Horseshoe Bay on a very difficult course. With six holes to go, Ben was leading. He told the others he would play left-handed the rest of the way. He shot those last six holes even par.

I have seen Ben on the course when it was so cold he was the only one playing. He would win a high school tournament, and then go play another round.

Ben's victory in the Masters in 1984 is one of the most popular wins of all time.

Ben's older brother, Charles, was just as talented a golfer as Ben when they were kids. But Charles starred in other sports and didn't concentrate on golf. It made me very happy when Ben gave up other sports and devoted himself to golf. Charles developed nongolf muscles, which are very difficult to overcome. He's in his forties now, and he can shoot 73 from the blue tees at Austin Country Club, no small feat.

I love Ben and Tommy like my own sons.

—1992

II.

The Idiosyncratic Nature

of Golf

The Social Aspect
of Playing Through

Peter Andrews

One group of golfers playing through another should be a simple matter. The basic law governing objects in motion is easy enough for even the most dense of us to comprehend. Faster gets to go ahead of slower. A race-track tout can understand this for heaven's sake. Even people who run in the New York City Marathon—and there can be no less mentally acute members of our citizenry than those persons who willingly lumber through city streets dressed in their underwear—realize that, sooner or later, the race is to the swift.

In golf, however, playing through can be as fraught with social peril as schooners trying to pass each other in the Strait of Magellan when the sea is up, as it always is.

The first problem in golf is that speed of itself carries no particular virtue. Although fast golfers assume a sense of superiority, they may, in fact, be good players or they may be dreadful. The only thing we know for certain is that they are fast. In an ideal world, and we haven't had one of those since the reign of Charles II, *that* should be sufficient to gain precedence on the golf course. But when the efficient golfer tries to work his way through, he has to deal with a series of moral issues that never occur to some little guy from Panama whipping a horse around an oval track under the hot sun. A host of conflicting social dogmata are raised: "respect your elders," "youth must have its fling," "age before beauty," "pearls before swine," "first come is first served" and "no jumping ahead in the chow line." The list goes on and on and the items must be carefully sorted out, particularly in these politically correct times.

Let us attempt to do just that.

The generally accepted rule is that if there is a foursome nipping at your heels and the hole in front of you is open, you should let the trailing foursome through. Immediately, we run into a qualitative question. What constitutes an "open hole"? Must it be entirely free of participants, or is a group putting on the green of a distant par 5 sufficient?

We will be arbitrary, which is one of the great fringe benefits of writing a column. If you are three shots behind the foursome in front of you, the hole is open. OK. But when and how do you let the trailing foursome through? Are you supposed to sense the urgency of their needs and wave them by as soon as they hove into view? Do you play for a bit to test their mettle or do you wait until they ask? I remember a time when the right to play through had to be freely offered. It was considered bad manners to ask to play through. To do so was to administer a social rebuff by in effect telling people they did not know how to act properly on the golf course. Of course, I remember a time when people made use of napkin rings, place cards and finger bowls, all of which puts me among the antediluvians. My daughter says I am from "The Olden Days." She calculates this as a rough and turbulent period of world history falling sometime between the collapse of the Roman Empire and the establishment of the first McDonald's humburger stand.

Perhaps so, but still I wait and wait and wait until I am asked. I sometimes adopt the exaggerated arms akimbo stance of the seasoned golfer whose contempt can be discerned from farther than I can hit, but I wait nonetheless.

The way to play through on par 3s has been well established by historical precedent. The leading foursome waits until all four balls are on the green and marked and then waves the trailing foursome on. This is a reasonable system, but perhaps a little stodgy. It seems to me that reasonable people can be more flexible and adopt a kind of "flying" play-through. Simply go to someone in the trailing foursome and say, "We know we are holding you up. Just play at your regular pace. We will watch out for you and you can come through whenever it is convenient." That way you don't have to play "Living Statues" while a foursome goes through.

All of this could go down as easily as sponge cake with a bit of jam if it were not for ingrained social attitudes.

Old men golfers don't like to let young men golfers through for a number of reasons not always connected with golf. Young men golfers hit too far, laugh too loudly, don't have to wear belts and get more sex. Let them wait.

Young men golfers don't like to let old men golfers through, even if the geezers are faster, because, well, just because they are old and should not be cluttering up the golf course in the first place. They should be like super seniors in an Eskimo society who are cast adrift on an iceberg with two days' supply of blubber and a sharp knife where they can contemplate entering into what Rabelais called "the grand perhaps."

Low-handicap players don't like to let high-handicap players play through because they are not good enough and should know their station in life. By the same token, high handicappers don't like to let low handicappers through because if low handicappers spent more time tending to their businesses they wouldn't be that good in the first place.

Some men would rather fall on their swords than let women play through. It wouldn't matter if the ladies were the four leading money-winners of the LPGA Tour. They just cannot play as fast as men. It is a known fact.

There is a course, where I play with some regularity as a guest, at which women are not allowed off the first tee on weekends until 1 P.M. Why the ladies have not burned down the clubhouse by now, I cannot understand. Although the tee is invariably clear by noon, the women are held back like teenagers waiting to get into a Michael Jackson concert. Why there are lines at a Michael Jackson concert I understand even less than I do the nonburning of the clubhouse. To worsen matters, there is a group of octogenarian male dubbers who make it a point to linger over their Welsh rarebit until exactly 12:55 P.M. before teeing off. They then meander down the course at the speed of yaks seeking summer pasturage and refuse to let anyone through. The foursome is known as "The Old Farts." A little ageism here, but defensible under the circumstances.

I suggested the women, most of whom could play any given hole faster than the men could add up their scores, should hit into the OFs and if they say anything, give them the finger. Sadly, my advice has not been taken, but it raises the point that some golfers, like neighbors who play loud rap music late at night, forfeit all expectation of being treated decently. How you handle such an individual situation may depend on how good your foursome is with their hands and how adept your attorneys are at handling assault and battery cases. You want to be firm but prudent.

Playing through has its own set of social requirements. It is axiomatic that when doing so, you will hit a squirrely shot, and this is accepted as part of the human condition. But you must play quickly. It's indefensible to spend a lot of time lining up putts while making others wait. Anything inside of five feet is close enough. And no search parties for lost balls on the next hole. Invoke the leaf rule and be gone.

Consider playing through on the golf course as you would bumping into someone on the street. It is a moment of possible social awkwardness, but one that can be easily handled by persons of good will. The group playing through is not saying they are more deserving than you, simply that at the moment they are faster. So let them through with a glad heart and wish them Godspeed. They will need it because that bumbling bunch of hackers in front of you will *never* let them through.

—1996

The Choke Factor

Thomas Boswell

The Year of the Gag

November 1989—

One thing elevates golf from the realm of games to the world of sports.

The choke factor.

Of all our American sports, golf is the most consistently humiliating for its stars. As Tom Watson once said: "We all choke. You just try to choke last."

What happened to Scott Hoch at the Masters, Tom Kite at the U.S. Open, Greg Norman at the British Open and Mike Reid at the PGA Championship—suffering a totally humiliating, self-inflicted collapse under pressure—is what makes golf a legitimate big-time, big-money sport, rather than a tofu-and-quiche pastime for yuppies.

Baseball, football, basketball, boxing, tennis, hockey, track and the rest can claim skill, grace, strength, speed, stamina, strategy and a dozen other virtues as their core source of attraction for us. Basically, golf offers us the spectacle of people under enormous strain unraveling before our, and their own, disbelieving eyes.

It's man against himself, with man usually losing quite badly.

A fellow proves, for several days in a row, that he can play a certain course in a dozen or more strokes under par. On most holes, he makes a birdie or finishes with a tap-in par. Then, when he only needs a final decent round on Sunday or perhaps one or two pars to get to the house and claim his prize, he suddenly turns into the rankest of amateurs.

"The pressure of golf can change you so you hardly know yourself," Joe Inman, a journeyman pro, once told me. "You have more electrical connections in your head than a whole city. You'll do anything to keep 'em from going blooey on you in the crunch. I have only one goal in golf—to leave it with my sanity."

No year in memory has left as many images of despair in defeat as 1989. At the Masters, Ben Crenshaw watched in horror as Hoch backed away from a twenty-inch putt to win a playoff against Nick Faldo.

"It's a good thing I don't carry a gun," said Hoch after he missed, then eventually lost to Faldo.

That April day, Reid also collapsed when it seemed he'd won. "Things happened so fast," he said. "One minute I was in control, then, faster than a blinking eye, bogey, double bogey. That's baseball."

On the seventy-first hole of the PGA, Reid got a second chance. He led again. That is, until he took four strokes to get down from the fringe, thirty feet from the hole, for a double bogey. His final blown putt was inches longer than Hoch's at Augusta.

Ironically, Reid sped up his normal ritual as much as Hoch had slowed his down. That didn't work either. As Reid's ball lipped out, who was standing behind him—a few feet away, his head turned so he could not watch the deed—but Scott Hoch.

At the post-tournament press conference, Reid said, "Somebody tell me this is only a game," then added, "Does anybody know where you can go around here for a good cry?" Pretty soon he was crying as he talked.

Between the Masters and the PGA came the most brutal unraveling of the year, all the worse because it took most of a round to complete and because it happened to such a superb player—Kite.

"A lot of people who entered this tournament don't have the opportunity to be scared to death tomorrow," said Kite, after taking the third-round lead in a major for only the second time in his long career. "I anticipate it. I welcome it. I want to be nervous. Do I have total control? Nah. Neither does anybody else. . . . It's you against yourself and you hope you can stand up to it."

Not even eighteen years of pro experience and millions of dollars in prize money could immunize Kite from playing himself on Sunday with a triple, bogey and two double bogeys—one of which included a wood from the rough that traveled less than fifty yards.

"I'll come back. And I will contend in more majors. I promise you. I'll survive," said the grim little Kite, who, like Hoch and Reid, has never won a major. 'But it's a bitter pill to swallow, to have a chance to win and perform the way I did. That's by far my worst round this year and probably the worst I've had in five years."

The longer you watch tournament golf, the more inclined you are to believe it's the most mentally torturous of all sports. Only in golf is a player given as much time as he needs to tie his own noose.

"You're completely alone, with every conceivable opportunity to defeat yourself," Hale Irwin once said. "What really matters is resiliency. There's going to come at least one point when you want to throw yourself in the nearest trash can and disappear. . . . It's like you're walking down the fairway naked. The gallery knows what you've done, every other player knows and, worst of all, you know. That's when you find out if you're a competitor.

"The longer you play, the more certain you are that a man's performance is the outward manifestation of who, in his heart, he really thinks he is."

Courage is grace under pressure. What a raw deal. How come it couldn't be something easier? In golf, at least, cruel demands for mental and emotional courage can be justified because the game demands no physical courage. The only bones that break are those in the skeleton of the personality. The only blood that flows is from an internal hemorrhaging of self-esteem.

Peter Jacobsen, another of those fine millionaire players who has never won a Big One, once explained how he felt about the prospect of someday playing a major-winning shot: "Am I going to have the guts to stand in there and hit the best shot I can and accept the consequences? All those practice shots don't mean a thing. You have to be able to stand on the last hole and say, 'It's due right now.' And then perform."

As if golf weren't cruel enough, you can actually perform too well. Norman shot a 64 in the fourth round of the British Open, then birdied two holes in the four-hole playoff. However, on that fourth and last playoff hole, Norman was so spectacularly pumped up that he hit his drive under the lip of a bunker that no one—not even he— ever dreamed could be reached. He ended with an "X."

Still, Norman should not forgive himself too quickly. With the exception of a couple of famous eighteenth-hole failures at the Masters, Norman's problems with pressure have come in the early rounds. He's like Johnny Miller, who once admitted, "The first round of the Masters has killed me for fifteen straight years."

Let's be honest. Everybody, in every sport, plays loosest and best when they're behind and have little to lose. Norman's closing rushes have something homely mixed with their handsomeness. If he's this good, then where was he for three days?

This has been a painful year for those close to the pro tour. Almost every cheer for Nick Faldo, Curtis Strange, Mark Calcavecchia and Payne Stewart has been balanced by a genuine note of sympathy for the victim of the day. Norman is as well liked as Kite is respected. No one could dislike Reid, and some who did not care for Hoch before the Masters found that he grew on them in defeat.

As Crenshaw once said: "The game embarrasses you until you feel inadequate and pathetic. You want to cry like a child." In the gentlemanly world of golf, so excessive a punishment for such small crimes is frowned upon as somehow unsporting.

Deep down, however, the pro's pain is secretly his badge of pride as well. He may not look like a Greek statue, but he has, in a sense, been forged in fire. Golf is serious sport because, of all our games, it is constructed in such a manner as to extract the greatest mental and psychological price. Four consecutive days of play. Deliberate pace of play. Constant scoreboard watching. No foe but yourself and, consequently, no excuses.

Still, following golf up close takes almost as good a stomach as watching Lawrence Taylor tackle Joe Theismann.

After he lost the Masters, Hoch carried his small son Cameron in his arms to the clubhouse as reporters followed. "C'mon over here. Daddy needs a hug," said Hoch.

When he got inside, Hoch—who once missed a playoff in the PGA because of a seventy-second-hole three-putt from eight feet—slammed his visor against a wall.

"Why did you do that?" asked Cameron.

"Because I goofed up," said Hoch.

"Daddy, did you goof up again?" asked the child.

"Boy," said Hoch with a pained smile, "you really know how to hurt a guy."

Don't Carry a Gun

Augusta, Georgia, April 10, 1989—

Ben Crenshaw watched Scott Hoch back away from his tap-in putt to win the Masters in a playoff. Two harmless feet. Probably less. Nick Faldo would be beaten. And Hoch, a dependable ten-year journeyman, would be a lovely sliver of golf history. "Jesus, hit it," implored Crenshaw, putting his hand to his mouth as he watched the TV screen.

As Hoch continued to circle and pace, working himself into putting paralysis, Crenshaw put both hands to his face in empathic fear and said, "Oh my God."

In the history of golf, no one had missed a putt so short to throw away—simply rip up and burn—a major championship. Although Hoch three-putted from six feet on the seventy-second hole to miss a playoff in the '87 PGA.

Hubert Green held the previous record for Major Squandering with a four-footer here on the eighteenth green in 1978. But that at least was a real putt. Not a slam-dunk, inside the-leather, collect-the-green-jacket gimme. By comparison, Doug Sanders's one-pace putt to reach a British Open playoff was lengthy.

When Hoch finally did the horrifying deed, knocking the ball entirely outside the hole and four feet past, Crenshaw's face fell forward in his hands. As a golfer—that is to say, a continual victim of inescapable humiliation—he couldn't watch such disproportionate crime and punishment.

Any child who watched the fifty-third Masters this sullen and soggy afternoon will, one assumes, never be tempted to become a professional golfer. Who'd choose such a thing? Finish second, win $120,000 and use it to buy cyanide.

At least Hoch could joke about it. "It's a good thing I don't carry a gun," he said after Faldo put him out of his sopping-wet misery with a twenty-foot birdie putt in the gloaming at the second playoff hole. "It's gonna hurt, knowing all I had to do was two-putt for all the immortality and all that other stuff that comes with these majors. I'da been sharin' that."

He hasn't figured out the worst of it yet. Although Hoch's won more than two million dollars on tour and a Vardon Trophy, not too many people know how to pronounce his name because he's only won three events.

It rhymes with choke. And after playing twenty-three holes in five under par this day, he deserves a far better memorial. After all, he simply fell on his sword last. What he did on the tenth green, the greatest men in golf had been doing all day.

Seve Ballesteros? His hopes and all his gallantry on a marvelous day splashed into the water at the sixteenth hole when he was just a shot off the lead. "I was thinking [birdie] two and got five," said the Spaniard, who, on his thirty-second birthday, led for a short time after making seven birdies in the span of ten holes. "When I saw my ball flying right at the flag . . . I could not believe what happened. It was only a matter of a couple of yards. Then, it spun back in the water and my tournament was over. . . . I guess my destiny was not to win."

Greg Norman? After thrilling the throng with three straight birdies to tie for the lead, he made a lame bogey at the seventy-second hole with a weak approach and a weaker pitch. All he needed was a par to get in the playoff. His thoughts? Don't ask. For the first time in all his major disappointments, he bolted for the parking lot. Perhaps the memories of 1986 here and 1984 at the U.S. Open, when he also bogeyed seventy-second holes and ended up a loser, were too strong even for his sharkish courage.

Crenshaw? He began the day at 9 A.M. with a four-shot lead with five holes remaining in the rain-interrupted third round. On a wet but windless day with the easiest possible scoring conditions, Crenshaw made nothing happen all day until he birdied the seventieth and seventy-first holes to tie for the lead. What'd he do? He collapsed instantly with a bogey.

"My glove was wet and slipped and I pulled it into the trap. And that was that," said Crenshaw, who, hard as it is to believe, had run out of towels. For want of a nail the shoe was lost, and so the horse, and so forth. "We thought we had one more," said Crenshaw in disbelief. "But we didn't."

Mike (Radar) Reid, the world's most accurate golfer in recent years? He had this Masters in his hands more securely than anybody except Hoch. But he three-putted the subtle fourteenth, then dunked a simple wedge shot into the water at the easy fifteenth for a double bogey.

Unfortunately for those who play it for a living, that's golf. Especially the Masters. "This is probably the hardest tournament in the world to win from the front. Probably ninety percent win from behind. . . . There's so much pressure here. This course asks for perfection," said Faldo.

In fact, Faldo never carried the burden of the lead for a second all weekend until he found himself in the playoff. Like so many others before him, like Gary Player (64) in 1977 and Nicklaus (65) in '86, he freewheeled it from the rear. Then, as soon as he had no one in front of him, Faldo lost this Masters with a bunkered bogey on the playoff's first hole.

Hoch just unlost it for him.

"You just stand there and watch," said Faldo of the awful feeling as Hoch prepared for his winning tap.

In golf, the wheel of karma never stops turning—so long as you keep plugging and let it work its will. For a decade, Crenshaw suffered. But he got a Masters. Tom Kite's long, stoic battle continues. Last year, Faldo lost a U.S. Open to Curtis Strange that he thought he should have won. "That slipped by," Faldo said. "But this makes up for it. Sure, certainly does. . . . What does this mean? Gosh, the world."

A world lifted, at any rate, from your shoulders. For strong losers like Faldo, the hour of vindication usually rolls 'round. Strange, for example, can joke about Rae's Creek. Now it's Hoch who'll have to relive his putt a million times. "I wasn't even that nervous," he said. "I didn't want to miss an angle. I said, 'This is for all the marbles. Just firm it.' Then I didn't line up the putter and I pulled it on top of that. . . . At that speed, I needed to keep it inside [the] left [edge]. But I pulled it. It was a terrible putt.

"There was a split second of indecision. I adjusted as I was over the ball. Between my brain and my hands, the message got criss-crossed."

Golf's most vicious illusion is that he who gags last gags worst. Actually, the penultimate victim has played better than anyone, except the champion. Some reward. "I feel good about myself," said Hoch, defiantly, almost convincingly.

Crenshaw, who has now finished second or been just a shot be-hind in six major championships, had the dank evening's wisest words—for himself and so many other brave failures here.

"I'm laughing now, but when the time comes [alone], it'll be painful, believe me. . . . [But] you're never cursed in this game. You just do your best and go on," said Crenshaw, adding with a rueful little chuckle, "Any way you can."

Father's Day

Brookline, Massachusetts, June 20, 1988—

Everyone in golf who knows Curtis Strange knew where his thoughts would turn as he walked up the eighteenth hole of the Country Club with the U.S. Open championship safely in his hands today.

He would think of his father, Tom, and their years together in his boyhood when golf was their bond and passion and almost a blood vow between them. He would think of the man who died when he was fourteen, nearly twenty years ago, leaving a paternal memory of superhuman size and demands, deep-carved demands, that would drive and lash Strange all his life.

Everybody knew, almost to the word, what Strange would say as soon as he had finished the work of beating British Open champion Nick Faldo, 71–75, in this eighteen-hole playoff. Strange would not talk yet about putts and sand shots, about "sheer guts," about how he ignored ten visits to the rough and five trips into sand traps. He would not talk about how he kicked the ball all over wind-whipped eastern Massachusetts, but willed his way to a dozen one-putt greens.

"I think you wait for a moment like this in your life to thank the people who've given you the advice, enthusiasm and knowledge to continue on," said Strange, picking every word, pausing as much as ten seconds between phrases as he cried quietly. "I have to thank my dad. This is for my dad." Then he waited.

"And that's all I can say. I've been waitin' to say that a long time," said Strange. "I just wish he could have been here. . . . I screwed up the '85 Masters. But let's not be bringing that up. Let's be havin' fun. . . . This is the greatest thing I have ever done . . . the greatest feeling I have ever had. My two kids don't even know [yet] what the hell this means to me."

This U.S. Open meant everything to Curtis Strange. More, perhaps, than it ought to mean to anybody. Even he has admitted that countless times, talked about the coiled spring of ambition inside him that drives and torments him, even as it pushed him to Arnold Palmer scholarships at Wake Forest and seasons as the number-one money winner on the PGA Tour. "I'm too hard on myself," he says. Yet this week he has barely slept. His eyes are bloodshot. And Sunday night, after coming so close to throwing away this Open, he couldn't even eat. For nearly twenty-four hours, he was a taut bow, "Waiting to go." Waiting to atone.

Faldo should have finished Strange when he had the chance, when he had all those cozy birdie putts on the back nine Sunday. He shouldn't have waited until this nasty, windy afternoon when both he and Strange would, inevitably, be blown off the short grass into the high heather and have a war of hearts, not swings. Eleven times Faldo missed the green and six times he ended up with bogey—five times in the last six holes as the long battle just wore him out.

Strange, the grinder's grinder, the bad boy with a bit of a sneer, just kept holing those heartbreakers: three feet, six feet. Sorry, Nick. No lip-outs today. Strange hit only seven greens all afternoon, but three times he set the huge crowds roaring with birdie putts of ten, twenty-two, and, finally, twenty-nine feet at the fifth, seventh and thirteenth holes.

Strange never trailed, not for a second. When he birdied the thirteenth, it was the day's kill shot. Faldo three-putted for bogey a moment later to put Strange ahead by three shots. "The turning point," said Strange, who never led by fewer than two shots thereafter.

The door opened only once after that, for a second at the fifteenth hole, when Strange was trapped and had to bogey. But Faldo slapped that door on his own foot. He fragged an easy chip shot all the way across the green into the fringe and bogeyed himself.

"I don't know what happened on that one," Faldo said.

Now Strange could come home on cruise control. When Faldo, gambling for birdie, bogeyed the seventeenth, Strange thought: It's over.

More than a golf tournament was over for the thirty-three-year-old who has won $3.6 million but, until today, never a major championship. Always money. Never glory. Never what his father, the romantic, valued most—stature in the game.

"We all have our egos and we want to be respected. Not just as a person but as a golfer," said Strange. "This [Open] means Curtis Strange might be looked at a little differently. . . . It means I got to that next level, damnit."

The earnings at the next level aren't bad either. Strange pocketed $180,000 for the victory; as runner-up, Faldo received $90,000.

Strange is the player that fellow pros on the tour always have worried about. Tears and fury ran just beneath his skin. His mask always was full of cracks, the rage or hunger waiting to erupt. Friends worried when he got publicly scalded by Palmer for his bad temper at the Bay Hill Classic a few years ago. They worried when he blew that Masters after being four up on the back nine. Think what that would do to any player. Imagine what it does to Strange.

The final round of the U.S. Open always falls on Father's Day—another bad break for Strange, who tries too hard, berates himself too much, on the best of days. Once, on an Open Sunday, a fan approached Strange between nines and said, "Win it for your dad."

"That did it," recalled Strange. "I was in tears on the tenth tee."

Now, the friends of Curtis Strange—a group that has grown enormously in the last three years after he met the indignities of Rae's Creek with fresh dignity of his own—don't have to worry anymore. He's come into the clearing.

Because he faced the worst when he lost the Masters, because he discovered that people forgave him, empathized with him and even liked him in failure, Strange was able to cope with his near-collapse here on Sunday. But it was far from easy. A night to regroup helped.

"After my [three-putt] mistake at the seventeenth on Sunday, I didn't want to lose today. . . . I just didn't want to face you guys if I lost. I hate to admit that, but it's true," said Strange at the postmatch news conference. "[A loss] would have been something I would have had to get over. But it would have been tough. Those things affect us."

Faldo seemed unfazed by his defeat. In fact, he seemed so proud that his nerve had held on his long shots—"I had it going in the right direction all day"—that his ineffectual putting hardly seemed to enter his mind.

"I just never put enough pressure on Curtis. . . . It felt like a helluva long day," he said, after roasting in the mid-nineties heat. "[And] I think my five spectators did a helluva job."

For Strange, the path to this Open title has been a long one. Along the way, he learned—although he'll be the first to concede not completely—how to relax, how to enjoy others, how to forgive himself, how to fail and how to carry himself like a champion of the game. "That Masters wasn't going to intimidate me or ruin my career," said Strange. "It even motivated me, to a point. What I've done since says, 'This was not going to devastate Curtis Strange.'"

As he came down the eighteenth fairway this hot, breezy evening, the throngs straining against the ropes to praise him, Strange raised both hands above his pepper-gray head in salute. In the gallery, his twin brother, Alan, almost a golf pro, hugged Curtis's wife, Sarah. Then, after the final putt, after he had joined Francis Ouimet and Julius Boros as Open playoff winners at the Country Club, it was Curtis's turn to hold his wife tight and saying nothing for a long time. Finally, Strange's lips moved. He seemed to whisper, "I made it."

And if he didn't, he might as well have.

—1989

Requiem for a Milkman

Tom Callahan

This is the story of a retired milkman named Emil Kijek, who wound up his life in the arms of a friend in the middle of a fairway on a Thursday afternoon.

The setting is southeast Massachusetts, on the rim of Narragansett Bay, where stories this small are usually thrown back. Lizzie Borden hailed from Fall River, right next door; Ishmael and Ahab sailed from New Bedford, just down the road.

As a center of drama, Rehoboth is not quite in their class.

It's a pretty little town though. Driving through, you might take it for hunting country if John Pellegrino weren't there to set you straight. "Shoot my deer" explained the owner of the Sun Valley Golf Club, "and I'll shoot you."

Pellegrino's operation is similarly unvarnished. Starting with the arrow sign on the highway, everything at Sun Valley could stand some paint. The roof wouldn't mind a little leveling. The clubhouse is mostly a bar. But the gray-haired men crisscrossing with pullcarts look well satisfied. The senior rate is thirteen dollars for eighteen holes.

Ron Collett, Morris Dumont, Jack Alexander and Emil Kijek were teamed up that Thursday in a tournament. Collett and Dumont were not Kijek's regular partners, although both knew "Ky" well. Everyone did. "He had a spirit about him, I tell you," said Dumont, a retired piano tuner. "Ky was the type who enjoyed the day better than the golf, who took the good shots and the bad shots as they came, always hoping the next one would be perfect."

Alexander, on the other hand, was Kijek's customary golfing crony and his closest friend. They served together in Hawaii during World War II, though they didn't know it at the time. Kijek had gone in and out of the Army before the war broke out. When it did, he came back as a Scabee, a builder, and eventually saw Saipan.

On Oahu, when Alexander only knew *of* him, Kijek was also a boxer, a middleweight. He was one of the staple attractions in the Friday night fights at Schofield Barracks, a model of that paradoxical gentleness you so often find in boxers.

His father was the same way. Back in Warsaw, Jacob Kijek had been a weaver's foreman preoccupied with keeping a certain loom operating, the one run by Caroline. Falling in love and emigrating to Pawtucket, Jacob and Caroline raised their boy in the weaving business. As he had been an only son, Emil grew up to have an only daughter, Sandra. Her childhood memories are of spontaneous picnics, Sunday rides and father whose only rule was kindness.

It was in the early 1960s that he embraced golf, when a cardiologist's first warning gave him four months off. After he retired—especially after losing his wife, Mabel—the golf course became home. He was a good, straight hitter, an 11- or 12-handicapper who held to that number (even as his distance waned) with increasingly better putting. This phenomenon is unheard of in the pros but well known in places like Sun Valley.

As a cardplayer, Kijek was a scratch, a legend at gin but even more partial to "pitch," the working man's rhapsody of high, low, jack and game.

"Deal the cards, old man," Alexander would say. Kijek would smile like a handsome child, and everyone else would laugh. At seventy-five, Jack was only four years younger, but lately they were telling years. Ky was losing his edge with the cards.

He could still putt. At the first hole that day, he made a twenty-footer for par. At the fourth, he knocked in another. "You're saving us, old man," Alexander said. The day looked bright

The sixth hole at Sun Valley is a 155-yard par 3. Kijek took a 3-wood.

"He hit that thing so beautifully," Dumont would say later. "It had this amazing trajectory."

"Emil, I can't see the ball," Alexander murmured after a moment. "I think it went in."

"Naw," Kijek said. He'd never had a hole-in-one.

"Old man!" Alexander sang as they reached the green. "Come get your ball out of the cup!"

Dumont recalled, "Ky was really happy, but there was no jumping up and down. He was such a humble man."

After driving nicely at the seventh, Kijek wavered over his second shot. "Emil, let somebody else hit first," Alexander suggested gently. "No, no, I'm OK, Jack," he said.

In the next instant, Ky started to fall, and his friend caught him. They settled softly in the grass. As the others ran for help, Jack said, "Emil, squeeze my hand. Don't stop until I tell you to." But Ky gave him that smile again and let go.

Who was he? He was a man who enjoyed the day better than the golf, who took good shots and bad shots as they came, always hoping the next one would be perfect. And it was.

—1995

We Know Who They Are

Tom Callahan

Nothing has been said this year in golf or in sports that rings with a sharper truth than the five words: "We know who they are."

To a leading question in a dinner setting, Tom Watson acknowledged in late winter that there were cheaters on the PGA Tour. "The game is a game of integrity," he told an Australian interviewer in Melbourne, "but you are talking about money and you're talking about livelihoods."

Invited to name names, Watson said icily, "We know who they are."

As if candor were calumny, Tom was slammed in the U.S. for once again sticking his blue nose where it wasn't wanted. But the slammers lost momentum when Nick Price told the *Fort Lauderdale Sun-Sentinel*, "There are two [players] I know of for sure on tour who cheat, and many others who I have come across in my travels. But once you do it, the guys all know who you are. Forever."

While PGA patriots were extolling Jeff Sluman's honesty at Bay Hill, Ben Crenshaw, of all gentle people, was saying, "Cheating is the absolute worst thing on tour, period. It's like the people who play golf are one big family, and once you get cast out of the family, there's no way to get back in."

If that were literally so, Watson and Gary Player, Greg Norman and Mark McCumber, Nick Faldo and Sandy Lyle, Seve Ballesteros and Paul Azinger—and all the other jousters who have tilted bloodily over honor—would never know peace in each other's company. (A few never will.) But time is a funny thing.

Many U.S. Opens ago, a large Californian named Lon Hinkle seemed to hang over young Ballesteros like a gargoyle at every green. Asked about it afterward, Hinkle said in a measured tone: "He is a great young player, but he is going to have to learn to mark his ball like a professional." Evidently, he did.

There's an American star on tour who, long ago, in the crucible of the Q school, left a birdie putt on the lip and angrily whiffed the tap-in. With a face whiter than Gold Medal flour, he proceeded to the next tee and drove off as if it were still his honor.

His two playing partners were so stunned that they said nothing. He won his card by more than a shot; all three qualified. But, late that night, the other two got to talking, and drinking, and one went to the telephone. "I just want you to know," he said in the alcoholic mist, "that I saw what happened out there today and you'll have to live with it the rest of your life." Only one word came back in rebuttal, softly: "OK."

Maybe a higher sense of obligation, some extra quality of effort, comes out of such a lonely start. Because, through the years, the player in question has gained the respect of the industry. But there are still whispers. Perhaps that's what Watson, Price and Crenshaw mean.

On the amateur level, the club level, the muny level, any level, "We know who they are" is the truest fact of golf, and maybe the only conforming law.

An old Kentucky newsman, Mike Barry, used to announce on the first tee, "You fellows go ahead and play whatever game you want. I'll be playing golf." In other words, he wouldn't be hitting a mulligan at number one, bumping his ball in the fairway or moving his coin to avoid an abrasion ("teeing it up on the green," as Jim Colbert calls that popular practice).

By the average hacker's code, none of these qualify as cheating, but they set a tone. Barry, who almost never broke 100, had a theory about amateur cheaters that is passed along here not for moralizing purposes but as practical advice.

Mike was convinced the cheaters weren't after his two dollars; they just wanted to shoot 88 instead of 93. But their machinations actually cost them strokes, and not just because teeing up a ball to miss a 3-wood is a ridiculous alternative to an honest 8-iron.

Besides defaulting on their own confidence, they were throwing away golf's most mysterious benefit, the springboard disguised as setback.

Jack Nicklaus will testify that he may never have won the 1986 Masters without a spike mark that popped up in his path at 12. That bogey meant more than any par to his round. It was what propelled him on.

Barry lived a rich life and died well, surrounded by family. In a bonus of timing, he narrowly outlived his archrival, the well-known governor, baseball commissioner and scoundrel, Happy Chandler.

When someone at Barry's bedside recalled Ol' Hap had "lied in state" at the Capitol, Mike came to for just an instant to say, "He lied in every state he ever went into." Then he settled back to sleep the blissful sleep of those who always played the ball down.

—1996

On Diegeling

Bernard Darwin

I diegel, thou diegelest, he or she diegels, we all diegel or are about
to diegel; and I trust that no golfer needs telling that the verb which
I am conjugating signifies to try to imitate the putting methods of
the hero, on the American side, of the Ryder Cup match.

Leo Diegel did not win the Championship. If he had we should
all have had cricks in our backs for the rest of our lives. Even as it is,
when it has been published far and wide that for one fatal round his
putting forsook him, I am sure that many backs have been broken
and elbows crooked to the point of agony in the attempt to get the
ball into the hole as he does. Not, of course, that these thousands
of sincere flatterers all over the country will admit what they are
doing. They will scoff at my statement should they chance to read
it, and then they will sneak away to that little corner of the lawn
screened by the laurel bushes, or to that spare bedroom floor over
the kitchen, knowing that the cook will not understand all that rolling and tapping over her head, or that, at any rate, she will not tell
tales in the drawing room if she does.

I will not myself be guilty of any such shiftiness. I will confess
that I have been evicted from room after room in the house while
openly and unashamedly diegeling. So far I have met with no conspicuous success, but then the Master himself is said to have taken a
year and a half to perfect his method, and I have been at it for only
a few days. Moreover, I am hampered by the fact that I do not pos-
sess a square yard either of floor or garden which is reasonably true;

the ball regularly misses the hole when it ought, were there any jus-
tice in the world, to have gone in, and, just as regularly, it hits the
table leg when it ought to have missed it. This leaves the student in
a state of painful uncertainty as to how he is getting on. I have not
felt my progress sufficient to justify diegeling in a real game on a real
green. The other day, in an essentially friendly match, being 3 up at
the fourth hole I announced my intention of doing so, but my courage failed me. First of all I thought that in the approach putt I had
better lay the ball dead in the ordinary manner; and I did lay it dead,
but when it was dead I utterly failed to indiegel it. Still I have a year
and twenty-four weeks left.

I have assumed that everyone knows in what the great man's
method consists. Many writers have described it and photographers
depicted it. Still there may be some whom the knowledge has passed
by; so perhaps I had better give a brief recipe. You take a putter, not
outrageously upright in the lie, with a reasonably long shaft. You hold
it at the very top of the grip with the left hand well under. You stand
square to the line of the putt, the feet spread rather wide apart. A
friend of mine, an instructor of innocent boyhood who ought to know
better, suggests that the stance should be called the spreadeagle
stance. You next crook the elbows, particularly the left elbow, till
you feel that something will break if you crook them any more. You
drop the nose—not the club's but your own—lower and lower, till
the top of the putter shaft lightly brushes the stomach. Then with
wrists perfectly rigid you take the club back a short way: you give the
ball a stiff little push, apparently with the right hand, and in it goes.

I have guarded myself by saying "apparently with the right hand"
because learned persons have argued in my presence, at almost excessive length, whether the motive power comes in fact from the player's
shoulders or from his feet. I am sure I don't know which is right, but I
also feel sure that for the elementary student it is essential to remember that the wrists are stiff. It is so particularly because the method has
been described as a pendulum method, and to many people the word
pendulum conveys the swinging of the club to and fro with flexible
wrists. It was in that sense that Mr. Horace Hutchinson used the word
in the beloved old *Badminton*, friend of my youth, when he wrote: "The

clubhead will be swinging something after the manner of a pendulum, and if the golfer gets the hanging arrangements of this pendulum correct, it cannot very well swing out of the true line." Mr. Hutchinson's putter did not swing out of the true line. With what pitiful envy, what smoldering fury have I watched him pendulum-ing the ball into the hole on those curly greens at Forest Row! But, though he crooked his elbow to some extent, he kept an insolently free wrist. To putt thus is to have genius, but it is not to diegel and I am writing about diegeling.

We all laugh at our friends and sometimes even pretend to laugh at ourselves for imitating the styles of the eminent. Yet there is this to be said, that if we are going to do it at all, the imitation of a putting style gives much the greater satisfaction. When we attempt a champion's driving swing, nobody by any chance recognizes our rendering of it. No total stranger will ever come up to us and say, "I beg your pardon, my dear sir, but I cannot help noticing that you are copying the effortless grace and free pivot of Mr. John Ball. I hope you are making good progress." On the other hand, we have only to contort ourselves for a single minute in front of the clubhouse windows and a dozen kind friends will shout "How is the diegeling getting on?" The ball may not go into the hole, but recognition is something. It encourages us to go on and, by the way, there comes to me, as I write, a most encouraging sound. It is a pleasantly purring sound as of one mowing. The gardener has been told to mow a patch for me and afterwards to roll it. Then I shall really be able to get down to it.

—1930

Golfing Winds

Bernard Darwin

The golfing winds have characters just as distinct, though no one has had sufficient imagination to christen them. The wind against is an implacable, relentless enemy, but he is an honest one, and plays the game according to his lights. He has no shifty tricks, and, mercifully, he is rather stupid. He can be rendered comparatively innocuous if you do not play his game by hitting too hard, and he affords you now and then, one of the most perfectly satisfactory of human sensations, in the cleanly-struck ball that flies low and straight into the wind's eye. Moreover, he is not nearly so formidable as he used to be in gutty days, since he has never discovered how to make a rubber-cored ball soar and soar till it comes back almost over the striker's head. That is, I suppose, because he is stupid, and for the same reason, he over-reaches himself when it comes to the approaching. By blowing so hard he makes things in some ways easier, since the ball can be pitched right up to the hole and will stop there of its own accord, with no need for recondite back spins.

The wind behind is entirely well meaning. He is a cheerful wind of rollicking and jovial disposition. If we could see him he would, I am convinced, wear a blue coat with brass buttons and drab breeches and gaiters like a jolly old gentleman in one of Caldecott's pictures. He would like to see everyone happy and, since he does not understand much about golf, he thinks everyone must be happiest when he is hitting the ball furthest. So he just takes the ball and whirls it along as far as he can, and, which is really friendly of him, minimises as far as possible any little tendency to slice or hook. In the short game he overdoes his good intentions. He thinks it a poor niggling business, which should not be taken too seriously. He cannot imagine anyone being really annoyed because a perfectly struck mashie shot has sent the ball bounding over the green into a bunker beyond; he cannot in the least understand the agonies of putting when you are being blown forward on to your nose. Golf, he thinks, is a game to be played with roars of boisterous laughter.

I wish I could think that the two side winds, the wind on your back and the wind on your face, had characters half so pleasant. They have nothing of the sort, being, in fact, cunning and evilly disposed persons. There is nothing honest and straightforward about them, and there is a good deal both of the bully and the snob. Thus they oppress most cruelly the poor player who has not strength or skill enough to resist them, but when they meet a really fine player, who cannot merely fight them but use them for his own ends, they become his allies. Watch such a player as Mr. Hilton at his best using the wind first with a pull and then with a cut, and you will see what curs these side winds really are, and how they cringe when they recognize their master.

Even much humbler players can, in a measure, conquer them. The poor terrified slicer with a wind on his back is apt to make more and more allowance for his weakness, and aim further and further to the left. The wind at once perceives that he has a beaten enemy to deal with, and hurtles the ball still further to the right. But if the slicer will stand up to him like a man, make no allowance, and even stand for something of a hook, the wind loses half its bluster, and lets the ball fly, not very far indeed, but reasonably straight.

—1922

The Day Joe Ezar Called His Shots for a Remarkable 64

Peter Dobereiner

The last time I heard of Joe Ezar he was working on the roads down in Florida. He was a nobody. And yet if Joe had been a different kind of person, a fraction more stable, and just a touch less fond of the bottle, he might today be enshrined in golf's Hall of Fame. Maybe not. For perhaps it was just that maverick streak in Joe that made possible the most extraordinary round of golf ever played.

The hands that today embrace a shovel were gifted with a golfing talent of rare quality. This is an appropriate moment to recall Joe's finest hour, which took place forty years ago—in July 1936—during one of his trips to Europe. And if it does not qualify him for the Hall of Fame it does at least deserve a footnote in the history of golf.

Joe, a swarthy Armenian-American, was a colorful character in those days. He won a lot of money, not in prizes so much as in fanciful side bets. He needed cash because he was a man with a very expensive thirst indeed.

Europe in 1936 was boiling up for war, and Joe fitted in perfectly with the mood of those who wanted to squeeze the last drop of carefree enjoyment out of a life that could not last. In Germany he won some cash, and when he found that he could not take it out of the country Joe invested the lot in the current status symbol of wealth, a flashy camel's hair coat. Joe loved that coat and lived in it. He refused even to leave it in the locker room when he played golf and draped it over his shoulders on the course, like a cape.

The precious camel's hair was never out of his sight, and he had it with him for the Italian Open of 1936 at Sestriere, up in the mountains near Turin. Henry Cotton, who had won the British Open in 1934 and was to win it again in 1937 and 1948, was the king of European golf; and on this occasion he had turned the Italian Open into a procession with two hot rounds, including a course record 68.

That evening he and Ezar were entertaining the crowd with an exhibition of golfing virtuosity, Cotton hitting the orthodox shots and Ezar producing an impressive repertoire of trick shots. Joe's final stunt was to drop three balls on the green thirty-five feet from the hole and invite bets that he could not hole one of them. Considering the rough state of the green, it was a fair bet and several people accepted the challenge. Joe holed the first two balls and laughingly collected his winnings.

The prime objective of the exercise had succeeded, to sort out those in the gallery with a taste for some action. One of them happened to be the president of the Fiat motor company. "What do you bet I can't equal the course record tomorrow?" asked Joe. The sporting tycoon smiled. "I'll tell you what I'll do. I will give you five thousand lira for a 66, and ten thousand for a 65."

"What about a 64?" asked Joe.

"In that case," said the president expansively, "I'll make it forty thousand."

"Very generous of you," said Joe. "Now I'll tell you what I will do. I will put down the score I'll make on each of the eighteen holes for my sixty-four."

He took a card and wrote down his target figures for every hole, finishing with a birdie 3 at the last. Cotton looked at the card and remarked: "You're mad." Joe headed for the bar.

In the morning Joe was in no mood for golf. His caddie pulled him out of bed and propped him under a cold shower. Joe protested that he was too drunk to play. "Oh no, you're not," said the caddie, who also had a wager going on the round.

Joe made it to the first tee and wanted to play in his camel's hair coat, to keep out the bitter morning air of the mountains. His caddie persuaded him to compromise; he could wear the coat between shots.

Cotton, his playing partner, advised him to forget the whole thing. "Nobody could do it. You're asking for eighteen successive miracles." Joe proceeded to rip off eight successive miracles. "You could call that round the biggest fluke of all time," recalls Cotton, "but the fact is that he did it. He had all the luck in the world, chipping in and holing impossible putts, but the figures came out just as Joe had predicted. Right up to the ninth. He had marked it down for a 3 but a poor tee shot cost him a 4."

However, he made the unlikeliest of 3s at the next hole where he had predicted a 4. And for the rest of the round Joe's luck stayed with him. Through the bedlam of the crowd Joe reeled off his predicted figures, all the while complaining to Cotton that he was too sick and nervous to hold a club. Still, he did it. He had his 64.

Like all golfers who specialize in trick shots, Ezar had a style that exaggerated hand-and-arm action and rather reduced leg-and-body movement. He played from a wide, flat-footed style and delivered a tremendous lash at the ball with those powerful arms. Cotton described his method as being composed of good points taken to excess. Ezar's right shoulder looked to be too much under his chin at impact; his head too far behind the ball; his eye fixed too firmly on his divot scrape long after the ball had departed; his clubface held square to the shot for too long after impact.

Yet Joe made it work and never better than on the final drive across the chasm of a dogleg—not unlike the layout of the famous sixteenth at Cypress Point—to hit the flagstick all of 290 yards away.

If he was almost sober by this time, he did not remain that way for long. Within weeks Joe was broke again, and he faced the problem of getting back to America. Here was a real challenge for the man who had once bet he could get his entry accepted for the British Open after the closing date, and, what's more, that he would lead after two rounds. He did exactly that, collected his two-thousand-dollar winnings and did not even turn up for the third round.

Joe had been present when Trevor Wignall, a columnist for the London *Daily Express*, was interviewing Cotton. Wignall mentioned that he was to sail on the maiden voyage of the *Queen Mary* to New York. Here was Joe's chance to get safely home. At Cherbourg he tagged his golf bag "Trevor Wignall" and saw it taken aboard. Joe followed, along with all the other well-wishers making their bon voyages, and hid in a closet in Wignall's stateroom. Twelve hours later, after the liner had safely cleared Southampton water, Joe emerged and told Wignall what he had done.

The writer asked Joe what he had done with the rest of his baggage. "This is all I've got," said Joe, indicating his precious camel's hair coat. Joe wanted to remain a stowaway, but Wignall fixed it with the purser for Joe to work for his passage by giving exhibitions of golf on deck. So Joe came home in style.

If you happen to be driving through Florida and come across an old man in a threadbare camel's hair coat shoveling gravel by the roadside, stop and shake his hand. And if you should have a spare fifth in the car he would certainly appreciate it. But do not, whatever you do, take him up on any bets.

—1976

The Mystery of Golf: Chapter One

Arnold Haultain

with a foreword by Herbert Warren Wind

Foreword

In the opinion of a numbers of leading scholars of the sports world what Izaak Walton's *The Compleat Angler* is to books on fishing, Arnold Haultain's *The Mystery of Golf* is to books on golf. Whether or not this is an excessive rating, there can be no disputing the fact that Haultain's treatise is both a historically important document and an extraordinarily evergreen entertainment. As such it is at least a minor classic, and it is a fine thing that, with this new edition, it is once again in print.

Not too much, really, is known about the author. Haultain, one gathers, was a Canadian belle-lettrist, born in 1857, who wrote authoritatively on a wide variety of topics from Cardinal Newman to love. As for *The Mystery of Golf*, it was first published in 1908 in a limited edition of four hundred copies and then republished in 1910 in a general edition by another publisher. By those dates, of course, golf was already well on its way to developing its exceptional literature—the finest, perhaps, of any game. For example, Horace Hutchinson's *Hints on Golf*, the game's first noteworthy humor book, had appeared in 1886, and, a year later, Sir Walter Simpson's *The Art of Golf*, the first considerable excursion into theory. Long before Haultain addressed himself to the subject many men had attempted to explain the game's indecent fascination, but what made *The Mystery of Golf* outstanding in its day was that Haultain, first of all, had the mentality to probe the enigma more deeply than anyone had ever managed to before, and then had the talent to articulate his findings with a brilliance and clarity that are quite astonishing. In my judgement, no later writer has equalled Haultain's performance, though, heavens knows, hundreds have tried.

I would suggest that you will enjoy Haultain most if you read him in relatively short takes. You will find him an amazing man, years ahead of his time in his knowledge not only of philosophy and psychology but also of anatomy and neurology. He knew his golf, too, but I doubt if he could have been much of a competitive player, not with all that on his mind.

—1965

The Mystery of Golf

Proem

Three things there are as unfathomable as they are fascinating to the masculine mind: metaphysics; golf; and the feminine heart. The Germans, I believe, pretend to have solved some of the riddles of the first, and the French to have unravelled some of the intricacies of the last; will some one tell us wherein lies the extraordinary fascination of golf?

The writer is astonied at the mysterie of the game ycleped golfe;

I have just come home from my Club. We played till we could not see the flag; the caddies were sent ahead to find the balls by the thud of their fall; and a low large moon threw whispering shadows on the dew-wet grass or ere we trode the home-green. At dinner the talk was of golf; and for three mortal hours after dinner the talk was—of golf. Yet the talkers were neither idiots, fools, nor monomaniacs. On the contrary, many of them were grave men of the world. At all events the most monomaniacal of the lot was a prosperous man of affairs, worth I do not know how many thousands, which thousands he had made by the same mental faculties by which this evening he was trying to probe or to elucidate the profundities and complexities of this so-called "game." Will some one tell us wherein lies its mystery?

And eke the zeale which yt evoketh.

I

I am a recent convert to golf. But it is the recent convert who most closely scrutinizes his creed—as certainly it is the recent convert who most zealously avows it. The old hand is more concerned about how he plays than about why he plays; the duffer is puzzled at the extraordinary fascination which his new-found pass-time exercises over him. He came to scoff; he remains to play; he inwardly wonders how it was that he was so long a heretic; and, if he is a proselyte given to Higher Criticism, he seeks reasons for the hope that is in him.

He confesseth his ignorance thereof;

And his afore-
time scorn of
its seeming
foolyshnesse;
also.

Well, I know a man, whether in the flesh or out of the flesh I
cannot tell, I know such an one who some years ago joined a golf
club, but did not play. The reasons for so extraordinary a proceeding were simple. The members (of course) were jolly good fellows;
the comfort was assured; the links—the landscape, he called it—
were beautiful. But he did not play. What fun was to be derived
from knocking an insignificant-looking little white ball about the
open country he did not see. Much less did he see why several
hundred pounds a year should be expended in rolling and cutting
and watering certain patches of this country, while in others artfully-
contrived obstacles should be equally expensively constructed and
maintained. Least of all could he understand (he was young then,
and given to more violent games) how grown-up men could go to
the trouble of travelling far, and of putting on flannels, hob-nailed
boots, and red coats, for the simple and apparently effortless purpose of hitting a ball as seldom as possible with no one in the world
to oppose his strength or his skill to their hitting; and it seemed to

He did up-
braid them
that played
thereat.

him not a little childish to erect an elaborate club-house, with
dressing-rooms, dining-rooms, smoking-rooms, shower-baths, lockers, verandas, and what not, for so simple a recreation, and one
requiring so little exertion. Surely marbles would be infinitely more
diverting than that. If it were football, now, or even tennis—and
he once had the temerity to venture to suggest that a small por-
tion of the links might be set apart for a court—the turf about the
home-hole was very tempting. The dead silence with which this
innocent proposition was received gave him pause. (He sees now
that an onlooker might as well have requested from a whist party
the loan of a few cards out of the pack to play card-tricks withal.)

Yet he
admitteth that
he may err;

Yet it is neither incomprehensible nor irrational, this miscon-
ception on the part of the layman of the royal and antient game of
golf. To the uninitiated, what is there in golf to be seen? A ball driven
of a club; that is all. There is no exhibition of skill opposed to skill
or of strength contending with strength; there is apparently no prowess, no strategy, no tactics—no pitting of muscle and brain against
muscle and brain. At least, so it seems to the layman. When the
layman has caught the infection, he thinks—and knows—better.

But, as a matter of fact, contempt could be poured upon any game by anyone unacquainted with that game. We know with what apathetic contempt Subadar Chinniah or Jemadar Mohamed Khan looks on while Tommy Atkins swelters as he bowls or bats or fields under a broiling Indian sun, or Tommy's subalterns kick up the maidan's dust with their polo-ponies' hoofs. And what could be more senseless to a being wholly ignorant of cards than the sight of four grey-headed men gravely seating themselves before dinner to arrange in certain artificial combinations certain uncouth pictures of kings and queens and knaves and certain spots of red and black? Not until such a being recognizes the infinite combinations of chance and skill possible in that queen of sedentary games does he comprehend the fascination of whist. And so it is with golf. All that is requisite in golf, so it seems to the onlooker, is to hit; and than a "hit" nothing, surely, can be simpler or easier—so simple and easy that to have a dozen sticks to hit with, and to hire a boy to carry them, is not so much a sign of pitiable insanity as of wilful stupidity. The puerility of the proceeding is enough to make the spectator irate. Especially as, owing to the silence and the seriousness with which the golfer plays, and his reticence as to the secret of the game—for none knows better than the golfer that the game renders up its secret only to the golfer, if even to him—this quiet, red-coated individual is surrounded with a sort of halo of superiority, a halo not made by himself. No wonder the onlooker's anger is aroused. That expertness in puerility of this sort should of itself exalt a man, make him possessed of that which obviously, yet unintentionally, raises him above the intelligent yet indignant onlooker—there is something in this past finding out. Nor does he find it out till he himself is converted. Golf is like faith: it is the substance of things hoped for, the evidence of things not seen; and not until it is personally experienced does the unbelieving change from the imprecatory to the precatory attitude.

However, the erstwhile aforesaid non-playing member of the golf club in question, the suppleness of his epiphyses, it may be, becoming (perhaps not quite imperceptibly) unequal to the activity and agility demanded of them by more ardent games, pur-

As many an other hath erred.

Nathelesse, golfe doth verilie contain matter for moche puzzlement.

The writer essayeth the game.

chased, first one club, then another, then a sheaf, and betook himself to the task of finding out *a posteriori,* by the experimental method, what there was in the confounded game that brought the players there by scores to play.—And to talk of their play. For it should be added that the talk at that club puzzled him as much as the play. It was not enough that keen King's Counsel, grave judges, erudite men of letters, statesmen, and shrewd men of business should play as if the end of life were to hole a ball; but they talked as if the way a ball should be holed were the only knowledge worth possessing. Well, he played; or, to be more precise, he attempted to play, and, fortunately for him, he persevered in the attempt. Then indeed did the scales fall from his eyes. He discovered that there was more in golf than met the eye—much more.

—1908

Hidden Extras

Henry Longhurst

Club selection snobbishness brings at once to mind one of the old-est golfing stories about the obstinate old Scottish caddie whose man, despite the caddie's advice to take a spoon, decided at a short hole to take his iron and holed out, whereupon the caddie said: "You'd have done better with your spoon."

However, I do think there is a lot of "snobbishness," if that is quite the right word, in the matter of length in golf. Perhaps "keep-ing up with the Joneses" is nearer the mark. It was first brought to my notice when, more than thirty years ago, alas, I used to play with my father. He was a typical enthusiastic but indifferent club golfer and never, if I remember rightly, reached a handicap of less than 16, which today would probably be nearer 24. We used to play mostly at Bedford, but during the annual family holiday we used to tour the courses of North Wales. Wherever it might be, when we came to a so-called short hole, i.e. bogey 3, he inevitably took out his iron. It was a short hole: therefore it must be an iron. Some-times it was manifestly impossible for him to reach the green with his driver.

Incidentally, he often used an expression which one does not seem to hear today but which I think is rather a loss to the game, since it seems to me so particularly graphic. As he hit one of those half-hit, half-foozled shots with which we are all so familiar, he would say: "Ach, *smudged him!*" Sometimes he would begin uttering it while the club was still on the down-swing.

At any rate he unwittingly taught me not to be a "snob" at short holes and I have never been proud since. I do not mind what club the other fellow takes. The other day I cheerfully took a driver to the short fourth at Worplesdon. Of course, swinging quietly, I hit it straight over the back of the green, but I like to think it showed a proper spirit of humility, which was increased when our opponents reached the green easily with an iron. Nevertheless there is a certain amount of useful gamesmanship that can sometimes be practised when the opponent is due to play first and takes out an iron. An audible request to the caddie to "give me the brassie" puts all sorts of uncomfortable thoughts in his head!

I think the mistake made by innumerable club golfers—but not by me—is that they tend to take a club with which they could reach the flag (but not probably the back of the green) if they hit their best shot with it. A man like, say, Peter Alliss knows virtually for a certainty that if he takes a number-seven iron it will go X yards and that if he takes a number six it will go X plus fifteen, or whatever the difference is. The rest of us are not in this happy position. Our shots with the number seven alone may vary by as much as twenty yards.

I do not often practise, but when I do I am often impressed by the extraordinary extra length that lies somewhere within me but is practically never revealed. I take, let us say, a 5-iron. The pattern is nearly always the same. Out of twenty balls about three will be a total loss—topped, scuffled or "smudged." Sixteen will be roughly in a group, about twenty yards wide and perhaps fifteen yards deep, i.e. in the difference between the longest and shortest. And one, just one, will be at least fifteen yards ahead of all the others. This one flew painlessly off the club and was hit with no evident force or in any way differently from the others. Yet there it is. That is what it lies within me to do with a 5-iron. All the same, in order to get that distance in actual play I should be a clot if I took anything less than a number three.

I know that I am always holding forth on the subject of carrying fewer clubs, but there does, I think, lie a very practical advantage in most of us doing so.

Personally I carry only the odd-numbered irons, and I do find, in so doing, that at least I am never in doubt as to what club to take. "Can you get up with a seven?" I often find myself saying to myself. "No, of course not. . . . Would you go over with a three? Yes, easily. Well, that settles it then. It's a five." In the old days I should have been waving between a six and a five and a four.

I do not so much mind playing bad shots—and it would not matter if I did—but to catch myself playing a stupid one has all through my golfing life made me extremely angry. Taking a 3-wood from a close lie on the fairway and topping it, when you could not have reached the green anyway and an iron would have moved you safely along; or hitting the face of a bunker when a more lofted club would have got you safely out, and so on. And, of course, the worse you are, the less you can afford this form of stupidity.

Nobody could say that my old partner, J. S. F. Morrison, was technically a very good golfer. He hit innumerable bad shots, but in all the years I played with him in the Halford Hewitt I do not remember him playing a stupid one.

—1962

Swingin' in the Rain

Charles McGrath

I took my troubles to the outdoor treatment facility. I wasn't alone
The guy with the arthritic back was there, grumpy as ever, and so
was the woman who moves her arms in slow motion. The guy with
the prosthetic devices was there—the ones you see advertised by grinning experts on late-night infomercials. He wore a rubber harness
that looped around his neck and bound his upper arms together, and
fitted onto his left elbow was a cyborg-like contraption—a miniature scaffold, made of titanium probably—that clicked whenever he
moved in a certain way. From time to time, as if in terrible pain, he
squeezed a rolled-up bath towel between his knees. But we were all
in pain from each of our little treatment booths there issued peri-
odic moans and sighs and, every once in a while, an anguished, teeth-
clenched "Oh no!" Cures have actually been found at this particular
facility (I once went into a two-week remission, after a long afternoon of therapy), but on this foggy Sunday, with the budding trees
black and slick from a late-morning downpour, the whole place gave
off a whiff—though that's a word that those of us who frequent the
place hate to use—of failure and futility.

Or maybe it was just me. There were other sounds, too: the usual
whomps, pings, dinks, and thwacks produced by the collision, felici-
tous or otherwise, of expensive metal alloy with balata. The facility,
I should have explained earlier, is a driving range, but what takes place
here is not really golf, any more than the individual Astro Turf tee
mats are really grass. What happens at the range is simpler and some-

times more therapeutic than golf: you buy a bucket of worn-out balls and then pound the daylights out of them. Some of us do this in the hope that by accident or mere repetition we might reform our swings. Some of us have much deeper troubles. The teenage boy two stalls down from me, for instance—the one with what looks like an inked-in diagram for a future goatee and with a baseball cap on backward. He lines up half a dozen balls in a row and then, clamping his driver in a modified baseball grip, advances quickly down the line, slashing them one after the other in the direction of the pick-up tractor, which has just made a turn, about seventy yards out, exposing the driver, in his little yellow cage, to a full barrage. (Can it be that this young man has some unresolved anger?) Or what about the guy who comes every week with his four- or five-year-old daughter in tow. For every thirty or forty shots he hits, he lets her hit two, with her little sawed-off 3-wood, and then, when she complains and asks to leave, he turns and shouts, "No, Melissa! I keep telling you—we're having fun!"

And, of course, all of us here at the facility are suffering from the collective, and very American, delusion that the expenditure of vast sums of money is the cure for whatever ails you. (An Asian delusion as well, to judge from the Japanese guys who throng the place.) The evidence is all around: Whales, Lynxes, Cobras, Berthas, Bears, Leviathans, Kongs, Godzillas—bulbous, almost weightless drivers with enormous sweet spots and whippy, non-torquing shafts fashioned from the rarest metals and state-of the-art fibres. Whenever anyone lays out four or five hundred dollars for a new one of these magical implements, there are always a few of us who will hang around begging just to heft it, to waggle it once or twice. The result, of course, is that our own drivers, year-old Big Boppers, made of anodized plutonium but without the special kryptonite power insert, immediately feel cheap and lifeless—all their good drives used up. No wonder we're so gloomy at the facility.

Whap! Whap! Whizz! Whffft! It's drizzling now, and we're really sweating and cranking, straightening our elbows, firming our grips, shifting our shoulders, shifting our weight—which we have already centered on our hips—trying to hit one last good one. The field in front of us is littered with thousands of range balls. In the gray and mist, they gleam a sickly yellow—like poisonous mushrooms. The tractor driver is still out there, like one of those Wordsworthian solitaries, raking them up. He'll lug them back in huge wire baskets and dump them, rumbling, into the big coin-operated storage bin, so that we duffers—clumsy, angry, depressed, but ever hopeful—can line up, like patients outside a dispensary, and pay some more money to hit them all over again.

—1981

What Makes the Ideal Clubhouse—and Club?

Jerry Tarde

A fellow came up during a round the other day and started telling me about the new clubhouse at a golf club of which he was the president. The clubhouse measures forty-seven-thousand square feet and cost twelve million dollars to build. It has front doors on it the size of Cadillacs and carpeting made of cashmere. It is magnificent, he said.

"Shows you what God could do if only He had money," I said.

Yeah, the fellow continued. He had just returned from a "final inspection" with the interior decorator and had found 124 more things that needed to be added.

I told him he had mistaken me for a guy who liked to hear about clubhouses. "I'm not a clubhouse guy," I said.

The truth is I am a clubhouse guy, but everything this forty-seven-thousand-square-foot clubhouse stands for, I am against. The kind of wasteful excess that grew up in the 1980s has no place in the '90s, despite the fact that people continue to build monuments to themselves. And who's going to pay for these Taj Mahals?

Either the members will write it off on their taxes as a business expense, which means you and I are going to pay for it, or the developer will get stuck with the bill and go bankrupt, which means you and I are going to pay for it.

All this high finance got me to conduct a survey on what is the ideal golf clubhouse. And the results at least should surprise the guy who just spent twelve million dollars, and didn't get one.

The clubhouse, my survey says, should be modest, quaint in its old-worldliness, a place that would impress your father-in-law, but not make your boss think he's paying you too much.

The locker room should be the focal point, not the dining room as many architects mistakenly think. Lockers should be made of wood, preferably oak. There should be no air-conditioning, but plenty of ceiling fans. If you can forget water conservation for a moment, the shower heads should be extra-large, the size of dinner plates, and the effect should be like you're standing under a heated waterfall. Nothing repairs the body or the spirit like a good shower after a bad round. You can drink your Scotch straight and use less water on the fairways to compensate for this indulgence.

There also should be a card room off the locker room where you can play gin rummy or roll dice while sipping drinks served by an old gentleman in dark trousers, white shirt and tie who gives the appearance that he once went ten rounds with Willie Pep. In his spare time, the old gent will refill the bowl of salted peanuts and have your shoes polished and bagged without your asking.

The ideal grillroom makes no distinction between men and women, but women tend to prefer the outdoor patio that overlooks the ninth or eighteenth hole. Inside, there is a television that is always turned to golf whenever golf is on, and the guy who switches it to baseball in July gets the bowl of peanuts thrown at him. The menu should be limited to a cheeseburger, a club sandwich, a salad for dieters and the kind of soup that a spoon stands up in. The food is served by a cadre of senior-citizen waitresses who call all the members "Honey." The walls are wood paneled, with a prominent plaque listing the club champions in hand-lettered script back to "1912 C. Wyckliffe Puffinfeathers III." There are no cliché Scottish prints anywhere in sight, but there is a framed map of the course drawn by the original architect.

Upstairs are a couple of Spartan bedrooms that serve as temporary quarters for the overserved guest or the member whose wife has put him out.

There is a dining room, but it is open only for special occasions, like the spring member-guest. There is no food minimum and no costly staff overhead, but the manager who doubles as the cook always asks if you need anything.

The golf shop is handy to the first tee, and it offers a 20 percent discount on everything. The members respond by buying all their clubs and balls from the pro and having him over for dinner.

Before I forget to mention it, there are no tennis courts or swimming pools. Carts are never mandatory, and the caddiemaster himself drives into town to round up enough caddies.

And that, my dear Mr. President, is all you need. If you want the ideal golf club, you should spend your money on one thing: the golf course. And don't spend too much of it on that, because all you're looking for is relatively green grass most of the time, a rake in every bunker, and eighteen greens that do not require a 5-iron loft on your putter. The minute they put flower beds around tee boxes, you know you've lost control.

Then you should spend your time, a more important commodity anyway, on taking care of the people who matter: the superintendent, the pro, the manager-cook, the caddies, the waitresses, the former Golden Gloves champion, and your fellow members who share these same values.

—1992

The Camaraderie of Golf—II

John Updike

Many men are more faithful to their golf partners than to their wives, and have stuck with them longer. The loyalty we feel toward our chronic consorts in golf acquires naturally the mystical and eternal overtones that the wedding ceremony hopefully, and often vainly, invokes. What is the secret? Structure, I would answer: the golf foursome is constructed with clear and limited purposes denied the nebulously grand and insatiable goals of the marriage twosome.

Like the golf course itself, golf camaraderie is an artifice, carved from the vastness of nature; it asks only five or six hours a week, from the jocular greetings in the noontime parking lot and the parallel donning of cleats in the locker room to the shouted farewells in the dusk, as the flagsticks cast their long shadows. Within this finity, irritations, jealousies, and even spats do occur, but they are mercifully dulled and dampened by the necessary distances of the game, the traditional reticence and mannerliness of sportsmen, and the thought that it will all be soon over. As in marriage, there is sharing: we search for one another's lost balls, we comment helpfully upon one another's defective swings, we march more or less in the same direction, and we come together, like couples at breakfast and dinner, on the tees and on the greens. But, unlike marriage, golf is war from the start: it is out of its regulated contention, its mathematical bloodshed, that the fervor of golf camaraderie blossoms and, from week to week, flourishes. We slay or are slain, eat or are eaten: golf camaraderie is founded on the solid and ancient ground of animal enmity, pleasantly disguised in checked slacks and small courtesies.

In many sport, such as tennis, one player's superiority over another is quickly established and monotonously reaffirmed. The inexhaustible competitive charm of golf, for the non-professional player, lies in its handicap strokes, whereby all players are theoretically equalized and an underdog can become, with a small shift of fortunes, a top dog. The drama of this shift, or the relative collapse of a stronger player, is appreciated by all, even those victimized by it. "Drama" is a key word, for golf is, within the arena of the foursome, not only war but theatre; each player has a golf persona, a predictable character, which the hazards of play subject to unpredictable shifts of fate by turns hilarious, thrilling, heroic, and pathetic. We are actors and audience in swift alternation; our love of one another is the love that enthralled spectators bear toward performers, heightened by the circumstance that the spotlight visits everyone, as the honor falls.

Much of the pleasure of golf, then, resides in the familiarity of the partners, and one's own security within a type-cast role. For years, strange to say, I played in a foursome in which I was considered the best. Not innately the best, perhaps; but another man, whose swing was sounder and who would have made short work of me in his prime, had become elderly, and had seen his scores succumb to ever-shorter drives and fits of senile chipping. In my role as tiny golfing giant, I felt tall, swung easy, and expected the putts to drop. And they often did, confidence and feeling comfortable being a significant part of golfing success. In the same era, as someone's guest on a strange course, a quick audition might establish me as the worst of the foursome, and I would play the part to perfection, straining too far back on every backswing, hurrying into every downswing, and feebly chuckling as the ball hobbled and sliced into every available rough, trap, and thicket. My only comfort, and a bleak one it was, lay in the consciousness of playing my part; I might be only Caliban, but I was saying my lines. On one such occasion, I recall, I inadvertently, combining the wrong club choice with a mis-hit, landed the ball on the green of a long par 3, and then helplessly fulfilled the unspoken expectation of my grim-lipped partner: I three-putted and once again failed to help our team. In my own comfortable foursome, I would have with contemptuous ease rolled the approach putt up for a tap-in par.

When I think of that dear old foursome, two of whose members are now dead, I think of my partner's choppy impatiently baseball swing, his right foot, for all of our urging to the contrary, inflexibly bolted to the earth, and of our other opponent's irrepressible tendency to look up and gronkle.* There is a comedy to consistency of character which we salute with laughter, as a kind of mechanical marvel (try to gronkle on purpose; it can hardly be done) and proof of the world's basic orderliness. And yet, when our friend the gronkler forgot to lift his head and so sent a shot singing into the air, this won the laughter that greets a surprise. Good or bad, there is joy on the golf course, and a curious sense of intimacy bred from repeated observation of this one strange physical act, the striking of a small ball with a long L-shaped stick. Without delving into politics, love-lives, or religious views, one seems to know golf companions very well.

In the quartet of comedians and agonists in which I now customarily play, I am type-cast as the third-best, or second-worst. It is a pleasant spot, suitable to my retiring nature; one can now and then ascend to second-best status without assuming any of the real responsibilities of excellence, and a descent into the worst has the compensation of immensely cheering up the fourth-ranked. We are dominated, the worst and I, by a fortyish former collegiate golf champ who, under a regimen of Buddhist meditation and no-starch diet, has become longer and longer off the tee—grotesquely long, in fact, so that even his half-wedge approaches tend to float over the green into areas rarely visited—and by an older, cannier man whose snatchy backswing and patchy vision are less of a handicap than they should be. He in his effervescence provides a running commentary on his

*This term may be less universal than I realize. In our local circles, it means, roughly, a topped ball, but a ball topped in such a way that it comes to a halt, behind some inconvenient undergrowth, about thirty yards distant from point of imperfect contact. It's as if the ball were struck with the edge of the end of a broad, somewhat warped board.

shots, and heightens our sense of being on camera, for some cosmic Viewer who sits in an easy chair behind the clouds, the passing birds, the swaying treetops. We are, my beloved comrades and I, that afternoon's entertainment; our camaraderie has the subtle frenzy of show business, the makeup and glitter of it, as our fortunes ebb and flow and we live up to our roles or momentarily step out of them. The good feelings that golf breeds are inseparable from its aura of being out in the open—of being enacted within a wide and breezy transparency that leaves no shortcoming hidden and no happy stroke uncongratulated.

—1987

III.

Fiction

The Year of Getting to Know Us

Ethan Canin

I told my father not to worry, that love is what matters, and that in the end, when he is loosed from his body, he can look back and say without blinking that he did all right by me, his son, and that I loved him.

And he said, "Don't talk about things you know nothing about."

We were in San Francisco, in a hospital room. IV tubes were plugged into my father's arms; little round Band-Aids were on his chest. Next to his bed was a table with a vase of yellow roses and a card that my wife, Anne, had brought him. On the front of the card was a photograph of a golf green. On the wall above my father's head an electric monitor traced his heartbeat. He was watching the news on a TV that stood in the corner next to his girlfriend, Lorraine. Lorraine was reading a magazine.

I was watching his heartbeat. It seemed all right to me: the blips made steady peaks and drops, moved across the screen, went out at one end, and then came back at the other. It seemed that this was all a heart could do. I'm an English teacher, though, and I don't know much about it.

"It looks strong," I'd said to my mother that afternoon over the phone. She was in Pasadena. "It's going right across, pretty steady. Big bumps. Solid."

"Is he eating all right?"

"I think so."

"Is *she* there?"

"Is Lorraine here, you mean?"

She paused. "Yes, Lorraine."

"No," I said. "She's not."

"Your poor father," she whispered.

I'm an only child, and I grew up in a big wood-frame house on Huron Avenue in Pasadena, California. The house had three empty
bedrooms and in the back yard a section of grass that had been
stripped and leveled, then seeded and mowed like a putting green.
Twice a week a Mexican gardener came to trim it, wearing special
moccasins my father had bought him. They had soft hide soles that
left no imprints.

My father was in love with golf. He played seven times every week
and talked about the game as if it were a science that he was about
to figure out. "Cut through the outer rim for a high iron," he used to
say at dinner, looking out the window into the yard while my mother
passed him the carved-wood salad bowl, or "In hot weather hit a high-
compression ball." When conversations paused, he made little putting motions with his hands. He was a top amateur and in another
situation might have been a pro. When I was sixteen, the year I was
arrested, he let me caddie for the first time. Before that all I knew
about golf was his clubs—the Spalding made-to-measure woods and
irons, Dynamiter sand wedge, St. Andrews putter—which he kept
in an Abercrombie & Fitch bag in the trunk of his Lincoln, and the
white leather shoes with long tongues and screw-in spikes, which he
stored upside down in the hall closet. When he wasn't playing, he
covered the club heads with socks that had little yellow dingo balls
on the ends.

He never taught me to play. I was a decent athlete—could run,
catch, throw a perfect spiral—but he never took me to the golf course.
In the summer he played every day. Sometimes my mother asked if
he would take me along with him. "Why should I?" he answered.
"Neither of us would like it."

Every afternoon after work he played nine holes; he played eighteen on Saturday, and nine again on Sunday morning. On Sunday

afternoon, at four o'clock, he went for a drive by himself in his white Lincoln Continental. Nobody was allowed to come with him on the drives. He was usually gone for a couple of hours. "Today I drove in the country," he would say at dinner, as he put out his cigarette, or "This afternoon I looked at the ocean," and we were to take from this that he had driven north on the coastal highway. He almost never said more, and across our blue-and-white tablecloth, when I looked at him, my silent father, I imagined in his eyes a pure gaze with which he read the waves and currents of the sea. He had made a fortune in business and owed it to being able to see the truth in any situation. For this reason, he said, he liked to drive with all the windows down. When he returned from his trips his face was red from the wind and his thinning hair lay fitfully on his head. My mother baked on Sunday afternoons while he was gone, walnut pies or macaroons that she prepared on the kitchen counter, which looked out over his putting green.

I teach English in a high school now, and my wife, Anne, is a journalist. I've played golf a half-dozen times in ten years and don't like it any more than most beginners, though the two or three times I've hit a drive that sails, that takes flight with its own power, I've felt something that I think must be unique to the game. These were the drives my father used to hit. Explosions off the tee, bird flights. But golf isn't my game, and it never has been, and I wouldn't think about it at all if not for my father.

Anne and I were visiting in California, first my mother, in Los Angeles, and then my father and Lorraine, north in Sausalito, and Anne suggested that I ask him to play nine holes one morning. She'd been wanting me to talk to him. It's part of the project we've started, part of her theory of what's wrong—although I don't think that much is. She had told me that twenty-five years changes things, and since we had the time, why not go out to California.

She said, "It's not too late to talk to him."

* * *

My best friend in high school was named Nickie Apple. Nickie had a thick chest and a voice that had been damaged somehow, made a little hoarse, and sometimes people thought he was twenty years old. He lived in a four-story house that had a separate floor for the kids. It was the top story, and his father, who was divorced and a lawyer, had agreed never to come up there. That was where we sat around after school. Because of the agreement, no parents were there, only kids. Nine or ten of us, usually. Some of them had slept the night on the big pillows that were scattered against the walls: friends of his older brothers', in Stetson hats and flannel shirts; girls I had never seen before.

Nickie and I went to Shrier Academy, where all the students carried around blue-and-gray notebooks embossed with the school's heraldic seal. SUMUS PRIMI the seal said. Our gray wool sweaters said it; our green exam books said it; the rear window decal my mother brought home said it. My father wouldn't put the sticker on the Lincoln, so she pressed it onto the window above her kitchen sink instead. IMIꓤꟼ 2UMU2 I read whenever I washed my hands. At Shrier we learned Latin in the eighth grade and art history in the ninth, and in the tenth I started getting into some trouble. Little things: cigarettes, graffiti. Mr. Goldman, the student counselor, called my mother in for a premonition visit. "I have a premonition about Leonard," he told her in the counseling office one afternoon in the warm October when I was sixteen. The office was full of plants and had five floor-to-ceiling windows that let in sun like a greenhouse. They looked over grassy, bushless knolls. "I just have a feeling about him."

That October he started talking to me about it. He called me in and asked me why I was friends with Nickie Apple, a boy going nowhere. I was looking out the big windows, opening and closing my fists beneath the desk top. He said, "Lenny, you're a bright kid—what are you trying to tell us?" And I said, "Nothing. I'm not trying to tell you anything."

Then we started stealing, Nickie and I. He did it first, and took things I didn't expect: steaks, expensive cuts that we cooked on a grill by the window in the top story of his house; garden machinery; luggage. We didn't sell it and we didn't use it, but every afternoon we went someplace new. In November he distracted a store clerk and I took a necklace that we thought was diamonds. In December we went for a ride in someone else's car, and over Christmas vacation, when only gardeners were on the school grounds, we threw ten rocks, one by one, as if we'd paid for them at a carnival stand, through the five windows in Mr. Goldman's office.

"You look like a train station," I said to my father as he lay in the hospital bed. "All those lines coming and going everywhere."

He looked at me. I put some things down, tried to make a little bustle. I could see Anne standing in the hall just beyond the door.

"Are you comfortable, Dad?"

"What do you mean, 'comfortable'? My heart's full of holes, leaking all over the place. Am I comfortable? No, I'm dying."

"You're not dying," I said, and I sat down next to him. "You'll be swinging the five-iron in two weeks."

I touched one of the tubes in his arm. Where it entered the vein, the needle disappeared under a piece of tape. I hated the sight of this. I moved the bedsheets a little bit, tucked them in. Anne had wanted me to be alone with him. She was in the hall, waiting to head off Lorraine.

"What's the matter with her?" he asked, pointing to Anne.

"She thought we might want to talk."

"What's so urgent?"

Anne and I had discussed it the night before. "Tell him what you feel," she said. "Tell him you love him." We were eating dinner in a fish restaurant. "Or if you don't love him, tell him you don't."

"Look, Pop," I said now.

"What?"

I was forty-two years old. We were in a hospital and he had tubes in his arms. All kinds of everything: needles, air, tape. I said it again.

"Look, Pop."

Anne and I have seen a counselor, who told me that I had to learn to accept kindness from people. He saw Anne and me together, then

Anne alone, then me. Children's toys were scattered on the floor of his office. "You sound as if you don't want to let people near you," he said. "Right?"

"I'm a reasonably happy man," I answered.

I hadn't wanted to see the counselor. Anne and I have been married seven years, and sometimes I think the history of marriage can be written like this: People Want Too Much. Anne and I have suffered no plague; we sleep late two mornings a week; we laugh at most of the same things; we have a decent house in a suburb of Boston, where, after the commuter traffic has eased, a quiet descends and the world is at peace. She writes for a newspaper, and I teach the children of lawyers and insurance men. At times I'm alone, and need to be alone; at times she does too. But I can always count on a moment, sometimes once in a day, sometimes more, when I see her patting down the sheets on the bed, or watering the front window violets, and I am struck by the good fortune of my life.

Still, Anne says I don't feel things.

It comes up at dinner, outside in the yard, in airports as we wait for planes. You don't let yourself feel, she tells me; and I tell her that I think it's a crazy thing, all this talk about feeling. What do the African Bushmen say? They say, Will we eat tomorrow? Will there be rain?

When I was sixteen, sitting in the back seat of a squad car, the policeman stopped in front of our house on Huron Avenue, turned around against the headrest, and asked me if I was sure this was where I lived.

"Yes, sir," I said.

He spoke through a metal grate. "Your daddy owns this house?"

"Yes, sir."

"But for some reason you don't like windows."

He got out and opened my door, and we walked up the porch steps. The swirling lights on the squad car were making crazy patterns in the French panes of the living room bays. He knocked. "What's your daddy do?"

I heard lights snapping on, my mother moving through the house. "He's in business," I said. "But he won't be home now." The policeman wrote something on his notepad. I saw my mother's eye through the glass in the door, and then the locks were being unlatched, one by one, from the top.

When Anne and I came to California to visit, we stayed at my mother's for three days. On her refrigerator door was a calendar with men's names marked on it—dinner dates, theater—and I knew this was done for our benefit. My mother has been alone for fifteen years. She's still thin, and her eyes still water, and I noticed that books were lying open all through the house. Thick paperbacks—*Doctor Zhivago, The Thorn Birds*—in the bathroom and the studio and the bedroom. We never mentioned my father, but at the end of our stay, when we had packed the car for our drive north along the coast, after she'd hugged us both and we'd backed out of the driveway, she came down off the lawn into the street, her arms crossed over her chest, leaned into the window, and said, "You might say hello to your father for me."

We made the drive north on Highway 1. We passed mission towns, fields of butter lettuce, long stretches of pumpkin farms south of San Francisco. It was the first time we were going to see my father with Lorraine. She was a hairdresser. He'd met her a few years after coming north, and one of the first things they'd done together was take a trip around the world. We got postcards from the Nile delta and Bangkok. When I was young, my father had never taken us out of California.

His house in Sausalito was on a cliff above a finger of San Francisco Bay. A new Lincoln stood in the carport. In his bedroom was a teak-framed king-size waterbed, and on the walls were bits of African artwork—opium pipes, metal figurines. Lorraine looked the same age as Anne. One wall of the living room was glass, and after the first night's dinner, while we sat on the leather sofa watching tankers and yachts move under the Golden Gate Bridge, my father put down his Scotch and water, touched his jaw, and said, "Lenny, call Dr. Farmer."

It was his second one. The first had been two years earlier, on the golf course in Monterey, where he'd had to kneel, then sit, then lie down on the fairway.

At dinner the night after I was arrested, my mother introduced her idea. "We're going to try something," she said. She had brought out a chicken casserole, and it was steaming in front of her. "That's what we're going to do. Max, are you listening? This next year, starting tonight, is going to be the year of getting to know us better." She stopped speaking and dished my father some chicken.

"What do you mean?" I asked.

"I mean it will be to a small extent a theme year. Nothing that's going to change every day of our lives, but in this next year I thought we'd all make an attempt to get to know each other better. Especially you, Leonard. Dad and I are going to make a better effort to know you."

"I'm not sure what you mean," said my father.

"All kinds of things, Max. We'll go to movies together, and Lenny can throw a party here at the house. And I personally would like to take a trip, all of us together, to the American Southwest."

"Sounds all right to me," I said.

"And Max," she said, "you can take Lenny with you to play golf. For example." She looked at my father.

"Neither of us would like it," he said.

"Lenny never sees you."

I looked out the window. The trees were turning, dropping their leaves onto the putting green. I didn't care what he said, one way or the other. My mother spooned a chicken thigh onto my plate and covered it with sauce. "All right," my father said. "He can caddie."

"And as preparation for our trip," my mother said, "can you take him on your Sunday rides?"

My father took off his glasses. "The Southwest," he said, wiping the lenses with a napkin, "is exactly like any other part of the country."

* * *

Anne had an affair once with a man she met on an assignment. He was young, much younger than either of us—in his late twenties, I would say from the one time I saw him. I saw them because one day on the road home I passed Anne's car in the lot of a Denny's restaurant. I parked around the block and went in to surprise her. I took a table at the back, but from my seat in the corner I didn't realize for several minutes that the youngish-looking woman leaning forward and whispering to the man with a beard was my wife.

I didn't get up and pull the man out with me into the parking lot, or even join them at the table, as I have since thought might have been a good idea. Instead I sat and watched them. I could see that under the table they were holding hands. His back was to me, and I noticed that it was broad, as mine is not. I remember thinking that she probably liked this broadness. Other than that, though, I didn't feel very much. I ordered another cup of coffee just to hear myself talk, but my voice wasn't quavering or fearful. When the waitress left, I took out a napkin and wrote on it, "You are a forty-year-old man with no children and your wife is having an affair." Then I put some money on the table and left the restaurant.

"I think we should see somebody," Anne said to me a few weeks later. It was a Sunday morning, and we were eating breakfast on the porch.

"About what?" I asked.

On a Sunday afternoon when I was sixteen I went out to the garage with a plan my mother had given me. That morning my father had washed the Lincoln. He had detergent-scrubbed the finish and then sun-dried it on Huron Avenue, so that in the workshop light of the garage its highlights shone. The windshield molding, the grille, the chrome side markers, had been cloth-dried to erase water spots. The keys hung from their magnetic sling near the door to the kitchen. I took them out and opened the trunk. Then I hung them up again and sat on the rear quarter panel to consider what to do. It was almost four o'clock. The trunk of my father's car was large enough for a half-dozen suitcases and had been upholstered in a gray medium-pile carpet that was cut to hug the wheel wells and the spare-tire berth. In one corner, fastened down by straps, was his toolbox, and along the back lay the golf bag. In the shadows the yellow dingos of the club socks looked like baby chicks. He was going to come out in a few minutes. I reached in, took off four of the club socks, and made a pillow for my head. Then I stepped into the trunk. The shocks bounced once and stopped. I lay down with my head propped on the quarter panel and my feet resting in the taillight berth, and then I reached up, slammed down the trunk, and was in the dark.

This didn't frighten me. When I was very young, I liked to sleep with the shades drawn and the door closed so that no light entered my room. I used to hold my hand in front of my eyes and see if I could imagine its presence. It was too dark to see anything. I was blind then, lying in my bed, listening for every sound. I used to move my hand back and forth, close to my eyes, until I had the sensation that it was there but had in some way been amputated. I had heard of soldiers who had lost limbs but still felt them attached. Now I held my open hand before my eyes. It was dense black inside the trunk, colorless, without light.

When my father started the car, all the sounds were huge, magnified as if they were inside my own skull. The metal scratched, creaked, slammed when he got in; the bolt of the starter shook all the way through to the trunk; the idle rose and leveled; then the gears changed and the car lurched. I heard the garage door slide up. Then it curled into its housing, bumped once, began descending again. The seams of the trunk lid lightened in the sun. We were in the street now, heading downhill. I lay back and felt the road, listened to the gravel pocking in the wheel wells.

I followed our route in my mind. Left off Huron onto Telscher, where the car bottomed in the rain gulley as we turned, then up the hill to Santa Ana. As we waited for the light, the idle made its change, shifting down, so that below my head I heard the individual piston blasts in the exhaust pipe. Left on Santa Ana, counting the flat stretches where I felt my father tap the brakes, numbering the intersections as we headed west toward the ocean. I heard cars pull up next to us, accelerate, slow down, make turns. Bits of gravel echoed inside the quarter panels. I pulled off more club socks and enlarged my pillow. We slowed down, stopped, and then we accelerated, the soft piston explosions becoming a hiss as we turned onto the Pasadena freeway.

"Dad's rides," my mother had said to me the night before, as I lay in bed, "would be a good way for him to get to know you." It was the first week of the year of getting to know us better. She was sitting at my desk.

"But he won't let me go," I said.

"You're right." She moved some things around on a shelf. The room wasn't quite dark, and I could see the outline of her white blouse. "I talked to Mr. Goldman," she said.

"Mr. Goldman doesn't know me."

"He says you're angry." My mother stood up, and I watched her white blouse move to the window. She pulled back the shade until a triangle of light from the streetlamp fell on my sheets. "Are you angry?"

"I don't know," I said. "I don't think so."

"I don't think so either." She replaced the shade, came over and kissed me on the forehead, and then went out into the hall. In the dark I looked for my hand.

A few minutes later the door opened again. She put her head in. "If he won't let you come," she said, "sneak along."

On the freeway the thermal seams whizzed and popped in my ears. The ride had smoothed out now, as the shocks settled into the high speed, hardly dipping on curves, muffling everything as if we were under water. As far as I could tell, we were still driving west, toward the ocean. I sat halfway up and rested my back against the golf bag. I could see shapes now inside the trunk. When we slowed down and the blinker went on, I attempted bearings, but the sun was the same in all directions and the trunk lid was without shadow. We braked hard. I felt the car leave the freeway. We made turns. We went straight. Then more turns, and as we slowed down and I was stretching out, uncurling my body along the diagonal, we made a sharp right onto gravel and pulled over and stopped.

My father opened the door. The car dipped and rocked, shuddered. The engine clicked. Then the passenger door opened. I waited.

If I heard her voice today, twenty-six years later, I would recognize it.

"Angel," she said.

I heard the weight of their bodies sliding across the back seat, first hers, then his. They weren't three feet away. I curled up, crouched into the low space between the golf bag and the back of the passenger compartment. There were two firm points in the cushion where it was displaced. As I lay there, I went over the voice again in my head: it was nobody I knew. I heard a laugh from her, and then something low from him. I felt the shift of the trunk's false rear, and then, as I lay behind them, I heard the contact: the crinkle of clothing, arms wrapping, and the half-delicate, muscular sounds. It was like hearing a television in the next room. His voice once more, and then the rising of their breath, slow; a minute of this, maybe another; then shifting again, the friction of cloth on the leather seat and the car's soft rocking. "Dad," I whispered. Then rocking again; my father's sudden panting, harder and harder, his half-words. The car shook violently. "Dad," I whispered. I shouted, "Dad!"

The door opened.

His steps kicked up gravel. I heard jingling metal, the sound of the key in the trunk lock. He was standing over me in an explosion of light.

He said, "Put back the club socks."

I did and got out of the car to stand next to him. He rubbed his hands down the front of his shirt.

"What the hell," he said.

"I was in the trunk."

"I know," he said. "What the goddamn."

The year I graduated from college, I found a job teaching junior high school in Boston. The school was a cement building with small windows well up from the street, and dark classrooms in which I spent a lot of time maintaining discipline. In the middle of the afternoon that first winter a boy knocked on my door to tell me I had a phone call. I knew who it was going to be.

"Dad's gone," my mother said.

He'd taken his things in the Lincoln, she told me, and driven away that morning before dawn. On the kitchen table he'd left a note and some cash. "A lot of cash," my mother added, lowering her voice. "Twenty thousand dollars."

I imagined the sheaf of bills on our breakfast table, held down by the ceramic butter dish, the bank notes ruffling in the breeze from the louvered windows that opened onto his green. In the note he said he had gone north and would call her when he'd settled. It was December. I told my mother that I would visit in a week, when school was out for Christmas. I told her to go to her sister's and stay there, and then I said that I was working and had to get back to my class. She didn't say anything on the other end of the line, and in the silence I imagined my father crisscrossing the state of California, driving north, stopping in Palm Springs and Carmel, the Lincoln riding low with the weight.

"Leonard," my mother said, "did you know anything like this was happening?"

During the spring of the year of getting to know us better I caddied for him a few times. On Saturdays he played early in the morning, when the course was mostly empty and the grass was still wet from the night. I learned to fetch the higher irons as the sun rose over the back nine and the ball, on drying ground, rolled farther. He hit skybound approach shots with backspin, chips that bit into the green and stopped. He played in a foursome with three other men, and in the locker room, as they changed their shoes, they told jokes and poked one another in the belly. The lockers were shiny green metal, the floor clean white tiles that clicked under the shoe spikes. Beneath the mirrors were jars of combs in green disinfectant. When I combed my hair with them it stayed in place and smelled like limes.

We were on the course at dawn. At the first fairway the other men dug in their spikes, shifted their weight from leg to leg, dummy-swung at an empty tee while my father lit a cigarette and looked out over the hole. "The big gun," he said to me, or, if it was a par 3, "The lady." He stepped on his cigarette. I wiped the head with the club sock before I handed it to him. When he took the club, he felt its balance point, rested it on one finger, and then, in slow motion, he gripped the shaft. Left hand first, then right, the fingers wrapping pinkie to index. Then he leaned down over the ball. On a perfect drive the tee flew straight up in the air and landed in front of his feet.

Over the weekend his heart lost its rhythm for a few seconds. It happened Saturday night, when Anne and I were at the house in Sausalito, and we didn't hear about it until Sunday. "Ventricular fibrillation," the intern said. "Circus movements." The condition was always a danger after a heart attack. He had been given a shock and his heartbeat had returned to normal.

"But I'll be honest with you," the intern said. We were in the hall. He looked down, touched his stethoscope. "It isn't a good sign."

The heart gets bigger as it dies, he told me. Soon it spreads across the x-ray. He brought me with him to a room and showed me strips of paper with the electric tracings: certain formations. The muscle was dying in patches, he said. He said things might get better, they might not.

My mother called that afternoon. "Should I come up?"

"He was a bastard to you," I said.

When Lorraine and Anne were eating dinner, I found the intern again. "I want to know," I said. "Tell me the truth." The intern was tall and thin, sick-looking himself. So were the other doctors I had seen around the place. Everything in that hospital was pale—the walls, the coats, the skin.

He said, "What truth?"

I told him that I'd been reading about heart disease. I'd read about EKGs, knew about the medicines—lidocaine, propranolol. I knew that the lungs filled up with water, that heart failure was death by drowning. I said, "The truth about my father."

* * *

The afternoon I had hidden in the trunk, we came home while my mother was cooking dinner. I walked up the path from the garage behind my father, watching the pearls of sweat on his neck. He was whistling a tune. At the door he kissed my mother's cheek. He touched the small of her back. She was cooking vegetables, and the steam had fogged up the kitchen windows and dampened her hair. My father sat down in the chair by the window and opened the newspaper. I thought of the way the trunk rear had shifted when he and the woman had moved into the back of the Lincoln. My mother was smiling.

"Well?" she said.

"What's for dinner?" I asked.

"Well?" she said again.

"It's chicken," I said. "Isn't it?"

"Max, aren't you going to tell me if anything unusual happened today?"

My father didn't look up from the newspaper. "Did anything unusual happen today?" he said. He turned the page, folded it back smartly. "Why don't you ask Lenny?"

She smiled at me.

"I surprised him," I said. Then I turned and looked out the window.

"I have something to tell you," Anne said to me one Sunday morning in the fifth year of our marriage. We were lying in bed. I knew what was coming.

"I already know," I said.

"What do you already know?"

"I know about your lover."

She didn't say anything.

"It's all right," I said.

It was winter. The sky was gray, and although the sun had risen only a few hours earlier, it seemed like late afternoon. I waited for

Anne to say something more. We were silent for several minutes. Then she said, "I wanted to hurt you." She got out of bed and began straightening out the bureau. She pulled my sweaters from the drawer and refolded them. She returned all our shoes to the closet. Then she came back to the bed, sat down, and began to cry. Her back was toward me. It shook with her gasps, and I put my hand out and touched her. "It's all right," I said.

"We only saw each other a few times," she answered. "I'd take it back if I could. I'd make it never happen."

"I know you would."

"For some reason I thought I couldn't really hurt you."

She had stopped crying. I looked out the window at the tree branches hung low with snow. It didn't seem I had to say anything.

"I don't know why I thought I couldn't hurt you," she said. "Of course I can hurt you."

"I forgive you."

Her back was still toward me. Outside, a few snowflakes drifted up in the air.

"*Did* I hurt you?"

"Yes, you did. I saw you two in a restaurant?"

"Where?"

"At Denny's."

"No," she said. "I mean, where did I hurt you?"

The night he died, Anne stayed awake with me in bed. "Tell me about him," she said.

"What about?"

"Stories. Tell me what it was like growing up, things you did together."

"We didn't do that much," I said. "I caddied for him. He taught me things about golf."

That night I never went to sleep. Lorraine was at a friend's apartment and we were alone in my father's empty house, but we pulled out the sheets anyway, and the two wool blankets, and we lay on the fold-out sofa in the den. I told stories about my father until I couldn't think of any more, and then I talked about my mother until Anne fell asleep.

In the middle of the night I got up and went into the living room. Through the glass I could see lights across the water, the bridges, Belvedere and San Francisco, ships. It was clear outside, and when I walked out to the cement carport the sky was lit with stars. The breeze moved inside my nightclothes. Next to the garage the Lincoln stood half-lit in the porch floodlight. I opened the door and got in. The seats were red leather and smelled of limes and cigarettes. I rolled down the window and took the key from the glove compartment. I thought of writing a note for Anne, but didn't. Instead, I coasted down the driveway in neutral and didn't close the door or turn on the lights until the bottom of the hill, or start the engine until I had swung around the corner, so that the house was out of sight and the brine smell of the marina was coming through the open windows of the car. The pistons were almost silent.

I felt urgent, though I had no route in mind. I ran one stop sign, then one red light, and when I reached the ramp onto Highway 101, I squeezed the accelerator and felt the surge of the fuel-injected, computer-sparked V-8. The dash lights glowed. I drove south and crossed over the Golden Gate Bridge at seventy miles an hour, its suspension cables swaying in the wind and the span rocking slowly, ocean to bay. The lanes were narrow. Reflectors zinged when the wheels strayed. If Anne woke, she might come out to the living room and then check for me outside. A light rain began to fall. Drops wet my knees, splattered my cheek. I kept the window open and turned on the radio; the car filled up with wind and music. Brass sounds. Trumpets. Sounds that filled my heart.

The Lincoln drove like a dream. South of San Francisco the road opened up, and in the gulley of a shallow hill I took it up over a hundred. The arrow nosed rightward in the dash. Shapes flattened out. "Dad," I said. The wind sounds changed pitch. I said, "The year of getting to know us." Signposts and power poles were flying by. Only a few cars were on the road, and most moved over before I arrived. In the mirror I could see the faces as I passed. I went through San Mateo, Pacifica, Redwood City, until, underneath a concrete overpass, the radio began pulling in static and I realized that I might die at this speed. I slowed down. At seventy drizzle wandered in the windows again. At fifty-five the scenery stopped moving. In Menlo Park I got off the freeway.

It was dark still, and off the interstate I found myself on a road without streetlights. It entered the center of town and then left again, curving up into shallow hills. The houses were large on either side. They were spaced far apart, three and four stories tall, with white shutters or ornament work that shone in the perimeter of the Lincoln's headlamps. The yards were large, dotted with eucalyptus and laurel. Here and there a light was on. Sometimes I saw faces: someone on an upstairs balcony; a man inside the breakfast room, awake at this hour, peering through the glass to see what car could be passing. I drove slowly, and when I came to a high school with its low buildings and long athletic field I pulled over and stopped.

The drizzle had become mist. I left the headlights on and got out and stood on the grass. I thought, This is the night your father has passed. I looked up at the lightening sky. I said it, "This is the night your father has passed," but I didn't feel what I thought I would. Just the wind on my throat, the chill of the morning. A pickup drove by and flashed its lights at me on the lawn. Then I went to the trunk of the Lincoln, because this was what my father would have done, and I got out the golf bag. It was heavier than I remembered, and the leather was stiff in the cool air. On the damp sod I set up: dimpled white ball, yellow tee. My father would have swung, would have hit drives the length of the football field, high irons that disappeared into the gray sky, but as I stood there I didn't even take the clubs out of the bag. Instead I imagined his stance. I pictured the even weight, the deliberate grip, and after I had stood there for a few moments, I picked up the ball and tee, replaced them in the bag, and drove home to my wife.

The year I was sixteen we never made it to the American Southwest. My mother bought maps anyway, and planned our trip, talking to me about it at night in the dark, taking us in her mind across the

Colorado River at the California border, where the water was opal green, into Arizona and along the stretch of desert highway to New Mexico. There, she said, the canyons were a mile deep. The road was lined with sagebrush and a type of cactus, jumping cholla, that launched its spines. Above the desert, where a man could die of dehydration in an afternoon and a morning, the peaks of the Rocky Mountains turned blue with sun and ice.

We didn't ever go. Every weekend my father played golf, and at last, in August, my parents agreed to a compromise. One Sunday morning, before I started the eleventh grade, we drove north in the Lincoln to a state park along the ocean. Above the shore the cliffs were planted with ice plant to resist erosion. Pelicans soared in the thermal currents. My mother had made chicken sandwiches, which we ate on the beach, and after lunch, while I looked at the crabs and swaying fronds in the tide pools, my parents walked to the base of the cliffs. I watched their progress on the shallow dunes. Once when I looked, my father was holding her in his arms and they were kissing.

She bent backward in his hands. I looked into the tide pool where, on the surface, the blue sky, the clouds, the reddish cliffs, were shining. Below them rock crabs scurried between submerged stones. The afternoon my father found me in the trunk, he introduced me to the woman in the back seat. Her name was Christine. She smelled of perfume. The gravel drive where we had parked was behind a warehouse, and after we shook hands through the open window of the car, she got out and went inside. It was low and long, and the metal door slammed behind her. On the drive home, wind blowing all around us in the car, my father and I didn't say much. I watched his hands on the steering wheel. They were big and red-knuckled, the hands of a butcher or a carpenter, and I tried to imagine them in the bend of Christine's back.

Later that afternoon on the beach, while my mother walked along the shore, my father and I climbed a steep trail up the cliffs. From above, where we stood in the carpet of ice plant, we could see the hue of the Pacific change to a more translucent blue—the drop-off and the outline of the shoal where the breakers rose. I tried to see what my father was seeing as he gazed out over the water. He picked up a rock and tossed it over the cliff. "You know," he said without looking at me, "you could be all right on the course." We approached the edge of the palisade, where the ice plant thinned into eroded cuts of sand. "Listen," he said. "We're here on this trip so we can get to know each other a little bit." A hundred yards below us waves broke on the rocks. He lowered his voice. "But I'm not sure about that. Anyway, you don't *have* to get to know me. You know why?"

"Why?" I asked.

"You don't have to get to know me," he said, "because one day you're going to grow up and then you're going to *be* me." He looked at me and then out over the water. "So what I'm going to do is teach you how to hit." He picked up a long stick and put it in my hand. Then he showed me the backswing. "You've got to know one thing to drive a golf ball," he told me, "and that's that the club is part of you." He stood behind me and showed me how to keep the left arm still. "The club is your hand," he said. "It's your bone. It's your whole arm and your skeleton and your heart." Below us on the beach I could see my mother walking the waterline. We took cut after cut, and he taught me to visualize the impact, to sense it. He told me to whittle down the point of energy so that the ball would fly. When I swung he held my head in position. "Don't just watch," he said. "*See*." I looked. The ice plant was watery-looking and fat, and at the edge of my vision I could see the tips of my father's shoes. I was sixteen years old and waiting for the next thing he would tell me.

—1988

The Dogleg on 5

Ward Just

The course at Oak Knoll is flat and easygoing, golf for middle-aged businessmen and their athletic wives. The front nine is shorter and more interesting than the back, and the fifth hole the most challenging, a dogleg with a great oak two hundred yards out where the fairway swings right. In that part of northern Illinois there are many huge oaks that were growing when Lincoln was living downstate. This one is prodigious and in the late spring beginning to fill with leaves, struggling in a dignified elderly way. The oak is the pride of the course and I remembered it from the last time I had played Oak Knoll, sometime in the sixties with Pat Bayley in the Member-Guest, a relaxed afternoon with Pat and two randy, storytelling surgeons. It was the reverse in every way from this April Tuesday, Mozart and I in an electric golf cart, a game arranged by a mutual friend who said that the old lawyer wanted to talk and that he would appreciate it as a personal favor if I would agree to listen to him, Oak Knoll, Elly Mozart, two sharp.

The members bore you to death with their flamboyant descriptions of 5, 490 yards from tee to green. The long hitter wants to aim slightly right of dead center and fade the drive; but the fade must be controlled or the ball will land in the rough near the oak or, worse, hit the god damned tree; all the members call the oak the god damned tree. Worst rough on the course, quack grass so thick and high that balls are lost every day. Three sand traps block the entrance to the green, which slopes up and then dips down. The pin is usually in the

dip. Behind the green are dark woods and the sixth tee. The fifth is
an easy hole for a long hitter with control. A very long hitter can
achieve the green in 2 and with the regulation putts get down in 4,
a birdie. Because the fairway is so wide and handsome and the turf so
soft and inviting, the romantic golfer always goes for the two big shots,
for locker room bragging rights, ha-ha. It's a pretty hole to play and
the big drive wonderful to watch, particularly if it's yours, the ball
rising swiftly ivory white and hard against the deep green of the turf,
and then fading and striking the fairway with a big bounce, rolling
beyond the oak, coming to rest white as a piano key on the horizon.
Hell of a shot, chief. But 5 is perverse because it offers such a temptation for the long ball, an appeal to recklessness and bravado; be-
witched by theater, the romantic golfer ignores finesse. The truth is,
5 rewards caution. Five is kind to the short hitter. Get the drive out
straight, second shot in front of the traps, a 7-iron to the green, two
putts, down in 5, par. Meanwhile the big hitter who thinks he's
Nicklaus is thrashing around in the murderous rough or one of the
three sand traps. Double-bogie 7 because he thought the drive would
look so pretty and he overclubbed it and hooked or, worse, turned
the fade into a slice. He forgot that at the end of eighteen it's the
score they add up. You can make a great entrance but if you forget
your lines in scene 2 it's a busted performance.

"Is that right," I said.

Mozart nodded. "I've seen a man go out three hundred yards and
take nine more blows to get home."

"Because he wasn't reasonable," I said.

"Because he didn't plan ahead," Mozart said.

We were waiting on the tee, stalled by the foursome in front. Two
men were searching for balls in the rough, having fallen victim to
5's false charm. They had motioned us through but Mozart had waved
courteously; we're in no hurry, take your time. There was no one
behind us and Mozart wanted a leisurely Tuesday game. He sat on
the bench next to the tee, his legs crossed as if he were at his office
desk. He was fascinated by the one-legged player ahead. Mozart explained that he had lost his leg in Korea but had always been a good

golfer and saw no reason to give it up; an explosion in Korea was no reason.

"Watch him," Mozart said.

Each shot was an agony. The one-legged golfer backed up to his cart, steadied himself on its chassis, took a huge swing and fell down. He fell down every time, always on his right hip. He had a detachable peg leg, which he put into the cart before each swing. When he fell down he hauled himself to his feet, using the golf club as a cane. Then he fetched his leg, fastened it, got into the cart, and drove on, always stopping the same distance from the ball. His partners paid him no notice and never helped him up. That was the bargain. The one-legged golfer had a 12-handicap and was valued as a partner for his competitive spirit. He never retreated. His swing was vicious and you could sense his fury and pain and frustration two hundred yards away. When the one-legged golfer waved us through, and Mozart refused, he stood scowling at us before he turned and hobbled off, as if he understood he was being observed and didn't like it.

"Never gives up," Mozart said. "He reminds me of you."

I said nothing to that and didn't believe it. I did not believe in Games as a metaphor for Life, though I knew when I accepted Mozart's invitation for golf that he'd get around to it sooner or later. And I had known a man who had been in the war and nothing that had happened in my life was the equal of what had happened in his, although he did not agree. I believed he was being modest.

"We think you could win, Jack."

"It'll be very close."

He nodded, concentrating on balancing the head of his driver on the toe of his shoe. "That's what our polls say. Too close to call. And the one hope she's got is that you're stalled. You're not moving, Jack. You're dead in the water. You haven't moved a point in a week and here we are, fourteen days until the primary. You've got the message but you can't get it out. You're a man with a bone in his throat. You've got to get the message *out*, to speak and be confident that you'll be heard. If you had her money, you'd win in a walk."

"That's true," I said.

"You're short on staff, short of time, you're short in everything."

"True again," I said.

"So near and yet so far," he said, rolling his eyeballs.

I said, "Yeah, Elly."

"She's breathing in an iron lung. And the iron lung's called television. She's paralyzed and the iron lung's keeping her alive because it's plugged into money. Pull the plug and she dies." He grinned, chuckling. "Every hour of every day, somewhere in the state, there she is on the tube in her cloche hat and her pearls and her dog and her husband. 'Give me your hand, give me your voice, give me your vote.' Sound familiar? JFK, 1960." Mozart looked up. The two golfers in the rough had given up, dropped fresh balls, and hit. They waited for the one-legged golfer, who balanced himself, hit a low line drive, and fell. Now the foursome was headed toward the sand traps, two golfers in each cart, the carts looking like toys as they bounced up the greensward.

"Your turn at bat, Jack. Take it nice and easy and you'll win the hole. It's a beast."

I drove and then it was Mozart's turn. He took his time, wagging the club head and flexing his fingers, muttering to himself. He took a half swing, slashing at the ball, popping it about 150 yards. I walked and he rode alongside in the cart.

"Notice the difference in her spots?"

"She doesn't say anything anymore," I said.

"Right. Hand, voice, vote; that's what she says, and that's all she says. And the spots're pretty. We take her to the lakefront and down to Galena and standing in a cornfield somewhere, Bement. Nice music in the background. Maybe a cuddly child or two at her feet with a couple of concerned citizens listening attentively as she speaks. And of course the mutt, Cookie. But you don't hear what she's saying. You hear music or a train whistle or the wind in the god damned willows. But she doesn't talk anymore, noticed that? She doesn't talk because *people don't like her*. They don't like her voice. Shows up in poll after poll. Tin-whistle voice, and people don't like it." Mozart addressed his ball and popped it another 150 yards. Ahead of us the one-legged golfer was chipping from the apron of the green. It was

only a twenty-foot chip shot but he put everything into it, swinging
and falling, and rising at once, watching the ball all the while.

"But it'll get us through the primary because the thing is, you're
stalled. You're stalled for keeps because you're broke and it's too bad,
because you've run a fine campaign, you've made every nickel count.
But you don't have money for the spots. You don't have the air force
for the carpet bombing. Kid who put our spots together is quite a lad,
twenty-five years old. They call him a genius. Can you imagine?
Unpleasant boy but shrewd and well spoken. Well-educated boy.
Watch his spots and you're reassured. You're reassured that she knows
what she's doing and that she's serious and tough, but feminine. As
long as you don't hear her voice."

"Might work in the primary," I said. "But you can't run Helen
Keller in the general. Speeches, press conferences, debates, every
night on the six o'clock news. They'll eat her alive."

"That's correct, Jack. You've spoken the truth. People aren't fo-
cusing on this primary. But they'll focus on the general. And when
they focus, she'll lose. We can win the battle but we'll lose the war if
she's the nominee."

"I'd get her a voice coach, Elly."

He sighed; evidently that was not the reply he'd hoped for. "More
complicated than that, I'm afraid. Her husband wants to take charge.
And he likes her voice. He thinks it's cute. He thinks she's cute, and
the trouble is that we've been holding her back. Let the tiger loose!
At least that's what he tells the campaign manager, on the nights
that he's fucking her instead of his wife."

I looked at him, but he was staring at the green. There was an
argument of some kind. We could hear raised voices, and the one-
legged golfer was waving his arms.

"I'd heard there was some sexual tension."

"He's pretty much of an idiot, Jack."

"Heard that, too."

"What you probably haven't heard is that he wants to go on the
attack because he thinks she's falling behind. I mean he wants her
to get personal, with you. He thinks that unless she does that, she's
going to lose."

"There are two theories," I said. "That's the second one."

He nodded. "His motives are not entirely clear, that's true."

"She does that, she loses."

"Perhaps. And perhaps not. You're stalled."

"I'm stalled in part because no one gives a damn. They'll give a damn in a hurry if there's something nasty to put on the six o'clock news. That's free time. I don't have to buy it."

"What the hell's going on up there?"

The four golfers were clustered around the pin. The one-legged golfer moved between two of the players. He staggered on his peg leg and seemed about to fall. He was shouting something. Then he did fall, sprawling on the green. The other three turned and walked off. The one-legged golfer did not move for a moment. You could see his chest heaving. He struck the turf once with his fist, then turned to grab the pin, hauling himself to his feet. It looked to be painful. The other three had disappeared into the woods, taking a cart on the narrow path to the sixth tee. The one-legged golfer waited a moment, clinging to the pin with its little pennant. He looked like a soldier planting the colors. Then after a moment he stumbled off, using his putter as a cane. His partners had left him the other cart. He climbed into it painfully and sat a moment. His chest was still heaving. He had the putter across his lap. Suddenly he rose and heaved the putter into the woods, slinging it backhanded. We watched it rise, glittering in the sun, and then we heard twigs and branches breaking. He shouted something, then sank back into the cart's seat, exhausted. In a moment the cart began to move, very slowly, off the apron of the green and down the path through the woods to the sixth tee.

Poor fellow, Mozart said. He took the game so seriously, each shot worth his life. Everyone understood but it didn't make it any easier. He'd fluff a chip shot or a putt and go on the boil, mad at himself and mad at his partners. He was in pain all the time and took it out on the world. He carried three putters in his bag because he'd always lose one of them in the woods or in the deep pond on 12. When he started to boil there was nothing to do but let him go, blow off steam. He always played in the same foursome, men who understood and respected him; but he could be an awful pain in the neck, poor fellow. However, everyone made allowances.

I was looking at my ball and listening to Mozart, whose voice had fallen as if he feared we would be overheard. The ball was nicely teed on a tuft of grass. I took a big swing and the ball exploded, fading at the end so that it dribbled off the green and out of sight.

"That's a hell of a shot, Jack. That's a fine golf shot, though you took a chance. I hope your lie's good, I didn't see where it went."

"It went off the green," I said.

"That's what I thought," Mozart said.

The old lawyer's third shot was straight, high, and short. He was in front of the big sand trap, a hundred yards from the green, a 7-iron for him.

"Do you think you can win it, Jack?"

"No," I said.

"That's my estimate. Funny the way you can feel it. You're stalled. You keep turning the key but the engine won't start, *rrr-rrr-rrr-rrrrrrr*. And it won't start because you're out of gas. You're out of money. It'd be all right if people were paying attention, but they aren't. It's only a primary and the winter's been so damned cold. Everybody's thinking about going to Florida."

"And taxes," I said.

"And there's only two weeks left."

"It's enough," I said.

"If there's money it's enough. Otherwise it's not enough."

"What are you offering, Elly?"

"The money," he said.

"How much?"

"As much as you'll need."

"She won't like it," I said.

"She won't know," he said. He had pulled the cart next to the sand trap and was now standing over his ball, looking at it. He sighed and took an 8-iron out of his bag. His ball was sitting high on the springy grass. Mozart moved his heavy shoulders and for a moment he looked twenty years younger, his torso motionless and his eyes steady, concentrating on his lie. Suddenly he swung and the ball clicked away in a high arc. I watched it fade right, strike the back side of the green, and bounce away; we were together in the woods. He replaced the club in his bag and smiled broadly, satisfied. "Normally I'd've taken a seven iron, but an eight felt right. I thought to myself, Eight will do the job. Sometimes you have to go with instinct and ignore experience, and the odds."

"That's what Pat Bayley used to say," I said.

"Pat was a champion," Mozart said.

The sun was lowering. I felt a breeze, damp and chilly from the lake only a mile away. The sun had been so warm, an early spring sun, unseasonable. Mozart had taken the cart around the back side of the green near the path to the sixth tee. He stood there waiting for me, idly swinging an iron. I walked, the turf soft and damp under my feet. I thought he had analyzed the campaign correctly. I was exhausted and my people were exhausted. Many of them were on half salary and I had money for one more payroll. The usual sources were dried up, waiting for the general election. We were stalled because I could not engage my opponent. She had refused to debate. I had done everything I knew how to do, and it had not been enough. Campaigns were waged on the small screen and I was not able to buy my way in, as Mozart had predicted at lunch months before. The kitty was small, and now it was almost gone. I had moved to within a few percentage points, then stalled. And she had sailed serenely on—hand, voice, vote. People had sacrificed for my campaign—and then I remembered the philosopher's answer to sacrifice. I spit on sacrifice, he said.

We moved off into the rough, searching for our balls. Mozart was whistling through his teeth, poking here and there with the blade of his 9-iron, and then he began to speak. He said he was retiring next year; he'd have an office but he'd be effectively out of it, "of counsel," except when they needed an old head to put a word in an old ear, ha-ha. His son had come into the firm. They had added half a dozen partners and had branched out. Not so much work at the Hall, he said. His son specialized in taxes and his daughter-in-law in communications law. Can you believe it? She was a living doll and smart as a whip. And they're very lucrative specialties, taxes and communications; and you'd be surprised how they fit, for example when one man's selling a radio station to another. They travel to Washington together, and his son spent his time at the IRS and his wife at the FCC, and at night they met at the Hay-Adams and had a cocktail and dinner with their friends. It makes a nice working holiday for them. And the other day his son brought up the possibility of a merger with a Washington firm, small firm, all young men and of course women, too. Smaller firm than Estabrook, Mozart. I said, Not while I'm alive. And my boy just laughed and a few days later his wife took me to lunch at the Tavern and told me they both want to go to Washington, take over the smaller firm. That's where it's at. And they were going to do it, whether I liked it or not; of course they wanted my consent, and my blessing. It would distress them if I fought it. But you can't stop us, Dad, because my mind's made up, she said. If you fight, you'll lose. I tell you, she's a pistol. So what's a father to do? And as everybody knows, Washington is just like Chicago or any other place: it's who you know. You have to know the right people, get a piece of paper from one part of the town to another without a lot of fuss and feathers. As you know, I can take it or leave it alone. Our nation's capital reminds me of Venice. It's a handsome city but it's dead. Nothing happens there. They collect money and they spend it but they don't make anything of value. They don't *produce*. They love to talk and they love to intrigue. They love to denounce people, and they've got their doge and their nobility and their importance in the world. They're news. It's glamorous but it's two grains of wheat in two bushels of chaff, as the man said. They want the rest of us to go away and leave them alone. Hard to tell that to young people, they don't want to believe it. They don't want to believe what's in front of their eyes. They want to believe the six o'clock news instead. My son and his wife love Washington. It excites them, bless their hearts. So what's a father to do?

"You want to buy them a senator as an anniversary present?"

He looked at me, grinning, and then he laughed out loud.

"Here they are," he said, pointing. He brushed away leaves with his 9-iron, uncovering his Titleist and my Top-Flite, both of them in impossible lies. The balls were about a foot apart behind low bushes. A trap was in front of the bushes and the green beyond the trap. The pin was thirty yards from where we were.

"Your go, Jack."

The Top-Flite was behind a tuft of grass in a little ragged trench, barely playable.

"I won't object if you improve that lie," Mozart said.

I swung and the ball ticked the top of the bushes, but had enough lift to clear the trap. I was this side of the green, off the apron.

"My goodness," Mozart said. "That's just a beauty. You're a man who came to play golf." He stood looking at his ball. The bushes prevented a direct approach to the green and the Titleist was behind a fallen branch. "Of course I want to buy them a senator, Jack. And not only them but some other good people I represent and have represented for many years, in good times and bad. They need a senator also. What's the matter? You so far up the ladder that you can't be bought?" He said all that without looking up. "Sometimes I've had a lie like this one, just impossible. Unplayable. So I did what I could." He shook his head and placed the blade of his 9-iron behind the ball, just so. Then he reached down and gently removed the branch and threw it away. Now there were only the bushes between him and the green. He said, "Time was, Springfield was all I needed or wanted. Butch Estabrook, too. God rest his soul. They never liked us downstate. We were too big, we muscled people even when we didn't intend to. The big fellow has to be careful where he sits. On the other hand, we had jobs to do and time was always of the essence. And Butch was often abrupt. He frightened people. *Chicago* frightened people, its sprawl and influence. Chicago moved its shoulders and the people on the edges got knocked out of the tree. But what are you going to do about that? Pretend you're a shrimp? Gosh, sorry. We're the engine and the engine makes a racket. The noise bothers some people. It just bothers the hell out of them. Well." He looked at me. "Tough shit."

"I can win without you," I said.

"No, you can't, Jack. You'll lose. Not by much. But you'll lose. And she'll lose too, in the general. Then we've all lost. You, me, her.

Three losers. Jesus, I hate to lose. Sometimes you can't prevent it and
so you swing with it, *c'est la vie*, and go on to something else. You
love the girl, but the girl doesn't love you back, so you say all right,
there're other girls. And those other girls have also got tits and nice
smiles. Win all the time and you know you've bought into an easy
game, and who wants that? But if you can prevent it, and still lose,
you're a horse's ass. You're selfish, you think you're Jesus Christ. You're
a stranger, you're living in another world, because that's not the way
we're built here, in this region. You know that, Jack. We don't believe in a perfect world here, we go with what we have; and if a man
extends his hand, we shake it or cut it off. There's no middle way.
And I'm wondering whether you belong on the first team or in a
sandbox, because it sounds to me like you believe in a child's history
of the world. Life's dirty, Jack. But of course you know that, too. Or
you did. Maybe you forgot." Mozart lifted his 9-iron and tapped the
grass behind the Titleist, then thought better of it, shrugged, and
picked up the ball. He rolled it on the tips of his fingers, removing a
speck of dirt and measuring the distance to the pin. Then he rocked
back and forth like a man pitching horseshoes, underhanding the
Titleist, lofting it over the bushes and the sand trap and onto the
fairway, where it bounced twice and rolled onto the green, about eight
feet from the cup.

I said, "Hell of a pitch, Elly."

But he was already moving away to the golf cart to fetch his putter.
His shoulders were square and his belly looked hard as iron, straining against the cardigan sweater. He wore old-fashioned golf shoes,
heavy brogans with cleats screwed into them. In his ensemble he
looked like one of the old-timers, Jimmy Demaret or Byron Nelson.
All he lacked were plus fours. He was standing behind the cart, looking at the Titleist on the green and smiling slyly. I wondered how
long he had thought about what he was going to tell me. I guessed
about five minutes. It was an old lecture, he had used the same material for fifty years; not that he had much occasion to use it, the times
being what they were. If I turned him down he would regard it as an
offense against nature, his own natural law, and he would find a way
to exact revenge. And that was what encouraged me to refuse him,

to let him know that the game was unimaginably complex, and that
there was no natural law beyond unpredictability; the universe was
in disorder, and Mozart and I were a misalliance. He had been buying politicians for fifty years. Politicians were his dearest, closest
friends; they came to the weddings of his children, and the christen-
ings of his grandchildren. They always needed money so they came
to him as a sick person came to a doctor, money a specific against
defeat. There were Mozarts all over America, some better, some much
worse, a fundamental part of the system. They were owed an article
of their own in the Bill of Rights to the Constitution.

He was standing on the green waiting for me. I felt that my life
had converged to this moment, that what I would do now would be
the sum of my actions in the past. He wanted me to submit to discipline, a novice to his confessor. We had been on the opposite side
of things for so long. I hated him for what he had done to Bayley;
or what I imagined he did, having no firsthand knowledge of anything. And at that I would be his last prize before retirement, the
old scoundrel's final fix. But I wanted the other, too; it also was the
sum of my actions, for better and worse. I wanted it as badly as I had
ever wanted anything material, in part as atonement for the years I
had lived on the margins, not evilly, but carelessly and without force
or conviction. It was part atonement and part compensation, though
I did not believe I was owed anything. I was not trying to regain something I had lost, but to seize something I had never had. I feared that
my goal was beyond reach, and the campaign lost.

Mozart was impatient, standing on the apron of the green and
looking at his wristwatch. I stepped up to the ball, not thinking about
it, not thinking about golf at all but what I would say to Mozart. I
realized suddenly that Charles Nierendorf would be the paymaster,
and that meant that when he called my office I would have to pick
up the telephone and listen to him and at the end of the conversation say Yes, or anyway not say No, hurriedly of course because it
would be late in the day and I was scheduled to meet young Mozart
and his wife and some boys from Chicago at the Hay-Adams. Probably it would be the young Mozarts, the boys from Chicago, and
Charles Nierendorf himself, the eight of us jolly at cocktails while

we discussed the problem at the FCC and who did I know over there? Can you make a call, Jack?

I tapped the ball, too weakly except that the green was fast. The ball was mis-hit and I groaned to myself, then looked up to see it jump and curl erratically toward the pin; and it dropped.

"My goodness, Jack!" Mozart cried. "You're a rascal. You're in the wrong business. You should be a golf professional. That's a par five!"

"Birdie four," I said. I could not believe it. I was grinning, elated. So that was how things worked out when you didn't pay any attention to them, didn't worry them, merely did them. The disorderly universe was not always malignant, only unpredictable. Frequently it was benevolent, usually when nothing was at stake.

"My, my," Mozart said, not acknowledging the error. "You just step right up, square yourself away, and bingo. I'd've sworn you didn't even have your mind on the game. I'd've sworn you were a million miles away. You don't need any help from anyone. You're a self-reliant fellow, Jack."

"That's what my father preached, self-reliance."

Mozart smiled. "Did he practice?"

"Not that I ever saw," I said.

Mozart concentrated mightily on his own putts, and took three of them. We walked off the tee and got into the cart and began the short drive down the path to the sixth tee. The woods were densely packed, the light pale and sullen. I realized with relief that we could not play eighteen; it would be dark soon; and it was chilly. Mozart was silent, steering the little cart down the winding path; he was irritated with himself for his three putts, and with me for taking so long and then holing the shot. I looked up, observing the crowns of the shagbark hickory and ash so black and twisted, anarchic against the April sky. It was quiet except for the hum of the electric cart and the crunch of gravel. High up in one of the hickorys something caught my eye. It glittered dully in the light, something balanced on the branches, its man-made linear symmetry incongruous. I shaded my eyes and looked at it, knowing at once it was the one-legged golfer's putter, stuck where he had thrown it in rage. It looked harmless enough now, and a good wind would bring it down. I supposed there were putters all over Oak Knoll, in trees and under bushes, and in the water at 12. The putter looked so fragile and insignificant, balanced on the thick limbs of the hickory, like something left over from a flood. I turned away, then looked back, and the putter was lost to view, concealed again in the tops of the trees.

Standing on the sixth tee, we looked down the steep sloping fairway at the foursome approaching the green. It was as if we had stadium seats, watching the playing field below. Six was a short hole, 250 yards. The one-legged golfer was leaning against his cart, preparing to chip. The club moved and the ball went wide and dribbled into a sand trap. He fell and then rose, painfully, and slapped the pitching wedge into the golf bag. He leaned against the cart a moment, his chest heaving. Then he got into the cart and slowly drove it around to the back of the green and into the sand trap. His companions waited for him on the green; they were ready to putt. The one-legged golfer got out of the cart, his club in his hand, and steadied himself. He looked from the pin to his ball and back again, calculating the distance. He swung, falling, the sand spraying in a fan, the ball moving a few feet and coming to rest. It was difficult for him to rise, the club head sinking into the sand. At last he stood, swaying; the one-legged golfer looked disoriented. He patted his trousers free of sand, got into the cart, and moved it forward so that he could lean against it and try again. Balanced, he swung, fell, and the ball was lost in the spray of sand. When he looked up, he saw that he had lifted it over the lip of the trap and onto the green's apron, a trifle. He drove the cart out of the trap and parked it, alighting with an aluminum rake that extended like a telescope. He leaned against the back of the cart and carefully raked the sand, back and forth a dozen times until the tire tracks and his own marks were erased, and the trap was as he found it. Then he collapsed the rake and replaced it in the cart, fastened his peg leg, fetched the putter, and hobbled onto the green. His companions had played out and now they stood silently, watching him. He took his time lining up the putt. At last he putted, lagging the ball about six feet beyond the cup. It took him two more to get down and when he moved violently to backhand the putter into the bushes, one of the men said something; a blast of rough laughter gusted up the fairway. The one-legged golfer wheeled on his friends, raising his fist, his face scarlet—and then, hesitating and lowering his fist, he made a little agonized gesture and limped back to the cart, laying the putter on the seat. The others sauntered away. He sat a moment, his head bowed, his chest heaving. I watched the one-legged golfer mark the scores on the card. "You win," I said to Mozart.

—1989

The Mower

James Kaplan

She ran every morning at six-twenty. At first I hardly noticed, but then it got so I'd look for her, and worry a little if she was late. She'd come out of the trees along the sixteenth fairway, run through the rough down the side, cut across the street, go down the seventeenth, then over the creek—there's a little wooden bridge—onto the third tee, and out of sight. I would never see her after that. If she finished where she started, though, she must have run four or five miles. Jesus. I couldn't run a mile if you paid me a million bucks. I never saw where she finished, because even though I was almost always on the fifteenth or sixteenth when she started—you cut them alternate days, usually—as soon as she got out of sight I had to go down the hill and do the eleventh or the tenth, and then back into the garage before the foursomes started showing up at seven. Benito, the greenskeeper, had his own special little system; he completely flew off the handle if you did it any other way, and he was always around, in that yellow cart with the flag on it, to make sure you did it right. Benito was *everywhere*.

Practically as soon as I began seeing her I hoped two things: one, that Benito wouldn't catch her—he'd love that—and two, that she got off the course before the foursomes came on. There's something about four guys together that I don't especially like. There's something about *golf* I don't like, as a matter of fact. But the course—that was different. Have you ever been on a golf course at six in the morning? It's very misty, kind of spooky; all the hills and bumps look like giant animals or something. Then the sun comes up—if you're lucky and it's clear out. I saw the sun rise every clear morning for six years. Not many people can say that. I'll take a sunrise over a sunset every time. But even if it's raining, it's beautiful out there. Ask most people what color a rainy day is, and what do they say? Gray. Not on a golf course. Everything is green—but not the same green. There are about eighty-two different kinds of green out there. Blue green, gray green, yellow green, orange green, brown green, purple green, green green. You name it.

I'd show up at five-thirty, try and steer clear of Benito, and get on one of the machines. Usually I'd do roughs first—not much fun. Then I did around the greens—kind of finicky work; the edges are the worst. But my favorite was the fairways. The big eighteen-foot mower—you feel like a king, going right down the middle. You have to use a different machine for each length of grass. They don't adjust like your little Lawn-Boy. There were three of us; we did nine holes every morning, three apiece. Benito had this whole complicated system worked out so you could trade machines with another guy when you were through. It was all done by the clock. Six-ten was when I started the sixteenth fairway, and six-twenty was when she came out of the trees.

It was nice watching her. Most people look terrible running. Most women, especially, don't look very good running. They don't seem to be built for it, usually. The only people I've ever seen that look any good running are these really skinny guys who run cross-country for the Catholic school across the mountain. They practice every afternoon; I see them when I drive home. They always look like they're about to die, extremely thin guys with sweaty undershirts and bony chests, their mouths open and their eyes staring. And their eyes kind of go dead every time one of their feet hits the ground. But there they are, running, mile after mile—you can't imagine them doing anything else. And then you see one of these fat guys huffing along in sweat pants and fluorescent shoes. Or one of these housewives. (I should talk. I could stand to lose twenty myself. Beer.) But you should have seen *her*. Once, when I was in high school—it seems like about thirty years ago—my music-appreciation class went to the ballet, and all of my friends and I were getting off on how faggoty it was, which is the kind of thing you get off on in high school. Most of the time I was pretty bored, I have to admit, but there were a couple of things I really liked, like when the guys jumped. Those guys can *jump*. And when they picked the girls up. You can't be that much of a fag if you can pick up somebody who weighs about a hundred pounds and make it look easy. I also liked it when the girls ran off the stage. I loved watching the way their behinds moved when they ran off the stage. That's just the way she ran. Exactly the same. Down the sixteenth fairway and out of sight.

She waved to me three or four mornings after the first time I saw her. I almost fell off my mower. Came out of the trees and waved at me, and did I wave back? Schmuck. I was too startled. But the next morning she waved again anyway. This will sound dumb, I know, but she had the nicest wave I ever saw. Most people just put up their hand and shake it back and forth, but she did something different—how can I describe it? It was sort of a periscope wave, or maybe like a little sea monster. Her arm was up, but her hand was at right angles to it, the back of her hand was arched, and she fluttered her fingers, like a pianist or something. When I got home, I did that wave at myself in the mirror. I felt like my hand didn't belong to me.

At the end of the month, it rained, hard, for a solid week almost. Sometimes when it's raining just a little bit, a lot of these guys who are nuts about golf will put on their funny hats or bring out their cute umbrellas and play anyway, but this was *rain*. I mean, there were swimming pools on the greens. Nobody was playing golf, running, anything. Or maybe she did run. I don't know. I wasn't out there to see her. When it was like that out, all you could really do was sit around the garage, pretending to repair stuff. The club paid you anyway. Big deal. I'd rather be outside. The guys I really felt sorry for were the caddies. What the hell could they do? But the four of us, mostly we'd just sit around, smoking, shooting the breeze, even playing poker. The funny thing was, when the weather got like that Benito was the first one to break out the cards. He'd make the amaz-

ing change, from a little rat into a sweetheart. Then he'd always worry
about the manager, Mr. Mahaffy. He'd talk real quiet while he dealt
the cards, and look over his shoulder a lot. I loved it. I loved the way
it smelled in the garage when it was raining out—sort of a combination of wet grass and gasoline and cigarette smoke. You could almost
go into a trance with the rain coming down on the roof. It was like
being high. Over on the wall, next to the fire extinguisher, somebody wrote in pencil: "JULY 2, 1961. RAIN." I used to stare at it and
wonder what the hell it was like on July 2, 1961. It seems like at least
four hundred years ago. What day of the week was it? Who was cutting grass? What did they look like? Were they playing cards? Was
the course still full of creeps then? Who was greenskeeper? (Benito's
only been there since '67.) Kennedy was President. Probably everyone had crewcuts. Then I wondered where *she* was then. Probably
not born yet. No, probably like three, four years old. I wondered if I
ever saw her someplace—a supermarket, maybe.

The rain finally stopped after five days. One afternoon it just
stopped, and the sun came out, and all of a sudden it was real hot,
and we had to go out and cut. Benito made us stay late. There were
still big puddles on the greens. Clouds of mosquitoes everywhere.
Clumps of wet grass stuck to the blades. Usually we didn't cut in the
afternoon, but Benito was panicking. Mahaffy was on his ass. So the
next morning the regular schedule was all screwed up. I was way the
hell on the other side of the course, and suddenly it hit me: I wasn't
going to get to see her come out of the trees. And it was killing me.
That's when I knew I was in trouble. I was cutting the seventh green,
going around and around in circles, cursing and punching the steering wheel. Around and around. Christ, I hated greens. And then,
bang, I see her, running down along the trees. And she waves, kind
of nonchalant, like we're old friends, like it hasn't been raining for
the past week, like we always meet this way on the seventh hole. But
what could I do? Bawl her out? I waved back—not a big wave, just a
little one. I was pretty mad. Then on an impulse, I cut the engine
and yelled to her. "Hey!" I said. She was on her way to the eighth
tee. "Hey!" I yelled. But she just sort of half turned around and gave
that wave of hers. Then she was gone. I got *really* wrecked that night.

You know how it is when you drink too much. It's pretty hard to sleep. Maybe I got four hours that night, I don't know, but I dreamed I was awake the whole time, and the room felt like I was riding that Goddamned mower around and around the seventh green. I dreamed about her. When I woke up, in the dark, I made up my mind that I would *definitely* talk to her at six-twenty. Definitely.

The sun came up through the trees like a giant orange golf ball sitting in the rough, the birds were making a racket, and I was riding down the sixteenth fairway at six-fifteen, with a head that felt like a piano or something, not a head. I was just riding, not cutting. I was really supposed to be on the fifteenth—Johnny D. had already done the sixteenth the day before. So I had the blades up, and I was just riding along, watching the trees. Benito would've murdered me. Out she came, right on schedule, and she waved. I was not feeling too sharp. I couldn't have looked too sharp, either, but I just cruised up next to her, about as close as I could get with the blade arm sticking out, and I said, "Hi!" She waved again. I don't think she heard me. The engine was pretty loud. We went along together for a little bit, just smiling at each other. Then I got up my courage. "What's your name!" I yelled. She smiled and put her hand up to her ear. I forgot to say she had really nice ears. She wore her hair up, and there were those little wisps of blond hair coming down. "Your name!" I shouted. "What's your name?" Then she said something, but I couldn't hear. I cut the engine. Now she was out ahead of me. I asked again. She called something back over her shoulder. Juliana?

I really think that's what she said. Juliana. What the hell kind of name is that? Practically all the girls I ever meet are named Cathy. Sometimes I think half the girls I've ever *known* have been named Cathy. Their favorite song is always "Cherish."

There was no rain at all the next month. Zero. Plus, it was about a hundred out every day. The course almost fried. We were allowed to water the greens but not the fairways. Town ordinance. Benito would just stand there and stare at his precious grass shrivelling up and look like he was about to pop a blood vessel. The weird thing was, every afternoon there were all these big black clouds, sometimes even some thunder and lightning—but no rain. There was always a lot of static on the radio. I wanted to say something to her about running on the fairways—Benito was at the point where he would've shot someone for taking a divot—but I was scared to talk to her. Can you believe it? The funny thing is, usually I'm never that way. Usually I'm just the opposite.

Then Benito put us back to just doing greens. My favorite. That's all that was growing. And he said if the weather didn't break he was going to have to let one of us go. He said we could draw straws. I should've told him what he could do with his straws. He assigned me to the first six, way the hell on the other side of the course from where she ran. I asked him if I could switch with somebody else, but he just gave me this look.

Then, next morning—it was *hot;* by six-thirty my shirt was soaked—I was coming over the hill to the fourth green when suddenly I just got goose bumps. I knew what was happening even before I knew, if you know what I mean. Way down the fairway, about 350 yards out, I could see this yellow dot and this red dot. That was all. I knew right away what was going on. I don't know why, but it reminded me of November of seventh grade. We were playing football one Friday afternoon, and Mr. Finelli, my gym teacher, came running across the field with his hands in his pockets. I knew it was bad news. I just knew. Everybody else on my team kept running, and I stopped in my tracks and watched him coming across the field. It was the same way now. I should've started on the green, but I headed down the fairway. We were only supposed to drive on the service roads, because the course was so dried out, but I just went right on down the middle. She was standing there with her hands on her hips, sweating like crazy, and Benito was shaking his finger in her face. I could've killed the little bastard. But I couldn't *get* there. It was like a bad dream: the stupid mower would only go about ten miles an hour. I should've just hopped out and run, but I probably would've dropped dead, my heart was beating so hard. Then

Benito heard the engine noise and turned around. He started jumping up and down—I swear it, jumping up and down. You should have seen it. I must have been trailing a dust cloud half a mile wide. And then she just took off. Vanished into the trees. I couldn't really blame her. I still can't. What was she supposed to do—wait around till Benito got finished with me?

So now I'm looking for work. My brother-in-law has this Arco station out on Route 17. Maybe I'll go there. Anything but cutting grass. I mean, in a way this whole thing might have been kind of lucky. Can you see me sitting on a mower when I'm forty? Every once in a while I miss the course a little bit. Not the job—the course. I liked the way the sky looked over it, all the different kinds of clouds. The way the grass smelled. The wind in the trees. You don't get that on Route 17. But I won't miss Benito. I won't miss the golfers.

For a while I kept thinking I was seeing her places—in the mall, walking down the street—but it was always someone else. Once, this white 280-Z pulled up next to me at a light and my heart almost stopped. She was at the wheel. I honked, but when she turned around I saw it was another girl. She gave me the finger. I gave it to her back.

—1981

The Golfomaniac

Stephen Leacock

We ride in and out pretty often together, he and I, on a suburban train.

That's how I came to talk to him. "Fine morning," I said as I sat down beside him yesterday and opened a newspaper.

"Great!" he answered, "the grass is drying out fast now and the greens will soon be all right to play."

"Yes," I said, "the sun is getting higher and the days are decidedly lengthening."

"For the matter of that," said my friend, "a man could begin to play at six in the morning easily. In fact, I've often wondered that there's so little golf played before breakfast. We happened to be talking about golf, a few of us last night—I don't know how it came up—and we were saying that it seems a pity that some of the best part of the day, say, from five o'clock to seven-thirty, is never used."

"That's true," I answered, and then, to shift the subject, I said, looking out of the window:

"It's a pretty bit of country just here, isn't it?"

"It is," he replied, "but it seems a shame they make no use of it—just a few market gardens and things like that. Why, I noticed along here acres and acres of just glass—some kind of houses for plants or something—and whole fields full of lettuce and things like that. It's a pity they don't make something of it. I was remarking only the other day as I came along in the train with a friend of mine, that you could easily lay out an eighteen-hole course anywhere here."

"Could you?" I said.

"Oh, yes. This ground, you know, is an excellent light soil to shovel up into bunkers. You could drive some big ditches through it and make one or two deep holes—the kind they have on some of the French links. In fact, improve it to any extent."

I glanced at my morning paper. "I see," I said, "that it is again rumored that Lloyd George is at last definitely to retire."

"Funny thing about Lloyd George," answered my friend. "He never played, you know; most extraordinary thing—don't you think?—for a man in his position. Balfour, of course, was very different: I remember when I was over in Scotland last summer I had the honor of going around the course at Dumfries just after Lord Balfour. Pretty interesting experience, don't you think?"

"Were you over on business?" I asked.

"No, not exactly. I went to get a golf ball, a particular golf ball. Of course, I didn't go merely for that. I wanted to get a mashie as well. The only way, you know, to get just what you want is to go to Scotland for it."

"Did you see much of Scotland?"

"I saw it all. I was on the links at St. Andrews and I visited the Loch Lomond course and the course at Inverness. In fact, I saw everything."

"An interesting country, isn't it, historically?"

"It certainly is. Do you know they have played there for over five hundred years! Think of it! They showed me at Loch Lomond the place where they said Robert the Bruce played the Red Douglas (I think that was the other party—at any rate, Bruce was one of them), and I saw where Bonnie Prince Charlie disguised himself as a caddie when the Duke of Cumberland's soldiers were looking for him. Oh, it's a wonderful country historically."

After that I let a silence intervene so as to get a new start. Then I looked up again from my newspaper.

"Look at this," I said, pointing to a headline, UNITED STATES NAVY ORDERED AGAIN TO NICARAGUA. "Looks like more trouble, doesn't it?"

"Did you see in the paper a while back," said my companion, "that the United States Navy Department is now making golf compulsory at the training school at Annapolis? That's progressive, isn't it? I suppose it will mean shorter cruises at sea; in fact, probably lessen the use of the navy for sea purposes. But it will raise the standard."

"I suppose so," I answered. "Did you read about this extraordinary murder case on Long Island?"

"No," he said. "I never read murder cases. They don't interest me. I fact, I think this whole continent is getting over-preoccupied with them—"

"Yes, but this case had such odd features—"

"Oh, they all have," he replied, with an air of weariness. "Each one is just boomed by the papers to make a sensation—"

"I know, but in this case it seems that the man was killed with a blow from a golf club."

"What's that? Eh, what's that? Killed him with a blow from a golf club!!"

"Yes, some kind of club—"

"I wonder if it was an iron—let me see the paper—though, for the matter of that, I imagine that a blow with even a driver, let alone one of the steel-handled drivers—where does it say it?—pshaw, it only just says 'a blow with a golf club.' It's a pity the papers don't write these things up with more detail, isn't it? But perhaps it will be better in the afternoon paper . . ."

"Have you played golf much?" I inquired. I saw it was no use to talk of any thing else.

"No," answered my companion. "I am sorry to say I haven't. You see, I began late. I've only played twenty years, twenty-one if you count the year that's beginning in May. I don't know what I was doing. I wasted about half my life. In fact, it wasn't till I was well over thirty that I caught on to the game. I suppose a lot of us look back over our lives that way and realize what we have lost."

"And even as it is," he continued, "I don't get much chance to play. At the best I can only manage about four afternoons a week, though of course I get most of Saturday and all Sunday. I get my holiday in the summer, but it's only a month, and that's nothing. In the winter I manage to take a run South for a game once or twice and perhaps a little swack at it around Easter, but only a week at a time. I'm too busy—that's the plain truth of it." He sighed. "It's hard to leave the office before two," he said. "Something always turns up."

And after that he went on to tell me something of the technique of the game, illustrate it with a golf ball on the seat of the car, and the peculiar mental poise needed for driving, and the neat, quick action of the wrist (he showed me how it worked) that is needed to undercut a ball so that it flies straight up in the air. He explained to me how you can do practically anything with a golf ball, provided that you keep your mind absolutely poised and your eye in shape, and your body a trained machine. It appears that even Bobby Jones of Atlanta and people like that fall short very often from the high standard set up by my golfing friend in the suburban car.

So, later in the day, meeting someone in my club who was a person of authority on such things, I made inquiry about my friend. "I rode into town with Llewellyn Smith," I said. "I think he belongs to your golf club. He's a great player, isn't he?"

"A great player!" laughed the expert. "Llewellyn Smith? Why, he can hardly hit a ball! And anyway, he's only played about twenty years!"

—1930

Golf in the Kingdom

Michael Murphy

I felt the land as we climbed the hill, the sea breeze, the grass beneath my feet. A film had dropped from my eyes, from my hearing, from all my senses. The smell of the sea and the grass, of leather and perspiration filled the air. I could hear a cry of delight in the distance, then tiny cheers. Something had broken loose inside me, something large and free.

I looked out from our vantage point; we could see for miles now. The sun was dipping behind the western hills, while purple shadows spread across the water and arabesques of grass below. The curving fairways and tiny sounds arising from them, the fields of heather, the distant seacaps were all inside my skin. A presence was brooding through it all, one presence interfusing the ball, the green, MacIver, Shivas, everything.

I played the remaining holes in this state of grace. Specters of former attitudes passed through me, familiar curses and excuses, memories of old shots, all the flotsam and jetsam of my golfing unconscious—but a quiet field of energy held me and washed them away. I can think of no better way to say it—those final holes played me.

Farrell's Caddie

John Updike

When Farrell signed up, with seven other aging members of his local Long Island club, for a week of golf at the Royal Caledonian Links in Scotland, he didn't foresee the relationship with the caddies. Hunched little men in billed tweed caps and rubberized rain suits, they huddled in the misty gloom as the morning foursomes got organized, and reclustered after lunch, muttering as unintelligibly as sparrows, for the day's second eighteen.

Farrell would never have walked thirty-six holes a day in America, but here in Scotland golf was not an accessory to life, drawing upon one's marginal energy; it *was* life, played out of the center of one's being. At first, stepping forth on legs one of which had been broken in a college football game forty years before, and which damp weather or a night of twisted sleep still provoked to a reminiscent twinge, he missed the silky glide and swerve of the accustomed electric cart, its magic-carpet suspension above the whispering fairway; he missed the rattle of spare balls in the retaining shelf, and the round plastic holes to hold drinks, alcoholic or carbonated, and the friendly presence on the seat beside him of another gray-haired sportsman, another warty pickle blanching in the brine of time, exuding forbearance and the expectation of forbearance, and resigned, like Farrell, to a golfing mediocrity that would make its way down the sloping dogleg of decrepitude to the level green of death.

Here, however, on the heather-rimmed fairways, cut as close as putting surfaces back home, yet with no trace of mower tracks, and cheerfully marred by the scratchings and burrows of the nocturnal rabbits that lived and bred beneath the impenetrably thorny, waist-high gorse, energy came up through the turf, as if Farrell's cleats were making contact with primal spirits beneath the soil, and he felt he could walk forever. The rolling treeless terrain, the proximity of the wind-whipped sea, the rain that came and went with the suddenness of thought—they composed the ancient matrix of the game, and the darkly muttering caddies were also part of this matrix.

That first morning in the drizzly shuffle around the golf bags, his bag was hoisted up by a hunched shadow who, as they walked together in pursuit of Farrell's first drive (good contact, but pulled to the left, toward some shaggy mounds), muttered half to himself, with those hiccups or glottal stops the Scots accent inserts, "Sandy's wha' th' call me."

Farrell hesitated, then confessed, "I'm Gus." His given name, Augustus, had always embarrassed him, but its shortened version seemed a little short on dignity, and at the office, as he had ascended in rank, his colleagues had settled on his initials, "A. J."

"Ye want now tae geh oover th' second boosh fra' th' laift," Sandy said, handing Farrell a 7-iron. The green was out of sight behind the shaggy mounds, which were covered with a long tan grass that whitened in waves as gusts beat in from the sea.

"What's the distance?" Farrell was accustomed to yardage markers—yellow stakes, or sprinkler heads.

The caddie looked reflectively at a sand bunker not far off, and then at the winking red signal light on the train tracks beyond, and finally at a large bird, a gull or a crow, winging against the wind beneath the low, tattered, blue-black clouds. "Ah hunnert thirhty-eight tae th' edge o' th' green, near a hunnert fifty tae th' pin, where they ha' 't."

"I can't hit a seven-iron a hundred fifty. I can't hit it even one-forty, against this wind."

Yet the caddie's fist, in a fingerless wool glove, did not withdraw the offered club. "Siven's what ye need."

As Farrell bent his face to the ball, the wet wind cut across his eyes and made him cry. His tears turned one ball into two; he sup-

posed the brighter one was real. He concentrated on taking the
clubhead away slowly and low to the turf, initiating his downswing
with a twitch of the left hip, and suppressing his tendency to dip the
right shoulder. The shot seemed sweet, soaring with a gentle draw
precisely over the second bush. He looked toward the caddie, expecting congratulations or at least some small sign of shared pleasure. But
the man, whose creased face was weathered the strangely even brown
of a white actor playing Othello, followed the flight of the ball as he
had that of the crow, reflectively. "Yer right hand's a wee bit froward,"
he observed, and the ball, they saw as they climbed to the green, was
indeed pulled to the left, into a deep pot bunker. Furthermore, it was
fifteen yards short. The caddie had underclubbed him, but showed
no signs of remorse as he handed Farrell the sand wedge. In Sandy's
dyed-looking face, pallid gray eyes showed the touches of morning
light; it shocked Farrell to suspect that the other man, weathered
though he was, and bent beneath the weight of a perpetual golf bag,
was younger than himself—a prematurely wizened Pict, a concentrate of Farrell's diluted, Yankeefied Celtic blood.

The side of the bunker toward the hole was as tall as Farrell and
sheer, built up of bricks of sod in a way he had never seen before,
not even at Shinnecock Hills. Rattled, irritated by having been
unrepentantly underclubbed, Farrell swung five times into the damp,
brown sand, darker and denser than any sand on Long Island; each
time, the ball thudded short of the trap's lip and dribbled back at his
feet. "'it at it well beheend," the caddie advised, "and dinna stop th'
cloob." Farrell's sixth swing brought the ball bobbling up onto the
green, within six feet of the hole.

His fellow Americans lavished ironical praise on the tardily excellent shot but the caddie, with the same deadpan solemnity with
which Farrell had repeatedly struck the ball, handed him his putter.
"Ae ball tae th' laift," he advised, and Farrell was so interested in
this quaint concept—the ball as a unit of measure—that his putt
stopped short. "Ye forgot tae 'it it, Goos," Sandy told him.

Farrell tersely nodded. The caddie made him feel obliged to keep
up a show of golfing virtues. Asked for his score, he said loudly in a
stagey voice, "That was an honest ten."

"We'll call it a six," said the player keeping score, in a forgiving, corrupting American way.

As the round progressed, through a rapid alternation of brisk showers and silvery sunshine, with rainbows springing up around them and tiny white daisies gleaming underfoot, Farrell and his caddie began to grow into one another, as a foot in damp weather grows into a shoe. Sandy consistently handed Farrell one club too short to make the green, but Farrell came to accept the failure as his own; his caddie was handing the club to the stronger golfer latent in Farrell, and it was Farrell's job to let this superior performer out, to release him from his stiff, soft, more than middle-aged body. On the twelfth hole, called "Dunrobin"—a seemingly endless par 5 with a broad stretch of fairway, bleak and vaguely restless like the surface of the moon, receding over a distant edge marked by two small pot bunkers, with a pale-green arm of gorse extending from the rabbit-undermined thickets on the left—his drive clicked. Something about the ghostly emptiness of this terrain, the featurelessness of it, had removed Farrell's physical inhibitions; he felt the steel shaft of the drive bend in a subtle curve at his back, and a corresponding springiness awaken in his knees, and he knew, as his weight elastically moved from the right foot to the left, that he would bring the clubface squarely into the ball, and indeed did, so that the ball—the last of his Titleists, the others having already been swallowed by gorse and heather and cliffside scree—was melting deep into the drizzle straight ahead almost before he looked up, with his head still held sideways as if pillowed on his right ear, just like the pros on television. He cocked an eye at Sandy. "O.K.?" asked Farrell, mock-modest but also genuinely fearful of some hazard, some trick of the layout, that he had missed taking into account.

"Gowf shot, sirr," the caddie said, and his face, as if touched by a magic wand, crumpled into a smile full of crooked gray teeth, his constantly relit cigarette adhering to one corner. Small matter that Farrell, striving for a repetition of his elastic sensations, topped the following 3-wood, hit a 5-iron fat and short, and skulled his wedge shot clear across the elevated green. He had for a second awakened the golf giant sleeping among his muscles, and imagined himself now cutting a more significant figure in the other man's not quite color-less, not quite indifferent eyes.

Dinner, for this week of foreign excursion, was a repeating male event, involving the same eight Long Island males, their hair growing curly and their faces ruddy away from the arid Manhattan canyons and air-conditioned offices where they had accumulated their small fortunes. They discussed their caddies as men, extremely unbuttoned, might discuss their mistresses. What does a caddie want? "Come on, Freddie, '*it* it fer once!" the very distinguished banker Frederic M. Panoply boasted that his had cried out to him as, on the third day of display-ing his cautious, successful, down-the-middle game, he painstakingly addressed his ball.

Another man's caddie, when asked what he thought of Mrs. Thatcher, had responded with a twinkle, "She'd be a good 'ump."

Farrell, prim and reserved by nature, though not devoid of pas-sion, had relatively little to offer concerning Sandy. He worried that the man's incessant smoking would kill him. He wondered if the tips he gave him were too far below what a Japanese golfer would have bestowed. He feared that Sandy was becoming tired of him. As the week went by, their relationship had become more intuitive. "A six-iron?" Farrell would now say, and without word would be handed the club. Once he had dared decline an offered 6, asked for the 5, and sailed his unusually well-struck shot into the sedge beyond the green. On the greens, where he at first had been bothered by the caddie's explicit directives, so that he forgot to stroke the ball firmly, Farrell had come to depend upon Sandy's advice, and would expertly cock his ear close to the caddie's mouth, and try to envision the curve of the ball into the center of the hole from "an inch an' a fingernail tae th' laift." He began to sink putts. He began to get pars, as the whitecaps flashed on one side of the links and on the other the wine-red electric commuter trains swiftly glided up to Glasgow and back. This was happiness, bracketed between sea and rail, and freedom, of a wild and windy sort. On the morning of his last day, having sliced his first drive into the edge of the rough, between a thistle and what appeared to be a child's weathered tombstone, Farrell bent his ear close to the caddie's mouth for advice, and heard, "Ye'd be better leavin' 'er."

"Beg pardon?" Farrell said, as he had all week, when the glottal, hiccupping accent had become opaque. Today the acoustics were especially bad; a near-gale off the sea made his rain pants rattle like machine guns and deformed his eyeballs with air pressure as he tried to squint down. When he could stop seeing double, his lie looked fair—semi-embedded. The name on the tombstone was worn away. Perhaps it was merely an ancient railroad right-of-way marker.

"Yer missus," Sandy clarified, passing over the 8-iron. "'Ere it's tae late, mon. She was never yer type. Tae proper."

"Shouldn't this be a wedge?" Farrell asked uncertainly.

"Nay, it's sittin' up guid enough," the caddie said, pressing his foot into the heather behind the ball so it rose up like ooze out of mud. "Ye kin reach with th' eight," he said. "Go fer yer par, mon. Yer fauts er a' in yer mind; ye tend t' play a hair defainsive."

Farrell would have dismissed Sandy's previous remarks, as a verbal mirage amid the clicks and skips of wind-blown Scots, had they not seemed so uncannily true. "Too proper" was exactly what his college friends had said of Sylvia, but he had imagined that her physical beauty had been the significant thing, and her propriety a pose she would outgrow, whereas thirty-five married years had revealed the propriety as enduring and the beauty as transient. As to leaving her, this thought would never have entered his head until recently; the mergers-and-acquisitions branch had recently taken on a certain Irma Finegold, who had heavy-lidded eyes, full lips painted vermilion, and a curious presumptuous way of teasing Farrell in the eddies of chitchat before and after conferences, or in the elevator up to the boardroom. She had been recently divorced, and when she talked to Farrell she manipulated her lower lip with a pencil eraser and shimmied her shoulders beneath their pads. On nights when the office worked late—he liked occasionally to demonstrate that, well-along though he was, he could still pull an all-nighter with the young bucks—there had been between him and Irma shared Chinese meals in greasy take-out cartons, and a joint limo home in the dawn light, through the twinned arches and aspiring tracery of the Brooklyn Bridge. And on one undreamed-of occasion, there had been an invitation, which he did not refuse, to delay his return to Long Island with an interlude at her apartment in Park Slope. Though no young buck, he had not done badly, it seemed to him, even factoring in the flattery quotient from a subordinate.

The 8-iron pinched the ball clean, and the Atlantic gale brought the soaring shot left-to-right toward the pin. "Laift edge, but dinna gi' th' hole away," Sandy advised of the putt, and Farrell sank it, for the first birdie of his week of golf.

Now, suddenly, out of the silvery torn sky, sleet and sunshine poured simultaneously. While the two men walked at the same tilt to the next tee, Sandy's voice came out of the wind, "An' steer clear o' th' MiniCorp deal. They've laiveraged th' company tae daith."

Farrell studied Sandy's face. Rain and sleet bounced off his brown skin as if from a waxy preservative coating. Metallic gleams showed as the man studied, through narrowed eyelids, the watery horizon. Farrell pretended he hadn't heard. On the tee he was handed a 3-wood, with the advice, "Ye want tae stay short o' th' wee burn. Th' wind's come around beheend, bringin' th' sun with it."

As the round wore on, the sun did struggle through, and a thick rainbow planted itself over the profile of the drab town beyond the tracks, with its black steeples and distillery chimneys. By the afternoon's eighteen, there was actually blue sky, and the pockets of lengthening shadow showed the old course to be everywhere curvaceous, crest and swale, like the body of a woman. Forty feet off the green on the fourteenth ("Whinny Brae"), Farrell docilely accepted the caddie's offer of a putter, and rolled it up and over the close-mown irregularities within a gimme of the hole. His old self would have skulled or fluffed a chip. "Great advice," he said, and in his flush of triumph challenged the caddie: "But Irma *loves* the MiniCorp deal."

"Aye, 't keeps th' twa o' ye taegither. She's fairful ye'll wander off, i' th' halls o' corporate power."

"But what does she see in me?"

"Lookin' fer a father, th' case may be. Thet first husband o' hers was meikle immature, an' also far from yer own income bracket."

Farrell felt his heart sink at the deflating shrewdness of the analysis. His mind elsewhere, absented by bittersweet sorrow, he hit one
pure shot after another. Looking to the caddie for praise, however,
he met the same impassive, dour, young-old visage, opaque beneath
the billed tweed cap. Tomorrow, he would be caddying for someone
else, and Farrell would be belted into a business-class seat within a
747. On the home stretch of holes—one after the other strung out
beside the railroad right-of-way, as the Victorian brick clubhouse,
with its turrets and neo-Gothic windows, enlarged in size—Farrell
begged for the last scraps of advice. "The five-wood, or the three-
iron? The three keeps it down out of the wind, but I feel more confident with the wood, the way you've got me swinging."

"Th' five'll be ower an' gone; ye're a' poomped up. Take th' four-
iron. Smooth it on, laddie. Aim fer th' little broch."

"Broch?"

"Wee stone fortress, frae th' days we had our own braw king." He
added, "An' ye might be thinkin' aboot takin' early retirement. Th'
severance deals won't be so sweet aye, with th' comin' resaission. Ye
kin free yerself up, an' take on some consults, fer th' spare change."

"Just what I was thinking, if Irma's a will-o'-the-wisp."

"Will-o'-the-wisp, d' ye say? Ye're a speedy lairner, Goos."

Farrell felt flattered and wind-scoured, here in this surging universe of green and gray. "You really think so, Sandy?"

"I *ken* sae. Ye kin tell a' aboot a man, frae th' way he gowfs."

—1972

The Pro

John Updike

I am on my four-hundred-and-twelfth golf lesson, and my drives still
have that pushed little tail, and my irons still take the divot on the
wrong side of the ball. My pro is a big gloomy sun-browned man—
age about thirty-eight, weight around 195. When he holds a club in
his gloved hand and swishes it nervously (the nervousness comes over
him after the first twenty minutes of our lesson), he makes it look
light as a feather, a straw, a baton. Once I sneaked his 3-wood from
his bag, and the head weighed more than a cannonball. "Easy does
it, Mr. Wallace," he says to me. My name is not Wallace, but he
smooths his clients toward one generic, acceptable name. I call him
Dave.

"Easy does it, Mr. Wallace," he says. "That ball is not going anywhere by itself, so what's your hurry?"

"I want to clobber the bastard," I say. It took me two hundred
lessons to attain this pitch of frankness.

"You dipped again," he tells me, without passion. "That right
shoulder of yours dipped, and your knees locked, you were so anxious. Ride those knees, Mr. Wallace."

"I can't. I keep thinking about my wrists. I'm afraid I won't pro-
nate them."

This is meant to be a joke, but he doesn't smile. "Ride those knees,
Mr. Wallace. Forget your wrists. Look." He takes my 5-iron into his
hands, a sight so thrilling it knocks the breath out of me. It is like, in
the movies we all saw as children (oh, blessed childhood!), the in-

stant when King Kong, or the gigantic Cyclops, lifts the beautiful
blonde, who has blessedly fainted, over his head, and she becomes
utterly weightless, a thing of sheer air and vision and pathos. I love
it, I feel half-sick with pleasure, when he lifts my club, and want to
tell him so, but I can't. After 411 lessons, I still repress.

"The hands can't *help* but be right," he says, "if the *knees* are right."
He twitches the club, so casually I think he is brushing a bee from
the ball's surface. There is an innocent click; the ball whizzes into
the air and rises along a line as straight as the edge of a steel ruler,
hangs at its remote apogee for a moment of meditation, and settles
like a snowflake twenty yards beyond the shagging caddie.

"Gorgeous, Dave," I say, with an affectation of camaraderie,
though my stomach is a sour churning of adoration and dread.

He says, "A little fat, but that's the idea. Did you see me grunt
and strain?"

"No, Dave." This is our litany.

"Did you see me jerk my head, or freeze at the top of the backswing, or rock forward on my toes?"

"No, Dave, no."

"Well, then, what's the problem? Step up and show me how."

I assume my stance, and take back the club, low, slowly; at the
top, my eyes fog over, and my joints dip and swirl like barn swallows.
I swing. There is a fruitless commotion of dust and rubber at my feet.
"Smothered it," I say promptly. After enough lessons, the terminol-
ogy becomes second nature. The whole process, as I understand it, is
essentially one of self-analysis. The pro is merely a catalyst, a random sample, I have read somewhere, from the grab bag of humanity.

He insists on wearing a droll porkpie hat from which his heavy
brown figure somehow downflows; his sloping shoulders, his hanging arms, his faintly pendulous belly, and his bent knees all tend toward his shoes, which are ideally natty—solid as bricks, black and
white, with baroque stitching, frilled kilties, and spikes as neat as
alligator teeth. He looks at me almost with interest. His grass-green
irises are tiny, whittled by years of concentrating on the ball. "Loosen
up," he tells me. I love it, I clench with gratitude, when he deigns to
be directive. "Take a few practice swings, Mr. Wallace. You looked

like a rusty mechanical man on that one. Listen. Golf is an effortless game."

"Maybe I have no aptitude," I say, giggling, blushing, hoping to deflect him with the humility bit.

He is not deflected. Stolidly he says, "Your swing is sweet. When it's there." Thus he uplifts me and crushes me from phrase to phrase. "You're blocking yourself out," he goes on. "You're not open to your own potential. You're not, as we say, *free*."

"I know, I know. That's why I'm taking all these expensive lessons."

"Swing, Mr. Wallace. Show me your swing."

I swing, and feel the impurities like bubbles and warps in glass: hurried backswing, too much right hand at impact, failure to finish high.

The pro strips off his glove. "Come over to the eighteenth green." I think we are going to practice chipping (a restricted but relaxed pendulum motion) for the fiftieth time, but he says, "Lie down."

The green is firm yet springy. The grounds crew has done a fine job watering this summer, through that long dry spell. Not since childhood have I lain this way, on sweet flat grass, looking up into a tree, branch above branch, each leaf distinct in its generic shape, as when, in elementary school, we used to press them between wax paper. The tree is a sugar maple. For all the times I have tried to hit around it, I never noticed its species before. In the fall, its dried-up leaves have to be brushed from the line of every putt. This spring, when the branches were tracery dusted with a golden budding, I punched a 9-iron right through the crown and salvaged a double bogey.

Behind and above me, the pro's voice is mellower than I remember it, with a lulling grittiness, like undissolved sugar in tea. He says, "Mr. Wallace, tell me what you're thinking about when you freeze at the top of your backswing."

"I'm thinking about my shot. I see it sailing dead on the pin, hitting six feet short, taking a bite with lots of backspin, and dribbling into the cup. The crowd goes *ooh* and cheers."

"Who's in the crowd? Anybody you know personally?"

"No . . . wait. There *is* somebody. My mother. She has one of those cardboard periscope things and shouts out, 'Gorgeous, Billy!'"

"She calls you Billy."

"That's my name, Dave. William, Willy, Billy, Bill. Let's cut out this Mr. Wallace routine. You call me Bill, I'll call you Dave." He is much easier to talk to, the pro, without the sight of his powerful passionless gloom, his hands (one bare, one gloved) making a mockery of the club's weight.

"Anybody else you know? Wife? Kids?"

"No, my wife's had to take the babysitter home. Most of the kids are at camp."

"What else do you see up there at the top of the backswing?"

"I see myself quitting lessons." It was out, *whiz*, before I had time to censor. Silence reigns in the leafy dome above me. A sparrow is hopping from branch to branch, like a pencil point going from number to number in those children's puzzles we all used to do.

At last the pro grunts, which, as I said, he never does. "The last time you were out, Mr. Wallace, what did you shoot?"

"You mean the last time I kept count?"

"Mm."

"A hundred eight. But that was with some lucky putts."

"Mm. Better stand up. Any prolonged pressure, the green may get a fungus. This bent grass is hell to maintain." When I stand, he studies me, chuckles, and says to an invisible attendant, "A hundred eight, with a hot putter yet, and he wants to quit lessons."

I beg, "Not quit forever—just for a vacation. Let me play a few different courses. You know, get out into the world. Maybe even try a public course. Gee, or go to a driving range and whack out a bucket of balls. You know, learn to live with the game I've got. Enjoy life."

His noble impassivity is invested with a shimmering, twinkling humorousness; his leathery face softens toward a smile, and the trace of a dimple is discovered in his cheek. "Golf is life," he says softly, and his green eyes expand, "and life is lessons," and the humps of his brown muscles merge with the hillocks and swales of the course, whose red flags prick the farthest horizon, and whose dimmest sand traps are indistinguishable from galaxies. I see that he is right, as always, absolutely; there is no life, no world, beyond the golf course—just an infinite and terrible falling off. "If I don't give *you* lessons," the pro is going on, "how will I pay for *my* lessons?"

"*You* take lessons?"

"Sure. I hook under pressure. Like Palmer. I'm too strong. Any rough on the left, there I am. You don't have that problem, with your nice pushy slice."

"You mean there's a sense," I ask, scarcely daring, "in which *you* need *me*?"

He puts his hand on my shoulder, the hand pale from wearing the glove, and I become a feather at the touch, all air and ease. "Mr. Wallace," he says, "I've learned a lot from your sweet swing. I hate it when, like now, the half-hour's up."

"Next Tuesday, eleven-thirty?"

Solemnly my pro nods. "We'll smooth out your chipping. Here in the shade."

—1966

IV.
Covering the Game

What It's Like to Be a Member:
A Look behind the Magnolia Curtain at Golf's Secret Citadel
Dave Anderson

I will not talk about what it's like to be a member. I don't want to jeopardize my membership. I'm at the age where I just want to enjoy it. The rules are, you're not supposed to talk about anything except the Masters.

—Longtime Augusta Member

The chairman who established those rules, the late Clifford Roberts, once wrote an elegant 256-page green-bound volume, *The Story of the Augusta National Golf Club,* that detailed his reign behind the high hedges and the white sentry box that separate the world's most prestigious golf club from the rest of the planet. Roberts' rules apparently didn't apply to him, only to the current 296 members from thirty-four states and the District of Columbia; another ten reside in Canada, Scotland, England and France.

Most members still don't dare challenge Roberts' first commandment: Thou shalt not talk about being a member. Even those who were willing to talk to *Golf Digest* requested anonymity.

Augusta National's mystique is such that some outsiders describe the membership as "almost a secret society." For that reason, just about anyone who has ever attended the Masters or watched it on television has wondered: Who are those guys in green coats up by the big oak trees and the green-and-white umbrella tables outside the sprawling white clubhouse? How did they get inside the green ropes? And what's it like to be there?

* * *

Mostly, those green coats match their owners' green dollars. Many are rich and powerful, but not necessarily famous. And not necessarily good golfers.

According to *Golf Digest* research, the membership's net worth is estimated at more than $10 billion. One member is worth $2.5 billion, nine others anywhere from $250 million to $630 million. If Augusta National had an alias, it would be The CEO Golf Club. Among its dozens of corporate honchos are the chief executive officers of American Express, Amoco, Citicorp, Du Pont, Emerson Electric, General Electric, IBM, Mobil, Morgan Stanley, Sara Lee, Sears, Roebuck & Co., Texaco, Textron, Travelers Insurance and USX (formerly U.S. Steel). More than half the members are on the board of directors of at least three companies. But by the nature of their business responsibilities, they are older men who spend more time in a board room than a golf locker room.

"You don't get to be where these guys are until you're fifty or sixty," one member says. "And you don't get there by playing a lot of golf."

"The bigger the man economically, the smaller the bet on the golf course," another says. "Usually they play a two-dollar nassau, maybe five dollars."

"There's no handicap board," another says, "but I'd say there are half a dozen golfers at three or under, maybe two dozen at seven or under."

"Some guys break eighty, and most break ninety," another says. "Or at least they did when they first drove up Magnolia Lane as a new member."

Once identified by the security guard at the sentry box, a member rides under a long canopy of magnolia trees to a grassy circle with yellow flowers in the shape of the United States with an Augusta National golf flagstick rising out of where Georgia would be. Then he strolls through the main entrance of what was once an indigo plantation house.

By the time you have reached the clubhouse, the guard has called the staff to inform them of your arrival and, if you are a member, your name is inserted into a plaque beside the front door. To the left is an oil painting of Robert Tyre Jones Jr., in his green coat, the club's patron saint, founder, co–course architect with Alister Mackenzie and Grand Slam golfer.

Beyond the switchboard desk and office on the right, a bronze bust of Dwight David Eisenhower, thirty-fourth President of the United States and the club's most celebrated member, glistens across the green-carpeted hall from an oil painting of Clifford Roberts in his green coat. Also on that wall are photo-engravings of Masters champions from Horton Smith in 1934 to Sandy Lyle in 1988.

Up a winding wooden staircase is the small Masters champions' locker room where Jack Nicklaus, Arnold Palmer, Tom Watson and Seve Ballesteros change their shoes at dark wooden lockers containing the green coats they wear, as honorary members, to dinner during Masters week.

Outside to the right is the men's grill, where peach cobbler is the favorite dessert. Just off the bar is the members' locker room where golfers who haven't won the Masters change their shoes during the tournament. Next door is the golf shop with its Masters souvenirs: green hats, green sweaters, green shirts, green slacks, green windbreakers, and beyond, the golf course itself stretching down a long grassy slope into scattered cathedrals of Georgia pine trees.

"For a golfer, it's heaven," one member says. "It's the ultimate."

It's also remote, one of the few complaints that members have.

"There are no direct flights from New York or Chicago to Augusta, so you've got to change planes in Atlanta," one member says. "It's a difficult place to get to unless you've got your own plane."

Many members do have their own planes, or the use of corporate jets. Even so, they might visit Augusta National only two or three times a year. But they enjoy it so much, that's enough.

"You're there to play golf, have dinner and a few drinks, play cards," one member says, "then get up and do it all over again."

Breakfast and lunch are served in the downstairs and upstairs dining rooms of the main clubhouse; dinner is in the Trophy Room where President Eisenhower, Bobby Jones and Cliff Roberts, each in their green coats, peer from oil paintings and where golf clubs that belonged to Jones and several Masters champions sparkle inside glass cases. Some members are lodged in motel-like suites just off the Trophy Room; others are in nine large white "cabins," each with a sitting room and at least four bedrooms, that drift down to the pines near the tenth tee; others are in small suites beyond the barber shop off the men's locker room.

"They can sleep ninety to a hundred guys, maybe more," one member says. "And when you arrive at your room, your green coat is hanging in your closet."

Members are asked to turn off the lights in the cabins by midnight. Nobody complains about that. But the influx of CEOs in recent years has stirred a quiet debate among some members disturbed by what they feel is a corporate takeover.

"We used to take in good guys," one member says, "but now the trend is to take the CEOs instead of just good guys. I think the club has lost a lot of its color."

"The CEOs are good guys," another says in rebuttal. "They're members because they understand golf and golf tradition, not because they're CEOs. If any of these CEOs wasn't a good guy and a golf guy, he wouldn't be a member."

Originally, the prerequisite for membership was that you had to be a "golf person." As Cliff Roberts once explained: "It is the membership that makes a club, rather than the other way around. Our roster has borne the names of many influential men. More important, from our club's standpoint, has been the high percentage of easy-to-like and interesting members who generate enjoyable companionship. There has always been a common bond throughout the membership, which can be attributed to a genuine devotion to the game of golf plus a concern for its best interests." Hord Hardin still holds to this ideal, but times have changed.

"It's a different club now than when President Eisenhower, Bob Jones and Cliff Roberts were around," says one member today. "Even with all the CEOs, we don't have three guys with the clout those three had."

Some clout exists. George Shultz, the Secretary of State during the Reagan Administration, is a member. So is Melvin Laird, once the Secretary of Defense and a longtime pal of President George Bush, an occasional golfer himself. But if Laird were to invite the President to Augusta National, the security surely would be tighter than it was the day in 1983 when President Reagan, as Shultz's guest, attracted an armed intruder who finally was apprehended in the golf shop.

Augusta National's tradition is even on its letterhead. The names of Jones (as "President in Perpetuity") and Roberts (as "Chairman in Memoriam") remain above that of Hord W. Hardin, the current chairman.

Once the president of the U.S. Golf Association, Hardin is a retired St. Louis attorney and banker with a better understanding of competitive golf than all members except Charlie Coe, a two-time U.S. Amateur champion, and Billy Joe Patton, who was leading the 1954 Masters after a hole-in-one at the sixth in the final round, but faded. As an amateur, Hardin qualified for the 1952 U.S. Open and four U.S. Amateurs. Now seventy-seven, he's the white-haired, soft-voiced gentleman in the green coat who, on behalf of the club, accepts the new Masters champion as an honorary member and "interviews" him on television. But to Augusta National members, he's the keeper of their keys, the one-man membership committee.

"You don't apply, a member suggests you to Hord," one says. "I think Hord talks to the executive committee, but I don't even know who's on the executive committee."

"They like to keep the membership around three hundred," another says. "If three or four guys die or resign in the course of a year, there's room for three or four new guys. Every once in a while, somebody really does resign, for whatever reason. But not often."

"You only get asked to join once," another says. "If you turn it down, that's it."

There are no women members and no junior members. Sons of members don't receive preferential treatment. And the best way to insure *not* getting into the club is to campaign for membership.

Occasionally a member will be expelled. During Roberts' reign, a member tried to persuade several other members to join a Florida golf club he had developed. To Roberts, that was treason. Stories still persist about members threatened with dismissal for such crimes as spilling a bottle of shampoo in the locker room. The uncertainty of membership keeps everyone on their best behavior.

"I never heard of any fights," one member says. "You just wouldn't do that."

"I don't know of any big bets on the golf course," another says. "Even in the gin or bridge games, I've never heard of anybody playing for more than a penny a point. Big betting is frowned on."

"If you drink too much or you're too noisy," another says, "you're gone."

"We're all appreciative of our membership. You don't bitch. If you want to suggest something about the course or the club, you do it very carefully. Maybe in a letter to Hord, but I think he listens more to the pros at the private Masters champions dinner than he does to any of us."

That sense of uncertainty annoys some members. They dislike the idea of always being on probation, so to speak.

"If you get a bill in late summer, you're still in," one member says. "If you don't get that bill, you're out."

That annual bill is relatively inexpensive. According to one member, the annual dues are under two thousand dollars and the initiation fee is around twenty thousand dollars, less than half of what some posh new clubs in Florida, Texas and California charge. There's no food minimum, and tipping is not allowed.

Thanks to income generated by the Masters Tournament, Augusta National assures its members of having "sufficient financial reserves to fund all operating expenditures and capital improvements." It also stipulates that it is "strictly a golf club that does not encourage social gatherings not related to golf." It has no tennis courts, no swimming pool, no corporate outings, no local Kiwanis luncheons, no weddings.

"It's not Augusta Country Club," one member says. "It's the Augusta National Golf Club."

With the emphasis on *National* and *Golf*. Only twenty-six members are from Augusta itself.

"It's like a college fraternity," one member says. "I'm a member at some other clubs, but when I go to Augusta, if a member on an adjacent fairway hasn't seen me in a while, he'll walk all the way over to my fairway to shake hands. I do it, too. They've shamed me into feeling like I ought to do it. But that never happens at other clubs. Guys might wave from another fairway, but they don't walk all the way over to shake hands. There's just more camaraderie at Augusta National than at most other clubs."

"If you belong ten or fifteen years," another says, "you'll know eighty percent of the members by their first name."

"Everybody from the waiters to the caddies to the people in the golf shop want you to have a good time," another says. "It's just a great warm feeling. You play golf, then you eat and drink and talk golf with all these guys. When you go there, you usually stay for three or four days. And lots of guys play thirty-six holes a day. Or they play eighteen and then go over to the little Par-3 Course."

"Most guys almost always play from the middle tees," another says. "Not many play from the back."

"Slow play is never a problem," another says. "Some days you might only have twelve or sixteen people."

Unlike most golf courses, Augusta National is closed during June, July, August and September.

Augusta National's schedule is backward from most other clubs: Its Opening Party is in October, its Closing Party in May. In between, it has a Governors Party in November and a Jamboree Party in March.

At each of those four-day gatherings, members only are allowed on the grounds (no wives, no exceptions), beginning at 6 P.M. on Wednesday through Sunday dinner. At the annual Thanksgiving Day Party, members are permitted to bring "their families." At other times, a member is limited to nine daily guests over October and November, another nine over March, April and May; there's no limit on daily guests in December, January and February.

"But you're only allowed three guests on the rounds at any one time," one member says. "If I leave, my guests have to leave." It's not unusual to hear stories of guests who were kept waiting at the front gates for the member to show up.

"I go there two or three times a year with clients," another says, "but it always creates mixed emotions. When those clients come back and rave about how great it was, my other clients say, 'When are you going to invite us?'"

While Masters champions get the green coat, they don't get the privileges of membership. If a former winner wants to play the course other than during tournament practice rounds, he must be a guest of a member. "After I first won in 1977," Tom Watson has said, "I assumed I could invite some people to play with me. I wasn't told I couldn't, but I was strongly advised against it. I got the message."

Members' wives also must follow the rules for "guests" and pay green fees accordingly. Some wives seldom go there; others often accompany their husbands.

"Unless your wife likes to play golf, it's hopeless," one member says. "There's nothing else for her to do in Augusta."

"My wife thinks it's the greatest," another says. "All the wives who like to go there know the guys are crazy about golf, but they're just as crazy about it as the guys are."

Since there are no women's tees, most women usually hit from the very front of the long tees.

"Wives play a lot more now than when Cliff Roberts was around," one member says. "Cliff used to say, 'On the golf course, women don't offend me, but stay out of my earshot and my eyesight.'"

Mulligans are allowed off the first tee, but playing in fivesomes or sixsomes is frowned upon. "And anything frowned upon," says a member, "you just don't do."

Green fees for guests are forty dollars each, except in December, January and February when they're twenty-five dollars each. The caddie fee is thirty dollars a bag. You can take a cart, but each player must also hire a caddie.

"Except for Masters week, the club menus never list prices," another says. "But judged against other clubs and resorts, Augusta National is not overly expensive. Your room is about ninety dollars a night before taxes. Dinner, from shrimp cocktail to steak and dessert, is about thirty dollars with wine. And they have the best wine cellar of any club in America."

"The wine is almost wholesale," another member says. "For a Château Lafite-Rothschild that would cost two hundred dollars in New York, you pay seventy-five dollars."

At the annual Jamboree Party, the wine is on the winners. But they can afford it. For what one member calls a three-hundred-dollar ante, a big winner can win as much as two thousand dollars. The rules of amateur status evidently do not apply at Augusta National.

"That's a two-man deal over four days," one member says. "But whatever you win, it'll cost you almost that much to buy the wine. At the other club parties, you're in a different foursome each day but the way the golf shop groups you is just outstanding. You have no say in it, but I've never heard anybody complain. In those other parties, you might win two hundred fifty dollars."

Tee times are never needed, not even at the Jamboree Party, which attracts at least one hundred members.

"They use the first and tenth tees, and it seems to work out," one member says. "The only really crowded day of the year at Augusta National is the Monday after the Masters ends. Most of the members have been there for the Masters and they all want to play that Monday."

Dozens of members seek to serve on the various Masters committees. Others prefer to avoid Augusta National that week.

"If I don't go," one member says, "it makes it easier to tell my friends that I can't get them Masters tickets."

Even for Augusta National members, the limit is four Masters badges, which they are allowed to purchase at the established price, ninety dollars this year. Once a member suggested a dear friend, a distinguished personality who had never attended the Masters, be permitted to buy two badges. But the member was told that those two badges would come from his usual allotment of four.

That wasn't exactly what the member had in mind. Sorry, dear friend. That is also what it's like to be an Augusta National member.

—1989

Teravainen

and

Locomotion

Michael Bamberger

For a long time, in the agate type of newspaper columns, I had followed the distinctive Finnish name of Peter Teravainen. I knew from golfing friends that he had been born and raised in Massachusetts and educated at Yale, and that he was living in Singapore and studying Buddhism with his Singaporean Buddhist wife. Teravainen was described as a hard-swinging, theory-spewing touring professional in his mid-thirties, the son of a gym teacher and a nurse, who reveled in the rough-hewn golfing life he had made for himself playing the European tour. I had written to Peter before our departure, asking him for a job as his caddie. I cited my previous work experience. He wrote back and said he'd take me on for two tournaments. After that, I'd be on my own.

I met him for the first time two days before the start of the Mediterranean Open in St. Raphael. Peter turned out to be a heartily built bespectacled man of nearly six feet, with thinning brownish-blond hair, strong tanned hands, and a lined, intelligent face anchored by a sturdy nose. He had small teeth, a broad forehead, pale blue eyes, and perfectly manicured fingernails, which somehow prevented him from looking haggard.

"I play a full schedule," Teravainen said on our first day together. We were climbing up and down the hills of a contrived Robert Trent Jones development course—the venue for the Mediterranean Open—and I had his bag on my back. I was a caddie again, and I was happy. "I feel that if there's a golf tournament somewhere and they're offering money and I can get in, I should be there." In the previous week, Peter had played in a small tournament in Girona, Spain, and after it he made the two-day drive to St. Raphael in a two-door rental car, sharing the cramped space with his traveling partner, Bill Malley, a former U.S. Public Links champion; Bill's wife, Rose; two huge golf bags; and a half a dozen suitcases. Prior to Girona, Peter had planned to play in a tournament in Dubai, United Arab Emirates, but it had been canceled—Peter thought unnecessarily—because of the war in the Gulf. So he played instead in a tournament in Singapore, his adopted homeland.

He was starting his tenth year on the European tour. He first came over in 1982 because he couldn't earn a spot on the lucrative U.S. tour. Though there was far less money on the European tour, there was far less competition, too. Before long, he was a regular.

In 1984, Peter played twenty-three tournaments in twenty-three weeks, with the burden of rugged travel between stops—ferries, rental cars, trains, buses, stand-by flights—always with the bag on his back and a suitcase in each hand. He thought nothing of playing in ten or eleven consecutive events. In Europe, most players regard five or six straight weeks as beyond grueling and on the U.S. tour four or five is considered the outer limit. Even three successive tournaments can turn a player's brain to mush: in a professional stroke-play competition, money changes hands on every shot and the stress can be overwhelming. To play as much as he wanted to play, Peter had to find ways to reduce the stress. That's why several years ago he stopped gambling during practice rounds. Some players want something at stake during their practice games so they can simulate the emotions of tournament play. Others need to make money; on the European tour there are still players trying to pay their motel rents through extracurricular play, as there once were on the U.S. tour. Peter's retirement from gambling put him in the minority. But he figured his mind was burdened enough during the four competitive rounds that comprise the typical tour event (two qualifying rounds, followed by a thirty-six-hole cut that eliminates about half the field, and then two more rounds). He viewed practice rounds as a chance to commune with the course. Often he played by himself, first thing in the morning, without even a warm-up. Before long, I realized that some of Peter's colleagues thought of him as antisocial, but that was a misunderstanding. He was just trying to preserve himself.

A friend once suggested to Peter that he might play better, and make more money, by competing in fewer events, but Peter ignored the suggestion, even though he acknowledged that it might be true. He believed that the life of a touring professional must include struggle: play hard, sleep rough, travel cheap, carry cash.

Teravainen developed certain attitudes toward his profession early in his career and they have stuck. In 1980 and 1981, he attempted to play the U.S. tour, but his game was too undeveloped, and he found himself always scraping to get to the next stop. He thought of his hardscrabble existence as a sort of apprenticeship until the day he realized it was, in fact, a way of life. That day came in the winter of 1980, during a practice round for a Monday qualifying round for the Bay Hill Classic, a tour event in Orlando, Florida. Peter and two other young players had joined up with Mike Hill, a thickly callused veteran. They were sitting on a bench, waiting for the group in front of them to get out of range when the discussion turned to John Cook.

"Who in the hell is John Cook?" Hill said.

Teravainen was surprised; he figured everybody knew who John Cook was.

"He's a former U.S. Amateur champ," somebody piped up cheerfully. Cook won the title in 1978, the year Teravainen graduated from Yale.

Hill thought the comment came from Peter and stared at him. "Amateur golf," he said, "don't mean shit."

Peter was embarrassed, but he immediately understood Hill's meaning: amateur golf was a pleasant diversion; professional golf was a life, a life of struggle that allowed no time for niceties like amateurism. For Teravainen, that one terse comment from Hill proved to be important in his professional education. It helped him develop his credo.

Since turning professional in 1979, Peter has had one goal above all others: to make a living solely by playing tournament golf, and to make it without the accoutrements common to the modern pro. As much as he can, he tries to go it alone. When I met Peter, he had no teaching guru, no travel agent, no manager, no psychologist, no equipment endorsements, no professional caddie, no clothing contract. He wanted to stay independent. He felt corrupting influences lurked everywhere.

I did not see him in danger of being offered a clothing deal. For any clothing manufacturer, an association with Peter would be dangerous. There was nobody left on the European tour, and probably nobody left in golf, who dressed like Peter. He was a fashion renegade.

Starting in the 1960s, and right through the middle of the 1980s, there was a uniform for the professional golfer adopted worldwide: snug polyester pans with built-in belts, often plaid but sometimes brown, worn with Munsingwear shirts, usually white or yellow, with stiff pointed collars.

Then there was a revolution. Golfers, lagging several years behind the rest of the free world, discovered the so-called preppie look: loose cotton pants, often khaki-colored, with four pockets and without a built-in belt, worn with loose-fitting polo shirts with soft, rounded collars. (Since then, there has been a counterwave, a drift toward loudness affecting only those players who will wear anything if they are paid enough money: shirts patterned with large, bright, dizzying geometric shapes, lavender sweaters with two-foot-high nineteenth-century golfers embroidered on the fronts.)

Peter took no part in the revolution. Had his sartorial tastes been influenced by the stereotypical dress codes of his schools—before Yale, he had attended the Tabor Academy, a prep school in Marion, Massachusetts—you might have expected him to feel right at home in the khakis and polos. If he had been modestly rebellious, you might have expected him to go one step further, to preppie dishabille: wear the khakis rumpled, wear the polo shirts faded, maybe wear red socks. But Peter, who attended both Tabor and Yale on scholarship, was a reactionary: he borrowed his style straight from Mike Hill, circa 1970, and held on to it. The collars on Peter's golf shirts were stiff enough to accommodate a tie. His favorite pants, made of wholly unnatural fibers, were slate gray and shiny, with an off-white pinstriping, tight at the hips and thighs, then slightly flaring from the knee to the tops of his shoes. Great trousers. He wore them twice in that first week on the Côte d'Azur.

His swing was distinctive, too. Teravainen belonged to the brute force school; off the tee, he was as long as anybody. Occasionally during his swing he grunted. Teravainen had so much unspent energy at the traditional concluding point for a full swing—hands neck-high, with the shaft of the club over the shoulder and pointing down the back—that he sometimes swung the club again, hard and in reverse, returning to his starting point. Among his colleagues, Peter's swing had a nickname: the Whiplash. Once, in a tournament in Switzerland, Peter swung so hard he fainted and in the fall sprained an arm. Peter's swing was unteachable. It came from within.

People said that if he refined his swing, there was no telling what he might do. But Peter was not interested. He expected that the refining period would cost him money—professional golfers are usually flubs when they are making changes—and by the time the adjustments took effect, *if* they took effect, Peter feared he would be too old for tournament golf. Moreover, seeking refinement would have required Peter to have a teacher, and that was not something he wanted.

That's unusual. Virtually every player on the U.S. tour has a person to whom they entrust their swing. Most players on the European tour, although a smaller percentage than on the U.S. tour, have golfing mentors, too. There are tournament weeks in which Faldo has his teacher, David Leadbetter, follow him around for eight or more hours a day: four on the course, a couple on the practice tee, a couple on the putting green. Bob Torrance—the father of Sam Torrance, a perennial Ryder Cup player—was formerly a Scottish club professional who now travels the European tour full time, giving instruction to a score of players, including Woosnam. Sandy Lyle, a former Masters and British Open champion, returns to his father, a retired club professional. There are notable exceptions. Ballesteros is largely self-taught and has no regular coach, although he'll talk to just about anybody. Olazábal is completely self-tutored. If he has a problem, he works it out himself. Teravainen's just the same.

Peter has his own method. His hands are low at address. In his grip, Peter's left thumb is exposed, in contrast to classical instruction, which preaches that the left thumb must be covered by the right hand. In his take-away, Teravainen defies the modern method, for he does not fan the club face open. Instead, he brings the clubhead back in a shut position, with the toe of the club pointing to *terra firma*, a somewhat Palmeresque move. Peter has a massive hip turn and shoulder turn and at impact, and in a blur, he throws his hands through the ball with a mighty, last-second flick. *Boom!* His swing is not lovely or pretty or poetic. It's deadly.

From the time he took up the game at age nine, through his graduation from Yale, Peter, for the most part, taught himself. He was the Ivy League golf champion in his junior and senior years and he was one of the better amateur golfers in New England in the late 1970s. But his game was not nearly advanced enough to earn him a living as a touring pro, which is what he wanted to be. So, after college he sought professional counsel for the first time. Peter drove to Florida in a borrowed van and took a job as a cocktail waiter at a rambling old golf resort called the Belleview Biltmore in Clearwater. When the Yale men on their annual winter trip to the hotel discovered that the person fetching their drinks was a fellow Blue attempting professional golf, they'd chuckle and ask, "Seriously, what is it that you intend to do with your life?" Teravainen didn't stick around to answer. He was playing golf every morning with a bartender and a piano player, hitting balls every afternoon and taking lessons thrice-weekly from a man named Irv Schloss. The first time Schloss looked at Peter's unorthodox, closed backswing he said, "You've got the best backswing of any player I've ever seen. Never let anybody talk you out of it." That was the major thought Peter took from Schloss, who died in 1984. Peter has not had a teacher since.

Unlike most professionals, Peter never sought an equipment contract, even after his best year, the year of Schloss's death, when he finished fifteenth on the European tour's Order of Merit. (The Order of Merit is the European tour's gently worded equivalent of the U.S. tour's "money list." Peter's fifteenth-place finish in 1984 earned him £40,503, equal then to about $55,000; Jack Nicklaus finished fifteenth on the U.S. money list that same year and won $272,595.) Teravainen plays Ping clubs, and has since 1981, because he likes them, because they're free, and because they come without compromising encumbrances.

Ping writes checks at the conclusion of the season to the players who use their clubs; the size of the check is based solely on how much the player earns in tournament play. The percentage rises as a player earns more—top players can double their income with the year-end bonus, while middle-of-the-pack players might increase their earnings by 10 percent with the post-season Ping check. But the company has no star system, no special contracts for big names. Every player begins the season under identical terms. The Ping player is not obligated to appear in any advertising or play in any corporate outings or appear at any social functions. Peter liked that. The Ping player is required to do only two things: employ at least nine Ping clubs, out of the fourteen clubs to which the rules limit a player, and carry the clubs in a Ping golf bag, an unaesthetic white, plastic sack with the company name pasted on the sides, lettered in a type style one might call computer text. Peter didn't find his standards jeopardized by any of that.

Peter didn't often need the cumbersome Ping bag, so the company gave him a small collapsible carry bag, the same model used by weekend golfers. He employed it when he caddied for himself, or when his wife, Veronica, caddied for him. He seldom employed one of the hundred or so roaming caddies who travel the tour; the few that he liked were out of his budget. And Veronica, living with her mother in Singapore and working as a United Airlines flight attendant, wasn't often around. Sometimes Peter hired a local teenager to carry his bag, but often, especially on the Continent, where the game is still taking root, local caddies weren't available. In those instances, Peter didn't mind carrying his own bag, which the European tour rules allow. (On the U.S. tour, each player is required to have his own caddie.) He figured he played just as well without a caddie as with one. As he explained this to me, I had the feeling that his approach to the use of caddies was just like all his other golfing decisions, ultimately rooted in his desire to keep costs down, to make it on his own, to have total independence, to succeed by himself, and to share blame for his failures with nobody.

I left my former life behind the moment I threw the strap of Peter's big Ping bag over my left shoulder. At the *Philadelphia Inquirer* I was in The Newspaper Guild and every week I received a paycheck. On the European tour, I was at Peter's mercy. With the British economy in a tailspin, there were scores of men, and a few women, traveling the tour, seeking caddie jobs. Certainly, there were more caddies than jobs. The handwriting was plain: if I could not earn a full-time job with Peter, I'd have trouble. And without steady caddie work, the whole concept of the trip was endangered.

Peter told me that he was an easy loop, but that was only his opinion. I fast realized that he was superstitious, fastidious, and fin-icky. And I fast realized that whatever caddie skills I had developed on the U.S. tour in 1985 had been pushed to the farthest recesses of my brain. I had to get back my caddie legs in a hurry, and to reac-quaint myself with the caddie mentality.

Early on, Peter told me that the clubs were rattling too much when I walked. I wanted to say, "Peter, don't you realize that the rhythmic clanking of clubheads is one of the great sounds produced by the game?" Instead I wrapped a towel around the clubs in a ser-pentine pattern, held a hand around the towel, and kept the clubs, and myself, quiet.

At the start of our first round together Peter handed me three new balls—balata-covered, one-hundred-compression Titleist 384s, each stamped with the numeral 8—and I was expected to give him the balls, as he needed them, in the particular order in which he wanted them. I found it difficult to distinguish one ball from the other, but Peter did not: he had custom-marked each ball with a series of elaborate pencil dots—the balls had no inherent order, but he had assigned them one. I think it was his attempt to reduce the innate capriciousness of the game.

Yet at other times, he succumbed to the game's mysticism. Peter played with balls stamped with an 8 because the numeral eight, he learned from his wife, was an ancient Chinese symbol for prosperity. Veronica also taught him the dangerous potency of red: Peter felt that wearing red set him up for an extraordinary round, one way or the other. Clothes, in general, were powerful to him: if he started a round in the cool of early morning in a heavy wool sweater and played well, the sweater stayed on, no matter how hot the day grew, until he made a bogey. He was particular about eating, too. If a specific breakfast served as a prelude to a 69 on a Thursday, which is what he shot in our first round together, he'd have the identical breakfast on Friday. "When you're going good," he said, "you don't change a thing." When Peter was on a cut-making roll, he didn't change drivers, putters, or even headcovers. I wondered if he extended that policy to caddies.

That Thursday opening round at St. Raphael went well. The weather was sunny and pleasant and Peter was relaxed and hitting the straight ball. On that day, he *was* an easy loop. Easy day, easy loop. But the Friday round, during which a steady rain fell unceasingly, was a different matter.

The ground was so wet that every time the ball landed it became encrusted with mud. A golf ball is difficult enough to hit without a half-ounce of glob sticking to its side, so the tournament officials invoked a rule allowing players to lift, clean, and place their ball when it was on the fairway. On one hole, Peter marked the position of his ball, picked it up, and tossed it to me for cleaning. While I wiped the dirt off and returned the ball to white, he walked ahead a hundred yards or so, umbrella in hand, to survey his ensuing shot. I put the ball in my pocket, to keep it warm, safe, and dry. Eventually, Peter returned with his palm stuck out—he wanted his ball back. I remember thinking, *He's waiting; he's waiting; don't keep him waiting.* I shoved a hand into a pocket and pulled out a ball and placed it on his outstretched palm. He returned the ball to the marked spot on the fairway and pulled a club from the bag.

Suddenly a realization came over me and I felt sick. In my haste I had shoved the wrong hand into the wrong pocket and pulled out

the wrong ball! A player can't change a ball during a hole unless the
ball is damaged, and only then with the approval of his playing partners. If Peter played the wrong ball, he'd be cheating! I alerted Peter
to my mistake.

Peter examined the pencil dots on the wrong ball while I produced the correct one. He was kind. All he said was, "Never put the
ball in your pocket." He sounded like a Kennedy: *Neva put the ball in
yaw pocket.* That was it.

I didn't think I could do much worse; I had nearly caused him a
two-shot penalty, and probably incalculable psychic harm. But a few
holes later I goofed again, and worse.

Peter routinely drank four or five cups of coffee before a round
and he flew around the course. To keep up with him between shots
I practically had to run. The worse he played, the faster he walked.
And he was not playing well in that second round.

On the tenth hole, he drove his ball under a tree. At first, he
considered punching out with a 7-iron. He gave the club a few
waggles and decided he'd be better off with an 8, so he handed the
7 back to me. He played his shot (hitting the ball fat, striking about
a half-inch of earth first) and set off after it. I replaced the divot
and went chasing after him. Eventually, he finished the hole and
we moved on.

As we gathered on the eleventh tee, I saw a man wearing knee-
high rubber boots and waxed jacket, yelling in French, waving a golf
club, and walking fast in our direction. Peter said to his two playing
partners, "Anybody lose a club?" He said to me, "You lose a club?"

I was just starting to say, "I don't think so," when I dipped my
head into the bag and saw, to my horror, that there were only thirteen clubs in it. When I looked up the Frenchman was on the tee,
standing in front of me, holding Peter's 7-iron and smiling idiotically.
One of the other caddies snickered. I felt myself turning red. I knew
that within a day virtually everybody on the European tour would
know that I had lost a 7-iron.

Did you hear what that guy working for Teravainen did?
Which guy, that ganky-looking American?
Yeah—he lost Tera's 7-iron!

You kidding me?

No, he lost the bloody thing—hasn't been seen since.

Caddies would tell players. Players would tell wives. Wives would tell other wives. Those wives would tell their husbands. Those husbands would tell their caddies. Before long, the 7-iron would turn into a putter, and the stories would have Peter finishing his round putting with his driver or his sand wedge or something. It dawned on me that if Peter fired me—which he should have, by all rights—I'd never find work on that tour again. My whole dream—to caddie my way to Scotland—was suddenly in jeopardy, to say nothing of the precarious balance of our financial existence, thousands of miles from home, which we had left with a big send-off party. Even if we returned home, my newspaper job wasn't available to me for another year. *I had signed papers, legal documents!* I couldn't get any air into my lungs. How was I going to explain to my wife of four months that I was a caddie failure! Stifling heat surged through my body. I wanted to sink into the soft Mediterranean soil. Peter said nothing. I could only imagine what he was thinking.

I don't know how I lost the club. Either it bounced out of the bag while I was running or I never put it back in the bag after the exchange of clubs under the tree. At that point, I figured only one of two things could happen. Either Peter would sack me, or I would improve. Worse was not possible.

O

I managed to go blunder-free in the third and fourth rounds of the Mediterranean Open, and when I asked Peter what time to meet him for the start of week two—the Balearic Islands Open on the island of Majorca, 120 miles off the east coast of Spain—he didn't say don't bother. So late on the Sunday night after the tournament, my wife and I, along with forty other caddies and a dozen players, flocked to the St. Raphael train station to catch the overnight train to Spain. No food till Port Bou.

The Mediterranean Open had concluded in mid-afternoon and the train out of town didn't depart until nearly midnight; caddie wallets were stuffed with post-tournament cash and the bars were open. These facts did not promote tranquility. When I saw an English-speaking caddie sticking his off-centered nose in the thin face of a French-speaking station official—they were debating the fine points of the open container law—I prayed that he would not be in our compartment.

My prayers were answered. Christine and I were in the same car as the barrister-caddie, but four or five compartments down. When we pushed open the door to our computer-assigned quarters, we found that the two lower bunks and the floor space in between them had already been claimed. A young professional golfer, an Englishman named Steve Bottomley, was on the left bunk, and his brother and caddie, Ian, was on the right. Sleeping on the floor in between them was the Bottomley golf bag encased in a canvas travel pouch. It looked like a gigantic cocoon. We shoved in our luggage, and my golf bag, and climbed in.

"How'd you go?" Steve asked me. He saw my bag and assumed that I was a player. He wanted to know how I had fared at the Mediterranean.

"I'm a caddie," I said.

"Traveling with your golf bag," Steve said skeptically.

"That's right."

"And your wife."

"Right."

"Are you sure you're not on holiday?"

I was quite sure of that. Problems at work consumed my thoughts.

There was conversation for a while, but the Bottomleys and Christine were asleep before the train was an hour out of St. Raphael. For me, sleep was impossible. The week's numbers kept running through my head. Teravainen had shot 69–75–72–74, a total of 290 strokes, 6 over par. He finished in a tie for twenty-ninth place, the middle of the pack, and won £3,540, which in February of 1991 was worth $7,000. (The Gulf War had weakened the dollar overseas; in late February, a pound was equal to nearly two dollars.) Ian Woosnam won the tournament and £66,000 by taking eleven fewer shots than Peter over the seventy-two holes. In my mind, I had no trouble slicing twelve shots off Peter's four-day score. Given another chance, balls driven into trees, onto rocks, and into streams, might have found fairways. Given better fortune, shots that bounced off hillocks and into bunkers might have bounced onto greens. This is the optimism upon which all golf is rooted.

I am optimistic by nature. Still, I wondered if I would have a job after Majorca. I knew Peter had to make the cut there if I were to have a chance of staying on his bag. Teravainen was a journeyman. In more than eleven years of professional golf, representing hundreds of tournaments, he had never won an event on any of the four major golf tours in the world: the U.S. tour, the European tour, the Japanese tour, and the Australian tour. His dream was to win one. His reality was that he made his living by making thirty-six-hole cuts. In 1990, Peter had entered thirty-one tournaments and made the cut in only eighteen of them. If you don't make the cut, you don't make a paycheck. Expenses are all out of pocket. The cutthroat, Darwinian capitalism of tournament golf was immensely appealing to Peter. Shoot score X, make amount Y. Peter ate numbers. He studied stock market tables. He studied racing forms. He had cut scores calculated long before tournament officials did. He had majored in Economics at Yale and he valued numerical analyses. But he believed in charms, too. I felt that if he made the cut in Majorca—*"two in a row with Bamberger; not bad"*—he wouldn't be so quick to dismiss me. That was my hope, anyway.

I did not put up a brave front for Christine. In the trough of our bed in St. Raphael, I had told her about the missing 7-iron, and about giving Peter the wrong ball. She knew my employment status was precarious. She was supportive. She never said, "Oh—I have married a caddie incompetent!" She told me not to worry. She said she could start a golf tour laundry service. Or a traveling tour barber shop. She said we'd get by.

I looked at her on the train's bouncing bunk bed. Its scratchy sheets did not bother her in the slightest. She was sleeping soundly, contentedly. As the train hurtled through the night and past the hamlets of coastal France, I enjoyed the simple fact that my wife and

I were sharing sleeping quarters with strangers. We were traveling loose. Our married life was off to an adventurous start.

I was afraid to go to sleep. The Bottomleys had warned us that thieving was common on overnight trains. They were sleeping with their pants on, and with their passports, watches, and wallets stuffed in their front pockets. Ian Bottomley, I noticed, didn't even risk taking off his expensive cowboy boots before retiring.

In the middle of the night, I saw those cowboy boots revolve 180 degrees, from heel up to toe up, and Ian—somehow sensing that I was awake and still reliving the strokes of the Mediterranean Open— suddenly asked, "So how'd your man go this week?"

I was pleased to have somebody with whom to talk, but for a moment I felt a conversational stymie: I could not regard Teravainen as my *man*. A caddie's man is his regular boss. The itinerant caddie has a *bag*. As in, "Whose bag you on this week?" By using the word *man*, Ian was paying me a compliment. He had assumed my job was steady. I didn't want to bore him with the small traumas of my professional life, so I said, "Tied for twenty-ninth. How'd you guys do?" In the language of caddies, *you guys* has an even higher standing than *your man*; *you guys* suggests that the caddie and the player are a single entity.

"Fortieth," Ian said. "Didn't make a putt, didn't hit a fairway."

I asked Ian how long he was out for. A tour caddie is *out*, until he returns home for more traditional work. Ian said his plan was to caddie for his brother for as long as the British economy slumbered. He had ambivalent feelings about the job, though. "Of all the arts," he said, "caddying's the most frustrating."

I asked him why.

"There's nothing really you can do for your man. You realize that at the end of the day. You can give him good yardages, tell him how you see the knobs of the greens, is it uphill, is it downhill, all that. You can throw your grass clippings in the air until the sky falls down, tell him the direction of the breeze and how hard it's blowing. You can warn him that he's got a flier lie or that the green is as hard as a motorway or that the pin position is for suckers only. You can make all the calculations, do all your considering. You can put the club in his hand, tell him to hit the soft six or the hard seven. But you cannot take the bloody swing for him."

I told Ian I wouldn't want to hit any shot for my bossman.

"I would," Ian said. "I play off two. When I'm playing well, I can beat Steve. I know his tendencies, his weaknesses. If the wind is blowing a certain way, if the ball is sitting a certain way, if it's a shot I know he's not comfortable with, I'd take that shot. Sometimes in a tournament I can predict the exact outcome of the shot before he makes it. When it's just the two of us in a friendly bounce game, he's more likely to make these stunning shots that just amaze you. That's because when we play at home there's no analysis. You just take in the shot: your eyes tell your head what to do, your head tells your body, and your body makes the shot. It's easy. In practice rounds before the tournament, same thing. It's the analysis that kills you. Once a tournament starts, it's like, 'OK, where's my left knee supposed to be at impact?' Who cares? How are you going to feel the shot when you're worried about the position of your left knee at impact?"

I listened attentively. Christine continued to sleep. So did Steve. The train roared on, Spain-bound. I suggested to Ian that maybe these seemingly minor technical swing fascinations were critical to success at a certain level of the game, that they gave the top player something manageable on which to blame success or failure.

"That's a theory," Ian said. That meant he didn't agree. "The thing with golf is that some people take to it like a fish to water and some people never figure it out. Anybody who's playing on one of the four major tours, they took to the game straight off. By the time these guys are old enough to get in a pub, they have *swings,* good, mature swings, swings with personalities all their own. Once the swing is developed, it doesn't change much. The magazines get all this yardage out of how David Leadbetter did a complete remake of Nick Faldo's swing, and that's how Faldo was able to twice win our Open and twice win your Masters in the space of three years. What are they talking about? The plane of his swing got a tiny bit flatter. That's it. The main thing is the head. Is it off? Is it on? His is obviously on.

He's got good thoughts going. I guarantee you that when he's on the golf course standing over his ball he's thinking only about executing the shot the way he wants to execute it. He's seeing the overall shot, the overall swing that's going to produce it, not a bunch of little pieces. Must be, or he wouldn't be making the shots he's making. That's the thing about Nicklaus. He started this idea of standing behind the ball and seeing in your mind's eye the entire shot before you get going. Now everybody does it. But a lot of players just go through the motions, they're not really seeing it. They're thinking, 'Do I have my left knee in the right position at impact,' or, 'Will that sponsor come through,' or, 'Does my shirt match my sweater.' People say Faldo's aloof on the golf course. You'd be aloof too if your brain was flooded with pictures like his is. This is high-level stuff, what Faldo's doing. People are so quick to dismiss it because they don't like his personality. They think he's a robot. They don't get it. He's made a breakthrough. There's probably only one level of golf higher than what Faldo is doing. I don't even know if this highest level is attainable, least not on a regular basis."

This is the nature of golf conversation. You start off with something simple. *How'd you guys do?* Soon you're hiking in the brain's most inaccessible hills. Highest level, higher than what Faldo is doing? "What, what is it?" I asked eagerly.

Ian didn't answer right away, and for a moment I was afraid that he wouldn't answer at all. Some people—Hogan among them, I believe—know certain secret things about the game that they don't want to reveal, not out of selfishness, but out of a fear that once the idea is spoken, it will be stripped of its validity, because no one else will understand it. In time, Ian Bottomley answered.

"You've probably experienced it, here and there. I have. The highest level is to be standing over your ball, playing your shot, and to be thinking about nothing at all." He paused. "Think about it," Ian said.

And with that, he spun around again and returned to sleep, leaving me in the dust of our perplexing little talk. What do you think about to think about nothing? And what was it that he said, that by the time you're old enough to get into a pub, your swing has a personality of its own? Does that mean if you're twenty-one years old—or, in my case, thirty-one years old—and your swing is still badly flawed your chances for improvement are improbable? If that is true, I thought, my game is in trouble. Can a swing really have a personality? I supposed that it could: some swings are jumpy, some are lazy, some are efficient, some are wasteful, some look good but accomplish little, some look ugly but are effective. Peter's swing was loaded with personality. My own had elements of a personality—rushed and tense. But were those the fundamental elements of my personality? I didn't think so; I hoped not. What happens if your personality is poorly suited to golf? Do you have to develop a personality well-suited to golf to become good at golf? Can you change your personality? What type of person am I, anyhow? Do I reveal my true self through my golf? My head swam. Finally, I felt drowsy. The train pushed forward.

—1992

The Cardiac Cliffs

Thomas Boswell

Ask every professional on tour what his five favorite golf courses are in the world, and the one name that will be on everybody's list is Pebble Beach.

TOM WATSON, PRACTICING FOR THE U.S. OPEN

Pebble Beach, California, June 16, 1982—

As he walked to the tee of the tiny, precipitous, sand-locked, surf-rocked, wind-wracked 110-yard seventh at the Pebble Beach Golf Links, Jack Nicklaus paused to look at the vista before him. Standing at the top of the tip of this peninsula, Nicklaus, playing a practice round before the U.S. Open, had the full panoramic sweep of Pebble Beach around him.

To his right was a sheer cliff drop down to Stillwater Cove, and, in the distance, the cypress-wooded promontory of Pescadero Point. To his left was blue-black, kelp-clogged Carmel Bay lapping on a mile of white Monastery Beach and, beyond that, the long rocky reach of Point Lobos. Around the tee was impenetrable barranca, full of wild-flowers, Scotch broom and sea grasses. On those huge ocean rocks not washed with waves were perched hundreds of sea birds. Behind Nicklaus, the foothills of the Gabilan Range began their climb, their heights covered with fog. Straight ahead lay the Pacific.

"This sure is beautiful," was all he said.

Like many who come here, Nicklaus has learned the foolishness of trying to hem in Pebble Beach with words. Robert Louis Stevenson called this Monterey Peninsula "the greatest meeting of land and water" anywhere on earth—and Stevenson got around some.

Even photographs are inadequate to the sight. They catch only a narrow arc of the place's 360-degree impact. And, inevitably, they tend to flatten what is, in reality, a wild and craggy place. Take two steps off the right side of the eighth fairway and it's two hundred feet straight down to the rocks and driftwood.

Occasionally, something in the world of sport actually surpasses expectations. Once in a while, Peggy Lee's wrong; that isn't all there is. Pebble Beach is natural, wild, stark and capricious. That's why it is, perhaps, the ideal U.S. Open venue. In February, at the annual Bing Crosby Pro-Am, Pebble Beach is wet, green, close-cropped and pretty, even if the weather is raw. But, in summer, with high rough and the general brownish tinge of longer grasses, Pebble Beach has the mean look it deserves. "It reminds you of a lot of British Open and Scottish courses. Yup, lotta Scottish golf in this course," said Watson. "From the seventeenth tee, for example, all you see is sky and ocean and flat grasses. It's a beautiful blue-gray setting."

"This is, basically, an unscorable golf course," says Craig Stadler. "It doesn't need to be tricked up or protected. If you can keep it in the fairway, you've got a shot at a real good round. If you don't, you're in a lot of trouble."

Rounds here have a compelling internal chemistry because Pebble Beach has such a well-defined personality. As Watson says, "There are a lot of birdies early on the first seven holes, and a lot of bad scores late."

The first five holes are completely inland and, by contrast with what follows, bland. The first, third and fourth are all short par 4s of less than 400 yards, the snug fourth being only 325 yards—just a 1-iron and a flip wedge; but all punish a shoddy drive severely. The 506-yard par-5 second hole is, for top pros, a gimme birdie hole. "This course has no weak holes, except number two," says Watson. Even the notorious 170-yard fifth hole, sarcastically called "the only dogleg par three in the world" because the tee shot had to be hooked to avoid trees, has a new tee and now provides a fair shot.

The truth of Pebble Beach begins with the majestic, uphill 515-yard sixth hole that begins in dense inland woods and culminates in a headlands heaven. In minutes, you've gone from the calm and familiar to a stretch of breathtaking holes that are the heart of this links. If Augusta has its Amen Corner, then Pebble Beach has its Cardiac

Cliffs. From the seventh through tenth holes, tournaments here are almost always decided.

The treacherous, wind-beaten 110-yard seventh sets the tone. Here, the balls start bouncing off rocks into the Pacific. Here, Sam Snead took a putter and deliberately bounced his ball down the hill into the front bunker to avoid an honest shot.

The eighth, ninth, and tenth may be the best stretch of hard par 4s on earth. He who comes to the eighth tee without a cushion of previous birdies may well end up wrecked; "Homero Blancos played the first seven holes six-under-par in 1972," recalls Watson, "but he finished the round even-par."

The 433-yard eighth is the most visually intimidating hole in America. The uphill tee shot is blind. The second shot must clear a 160-yard gorge that is so deep and beautiful that the only defense is not to look at it. From the green, approaching players look like specs as they swing atop a bluff.

The 467-yard ninth and 424-yard tenth—with their fairways tilting ridiculously toward the cliffs and ocean on the right—are actually tougher holes. They are impossible; the eighth just looks that way.

From the eleventh through the sixteenth, Pebble Beach regains its sanity once more, weaving inland again, but this time offering stern pars, not birdies. Even the 565-yard par-5 fourteenth hole is an honest par.

Finally, comes the signature finish. The 209-yard seventeenth, into prevailing winds, looks bleak, barren and intractable. Every other hole is aesthetically pleasing: the nasty, charmless seventeenth is, in the best British sense, hideously ugly. "Take your bogey—if you're lucky—and shut up," it says.

The eighteenth is better. Better than what? Better than you think it is. Better than its photographs or its reputation. And its reputation is that it's the best finishing hole on earth. What TV doesn't show is the complete sense of desolation and vulnerability on the exposed tee. All around you is crashing surf. Between there and home is 548 yards of prehistoric sandstone and tumbled rock. You know the fairway is way over there on the right, but every misguiding instinct in the subconscious is going to pull you left to oblivion. Pros say this might be the most difficult shot to align properly in all of golf.

The man who comes to this seventy-second hole on Sunday of a U.S. Open and survives it for victory, is, in the truest sense, the American champion, because he has won the title on the course that may be this country's most beautiful—and thorough—test.

—1982

Westchester Keeps a Tournament and Loses an All-Male Sanctuary

Marcia Chambers

One expects that Oakland Hills will resolve this problem before the 1996 Open. In case the good men there are still thinking about it, they ought to know what happened at Westchester Country Club in Rye, New York, in 1992. Westchester has been the site of the Buick Classic for several years, a PGA Tour event that attracts television coverage and thousands of fans to the club each June.

When the Buick Classic arrived in 1992, it was met with picket signs held aloft by members of the National Organization for Women. The signs spoke of discriminatory tee times and the men's grill. Buick was stunned. Stunned.

Women, they knew, bought cars—their cars.

Buick wrote to the tournament's sponsors, telling them that they would withdraw as chief commercial backer unless the club opened the men's grill to women.

The club decided to end the men's grill, a gesture that drew protests from some five hundred members, who petitioned the board to retain the grill. Faced with such overwhelming opposition, the club confronted a dilemma: give up the Classic and its lucrative financial benefits, which helped to offset the club's expenses, or integrate the grill.

"Westchester Country Club is a private club. The choice to hold the Classic and other outings at the club, however, brings our private rules into the public eye," a letter to the members said. "Your view of whether the men's grill is a discriminatory practice or an expression of freedom should be weighed against the desire of the companies which hold outings at the Club, including the Buick Classic, to avoid the negative publicity that has and could result from sponsoring an event at a club that maintains a men's grill. Some companies may decide not to hold outings at the club if a men's grill is maintained, and may even question paying for club membership fees. Some members may be forced to resign if discriminatory policies come into conflict with their own business policies, associations and community activities."

Their next step was a survey. Of the club's 985 members, 616 persons responded, a large number for a mail survey. Although a majority, 55 percent, felt that in principle the club was entitled to have a men's grill, fully 75 percent voted to keep the Buick Classic and 71 percent favored a mixed grill.

In the end, economics had won out over the social pressure to keep the grill all-male. The prospect of losing the prestigious event, which helped finance the club's activities and generated funds for a local hospital, convinced even the diehards. The grill opened its doors to women. Buick stayed on. The negative publicity ended.

—1995

A Woman's Trophy
and a Men's Grill

Marcia Chambers

> There are many things that hold a woman back in golf that are not
> common to the two other popular sports—tennis and swimming. I
> know of no tennis clubs that bar women, and there are no restrictions
> at all on the use of the ocean.
>
> —GLENNA COLLETT, 1928

The most poignant tale about men's grills did not concern locker
rooms or picket lines. After renowned amateur champion Glenna
Collett Vare died, in 1989, Metacomet Country Club, the Rhode
Island club where she learned to play and where her father was president, wished to create a memorial in her honor.

Mrs. Vare, the acknowledged first lady of women's amateur golf
in the U.S., holds the record for winning the most United States
Women's Amateur golf championships—six in all—from 1922
through 1935.

She had spent a day at Metacomet when she was fourteen. "Standing on the broad verandah, perched high on a Rhode Island hill, I
watched Dad send a long, raking tee-shot through the air. It drove
far down the fairway," she wrote in her book, *Ladies in the Rough*.
"Tremendously impressed, I hurried out on the course and asked for
permission to play along with him. With beginner's luck my first shot
off the tee went straight down the fairway. . . . 'The coming champion!' shouted one sun-browned veteran, who asked me to duplicate
my swing. His comments were followed by others of lavish praise and
warm encouragement as I moved from hole to hole. I had a natural
golf-swing. . . . Dad was elated and my head was bursting with the

soaring dreams that only the very young and ambitious live and know. As I came off the course after the first game, my destiny was settled. I would become a golfer."

Many years later Mrs. Vare's two grown children, Glenna and Ned, named after their mother and her brother, may have remembered that passage when as adults they read with pride a proposal from Metacomet to honor their mother.

The club's decision to honor Glenna Collett Vare came shortly after she died. The club president asked the children "for memorabilia from your mother's great golfing career in order to have a permanent memorial in her honor here at Metacomet." The children decided on an early trophy and they were invited to present it to the club at a ceremony on October 30, 1991.

Just before the ceremony, the club's top officials, including a man who had been a golf partner of Ned's for years, took Glenna's husband and Ned for a celebratory drink at the bar in the men's grill. Glenna and the wife of another friend who was there were not invited in. They were left to sit on a bench outside. Glenna was stunned. Ned later said that he went inside in deference to his long friendship with one of the members who was present that night. "I was appalled," he later said, by "its discourtesy, especially as it became prolonged."

Glenna Collett Vare's daughter was upset. "I was angry. I kept thinking to myself, How can I get out of here, how can I get the car keys and go home?" She said later, "No one has ever done anything like that to me in my life. It was so crassly done. It had never occurred to me that I was a second-class citizen."

As Ned and his sister reflected afterward on the incident, they thought about their mother. "Our mother would never have stood for such treatment," Mr. Vare said. "And had she known about Metacomet's policies toward women, she would not have donated anything to honor such a club. Had my sister and I known about the rules, we would not have donated anything, either. . . . There would have been no ceremony."

The club's president sought to explain, but offered no apology. In a letter to Vare and his sister, in February 1992, then club president Robert Verri asserted that there was no discrimination against women. He said they had their own locker room, grillroom, and card room. Mr. Verri remarked that no member had ever complained about the arrangement, and he added, "we allow our women more favorable tee times than other clubs in the area." The club's president went on to urge the Vare children not to deprive the club of their mother's memory "by removing her trophy."

Vare and his sister thought about it. They then told the club they would give them time to change their discriminatory rules against women, but "our request remains that Metacomet put into writing that it disallows discrimination by sex." If the club could not do that, then it must return the trophy, the children wrote.

The answer came by registered mail. Without comment, the club returned the trophy.

—1995

The Finest Course of All

Peter Dobereiner

The late Bernard Darwin, the father of golf journalism and, indeed, the pioneer along with Neville Cardus of literacy on the sports pages, was a considerable player as well as a fine essayist. When he sailed to America to cover the inaugural Walker Cup match the captain fell ill and the man from the *Times* was co-opted to play and take over the duties of leading the side.

It was from Darwin that British golfers first learnt about Pine Valley. The course already had a fearsome local reputation by the time Darwin was taken there on a private visit in the twenties.

He played the first seven holes in level 4s and then came comprehensively to grief at the eighth. He picked up his ball and, sad to relate, retired to the clubhouse after delivering judgment: "It is all very well to punish a bad stroke, but the right of eternal punishment should be reserved for a higher tribunal than a green committee."

So far as the outside world was concerned that peppery diatribe set the tone for all subsequent writing about Pine Valley. The course had its label and there was no shortage of lurid anecdote to fuel that myth.

The members relished these horror stories and took pride in Pine Valley's growing notoriety as the most penal, the most difficult and the most malicious course in the world. They offered bets that visitors could not break 100 at the first attempt, or beat the par 18-up with the benefit of five strokes a hole.

So my brain was thoroughly washed by doom and despondency before I set out for the backwoods of New Jersey to tilt my feeble lance at the gorgon of golf. A friend sped me on the way with the words: "It is all very well for golfers of Walker Cup calibre but for the likes of you and I it is simply unplayable."

As to that, and to all the rest of the weeping and wailing and spitting of blood about Pine Valley, I am now ready to respond with a cheery cry of "Rubbish!" True, it demands a standard of accuracy which is beyond most golfers, myself near the top of the list. Equally true it exacts a scale of punishment which is positively Old Testament in its severity, six strokes being a common sanction for missing a fairway or one of the greens which rise like islands in a sea of unraked sand.

As for the bunkers, there is one turf-walled brute at the front of the short tenth whose name is prudishly rendered in official publications as the Devil's Advocate or the Devil's Pit or, getting closer to the truth of the matter, the Devil's ah, Aperture, or just DAH. It is about eight feet in diameter and the same depth, with steps set into the sand to assist the exhausted and disgruntled golfer to get back to the surface at the end of his shift.

One player, accomplished enough to have scored 35 on the first nine holes, found this bunker off the tee and took 23 for the hole. Devilish intervention caused one four ball to run up an aggregate of 88 strokes at the tenth and another player, having ruined his card and his disposition by taking seven strokes to extricate his ball from the pit, sat on its rim with his feet dangling into the abyss and howled like a baby.

My favourite Pine Valley story is of the four ball which lost one of its members in the woods. Three of them sliced into the trees and the fourth hooked his ball wildly. After playing back into the open country the three slicers crossed the fairway to help their companion's search. They found his ball but he was nowhere to be seen.

The police delivered him back to the clubhouse late at night, somewhat the worse for drink. He had lost his bearings and wandered for miles through the forest and had celebrated his eventual contact with civilisation in the time honoured tradition of *après* golf.

All these tales—and everyone who has enjoyed the privilege of playing Pine Valley has a personal disaster to relate—bear out the horrific reputation of the course. But they tell only the lesser half of the story. Because of the perils which beset the golfer on every side, the charge of exhilaration he receives when he successfully carries his drive over 170 yards of sandy waste is proportionately increased.

The hitting of a green, a routine enough experience at your home club, becomes a thrill. As for holing across those undulating greens with surfaces as slick as polished marble, watching the ball swing as much as twenty feet on its roller-coaster route, the afterglow of achievement lasts for weeks.

So, while playing Pine Valley can be a penance, and nearly always is somewhere during the round, the agonies are the price which must be paid for the ecstasies. Provided you leave your ego back in the locker room, Pine Valley is a delight. The scenery alone is intoxicating and enhanced by the wildlife of what is in effect a 650-acre nature reserve.

When my friend asks what I scored, he will doubtless say: "I told you that you could never get around it." In terms of numbers that is a just comment but numbers, far from being the be all and end all of golf, are the least part of the game.

After Pine Valley, by a long way the finest course I have experienced, other courses will seem humdrum so I may very likely retire, to take up pursuits more suited to my creaking bones. It would be a pity to end on a high score but fitting to go out on the highest note of them all.

—1985

The Glory Game at Goat Hills

Dan Jenkins

Goat Hills is gone now. It was swallowed up by the bulldozers of progress, and in the end it was nice to know that something could take a divot out of those fairways. But all of the regulars had left long before. I suppose it will be all right to talk about it now, about the place and the people and the times we had. Maybe it will explain why I don't play golf so much anymore. It's swell to get invited to play Winged Dip and Burning Foot and all those fancy clubs where they have real flagsticks instead of broom handles, but I usually beg off. Frankly, I'm still overgolfed from all those years at Goat Hills in Texas. You would be too if . . . well, let me tell you some of it. I'll try to be truthful and not too sentimental, but where shall I begin? With Cecil? Why not? He was sort of a symbol in those days, and . . .

We called him Cecil the Parachute because he fell down a lot. He would attack the golf ball with a whining, leaping move—more of a calisthenic than a swing—and occasionally, in his spectacular struggles for extra distance, he would soar right off the end of elevated tees.

He was a slim, bony, red-faced little man who wore crepe-soled shoes and a heavily starched shirt that crackled when he marked his ball, always inching it forward as much as possible. When he was earthbound, Cecil drove a truck for Grandma's Cookies, and he always parked it behind a tall hedge near the clubhouse, out of sight of passing cars, one of which might have Grandma in it.

Anyhow, when the truck was there, you could be pretty sure that not only was Cecil out on the course but so, most likely, were Tiny, Easy, Magoo, and Foot the Free, Ernie, Matty, Rush, and Grease Repellent, Little Joe, Weldon the Oath, Jerry, John the Band-Aid, and Moron Tom—and me. I was known as Dump, basically because of what so many partners thought I did to them for money.

There would be an excellent chance that all of us would be in one hollering, protesting, arguing, club-slinging gangsome, betting huge sums of money we didn't have. In other words, when Cecil's truck was hidden behind the hedge, you knew the game was on.

The game was not the kind the United States Golf Association would have approved of, but it was the kind we played for about fifteen years at a windy, dusty, seldom mowed, stone-hard, practically treeless, residentially surrounded public course named Worth Hills in Fort Worth, Texas.

Goat Hills we called it, not too originally.

It was a gambling game that went on in some form or other, involving anywhere from three to twenty-two players, almost every day of every year when a lot of us were younger and bored silly. The game not only survived my own shaft-breaking, divot-stomping, club-slinging presence, it outlasted rain, snow, heat, wars, tornadoes, jobs, studies, illnesses, divorces, births, deaths, romances, and pinball machines.

Nearly all of the days at the Hills began the same way. Some of us would be slouched in wicker chairs on the small front porch of the wooden clubhouse, smoking, drinking coffee or Cokes, complaining about worldly things, such as why none of the movie houses in town had changed features in five or six weeks, and why most of the girls we knew only wanted to hump rich guys—didn't they care anything about debonair?

Say it was August. We would be looking across the putting green and into the heat. In Texas in the summer, you can see the heat. It looks like germs. In fact, say it was the day of the Great Cart Wreck.

There on the porch, Matty, who had a crew cut and wore glasses, was playing tunes on his upper front teeth with his fingernails. He had learned how to do this in study hall in high school, and for money he could play almost any tune, including "Sixty-Minute Man" and "Saber Dance," and you could actually recognize it.

I was reading a book of some kind as usual. Something light by a Russian or a German.

Tiny, a heavyset railroad conductor, came out of the clubhouse in his flaming red shirt and red slacks, and said, "Dump, what you gonna do with all that book crap in your head?"

"None of it stays there," I said.

Foot the Free, which was short for Big Foot the Freeloader, was practice-putting at a chipped-out crevice in the concrete, a spot that marked the finish of the greatest single hole I've ever seen played—but more about that later.

Little Joe as out on the putting green, trying to perfect a stroke behind his back, a trick shot, in the hope that somebody would one day suggest a behind-the-back putting contest.

Magoo was sitting next to me on the porch.

"Anything about God in that book?" he asked.

"Some."

"Anything in there about what God did to me on the back nine yesterday?"

Around the corner came John the Band-Aid, cleats on, clubs over his shoulder, handkerchief around his neck, impatient as always.

"You, you, you, and you, and you too," he said. "All of you two, two, two, automatic one-down presses, get-evens on nine and eighteen. Whipsaw everybody seventy or better for five."

We began tying our golf shoes.

John the Band-Aid removed three clubs from his bag, dropped the bag on the gravel, and started swinging the clubs in a violent limbering-up exercise.

"Me and Little Joe got all teams for five match and five medal—dollar cats and double on birdies," he said.

Little Joe, who played without a shirt and had a blond ducktail, said, "Damn, John, I'd sure like to pick my own partner someday. You gonna play good or scrape it around like yesterday?"

John the Band-Aid said, "Well, you can have some of *me*, if it'll keep your interest up."

"I try five," said Little Joe in his high-pitched voice. "Five and a R-ra C."

Little Joe and I took a cart. So did John and Magoo. We had won money the day before, so we could afford to ride. The others walked, carrying their own clubs. We were an eightsome, but others would no doubt join us along the way. It wasn't unusual for other players to drive their cars around the course, find the game, hop out, and get it on.

It was Matty one afternoon who drove his red Olds right up to the edge of the third green, jumped out with his golf shoes and glove already on, and said, "Do I have a duck in the car?" He had driven straight to the game from the University of Oklahoma, a distance of some two hundred miles, and he had the duck in the car in case somebody wanted to bet him he didn't have a live duck in the car.

We played the first eight holes and then came the long interlude of bookkeeping on the ninth tee.

John the Band-Aid had earned his nickname by bleeding a lot, such as he did this day because he had shot even par but was losing to everybody. Which was why he had teed up his ball first—the game worked in reverse etiquette.

"All right, Magoo," he said, "you got me out, out, even, even, one down, and one down. I press your young ass for ten. Foot, you got me out, out, out, and one down. You're pushed for eight. Window closed?"

And so it went.

The ninth tee at Goat Hills was on a bluff, above a steep dropoff into a cluster of hackberry trees, a creek, rocks, and weeds. It was a par 4. The drive had to carry the ravine, and if you could hit it far enough, you had about a 7-iron to the green, going back toward the clubhouse.

John the Band-Aid tightened his straw hat and dug in for the tee shot.

"I'm gonna hit this summitch to Dallas," he said.

"Outhit you for five," Magoo said.

"You're on. Anybody else?"

"I try five," Little Joe said.

"You're on."

John the Band-Aid then curved a wondrous slice into the right rough, and coming off his follow-through, he slung his driver in the general direction of Eagle Mountain Lake, which was thirty miles behind us.

He just missed hitting Little Joe, who was nimble enough to dance out of the way.

Little Joe said, "Man, they ought to put you in a box and take you to the World's Fair."

John's arms were folded and he was staring off in an aimless direction, burning inside. Suddenly, then, he dashed over to his bag, jerked out his 2-iron, and slung it against the water fountain, snapping the shaft in half.

"That club cost me a shot on the fourth," he explained.

I wasn't all that happy myself. One under and no money ahead. Maybe that's why I pointed the three-wheel electric cart straight down the hill, full speed ahead, a getaway cart.

Over the rocks and ditches we went darting, and that's when the front wheel struck a large stone in the creek bed. All I recall hearing was Little Joe's voice.

"Son of a young . . . !"

We both went over the front end, headfirst, the bags and clubs flying out over and behind us.

I guess I was knocked out for ten seconds. When I came to, the cart was pinning down my left leg, battery acid was eating away at my shirt, and broken clubs were everywhere.

Little Joe was sitting down in the rocks examining his skinned elbows, and giggling.

The others were standing around, looking down at us, considering whether to lift the cart off my leg, or leave me there to lose all bets.

Magoo glanced at Little Joe's white canvas bag which was already being eaten into by battery acid.

"Two dollars says Joe don't have a bag by the fourteenth," Magoo said.

My ankle was swollen. I had to take off my shoe and play the rest of the round in one shoe.

It is a remarkable footnote in golfing history that I birdied that ninth hole, to which Matty said, "I done been beat by everything now. Dead man comes out of the creek and makes a birdie."

Little Joe's bag lasted exactly until the fourteenth hole. After holing out a putt, he went to pick it up but there was nothing left but the two metal rings and a shoulder strap.

And most of his left trouser leg was going fast.

"Two says Joe is stark naked by the seventeenth," Magoo said.

That day, Little Joe and I both managed birdies on the eighteenth, winning all presses and get-evens, and Magoo and John the Band-Aid talked for weeks about the time they got beat by a cripple and a guy who was on fire.

On other days at the Hills, purely out of boredom, we played the course backward, or to every other hole, or every third hole, or entirely out of bounds except for the greens, which meant you had to stay in the roads and lawns. We also played the course with only one club, or just two clubs, and sometimes at night.

One game we invented was the Thousand-Yard Dash.

This was a one-hole marathon that started on the farthest point on the course from the clubhouse—beside the twelfth green—and ended at the chipped-out crevice in the concrete on the clubhouse porch.

I'm not sure, but I think this game was the brainchild of either Foot the Free, Matty, or me. We had once played through six blocks of downtown Fort Worth, from Seventh Street to the courthouse, mostly on Commerce Street, without getting arrested.

On the day of the first Thousand-Yard Dash, some of us went to the left of the rock outhouse perched atop the highest point on the course, and some played to the right of it. I followed Foot the Free because he could never afford to lose—he carried the same five-dollar bill in his pocket for about eight years.

We hooked a driver, hooked another driver, hooked a third driver, then hooked a spoon—you had to hook the ball to get distance at Goat Hills—and this got us within a pitching wedge of the porch.

Most of the other twelve were out of it by now, lost in creeks or the flower beds of apartment houses bordering the first fairway.

My approach shot carried the porch, slammed against a wall of the clapboard clubhouse, chased Wells Howard, the pro, inside the front door, and brought a scream from Lola, his wife and bookkeeper. The ball came to rest about twenty feet from the crevice and was puttable, if I moved a chair.

Foot played a bounce shot at the porch. He lofted a high wedge, let it bounce off the gravel. It hopped up over the curb, skidded against a wall, and stopped about ten feet from the crevice.

We borrowed a broom from Lola and swept dirt particles out of our putting lines.

The other players gathered around to make side bets.

Two rent-club players came out of the clubhouse and stepped in our lines.

"Hey!" I said to them. "This is business!"

"Smart-ass punks," one of them mumbled.

I gave my putt too good a rap. It went past the crevice and wound up in a row of pull carts at the end of the porch.

"Unnatural hazard," I said. "Free drop."

An instantly formed rules committee consisting of Magoo, Matty, and Grease Repellent, who worked at a Texaco station, basically decided that my request was bullshit.

I had to play it out of the pull carts, which was why I eighteen-putted for a 23.

Against anyone else, I might have still had a chance, but Foot was one of the great putters in history, on any kind of surface. If anything, the concrete looked like bent to Foot compared to the texture of the gnarled Bermuda greens out on the course.

He calmly tapped his ten-footer and it wobbled slowly, slowly, slowly over the concrete, wavered, and went in!

That was one of the two greatest holes I ever saw played. The other was when my friend Bud Shrake made a 517 on a five-block hole that stretched from Goat Hills' first tee to a brown leather loafer in another friend's apartment.

The longest hole we ever played was from the first tee at Goat Hills to the third green at Colonial Country Club, roughly fifteen blocks away.

The first time we played it, Rush's dad, a retired oilman, caddied for him in a black Lincoln, and Cecil got bit by a cocker spaniel.

Playing through neighborhoods required a unique shot, we discovered. A blade putter was an ideal club to keep the ball low so it would get extra roll on the pavement.

Some of us went down Stadium Drive, past the TCU football stadium, then left on Park Hill and over the houses. Others went the back way, down Alton Road.

I happened to have sliced a blade putter into a bed of irises on Alton Road and was looking for it when I saw Cecil down the driveway.

He was contemplating a shot that would have to rise quickly to clear a cyclone fence, then duck sharply under an oak, then hook severely to get around a tile roof, and then slice to land in the street.

As Cecil studied the shot, a dog was barking at his ankles.

Cecil leaped at the ball in his customary manner and drove the ball straight into the fence, about eight feet in front of him, and his follow-through carried him forward and onto the ground on his elbows and stomach. He slid into the fence, and the spaniel chased after him as if it were retrieving a sock.

Cecil scrambled to his feet and tiptoed back down the driveway, and withdrew from the competition.

"Hurried the shot," he said. "That sucker was growlin' at me, and just when I started to swing, I seen a lady cussin' me through the kitchen window."

Tiny quit at a fishpond. Grease Repellent lost his ball when he struck a sundial. Easy Reid met a fellow and stopped to sell him some insurance. John the Band-Aid broke his blade putter when he sailed it at a chimney. Foot and Magoo were the only two who finished, and they had to play out fast after they climbed over the Colonial fence because some members sent a caddie back to the clubhouse to get the club manager, who would, in turn, call the police.

There was an argument about who won, and a playoff was decided upon. Magoo wanted to play back to Goat Hills, to the cold-drink box in the lunchroom. Foot wanted to play to Herb Massey's Cafe, about three miles away, to the third leg of the shuffle-bowl machine. Herb's was where Matty once showed up one day with his shirt and pants on backward, and his glasses on the back of his head, and posted a score of 280 on the shuffle bowl, sliding the puck backward.

Foot and Magoo wound up splitting the money, and we all went back to Goat Hills and got in a putting game that lasted until midnight.

Why we did such things was because we lived in Fort Worth, the town that gave you Ben Hogan and Byron Nelson, and offered little else to do.

Besides, it was Texas.

Golf had always received lavish attention in the newspapers, and it was at a very early age that you knew about Hogan and Nelson and others: Jimmy Demaret, Lloyd Mangrum, Ralph Guldahl, Jackie Burke, Gus Moreland, Harry Todd—all Texans.

There was also a vast amateur circuit you could travel, if you wanted to take your game out of town. All summer long, you could go play in invitation tournaments in towns like Ranger, Midland, Abilene, Wichita Falls, Waxahachie, Longview, Corpus Christi, everywhere.

In these tournaments, you would win shotguns, radios, silverware, lawn tools, and quite a lot of money in calcutta pools.

It was this amateur circuit that gave us Hogan, Nelson, and Demaret from the old days, and then Jackie Burke, Jr., Tommy Bolt, Billy Maxwell, Don Cherry, Don January, Earl Stewart, Dave Marr, Bill Rogers, Charlie Coody, Bobby Nichols, Miller Barber, Howie Johnson, Ernie Vossler, Homero Blancas, Fred Marti, Jacky Cupit, and then in later years your Ben Crenshaws, Tom Kites, and John Mahaffeys.

Ernie Vossler, who got richer than A-rabs in Palm Springs, came right out of our game at the Hills.

Even then, he was a relentless competitor who never understood why anybody but him ever made a putt.

Sometimes, when Weldon the Oath, a postman, made a putt, Ernie would walk off the course, fuming.

Ernie was never as proficient as myself or John the Band-Aid at breaking clubs. I once broke the shaft on my 8-iron nine days in a row at the seventeenth because I couldn't make the ball hold that green, a par 3. But Ernie had his moments. He bladed a 6-iron one day in the sixth fairway and almost killed everybody. He hurled the club into the brick fairway, and the shaft snapped, and both parts of the club went into the air, and one jagged end sprang back and hit Ernie in the palm, causing five stitches, and another jagged end caught me in the leg. As the shafts sparkled in the sun, it was as if we were being attacked by lightning bolts.

And this was the man who knew nothing of golf before I had once recruited him for the golf team at Paschal High. He went on to win the Fort Worth city championship, which was something that Hogan, Nelson, and I could never do—we all finished second in our best effort—and Ernie won the State Amateur, and then some tournaments on the PGA Tour, and then h e got into real estate and bought Oklahoma City and Palm Springs. Ernie Vossler became our honor graduate.

But our most intriguing graduate was Weldon the Oath.

Weldon had talking fits—talking to the ball.

He would take oaths. He would rush out to the game so quickly, he would play golf in his postman's cap and without golf shoes, which could have had something to do with his chronic slice.

"All right, this is your last chance," Weldon would say to the ball as he waggled his driver. "You lousy little crud, if you slice on me one more time I'm gonna bite you in half and chew your rubber guts up. You're goin' straight this time, you hear me? You *hear* me tellin' you this? All right, then. Geeeeooood, daaaammmmmm, aaaaiii, ga!"

And Weldon would hit another slice.

It would cross two fairways to his right, a marvelous half-moon of a shot.

The ball would scarcely leave the club face before Weldon would start to spin around in circles, pawing at the air, slugging at imaginary evils. Frequently, he would dash over to the tee marker and start beating the driver on it. He would stomp on the club.

Then just as quickly, he would calm down and say, "Let me hit one more, I got to figure out what I'm doin' wrong."

And he would slice again.

That's when he would break the shaft over his knee. "Geeeeaaa, rrreeeeaaa, aaaddd," he would snarl. "This is my last time on a golf course, you can book it! Gaaddd raaaap son of a baddred bat rop ditch bastard." When Weldon was hot, the words didn't come out right. "You picks have guyed me damn stick—this rotten, stinking, miserable, low-life spicky dop whore bubbin' game—feck it, babber sam!"

Weldon would hike to the clubhouse, but of course he would be back the next day.

It was in the last couple of years at Goat Hills, shortly before the city sold those 106 acres to TCU so the school could build more cream-brick buildings, that the games grew too big, too expensive, for working men and college students.

Some of the guys got to where they couldn't pay when they lost, and others didn't want to collect it, and some of us were developing other interests—snooker, eight-ball, newspapers, divorces.

Moron Tom had something to do with the games disappearing, going the way of other endangered species.

He was a muscular, likeable West Texan who had come to Fort Worth on a football scholarship at TCU, but had quit football when he found out you had to work out every day in the fall. He hit a long ball and he loved to bet, on anything. He could hold his breath longer than anybody, for money, or inhale a can of beer in four seconds, for money, and he rarely spoke English.

Everything was quadruple unreal to Moron Tom, or "Hit it fine, pork-e-pine," and many of the words he uttered were something else spelled backward.

"God Ee-rack Fockle-dim," for instance, was Dr. Cary Middlecoff spelled backward.

The day of one of the last big games, Moron Tom walked onto the porch and said, "I'll take toops and threeps from Youngfut, Youngjun, and Youngdump."

This meant Moron Tom wanted 2 up and 3 up from young Foot, young John, and young me.

"Ten and ten with Grease's men," he added, "and two and two with Joe-Magoo."

Everyone drifted out to the first tee.

Wagers were made, partners chosen, practice swings taken.

Moron Tom brought a big hook in from over the apartment houses and found the fairway.

"Think I can't, Cary Grant?" he said.

Magoo and I wound up as partners against all other combinations, and this was not altogether good—neither of us knew how to play safe, and Magoo was also unlucky. Once in the Glen Garden Invitation in Fort Worth—that's the course where Hogan and Nelson caddied as kids—Magoo hit a 285-yard tee shot but found his ball in a man's mouth, being cleaned.

We were in good form today, however. Teamed well for a blaze of birdies and had everybody bleeding to death by the time we got to the eighteenth.

I would hit a good drive and Moron Tom would say, "Cod Ee-rack Fockle-dim," and Magoo would hit a good drive, and Moron Tom would say, "Wod Daw-ret-sniff," meaning Dow Finsterwald spelled backward.

When either of us holed a putt, Moron Tom would say, "Take a nap, Einra Remlap," which was Arnie Palmer spelled backward.

By the time we came off the seventeenth green, Magoo and I had somehow birdied six holes in a row, and we calculated that if we only parred the eighteenth, we would win so much money we wouldn't be able to haul it home in Cecil's cookie truck.

Everybody pressed to get even, of course, on the eighteenth tee.

John the Band-Aid summed it up for most of the players, who must have numbered twelve in all, when he said, "I'm out, out, out, out, out, and out, and one down, one down, one down, one down, one down, and even. Want me to bend over?"

The eighteenth at Goat Hills was slightly uphill. You drove from a windy knoll with the south wind usually helping and aimed across a tiny creek and a couple of sycamore trees. A big drive would leave you only thirty or forty yards short of the green, a flip and a putt from a birdie or a flip and two putts from an easy par.

Not to birdie the eighteenth often resulted in a wedge being broken, and not to par the eighteenth was unthinkable.

The only conceivable trouble was far, far to the right, across the tenth fairway, where Stadium Drive was out-of-bounds. But nobody had ever sliced that badly, not even Weldon the Oath, until Magoo did.

At the height of Magoo's backswing, when he was coming out of his shoes to try to drive the green and make us richer, Moron Tom quietly said, "Tissim, Oogam." Which was "Miss it, Magoo," backward.

Needles were commonplace in the game. Coughing, sneezing, dropping a full bag of clubs, yelling, burping, all such things could be heard on backswings at times—you took it for granted and dealt with it.

But Magoo came apart with laughter at Moron Tom's remark and almost fell down like Cecil when he swung at the ball.

Even Magoo had to laugh again when Moron Tom said, "Oogam dewolb the Nepo," which translated into "Magoo blowed the Open."

To say this put extra pressure on me, with Magoo out of the hole, would be to say that the meat loaf in the lunchroom at Goat Hills contained grease.

Right here, I should explain that on the other side of the creek at the eighteenth, set upright into an embankment, was a storm drain about three feet in circumference. We often pitched at it with old balls from the ladies' tee, but it was a remarkable thing if anybody ever got one in there.

And from up on the men's tee, a hundred yards or so back, it was an incredibly small target. In fact, I didn't even think about it as I got set to drive the green and make another birdie, or know the reason why. All I wanted to know was what everybody wanted engraved on their tombstones.

But at the top of my swing, Moron Tom whispered something else.

"Glutch, Mother Zilch," he said.

The club head hit about two inches behind the ball, and the drive snap-hooked into the ground just in front of the ladies' tee, took a big hop to the right off of some rocks, and—I swear to you—went straight into the storm drain.

It remains the only hole in one I ever made, and it was, you might say, the shot which semi-retired me from golf forever.

—1970

My Semi-tough Return
to Playing Golf

Dan Jenkins

It is no big secret that the game of golf requires grave concentration to be played decently, so let me say right off that it is not altogether to your advantage while you're standing over a 5-iron shot to be thinking: "I've got to remember to get some Freon in the Toyota."

Freon shots are my life these days. They are the kind of shots, which, after you hit four inches behind them, float lazily into a lagoon, forest or marsh. Freon shots are what happen to you all too often when you take up the game again after a ten-year layoff.

I call them Freon shots but they have other names, such as:

1. The Phillips screwdriver shot, as in, "I know there used to be one in that drawer."
2. The frozen dinner shot, as in, "I'm sure we're out of creamed chipped beef and chicken pot pie."
3. The electrician shot, as in, "It's usually the circuit breaker but this time it's not."
4. The VCR shot, as in, "You'd think the manual would tell you how to set the damn timer."

And most familiarly:

5. The no-count, low-life, rotten summitch.

Actually, the Freon shot comes later. When you take up the game again after a long absence, there is a more urgent problem.

The first thing you discover is that a golf club weighs in the neighborhood of 180 pounds and feels like you're trying to swing a parking meter.

A golf club didn't used to weigh this much, as I recall. Not during all those years when I played at scratch around Fort Worth and won some tin against a pillaging bunch of barbers, filling station attendants, petshop owners, insurance salesmen and deliverymen.

A golf club weighed next to nothing and the only thing I ever thought about it was that it better not betray me on a crucial shot in a heavy-duty gambling game unless it wanted to get drowned or have its neck broken on the trunk of a pecan tree.

Also, the golf club listened when I spoke to it.

It would perk up its little MacGregor head and pay attention when I would say something like, "I'll tell you one thing, Slick Grip. Show me that banana ball again and I'll stuff your ass inside the trunk of that car over there and we'll see how you like it when you suffocate!"

The golf club would go quietly into the white canvas bag and vow never to hook again.

Nowadays, however, my Hogan Apex 9-iron, for instance, just sits there and glistens in the Florida sunlight while its shaft gets mysteriously longer and the clubhead gets mysteriously heavier—it can't wait for me to hit a cold shank or plow up a square foot of Bermuda on a simple pitch shot.

Once I even heard it call me a name off a Chinese menu. That was after it made me hit a foot behind the ball from only one hundred yards out and never even finish the easiest par 4 in North America after my best tee ball of the round.

"LOIBIP," is what it called me, as in Loss Of Interest, Ball In Pocket.

I think that's what it means, although it could mean minced pork in lettuce.

If I had hit a shot like that in the old days, I would have taken that whole bag of clubs and thrown them to the reptiles, and played out of somebody else's bag, and pressed everybody to get even, and tried to prove how much money I could lose in a single afternoon.

But when I commit such an atrocity today, inasmuch as score no longer matters, I just shrug and casually climb in the golf cart and smile at someone, and say, "Part of the charm."

Of course, there's another reason why you can't dump a whole bag of clubs into a haunting lagoon or river. That's because golf clubs today cost $4,768 apiece, and a full set of clubs that are perfectly suited to your swing takes 112 months for delivery.

The reason it takes so long to get them is because the director of golf at your country club, who used to be known as the club pro and only had one assistant instead of eight, is on the staff of the manufacturer.

As a golf writer, I had never stopped being *around* the sport, but the reason I started playing again is because I recently moved to Ponte Vedra, Florida, after living in New York City for twenty-six years, and if you don't take up golf in Florida, there's not much else to do except become a real-estate developer.

Growing up in Fort Worth, the exotic town that gave you Ben Hogan, Byron Nelson and my once-fabled hook, I had played golf almost every day of my life for about twenty years, from the age of eight to the age of twenty-eight. I had kept on trying to play once or twice a month for the first twelve years or so that I lived in Manhattan, which wasn't easy. If you live in Manhattan, a round of golf in Westchester County, or out on Long Island, or up in Connecticut, or over in New Jersey, takes two days, counting travel time, and a year off your life, counting the aggravation.

But up until the late 1970s, possessing what some would call a natural swing, I could still go out and break 80 on any course you wanted to drop me on, and I could do it from the blues, which used to be known as the tips before some dirt salesman invented the gold tees, the platinum tees, the uranium tees, the Tiffany tees, and finally, at long last, four condos later, the championship tees.

Muscle memory would help me accomplish this. That and the fact that I was tournament-tough from all those earlier years of competing in high school and college and on the Texas amateur circuit against such legends as Morris Williams Jr., Billy Maxwell, Don January, Joe Conrad, Don Cherry, Earl Stewart, Ernie Vossler, and on and on; guys who could waltz me around the dance floor like I was some kind of Ginger Rogers.

Not that I didn't have my moments of glory as a Respectable Golfer, caps, italics or unquote.

In 1955 I was a serious contender for the Fort Worth City Championship, which at the time was thought by some of us to be second in importance only to the U.S. Open. That year, the tournament was contested at 72 holes of stroke play on a wind machine and gravel pit known as Rockwood Muny.

I stayed within a shot or two of the lead all the way and then a demon inhabited my body and I birdied four of the last five holes of the final round. But while I was sitting on the clubhouse porch rehearsing my victory speech, I finished second to a college player from North Texas State in Denton, who had taken the precaution of eagling one of the holes I had birdied, and that was the difference.

"Nice going, Harold," I said. "Spending a lot of time in the city these days?"

Just teasing. I knew he was originally from Arlington, which was in the county, and that made him legit. Besides, he could beat me any day of the week and deserved to win.

Anyhow, I was already amusing myself with a thought. I now had something in common with Ben Hogan and Byron Nelson. They never won the City either.

The closest they came was back in 1929. That summer, the City was conducted at match play over a meandering creekbed and copperhead convention known as Meadowbrook Muny, and it is part of Fort Worth golfing lore that a gentleman named Joe Ballard beat Ben Hogan at the semifinals and Byron Nelson in the final, never mind that Ben and Byron were only about sixteen years old at the time.

All through the 1950s, I would play the occasional round with Hogan, out at Colonial Country Club, while also covering his remarkable deeds for the *Fort Worth Press*.

Having a sense of history, I realized even then what an incredible privilege this was.

"Who did you used to play golf with, Daddy?"

"Oh . . . Ben Hogan."

I would wander out to Colonial and find Ben practicing some-where, hitting knocked-down 3-irons he might need at Oakland Hills or Oakmont or Olympic. I would say, "What the hell is *that?*" He would say he needed it at Oakland Hills.

Once in a while he would say, "Let's go," and we would play eigh-teen, whereupon he would shoot what I thought was a flawless 66, though never holing a putt, and I would shoot a paraplegic 76, though never missing a putt.

Ben squinted at my putter a lot, I remember. Now and again, he would take the Armour or Cash-in from me and look at it curiously and practice a few strokes with it but eventually hand it back and walk away toward the next tee, shaking his head with an expression I sensed to be a combination of disgust and disbelief.

One afternoon I got a critical tip from him.

On a par 4 at Colonial with only 115 yards to the pin and a stiff south breeze behind us, I watched him take out a 7-iron of all things and bounce it up for a gimme birdie.

"What in God's name was *that?*" I asked.

"You always overclub downwind," he explained.

Swell. I've been overclubbing downwind ever since, and it would be impossible to total up the number of balls I've hit over greens and into bunkers, rivers, orchards, backyard cookouts and city streets.

In the spring of 1956, Ben invited me to join him and two other players out at Colonial in an eighteen-hole exhibition for the ben-efit of the United States Olympic Fund. This was the Olympics where we were going to send Bobby Morrow of Abilene, Texas, over to Melbourne, Australia, to whip up on the foreigners in the sprints, and Ben wanted to help out.

The other members of the foursome were Royal Hogan, Ben's brother, a former City champion, and Raymond Gafford, the pro at Fort Worth's Ridglea Country Club, a bettor's haven back then and something of an historic landmark in that it used to be one of Ti-tanic Thompson's hangouts.

Raymond was a very stylish player, a guy who could have made it on the PGA Tour if he had wanted to take a cut in pay from bury-ing everybody in the high-rent gambling games at Ridglea.

I could only assume I was invited to be a part of the exhibition because in those days I was writing a daily column with my picture in it. Actually, it was the picture of a person I had never seen before in my whole life.

Owing to some idiotic delay at the newspaper office—no doubt a discussion with the editor-in-chief about an excessively cosmopolitan business trip I'd taken to Wichita Falls—I arrived at the first tee just in time for the game.

I didn't really expect to find three thousand people lining the first fairway, but I would deal with that later. I ripped off my coat and tie and rolled up the sleeves on my light blue buttoned-down shirt, teed up a ball and waggled a driver.

No glove and no golf shoes yet.

"Wait a minute," said Hogan, staring at my ball. It was an old Spalding Dot that was turning the color of pewter. Ben came over and handed me two boxes of new balls.

"And put on your shoes before you hurt somebody," he said.

I got off the first tee without injury to anyone, but for the first four holes, with a severe case of gallery nerves, I either cold-topped or dart-hooked everything.

My swing must have looked as jerky as Charlie Chaplin in a silent movie because, as we were walking down the fifth fairway, Ben said, "You could probably take it back faster if you really tried."

I got the point.

I settled down and somehow managed to get around in 77 while Ben shot what I thought was the best round of recreational golf, tee to green, I had ever seen, a 3-under 67. He hit every fairway and every green in regulation and the longest putt he made was a tap-in.

By the way, in those years Colonial was an unspeakably hard golf course. The fairways were brutally narrow, the rough was deep and uncultivated and the Trinity River came more fiercely into play. The bent greens, first in the southwestern part of the U.S. (circle 1936), not only seemed to be the size of throw rugs, there were diabolical levels to them and they were guarded by huge oaks that have since died.

"What a great round," I said to Ben of his 67 later that day in the grillroom.

"That wasn't a good round of golf," he said, and his look told me he was serious.

I tried not to appear astonished.

He said, "A good round of golf is if you can hit about three shots that turn out exactly as you planned them. I didn't have any of those today."

"Well," I grinned, "I wish I could miss every shot and shoot sixty-seven."

"It's possible," said Ben. "That's what's wrong with tournaments."

Hogan witnessed the best shot I ever hit in competition, but let me set it up properly.

It was a few years earlier, in 1950, my sophomore year at Texas Christian University, a thrilling time in the annals of Horned Frog golf, for I was the team's number-one player despite my double bogeys that traveled extremely well.

Somehow that spring, however, our team won enough matches and tied enough matches against Bears, Owls, Aggies, Mustangs and Razorbacks that we came down to the final match against the University of Texas at Colonial with the Southwest Conference championship on the line.

I, of course, knew the championship wasn't on the line. There was no living way we could beat Texas—Texas had Morris Williams Jr.!

The son of an Austin sportswriter, Morris was a slender, wiry, supple, good-looking guy who never hit a crooked drive, never struck an iron that didn't sound pure and wasn't clotheslined to the flag, and never missed a putt he needed to make. He had a quick smile and a friendly nature, but on the golf course there was an ax murderer struggling to climb out of his heart. He had a beautiful upright swing and played along in the quick-hitting style of a Lanny Wadkins or Tom Watson. He had become a friend, through the Texas amateur circuit, but I was in helpless awe of his talent.

Morris Williams Jr., was invincible, unbeatable, incomparable and otherwise stupendous—the Ben Crenshaw of his day. I think he remains the only golfer who won the State Amateur, State Junior and Texas PGA all in the same year—as an amateur, against the best pros in the territory—a Texas Slam.

That I knew of, the only match he had ever lost was to North

Carolina's Harvie Ward in the thirty-six-hole final of the 1949 NCAA championship, which was no great embarrassment if you knew anything about Harvie Ward.

This was during a more romantic time in our history when prominent members of TCU's varsity football team would come out to Colonial to caddie for us in college matches. School spirit deal, they said. It was a flattering thing, though very few of the gridiron heroes knew anything about golf.

The caddie for my match against Morris Williams Jr., that day was a burly, maniacal defensive end from Odessa named Billy Moorman.

As we were all fooling around on the putting green before the matches started, Billy quietly said to me, "We're gonna mop up on them tea-sippers today."

"Speak for yourself," I said.

"Naw, really," he said. "Look how skinny they are."

I figured there were two things that might keep me from being totally humiliated by Morris. One, he never played Colonial before, and two, Ben Hogan would be following us in a golf cart. Ben had read about this celebrated kid from Austin and wanted to take a look at him.

We played the back nine first to avoid a collision with some of Colonial's grumpiest members, and through fifteen holes, rather miraculously, I was all square with Morris and we were both even par. Quite frankly, I was playing my career round. I might even have been 1 up or 2 up if God had been wearing the purple of TCU instead of the orange of Texas.

But now we were at Colonial's par-4 seventh hole—our sixteenth—which back then called for a 1-iron or 4-wood off the tee and a 6-, 7- or 8-iron to the green unless you wanted to try to thread a needle with the driver, in which case you'd have a pitching wedge to the green, the green being one of those shadowy throw rugs sheltered by tall, overhanging trees.

Smart money usually played it safe, but I was never known for that. So I sky-sliced a driver into the right rough behind a tall cluster of oaks.

I looked over at Hogan, who was sitting in the golf cart with Marvin Leonard, his old friend and the man who built Colonial. I put my hand to my throat and smiled weakly. Ben shook his head sadly. Meanwhile, Morris nailed it down the gut with a 4-wood.

I had a remote chance to reach the green on my second shot if I could get a 6-iron out of the Bermuda rough and up quickly over the trees and then down quickly over some more trees, which, curiously, is what happened. Don't ask me to write an instruction article on it. All I did was swing the club, and mostly out of anger at my tee shot. The ball barely cleared the trees going up, and barely cleared a front bunker coming down, and bit into the green and stopped about six inches from the cup.

"Gosh, Dan, great shot," said Morris from out in the fairway.

I said thanks and tried to act like the shot was merely a part of my normal repertoire.

The defensive end, my caddie, said, "There you go, bubba— nothin' two more of those won't cure."

I looked at him incredulously.

For the next long moment, while I waited for my opponent to spray his own approach out of shell shock, I entertained some wonderful thoughts. I had a gimme birdie, thus I was going to be 1 up on Morris Williams Jr., with only two holes to play. I was going to *beat* Morris Williams Jr. I was going to win the individual championship in the conference tournament next month. I was going to turn pro, go on the tour, wear beltless slacks and complain about courtesy car drivers the rest of my life. I was . . .

This is about the time that Morris holed out his 7-iron for an eagle 2.

Yeah. Holed it out. Hit a 7-iron in there about ten feet short of the flag. The ball took a gash out of the lush bent grass and rolled slowly past my six-inch birdie and died in the cup—a deuce.

All I could do was laugh. All Morris could do was laugh, though apologetically.

Still laughing, I looked over at Ben Hogan. He was shaking his head again as he turned the cart around and headed for the clubhouse. I guess he knew the match was over.

Needless to say, it was. We both parred the last two holes, so with the lowest round I ever had on old Colonial, a 1-under-par 69 from the tips, I lost 1 up, didn't win the conference the next month, never won the conference, didn't turn pro and only went out on the tour with a typewriter.

(Although I'm not generally fond of parenthetical information, it would be incorrect for me not to mention here that Morris Williams Jr., one of the nicest guys I ever knew and one of the best golfers I ever saw, was tragically killed in the crash of an Air Force jet in 1953. He had planned to go on the PGA Tour when he got out of the service. I don't have any doubt that he would have been a big star out there and would have given Arnold Palmer a run for his charisma.)

So much for the glory moments. I have relived a few of them only to acquaint you more intimately with the man who gave up the game completely for ten years.

I can't blame my loss of interest entirely on living in Manhattan. I think it had more to do with the time I went up to Winged Foot and discovered that, virtually overnight, I could no longer get my swing around my stomach.

What had once been a reasonably controlled hook off the tee that would go 250 yards or so had suddenly turned into a pitiful slice of, oh, 174 yards.

Moreover, I had gone from a deft chipper and putter to a person more interested in idle gardening. And all of the clubs between the driver and putter were achieving the results of rakes and shovels.

I couldn't break 95. Thus, having once played well enough to tell tales and collect a cupboard of trophies my kids could throw away someday, it was no fun at all to play disgusting, rancid golf.

So I quit.

You may ask what I did for recreation for those ten years. Well, to start with, golf was never recreation for me. Golf was never anything but vicious competition and cerebral gambling—learning how not to get out-bet. I played a little family tennis, only because I discovered you can smoke at the net in family tennis. Largely, I drank a lot, traveled a lot and worked.

It seems clear now that the most pleasure I got out of quitting golf was turning down some invitations to play in the Crosby, as many of us still refer to it. It was most satisfying to turn down the Crosby, knowing there were so many CEO's who would sell their daughters to get invited.

I fondly treasure the many happy years of covering the Crosby and lifting beverages in Club XIX of the Pebble Beach Lodge for a week, secure in the knowledge that I didn't have to get up at 6 A.M. and wade through the ice plant.

As my friend Steve Reid, the ex–touring pro turned TV producer, once said, "There's nothing more boring than a golf tournament in the daytime."

Almost everything looks different when you reenter golf after a long layoff.

Take the clubs. In most any golf shop I've entered, I've been able to find nothing but long rows of things that look like parts that have fallen off a DC-10.

I inquired and found out that these things are called metal woods. All of my golfing friends love them, but I can tell you that if you ever find a metal wood in my hands, you'll know I've retired again.

They are, to me, as unsightly as the long rows of unfinished irons in the golf shops. I know they're unfinished because all of their backs are missing. You could pour a cup of soup in them or use them for a soap dish.

I happen to be a traditionalist. I play with an old rebuilt set of Haig Ultra woods, which are made of wood, and a new set of Hogan Apex irons, which look like irons and don't have the backs missing, and an old Tommy Armour putter—I don't want my putter to sound like a door chime or look like a power tool.

I *do* carry a 5-wood and a 7-silly, or what is more accurately known as a 7-wood. These clubs are the best of the modern inventions, especially the 7-silly, which eliminates the 1-iron, 2-iron and 3-iron from your bag forever.

Off the pro tour, nobody has ever been able to hit a long iron with consistency or confidence. The only way to attempt it is with a debonair casualness while humming a medley of Broadway tunes.

People say my resentment of the new technology costs me three shots a nine these days, but since I only keep score on rare occasions, what difference does it make?

Peculiar questions are now asked of me in golf shops.

When I went up to the counter to buy my first dozen Titleists in ten years—Titleist being the only golf ball I remembered with fondness—a young assistant pro said, "Surlyn or balata?"

"My name's Jenkins," I said. "I'm playing with Mr. Herring at one-fifteen."

We straightened out that confusion and then the assistant pro said, "Do you want nineties or one hundreds?"

"I suppose I'd rather shoot in the nineties," I said intelligently.

On another day at another club, I asked another young assistant pro if he had a set of leather head covers for sale.

He looked at me oddly and said, "Leather . . . ?"

Apparently, if you want a set of leather head covers today, you have to buy a calf, kill it, send it off to Dornoch in the north of Scotland, and wait two years for the owner of a primitive arts and handicrafts shop to sew it together.

In the meantime, you can buy a set of furry-fuzzy head covers in pink, red, green, blue and yellow. This way your golf bag looks like dueling drum majors, or a hot new rock group on MTV.

I understand how fortunate I am to live where I do, which is on Florida's "First Coast," halfway between Jacksonville and St. Augustine. My reentry to golf wouldn't have been possible otherwise. I'm only a matter of minutes from the first tee at Marsh Landing, Ponte Vedra, Sawgrass or the TPC, four elegant clubs offering a total of 117 fascinating holes of golf, clubs I've been able to join for only a third of what it would cost to join Colonial back in Fort Worth, which still didn't have an ocean the last time I checked but did have a waiting list for both memberships and starting times.

In the beginning, my comeback was a festival of shanks and tops, plinks and pop-ups, scoops and scuffers. Agony. Torture. Nonsense.

I would play the front nine in 6, Pocket, Pocket, 5, Pocket, 6, Pocket, Pocket, Pocket.

What did you shoot on the front?"

"Seventeen."

I would then play the back in 6, Pocket, 5, 6, 6, Pocket, Pocket, 6, Pocket.

No card.

For the first time in my life, I was forced to seek advice about hitting a golf ball. "Slow it down" was easier said than done. "Hold on tighter" was next to impossible. "Get back on your heels" was helpful if I wanted to hit another foot behind it.

Roger Maltbie, one of the tour's venerable cigarette smokers and therefore someone I like, was the first person who told me something useful. When we happened to be in the same tavern one evening, I said, "Roger, in one sentence, cure my shank."

He thought about it a few seconds, and said, "Try to hit it left."

It worked. I no longer shank, but now I have to ask him another urgent question: How do I keep from hitting it left so often?

Early on in the agonizing, torturous, nonsensical days of my comeback, golf tried to kill me.

On the South Nine at Sawgrass in late spring I was hacking around with a couple of friends one day and we came to the sixth hole, a par 5 that requires a drive, a lay up and a pitch over a lagoon. The lagoon is supported near the green by a bulkhead to keep the alligators from gnawing on the flagstick, or golf carts, and to keep the water moccasins from swallowing the Surlyns and balatas, or pecking at your ankles.

My pitch shot, a sickly thing, came down in the grass between the green and the bulkhead, and then my chip left enough to be desired that I spoke to it in Swahili, backed up, and smoldered.

But not for long. What I had forgotten is that the bulkhead and lagoon were directly behind me. Suddenly, I was standing on top of the bulkhead, losing my balance, flapping my arms like a demented person trying to fly, gaping over my shoulder at the lagoon, my eyes ablaze, knowing what horror existed in the watery deep.

"Geeeaaad damn, aaaiiigh," is close to what I was saying before the splash, five feet down and into the mud and dark water, as two things raced through my brain. Alligators kill you; they drown you first, then chew you. If that wasn't my fate, I was probably going to reenact the "river scene" from *Lonesome Dove*.

Fortuitously, the gators and moccasins were all preoccupied with other interests while I waded around, waist deep, in the lagoon, and I guess I don't have to tell you that I may have set a new gym, school and conference record for the Terror-Stricken Sportswriter's Bulkhead Climb.

Splattered with mud and lagoon-drenched, I finished the round in the grand style of LOIBIP.

Since that day, I've slowly discovered that it's possible to enjoy golf, but only if you follow certain rules.

a. Play from the white tees only. Any 12-handicapper, square-groove, metal-wood, hot-ball, macho nitwit who wants to drag you back from the whites, shoot him.

b. Roll it over everywhere and don't swing at it until you have it sitting up perfectly. You won't be able to hold onto the club for weeks after you take up the game again, and airborne balls are most encouraging.

c. Keep in mind that you or others in your foursome can't make worse than a double bogey on any hole. Speeds up play.

d. Never look for lost balls more than five seconds. Drop one without penalty.

e. Hit till you're happy off the first tee, or any other tee if it suits your mood.

f. Don't try to blast out of bunkers. Either putt it or take a free drop. Why risk blindness?

g. Tell the club manager you want to see the girl in the beverage cart every six holes or he's dogmeat.

h. Mulligans are free. Use them without guilt or embarrassment.

i. There is only one thing to say after hitting a shot into the water. "Surf's up, dude."

j. Never keep score unless by some weird coincidence you have a chance to break 80, 85, or 90 for the first time. Not keeping score eliminates much of the game's frustrations. On the other hand, if you come within a stroke of breaking 80, 85, or 90 for the first time, by all means count the practice shot you hit from the twelfth fairway, the one that went on the green. It was, after all, the shot you would have hit if you hadn't been thinking about Freon.

Even by the above rules, it took me a long four months of playing two and three times a week to get it down to where I could reasonably expect something decent to happen. Not long ago, I finally broke 80 at Marsh Landing.

Nobody wants to hear about anybody else's round, of course. I certainly don't. Start to tell me about your round of golf and I bolt for the door. Or my eyes glaze over and I topple out of my chair. I wouldn't think of doing this to anyone. But the first hole at Marsh Landing is this sporty little par 4 with big trouble on the right, so I cut my drive down the left side of the fairway, and . . .

—1990

They Might Be Giants

John Paul Newport

The hardest-working man on the Space Coast Tour is Gene Jones, Jr., a.k.a. Gene the Machine. Granted, that's not saying an awful lot, since many of Jones's peers, especially the youngsters, spend as much time honing their personalities as honing their games. Unlike on the PGA Tour, where wit and colorful behavior are relics of the past, in bush-league professional golf personality counts for a lot. That's because most of the players are just giving the pro game a shot for a few years before moving on to their true life's work: conducting golf seminars for the plaid-pants crowd at backwater country clubs or selling universal life-insurance products for Prudential.

Jones is like the nerd in your college lit class who always read every assignment. After a tournament round, he will pound balls at a driving range, go home to videotape his swing in the search for tiny flaws and then practice putting and chipping for an hour or two. On days when the Space Coast Tour doesn't stage an event, he finds another tournament to enter. On Sundays he practices some more and then usually takes his ten-year-old daughter, Amberly, out for a round of golf. What drives Jones to pursue golf so maniacally is a matter of considerable speculation among his fellow competitors. But obviously, he's very serious about the game.

I first encountered him as I was standing near the scoreboard during the first round of the DeBary Plantation tournament, north of Orlando, last fall. Around me, young Space Coast cadets were offering preposterous excuses for why they had scored so poorly. "I'd have shot a sixty-eight if I hadn't triple-bogeyed number eight," a curly-haired fellow from Colorado assured me, explaining his round of 77. Another player, this one from Georgia, pointed toward the neat, handwritten row of 4s, 6s and 7s that appeared after his name on the scoreboard and complained, "How could someone as studly as me have shot a dip-shit round like that?" He didn't seem overly upset, however, as he lounged in his golf cart, feet on the dash, guzzling a Coors. He was young and good-looking, he had a rich sponsor somewhere paying all his bills, and there would always be tomorrow.

This was when Jones drove up, making the turn after nine holes of play, his eyes scanning the scoreboard like antiaircraft sensors. At thirty-five, he is a short, sturdy-looking man, with blond hair, plump cheeks and a forlorn, distracted air. In baggy black shorts, a Nike cap and saddle-oxford golf shoes, he looked more like a schoolboy than the tour's leading money winner. Nevertheless, his arrival silenced the cadets.

"What's the low score?" he asked in a taut North Carolina accent.

The question was precisely worded. Not "Who's in the lead?" because Jones didn't care about the person attached to the score. Not "What's in the money?" because finishing high enough to earn a check is not the issue; Jones almost always does. Rather, simply, "What's the low score?" What number precisely did he have to beat to take the lead?

"Uh, three under, Gene," someone said.

"Thanks," Jones replied and gunned the cart up the path. No one dared ask after his score, which happened to be even par.

After a pause, the banter resumed. "No one can play well *all* the time," my pal with the Coors continued in defense of his dip-shit round. But then he added, with a none-too-friendly edge in his voice, "Unless your name is frigging Gene the Machine."

The Spalding Space Coast Tour is golf's version of Bull Durham baseball. Most of the players are in their twenties, and every one thinks he is on the brink of Big Tour stardom. Pitted against them is a handful of cagey veterans and downward-spiraling former tour pros with names like Tony Cerda and Doug Weaver. The latter group almost always cleans up.

The biggest difference between Bull Durham–style minor league baseball and the Space Coast Tour is that in baseball the players earn a living. On the Space Coast Tour, which operates most of the year except for the hot summer months, probably fewer than a dozen golfers actually support themselves out of winnings. The rest, mostly the young guys, hit up Mom and Dad for cash transfusions, wangle financial-sponsorship deals from wealthy sportsmen who might otherwise back a racehorse, hustle amateurs at the approximately 140 Orlando-area golf courses or work part time.

The Space Coast Tour is essentially an open-air golf casino: Players put down their bets in the form of $300 to $350 entry fees, and the top few finishers walk off with most of the loot. The Spalding Company, hoping to curry favor with the club professionals of tomorrow, kicks in $100,000 a year to the kitty. And the house—in the person of J. C. Goosie, sixty-four, sole owner and proprietor—sweeps away 12 percent after course expenses. Last year the total purse was about $1.2 million, compared with more than $54 million on the PGA Tour.

"Our operation is simple," Goosie told me over the telephone. (He doesn't show up at Space Coast events when he qualifies for tournaments on the Senior PGA Tour.) "We want ex-college players to come down here and spend about sixteen thousand dollars to seventeen thousand dollars—that's for everything, entry fees, living expenses, everything—and play for a year. If a guy's good, he's gonna make twelve or thirteen thousand dollars of that back. If he's very good, he may break even. So for fifteen to thirty cents on the dollar, next to nothing, he's gonna get experience he can't buy nowhere else."

J. C. Goosie invented the minitour concept twenty years ago, basically because he and his pals who couldn't get on the regular tour needed a place to play. The idea caught on. Over the years quite a few Space Coast alums have made names for themselves on the

PGA, including stars like Paul Azinger and Craig Stadler. Recently, however, the best subtour talent has gravitated to the PGA Tour–sponsored Nike Tour (formerly the Ben Hogan Tour) and the four-year-old T. C. Jordan Tour. That leaves Goosie and a few other upstart minitours, like the Golden State Golf Tour, in California, defending the honor of single-A golf.

Conditions are what you'd expect: spiky greens, sprinkler systems that occasionally burst to life in the middle of a player's backswing, passing motorists yelling "Fore!" as a joke and no sign of a gallery anywhere. The absence of fans has advantages: Players feel free to relieve themselves in the woods whenever they like and to indulge in the same colorful expletives that golfers everywhere enjoy. The day-to-day manager of the Space Coast Tour is a former pro and real estate agent named Bobby Simpson, who has an odd way of holding his head, like a turtle peeking out of its shell. The starter is an affable Cajun nicknamed Crow, who spends the balance of his week at the dog track. And the rules officials include retired old pros who disperse around the course in golf carts and can often be spotted snoozing.

Such is the sweet narcotic bliss of golf, however, that nobody seems to mind.

I followed Jones around the back nine at DeBary, and it took me a while to identify his value-added as a golfer. His drives, though accurate, were not particularly long, and his swing, though serviceable, was brusque and pared down, pistonlike—not at all the elegant, modern Fred Couples ideal. He did appear perfectly comfortable standing over the ball, which is not always the case with golfers on the Space Coast Tour, many of whom bounce up and down neurotically and back way from the shot so often you begin to wonder if they might be afraid of hurting the ball.

After a few more holes, however, I began to understand that Jones's distinction is not his ball-striking ability so much as his raw animal hunger to score birdies. He works the course like a perpetual-motion machine, darting after his balls with the ferocity of a terrier, swinging extra clubs to groove the right feel, pacing like a CEO in a doctor's office whenever he has to wait, sizing up putts from every angle of the compass. On the eleventh hole he missed a seven-foot birdie putt and stayed on the green for several minutes afterward, inspecting the turf around the hole with the disgust of a surgeon try- ing to comprehend a botched operation.

Jones's attitude stood in marked contrast to that of his playing companion for the day, D. W. Smith, forty-two, a courtly Mississip- pian wearing a straw fedora. Smith, a very fine golfer himself (dur- ing one seventeen-round stretch last summer, he shot 90 under par), lolled about in the cart between shots chatting with other golfers like a pastor at a church social. "Look at D.W.," Jones said derisively, nodding as Smith nonchalantly got up to arch his back like a cat enjoying the sun. "If I was two over, I'd be eyeballing down the fair- way to see how I could get me a birdie."

During a brief delay on the fourteenth tee, Jones took me aside to apologize for a minor display of temper—he had tossed a club—on the previous hole. "I expect a little more out of myself is all," he said. "When you're playing this bad, it just gets under your skin, that's all. You gotta get after yourself, gotta get a little bit mad." The day be- fore, he said, he had shot 67 in a hurricane to win the one-thousand- dollar first prize at a tournament in Lady Lake.

With that he stepped up to his ball, mumbled something like "Come on, now, just gimme a chance" and sizzled a 3-iron straight down the center of the fairway. "Whoo-ee, Jethro," Smith cooed in appreciation. Jones acknowledged the compliment with a tight-lipped smile and stood aside, practicing his hip turn as the others hit.

"Personality-wise," I jotted in my notebook, "this guy's a natural for the PGA Tour."

I had hoped to talk with Jones more extensively after the round. But before I could collar him, an entertaining golfer named Billy Glisson asked me for a ride to his car. I had met Glisson a few days earlier. He claims to be the World's Leading All-Time Minitour Winner, and he probably is, though many would consider that a dubious honor.

"I come down here for one thing and one thing only, and that's to win," he told me in his hurry-up South Carolina accent as we barreled down a derelict stretch of highway. He was dragging on a Viceroy and blowing smoke out the window. "Coming in second don't cut it. That's why I've won ninety-one-plus minitour events. I reckon it's like Nicklaus."

Glisson, forty-six, is a friendly, lackadaisical mess of a man. He has a broad, blunt nose, longish, dirty blond hair that curlicues out the back of his golf cap and such a monster belly that he never even tries to tuck his shirttail in. He tends to wear the same pair of baggy gray shorts day after day and leaves a butt trail of Viceroys around the course which Hansel and Gretel would envy. I estimate he smokes three packs per round. Glisson also engages in the disturbing habit of popping his ball in his mouth between holes despite all the insecticides around.

If the Space Coast Tour attracted media attention the way the PGA Tour does, Glisson's personal history would be the stuff of legend. During the early years he supported his golf habit by working as the night manager of an Orlando brothel that operated out of a beauty salon. He got so good at golf, however, that by the early eighties he was supposedly winning more than fifty thousand dollars a year on the minitours. In 1981 he made it to the big tour and did pretty well. "Got on TV four or five times," he bragged matter-of-factly. Unfortunately, he soon suffered a nearly fatal stroke—"Too much drinking and carrying on, I reckon"—and so, after a couple of years' recovery, it was back to the minors.

Glisson lasted long enough on tour to make a mark, however. He is remembered, among other reasons, for confusing the courtesy-car volunteers with his frequent requests to pick up more than one "Mrs. Glisson" at the airport. At one tournament, the real Mrs. Glisson spotted her husband strolling the fairway holding hands with a Mrs. Glisson not herself and stole his Corvette out of spite, leaving only his street shoes in the parking space.

Despite a too-quick backswing and constant exasperation at slow play, Glisson still wins his share of minitour events. That's why the 79 he had shot that morning was such a thorn. "Couldn't make a putt," he grumbled as we drove. "When you play golf for a living, you gotta have total concentration. All I could think about was my damn car."

His car, a black 1983 Eldorado with an I'D RATHER BE GOLFING bumper sticker in the rear window, had broken down that morning on an I-40 exit ramp. He had had to hitch a ride, by chance with Gene the Machine, to make it to the tournament on time. We found the car, apparently repaired, tilting half-in, half-out of a muddy ditch beside the weather-beaten combination garage and sign shop where he had left it. The proprietor charged Glisson only thirty-five dollars. "Hot damn," Glisson said, beaming like he'd just holed out a pitching wedge from a hundred yards. "I thought they'd take me to the cleaners."

Even so, he had to borrow twenty dollars to make it back to the friend's apartment where he stays, sleeping on the couch, while competing in Orlando. And a few days later the Eldorado broke again. This time the repairs cost eight hundred dollars.

Glisson has a new wife and two children back in South Carolina. I asked him why he still plays tournament golf. "It just gets in the blood, I reckon," he replied, "and you can't get it out."

The next day, back at DeBary Plantation, Gene the Machine failed to win the tournament. He cranked out what for him was another disappointing round of even par to finish three shots off the pace. The winner, in a sudden-death playoff, was Doug Weaver, another former tour pro like Glisson but unlike Glisson in nearly every other possible respect. I realized this immediately when I offered to buy him a drink at the clubhouse bar to celebrate his exciting victory, and he enthusiastically accepted by ordering milk.

Weaver, thirty-three, is a solidly built redhead with a deep southern voice and a lightly pocked face. I thought he was joking about the milk, of course, but he wasn't. He ordered a tall glass of it, took one sip, then dashed off to a telephone to tell his wife the good news of their forty-three-hundred-dollar payday. "God must be teaching us to be very dependent on Him," Weaver said when he returned, "because every time we get almost broke, I win a tournament."

Two years earlier, he said, the family had been in a similar pickle. Their bank account was practically zero, his wife was pregnant, his swing was incoherent, and he had just shot 81–82 in a pro-am tournament at Pebble Beach. After the tournament, he and his wife, Patricia, walked down to the beach below the course and prayed, "Dear God," they beseeched, "if we're going to play golf in 1991, You're going to have to put the money in our hands because we're too embarrassed to ask anyone for it ourselves anymore." Sure enough, a few days later Weaver received an offer from a potential sponsor—one of his partners in the disastrous Pebble Beach pro-am, no less—of thirty thousand dollars over the next two years. He was back in business.

I asked Weaver what keeps him golfing when the financial abyss yawns. "I realize I could go back to South Carolina and get a good job," he replied. "But the Bible says a young man without vision shall perish. That doesn't mean really perish, but he just won't have a good life." He paused to take his last gulp of milk. "This is the dream God has laid on our hearts."

The shocking thing about the pro-golf scene in Orlando is the sheer number of men, like Weaver and Glisson and all the cadets, who manage to arrange their lives to play golf every day "for a living." Because in addition to Goosie's operation, two other, even lesser minitours operate in the area: the Tommy Armour Tour and the North Florida PGA Winter Tour. Together the three tours qualify Orlando, without a doubt, as the Bush-League Professional Golf Capital of the Universe.

I called on the Tommy Armour Tour one Saturday during its one-day tournament at the Overoaks Country Club. First-place prize money was one thousand dollars, and the second-place check (which went to Gene the Machine for shooting 67 again) was six hundred dollars. When I arrived, the players who had already finished were standing around in a grove of live oak trees, the branches hung with Spanish moss, sipping beer or soft drinks and chatting amiably amongst themselves. It looked a lot like a big southern picnic or family reunion. "No offense," a competitor recently arrived from New Jersey told me, "but this is the lamest tour I've ever played in."

The man who owns the Tommy Armour Tour is a perplexed-looking forty-nine-year-old named Terry Fine. Fine plays in his own tournaments as a way of tuning up for the Senior Tour. The day I visited, he shot an 81. "The biggest complaint the players have down here in Florida," he said, "is the blatant stealing out of the purse that takes place on some of the other tours." By "other tours" he was clearly alluding to Goosie's, though Fine later said he did not mean to suggest by "stealing" that Goosie was doing anything illegal—merely that he was keeping too high a percentage of the pot for himself.

No love is lost between Fine and Goosie. For Goosie, the Tommy Armour Tour is "kind of a sore thumb." He claims not to mind the competition—"good, honest competition we can handle"—as much as the way Fine "slipped around behind my back, giving my players his cards, that sort of thing," when Fine was getting his tour off the ground three years ago.

As for Fine, he likes to portray himself as the golfers' true friend. He prides himself on keeping a higher percentage of the players' money in the pot, after expenses and profits, than does Goosie. But since his major sponsor, the Tommy Armour Golf Company, contributes less to his tour than the Spalding company does to the Space Coast Tour, the players still get a better return with Goosie. To compensate, Fine was working on a deal to offer all Tommy Armour Tour members in good standing a 10 percent discount at Wolf Camera outlets across the South. "One thing we're trying to do at the Tommy Armour Tour is add a little dignity," he said. Earlier, the tour had been known as the Hooters Tour, after a restaurant chain that features busty waitresses in tight T-shirts and hot pants. So dignity-wise, that's progress right there.

I wandered over to the clubhouse porch, where a number of competitors were loitering after their round. They constituted the usual assortment of oddballs one finds in bush league golf: a bartender and occasional dancer at a Chippendales-like club, a frightened-looking kid from South Africa who appeared to be no older than twelve, a forty-one-year-old tenured Delta pilot who competes regularly by virtue of his eighteen off days per month and a surly, ponytailed, practice-range pro who was griping about how much Fred Couples earned for switching to Parallax clubs (supposedly four million dollars) and showing off his own abnormally long driver. This club's head weighed about ten pounds and was made of Kryptonite or plutonium or something and if manipulated correctly could propel the ball, he said, 339 yards. He let me try it on the range. It was like swinging a maypole with several small children attached. My best attempt almost reached the 100-yard marker.

As I was preparing to leave, a twenty-four-year-old golfer named Joe Shahady took me aside to suggest privately that I might want to mention in the article how much he enjoys eating PowerBars. PowerBars, according to some information Terry Fine made available, provide delicious, nutritious, *sustained* energy to help golfers maintain the focus required for hitting straight drives and making crucial putts. I forgot to mention earlier that the PowerBar company is an official sponsor of the Tommy Armour Tour. Any player quoted in the press singing the praises of PowerBars gets a five-hundred-dollar bonus.

I finally had a chance to sit down and talk with Gene the Machine after the first round of the next Space Coast tournament, a two-day affair at the Kissimmee Bay Country Club. He had just shot a 66 but couldn't resist complaining about a couple of knee-knocker putts he missed. "I just couldn't get anything started on the front nine," he grumbled.

Off the course Jones is not nearly as daunting as he is when stalking a golf ball. He has a mild, fidgety manner and a hang-dog vulnerability. During the interview, whenever a subject arose that he didn't feel comfortable with, such as the past, he flitted off to something more benign, usually golf. "I used to be down on myself because I didn't have any money and all, but the insight I had was that the more failures you go through, the higher you can achieve," he said. "You can work hard in golf and make it."

Reportedly, Jones was a superstar in high school in Orlando. He won the Florida PGA Junior title and the U.S. Olympic Junior championship before turning pro at eighteen. Then something happened, all the details of which I could not discover. A car wreck was part of it; for five years he wore a neck brace. Apparently, too, he didn't get along with people; he was introverted and, as he puts it, "too hardcore" about golf. For a long time he drifted. He sold pots and pans in Fort Worth, cleaned swimming pools in Orlando and mowed the grass at a country club in South Carolina. "I had went as low as I could go," Jones says, "but I won't say I was going crazy, because I still always believed that I could play."

His rescuer was Malcolm McDonald, an Orlando-area surgeon and friend of the family. Dr. Mac, as Jones calls him, remembered what a fine player Jones had been as a youth and convinced him four years ago to move back from South Carolina. To make that financially possible, McDonald bought Jones and his wife a trailer and a few acres of land outside Orlando and encouraged him to reconcile with his dad, a teaching pro.

The turning point for Jones, golfwise, seemed to come last year when he qualified in a preliminary round to compete in the Greensboro Open, a PGA Tour event. "At Greensboro, you'd hear ten thousand people giving you the clap, and it was really motivating," Jones said. "I'm not gonna say I belong out there on the tour, but that experience made me think I might."

In 1992, by the time we were talking, Jones had already won seventeen tournaments on the minitour scene. "It scares me how well I'm doing," he said. "Right now I'd be afraid to take a week off."

Then he excused himself to go home and practice for the next day's final round. He was tied for the lead.

To get to Kissimmee Bay from DeBary Plantation, you motor down the interstate past the fantasy factory at Universal Studios and the counterfeit reality of Walt Disney World. Then you turn left into a nightmare strip of bogus American roadside attractions. You pass Gatorland, Pirate's Island, Medieval Times and Fun 'n Wheels. By the time you reach the county jail, where you turn right, Long John Silver's seems like a high-class seafood shoppe.

I mention this because it occurred to me as I drove to Kissimmee that it's no coincidence that the Bush-League Professional Golf Capital of the Universe should be in a city like Orlando, which is wholly predicated on the suspension of disbelief. Because that's what golf is all about, too. For ostensibly mature adult men to persuade themselves that the possibility of slicing a dimpled ball into some completely artificial, blue-dyed lagoon is a risk with as dire and pulse-quickening consequences as being eaten by a bear or ambushed by the Viet Cong demands not only the suspension of disbelief but also the collusion of an entire social ecosystem. That the players are engaged in *professional* golf (albeit third-rate professional golf) only adds to the gravitas and urgency of the adventure. The delusion grows that these rounds really matter, that the players' very careers hang in the balance on each and every shot. This, I concluded, could be the ultimate source of professional golf's dark and addictive thrill and possibly the key to understanding why men of the bush league so willingly sacrifice all the nice things that their wives would like them to buy with the money they don't earn, such as new drapes for the living room and higher-quality knickknacks.

That was my thinking, anyway.

For the final round of the Kissimmee Bay tournament, Jones was paired in the next to last foursome with three cadets named Scott Pleis, Bo Fennell and Chris Hehmann. Hehmann was a rookie who had apparently never before been so high on the leader board for a final round.

Diluting the potential tension of the round was the observational presence, in a golf cart, of Steve Pleis, Scott's brother, and Brad McClendon, a brawny, crew-cut, good old boy from Louisiana. Steve Pleis and McClendon, having gone out in the first group of the day, had already finished their rounds. They had zipped around the course in near record time—"They played like they were in some kind of hurry to take a shit," a rules official told me—and now had a bad case of the giggles, especially when it came to Hehmann.

"He's playing out of his ying-yang," McClendon chortled at 11 when Hehmann mis-hit an approach shot but then chipped in from fifty feet for a birdie. On 14, when Hehmann left a forty-foot putt almost fifteen feet short, Steve said, "There's a lot of chicken left on that bone," and he and McClendon sat stifling their laughter like Sunday schoolers in a church pew. Eventually Hehmann self-destructed.

Jones, of course, was having none of it. He continued to play nearly flawless golf, hitting most greens in regulation and rolling his lag putts to within inches for tap-in pars. If Jones even noticed Pleis and McClendon trailing the group, he didn't show it. The Machine was focused, readying himself for what he had told me the day before was his primary focus and favorite part of a tournament: the final three holes. Coming off the fifteenth green, Jones said he figured two birdies out of three would give him a chance to win. "We'll see what we can do," he said.

He got one birdie at the par-3 sixteenth, draining a forty-footer. On 17, a 416-yard par 4, he parked his approach shot five feet from the pin, and I had no doubt the Machine would hammer home the putt. But he didn't. The ball gave the hole a smell but then lipped out. On 18, all Jones could muster was a routine par.

His 69 tied him for fourth. "One of these days," he said tersely and walked off the course.

In the clubhouse bar afterwards, a couple of dozen players were waiting around to pick up their prize checks. Roger Rowland, a towheaded cadet from nearly Ocala, was hunched over his beer at the bar and shaking his head from side to side. He had just won the tournament with twin 66s. "Man, I'll tell you," he was muttering, "you plain gotta play some golf to win one of these things."

Billy Glisson was there, chain-smoking Viceroys and throwing back Seven and 7s as he regaled the Pleis brothers with tales from the good old days. "There was a lot more going on in those chairs than just blow-dries, I guarantee" was one line I overheard, presumably in reference to the beauty parlor/brothel where he used to work. For some reason he was carrying a jumbo driver and waggling it, Bob Hope–style, as he delivered his shtick. The Pleis brothers seemed only mildly amused.

To my surprise Gene Jones walked in and took a stool at the bar. I had the impression that drinking with the boys was not something he did very often.

"Hey, Machine," someone called out. "There's a rumor going around that you're making so much money you don't even cash your checks."

The barroom grew quiet to hear his response. "That's right," Jones said and took a long sip of beer. "I just go home every night and stare at 'em."

The line got a laugh, and that seemed to relax him. When a relative old-timer sauntered by and said, "Hey, Gene, what happened out there? I'm not used to seeing your name that far down the list," Jones smiled and seemed to relish the implicit compliment.

I took the stool next to Jones and offered to buy him a beer, but he bought me one instead. I asked him about his round. "Golf's a tough business," he replied with a shrug. "It's all about making the short ones."

He got out a pencil and calculated on a cocktail napkin that the missed five-footer on 17 had cost him eight hundred dollars. "But I still had a two-thousand-dollar week. I'll be getting fourteen hundred dollars from Goosie and another six hundred fifty dollars from the Spalding bonus pool. That's pretty good money for a country boy." Then he began pulling jewelry out of a pouch that he carries around in his golf bag: a gold Rolex, a gold pinky ring with a gaudy dollar sign on its face and a key ring hung with a tiny gold golf club and a spike wrench.

Finally, the tour manager, Bobby Simpson, began circulating with the checks: large, yellow Space Coast bank drafts signed by J. C. Goosie himself. Jones folded his neatly into quarters and tucked it in his wallet beside two suspiciously similar-looking pieces of paper. "What are those?" I asked.

He took them out and showed me: uncashed Space Coast checks

for three thousand dollars and one thousand dollars. "I guess I am getting a little behind," Jones admitted sheepishly. But as he returned the checks to his wallet, he held my glance for a moment, and I could see how powerfully proud he was of winning checks that large. He was proud of all that he had accomplished with his life in the last few years. Maybe he does take the checks home and stare at them, I thought.

The instant Jones left the bar, a journeyman pro named Dan Oschmann said: "The son of a bitch. I wish he'd get the hell out of here and let the rest of us make some money." He meant it as a joke, but he was serious, too.

In the PGA Tour Qualifying Tournament, which began two weeks later, Jones obliged. He was one of only forty-three players out of nearly nine hundred entrants—including a large proportion of the Space Coast irregulars—to win a coveted tour card for 1993.

I talked to the Machine by telephone afterward. "I'm looking to earn a million dollars," he said. As of late April, however, Jones had made the cut in just two tournaments, earning a total of $4,340.

—1993

Grown Men on Spring Break

David Owen

In terms of optimum clubhead speed, the length of the hosel and the apparent angle of the groove-to-punch mark declination, minus the reciprocal of the angle of the axis of the shaft as it relates to the heel, must under no circumstances exceed the distance in millimeters between the axis of the shaft or the neck or socket and the back of the heel.

There. That ought to take care of my wife. I don't think she would read this anyway, but she'll definitely never get past that paragraph. We can now speak freely.

Why does my wife—and, by extension, virtually everyone else's wife—hate golf? One reason, I suppose, is that Ethel (not her real name) does not herself play golf. She doesn't get the point of competitive sports and, in fact, won't even play cards. She will occasionally play Scrabble, but if you get a big word in your first few turns she will insist on starting a new game. (Why not simply press?) In addition, she doesn't like anything that she isn't good at immediately—a character trait that rules out putting, chipping, pitching, sand play, short irons, medium irons, long irons, fairway woods, and driving.

I don't necessarily view any of this as a drawback; I'm glad Ethel doesn't play golf. I have several friends whose wives reluctantly took up the game in an effort to share their husbands' lives but ended up merely adding to their own already hefty burdens of resentment. They used to be angry at their husbands for spending so much time playing golf. Now they're angry at their husbands not only for that, but also for never wanting to play with them.

Obviously, not all golfing wives are like this. I have a 0-handicap friend who made it to the quarter-finals of the British Amateur a decade ago; when he plays with his wife, she gives him a stroke a side. They have what may be the perfect marriage—my concept of the ideal woman has changed in the last few years—but their relationship is very unusual. More typical of golfing wifedom are the four women my friend Jim and I encountered one day at our local nine-hole golf course. Jim and I were playing twenty-seven holes, and the women were playing nine, and we played through them three times. The problem wasn't so much that they were terrible golfers, although they were. The problem was that they approached the game with a baffling sort of lackadaisical vagueness that precluded, for instance, making any effort whatsoever to control the direction or speed of a putt. A round of golf, for them, was a social outing; it wasn't a round of golf.

Everything I've said so far is pigheaded and unfair, but it is positively enlightened in comparison with the things that Ethel says about golf. In her view, the game is beneath contempt, like vivisection. When I say, "I'm going to play golf," she looks at me as if I had said, "I think I'd like to start dating our daughter." She approves of flower arranging, liposuction, psychotherapy, hair dye, and aimless, irrational driving—but a nine-hundred-year-old game played by the president of the United States she can't stand.

The paradox, I suppose, is that Ethel's feelings about golf seem to increase my enjoyment of the game. It may be that men are chromosomally predisposed toward doing virtually anything their wives don't want them to do. (My literary agent, an enlightened woman, provides ironic support for this hypothesis. For many years, she has tried to persuade her husband to take up golf—"I *want* to be a golf widow," she says—but he has refused.). This innate contrariness must have given our humanoid ancestors some powerful evolutionary advantage. A possible scenario: Female cave people implored their mates to spend more time around the cave, picking up woolly-mammoth bones and entertaining the children; those who complied watched their families slowly starve to death, while those who ignored their mates and went hunting instead survived. In such beneficent behavior we may be seeing evidence of the forerunner of the modern golfing gene.

Whether or not our intention was to infuriate our wives, my brother, John, my friends Jim and Mike, and I spent a good bit of the fall and winter planning an early-spring golfing trip to Myrtle Beach, South Carolina. We sent away for catalogs listing courses and motels, then spent several happy weeks poring over them, like sorority sisters dreaming of the perfect honeymoon. In and around Myrtle Beach are dozens of motels and hotels that offer inexpensive golf packages. Some include a room, breakfast, and a round of golf for less than thirty dollars a day, depending on the season.

After much heated but essentially ignorant deliberation, we settled on a motel in North Myrtle Beach that, for legal reasons, I will refer to as the Bates Motel. We called the proprietor to tell her when and where we wanted to play, and that was that. She made all our golf reservations for us. All we had to do was survive two more months of snow.

On a golf-hole-per-square-mile basis, Myrtle Beach is far and away the springtime golf capital of eastern North America. There are something like eighty courses on the strip of Carolina seaside known as the Grand Strand, and so many more are under construction that the maps on the placemats in the restaurants are invariably out of date. During the peak spring season—which runs roughly from the middle of March until the first of June—the area fills with men from the North whose veins are throbbing with resurgent golf hormones. During the two months before our late-February departure date, I remembered what it felt like to be a child waiting for Christmas. By the time the great day arrived, my partners and I were so excited that we could scarcely make intelligent conversation with our wives, who were no longer speaking to us anyway.

We were nearly an hour late in taking off from Charlotte, North Carolina, for the final leg of our journey. Bad weather elsewhere in the country had played havoc with connecting flights, and ours was the last plane bound for Myrtle Beach that night. The plane by that point was filled almost entirely with Myrtle Beach golfers, of which there are two broad species: Golf-Dependent Personalities and Arrested Development Cases. These species are easily distinguishable. The GDPs go to bed early, play thirty-six holes a day, and lose sleep worrying about frost delays. The ADCs are former high school bad boys who haven't quite surrendered to the constraints of married life. They smoke cigars, cruise the strip joints at night, play only one round a day, and never have a morning tee time. Members of both species are exclusively male and closing in on middle age. None would remember to call home if his wife didn't give him a Post-it reminder to stick to the telephone in his motel room.

On the plane, the GDPs were wearing golf hats, reading golf magazines, and debating the merits of penal versus strategic course architecture. The ADCs were angrily complaining that they hadn't been allowed to sit out the delay in the terminal cocktail lounge. A linebacker-sized ADC sitting behind me grumbled, "We're going to miss our tee time at the Doll House," referring to a well-known Myrtle Beach strip joint. The stewardesses, who had been forced by the collapse of the Soviet Union to take early retirement from Aeroflot, were surly and unapologetic. Through my window I anxiously watched cadaver-shaped golf bags ride the dark conveyor belt into the belly of our plane. Was that one mine? Finally, just as the last liter of oxygen in the cabin had been converted to man breath, we took off.

Like most GDPs, my partners and I rented a minivan when we arrived in Myrtle Beach. (ADCs rent, and often wreck, Lincoln Town Cars.) A Grand Voyager is exactly the right size to hold four tubby men, four golf bags, and four poorly packed suitcases. Plus, it has drink holders, and you can dry two pairs of golf shoes at a time by wedging them between the windshield and the defroster. In the nation at large, the minivan is an icon of family values; on the Grand Strand, it's just an oversized, all-weather golf cart. We called ours the Man Van.

It was close to midnight when, after approximately an hour and a half of being hopelessly lost, we pulled into the parking lot of the Bates Motel. A cold, stinging wind was blowing off the Atlantic, causing sand, newspapers, plastic foam cups, and a big garbage can to tumble around the swimming pool, which had been covered with

a flapping tarp. Rain, if not snow, seemed imminent. Ghostly breakers slammed into the beach. The motel's office was dark, empty, and
locked. Taped to the door was an envelope that turned out to contain our golf vouchers and a note explaining that our room keys could
be found under the mats in front of our doors. We lugged our bags up
to our rooms—two tenement-quality two-bedroom suites, each with
a minimalist living room and kitchenette—turned on the rasping
wall-mounted heaters, and fell into bed. Comfortingly, just as I was
about to doze off, I heard a golf ball bounce and roll on the floor of
the room above. I got up half an hour later to look for an extra blan-
ket, but couldn't find one, and ended up unpacking my suitcase on
top of my bedspread in an effort to raise the R-value of my bed.

A little over four hours later, when my alarm went off, an icy
rain was lashing the broken window at my head. Stumbling out of
bed, I discovered with sorrow that I had packed too many golf shirts
and not enough Arctic-weight down-filled Gore-Tex jumpsuits. Our
first tee time was seven-sixteen, at the Legends, a three-course complex virtually all the way back to the airport, some forty-five minutes away. On our way south, we stopped at one of Myrtle Beach's
ubiquitous pancake houses to choke down bacon, eggs, and Advil.
Two men who didn't look like golfers were the only other diners. They
eyed us coldly as we pestered the waitress for additional coffee. Then,
back into the Man Van. As we drove, I kept the windshield wipers
on intermittent speed, even though I could barely make out the car
ahead of me, because I didn't want to encourage the rain by seeming
to give in to it. "I think the clouds are breaking up," Jim said hopefully, as thunderclouds collided above us.

Myrtle Beach is the sociological equivalent of the inside of a single
man's refrigerator. Driving to the course from our motel, I got an
inkling of what the world would be like if wives did not exist. There
were gas stations, cheap motels, a topless karaoke bar, liquor stores,
pawn shops, hangar-sized fried-food restaurants, golf-equipment stores
that stayed open until ten, and very little else. A white frame bun-
galow that looked like a farmer's vegetable stand turned out to be a

used-golf-ball store. You can find anything you need in Myrtle Beach, as long as it isn't broccoli or a diaper.

Myrtle Beach's history as a low-cost golf destination stretches back about a quarter-century. The first golf package was offered in 1959 by the Dunes Club and the Caravelle Hotel. Golfers could stay at the Caravelle and play at the Dunes, which had opened a decade earlier (and is still one of the prime courses in the region). At that time, there were only three eighteen-hole golf courses in the Myrtle Beach area. The antifeminist spectacle that the Grand Strand would later become was yet undreamed of. But the Dunes package was a hit, and it inspired imitators. By 1979, there were more than thirty courses operating, and many packages. Truly explosive growth came in the eighties, when more than forty new courses were built. By 1990, there wasn't a compulsive golfer in America who didn't know about Myrtle Beach. The Grand Strand was the place to go for a quick, cheap fix.

Myrtle Beach's reputation for high-quality golf was slower to develop, but—surprisingly, given the distinctly seedy atmosphere—it is deserved. In recent years especially, a large number of excellent courses have been built, making it possible for diehard GDPs to get their daily fixes on courses that are actually quite decent. The courses tend to be crowded, but the crowds have their positive side: They generate the revenues that make premium-course construction possible.

The three courses that make up the Legends—Heathland, Moorland, and Parkland—are among those frequently cited as being tops. Heathland, which opened in 1990, was designed by Tom Doak, who is one of the most interesting young American course designers. Doak majored in golf-course architecture at Cornell and spent a fellowship year in Britain, where he visited 172 different courses. He also worked as a caddy at the Old Course. After graduation, Doak served his design apprenticeship with Pete Dye. He came away from these experiences with a firm grounding in classical design coupled with more than a touch of Dye-esque inventiveness. Ben Crenshaw, who has a reputation for being the PGA Tour's resident keeper of the flame, views Doak as a kindred spirit and has called him "a *real* lover of the game."

Heathland represents one of Doak's highly satisfactory efforts to build a linkslike course in the United States. We certainly had Scottish-style conditions. The rain fluctuated in intensity but never entirely disappeared, and the wind picked up. After wavering briefly in the pro shop, we decided to cough up an additional twenty bucks for plastic covers for our carts. These provided a certain amount of protection from the gusty, twenty-five-mile-per-hour wind and the steady, enervating rain. Curiously, though, I think the carts made the weather seem even nastier than it was. I had played in worse weather in Ireland but minded it less—mostly, I think because walking kept my muscles warm and my blood circulating. At Heathland we were constantly climbing in and out of our absurd vehicles, zipping and unzipping the plastic covers, sitting in chilly puddles, and rolling back or tying together the dripping flaps that covered our clubs. The roofs of the carts amplified the sound of the rain, making a drizzle seem like a downpour. The windshields were merely translucent. The runoff from the roofs drained directly into our golf bags. All day long, I felt *encumbered*. Worse, a cart makes it very hard to get a sense of what a course is actually like. A hole doesn't unfold to you the way it does when you are on foot—especially if you can't see out the windshield.

Still, Heathland is a very good golf course. It doesn't make you think you are in Scotland, but it wears its influences very well. Several holes were directly inspired by favorite holes of Doak's in Britain (the fifteenth is modeled after the third at Royal St. George's; the eighteenth is Doak's tribute to the eighteenth at Royal Lytham and St. Annes). Once or twice I was reminded of Carnoustie. Someday I would like to go back.

My hands were so numb by the end of our first round that I could scarcely grip the hotdog that I didn't have time to eat as we raced around the back of the clubhouse to sign in for our second round. The proprietor of the Bates Motel had scheduled our two rounds just five hours and four minutes apart, an overoptimistic spacing considering the glacial pace of play at most Myrtle Beach golf courses. We played our second round on the Parkland course, which is the newest of the three Legends. It was designed by Larry Young, who owns the entire complex and is responsible for several of the more distinguished courses on the Grand Strand. (Moorland was designed by P. B. Dye, who is the son of Pete.) Unfortunately, my memories of Parkland are few and indistinct. The forecast we had checked at five that morning had said the rain would end by midday, but it did not. There were many occasions when the clouds seemed to be breaking up, or when the splashes on the ponds seemed to be thinning, and there was a moment when we actually took off our rain jackets, thinking the sun was about to break through. But the weather never really changed. We were cold and wet, and we had trouble paying attention.

Shortly after five o'clock, we drained our last four feeble putts and staggered into the nice, big bar in the clubhouse. Silently, we drank beer, ate potato chips, and stared at the two huge television sets, one of which was showing a tape of the 1992 U.S. Open, and the other of which was tuned to the Weather Channel. Obsessive viewing of the Weather Channel is the closest thing in Myrtle Beach to an organized religion. The guys at the bar were all gazing at the radar map and arguing about the significance of the shifting pattern of green and orange splotches, which signified rain. The forecast for the next day seemed to be better. Or maybe it wasn't.

A little later, we stowed our soggy equipment in the back of the Man Van and headed north again. We stopped for dinner at a Myrtle Beach institution called Dick's Last Resort, where we drank Big Ass Beers (from glasses so labeled) and ate buckets of fried and barbecued food. Dick's is a sort of human feedlot with long, greasy tables in it. Our waiter gave us matchbooks with pictures of naked women on them and promised us free drinks if we could figure out which one of the naked women was now a (fully clothed) waitress in the restaurant. Every few minutes, a quartet of weary golfers would stumble through the front door and ask for a table. (In Myrtle Beach, the basic social unit is not the couple or the family but the foursome. Every hour or so, at least one member of every foursome will grin smugly at his mates and say, "It just doesn't get any better than this," usually at a moment when the statement is obviously and even poignantly not true.) As we waited for our check, a tall man surrounded by half a dozen beautiful young women strolled into the bar. He wore a hat that looked like a condom. A golfer at the next table said, in a hushed voice, "That's Dick."

On our way home after dinner, we spotted a brightly illuminated after-dark executive golf course on the main drag. John and I wanted to stop for a few bonus holes under the halogen lights, but Jim and Mike were still emotionally distraught from our day at the Legends, and they insisted on returning to the Bates Motel. John and I dropped them off, then drove back downtown and stopped at Martin's, a massive golf-equipment store that's open till ten o'clock five nights a week. We bought Jim and Mike each two bags containing twenty-four sepia-colored used balls, for $4.95 a bag (Jim and Mike had each lost at least a couple of dozen balls that day). For myself, I bought a dozen new balls, several pairs of socks, a map of Myrtle Beach, and some tees. John and I tried out various putters. Then we went home.

Jim and Mike were semicomatose when we returned, but John and I still hadn't had quite enough golf, so we putted on the floor of our living room, then used 9-irons to hit nickels from the carpet into the heavy curtains covering the front window. John had learned this trick while staying in motels during various away matches with his golf team in college. If you keep your head fairly still, you can pick a coin cleanly off a rug that has a decent pile, and the big double curtains protect the windows. When we got tired of hitting money, we switched to balls and laid out a short but challenging course that wound through the three and a half rooms of our suite. We got into quite an analytical discussion concerning the difference between hitting off our beds and hitting off the couch, and whether it was better to putt or chip from the linoleum floor of the kitchenette onto the carpeted floor of the living room. All in all, we made only a few dark marks in the popcornlike acoustical finish on the ceilings, mostly with overenthusiastic follow-throughs.

Not every hotel or motel room is ideally suited to golf. In most rooms, there's a big window (with the requisite heavy curtains) at one end, a big bed or two on one side, and a bureau, desk, and so forth on the other side. If you are a right-handed golfer and the beds are on the left as you face the window, you have plenty of room to take a full swing without unduly damaging furniture. If the beds are on the right, however, you run the risk of smashing the TV at the top of your backswing. In such a room, a golfer is limited to putts, chips, and three-quarter knockdown shots. The wisest course is probably to specify the type of room you need when you make your reservation: "I'd like a nonsmoking single for a right-handed golfer, please." Of course, the ideal room also has a big mirror on the wall over the bureau, so that you can stand on your bed and check your takeaway from three different angles. The mattress makes any weight-shift errors instantly obvious, but only in the older, more luxurious hotels—those with high ceilings—is it possible to take a full swing while standing on the bed.

While John and I were playing, we were also drying our equipment. We had removed all our clubs from our bags and leaned them against the walls, so the grips could dry. I had Velcroed my five sopping golf gloves to a wire hanger and dangled them in front of the heater. We had already discovered that we could dry our shoes in about an hour by placing them upside down on top of the shades of our bedside lamps. When my gloves were dry, I draped my wet towel (which I had stepped on at the Legends and stuffed into the bottom of my bag) over the vents of the heater and promptly forgot about it. While John and I chipped from chair to couch, the towel slowly turned to the consistency of tree bark, while gradually humidifying and odorizing our room.

A world-class drunk can cheerfully hop out of bed without a trace of a hangover the morning after downing a couple of quarts of gin. Similarly, a Golf-Dependent Personality can cheerfully whistle while screwing new spikes into his golf shoes the morning after playing two rounds of dreary, life-threatening golf. Although all of us had suffered mightily in the wind and rain the previous day, all of us were smiling and eager to begin again when our alarms went off at five-thirty on the second morning. All of us, that is, except Mike, who kept us waiting for twenty minutes while he sulked in the bathroom, covering virtually his entire epidermis with Band-Aids. "Would you like some of my Advil?" asked my brother, who was playing with two broken ribs, the result of a skiing accident. "I don't need Advil," Mike said gloomily. "I need Prozac." Fortunately, the Weather Channel at that very moment was promising that the rain would not return.

Our first round of the day was at Marsh Harbour, a wonderful course that wanders among the salt marshes along the Intracoastal Waterway. Marsh Harbour was designed by Dan Maples and by Larry Young, who owns and built this course in addition to the Legends. The signature hole is the seventeenth, a lengthy par 5 with intimidating carries over marsh for both the second and third shots. I managed to par that hole while my brother got a bogey—one of the few holes on which I bested him, despite his broken bones. Jim and Mike launched perhaps a dozen balls into various portions of the marsh before retiring glumly to their cart. (That morning, they had dumped their bags of used balls into the wire-mesh baskets on the back of their cart, and they dipped into these stores frequently, as though the baskets were bowls of peanuts.) The entire course was challenging and thought-provoking, and it was full of photo opportunities. We saw several herons, a pair of eaglelike birds called oslos, and a woodpecker the size of a pterodactyl. Once again, the day began chilly and got cooler, but there was no rain, and the intermittently bright sun provided the occasional illusion of warmth.

We played our second round, after a real and relatively unhurried lunch, on the other side of the waterway, at a course called Ocean Harbour. (Both courses straddle the border between the Carolinas, making it possible to hit shots from one state to the other.) None of us liked Ocean Harbour very much, even though the staff was extremely solicitous. "If you have any trouble with this cart, let me know and we'll get you another," a friendly attendant said as we set out. Six holes later, we found out why he had been so friendly. The cart stopped dead. Jim got out and pushed it for a while, trying to reinspire

it. Mike sat morosely in the seat, nursing blisters that made it difficult for him to limp even from one greenside bunker to another.
Finally, we managed to flag down a ranger, and traded carts with him.
The ranger's cart had a jagged, ball-sized hole in the middle of the
windshield, but it moved along quite briskly.

The groups ahead of us for as far as we could see were playing at
the pace of weary tortoises, and darkness began to fall long before
we were finished. We played the fifteenth, a 140-yard par 3, without
being able to see the flag, but all miraculously hit the green. By the
time we reached the eighteenth, a par 4 that is edged along its entire
right side by the Calabash River, we could see nothing except the
clubhouse lights. We fired all of Jim and Mike's remaining balls out
toward the fairway, hoping to find at least four in play. We turned
up six, and fired all of them toward what we presumed to be the green.
One of the shots was followed at a suspect interval by the sound of
crunching metal—the roof of a car in the parking lot?—but we never
saw any of those six balls again, on the green or anywhere else.

That night, we ate dinner at a restaurant whose name, if memory
serves, was Homer Simpson's Calabash Deep-Fat Aortic Aneurysm.
The blue-roofed barn was brightly lit, and it was filled with senior
citizens plus a sprinkling of foursomes. Our waitress was young and
cute. Giving her our orders was as close as we had come so far to
having any sort of sexual adventure in Myrtle Beach (no lap danc-
ing for us). Jim, John, and I ordered the seafood special: lobster tail,
fried shrimp, fried oysters, fried clams, fried scallops, fried "fish," a
basket of hush puppies. Mike ordered something called, I believe,
Hoof and Brine: a steak and various fried seafood items. John suddenly felt queasy and ate only one hush puppy, which, he said, instantly expanded to a size slightly greater than that of his stomach.
We were all entitled to eat all we wanted at the seafood bar, which
consisted mostly of teeny shrimp that appeared to have spent less time
in the sea than in a can. We all left feeling ill, especially John. On
the way back, we stopped at Revco (to buy Band-Aids, moleskin, and
Advil) and at a fairly tony golf-equipment store (to buy more balls
for Jim and Mike). Back at the Bates, we all went straight to bed—

John and I didn't even putt—after our customary evening devotional with the Weather Channel. The forecast: sort of good.

We were all a little poky in the mornings, but none of us was slower than Mike. After the first night, Jim had set his alarm clock half an hour ahead, to trick Mike into thinking he had less time to gird himself for battle than he did. This ruse worked pretty well, and Mike never caught on. On the third morning, Mike told Jim that the mornings were his favorite part of the trip, an astonishing statement that Jim initially took to be a joke. But it turned out that Mike was serious. "I can't believe how cheerful and optimistic I feel each morning," he said, "given what the reality is."

The third day of our trip was Mike's tenth wedding anniversary. His wife had assured him that she didn't mind his being away on the big day, but a friend of his wife's had been appalled, and she had been trying to make trouble. As we drove to breakfast (with two pairs of damp golf shoes drying on the dashboard) we debated what to do. "Maybe we should call your wife's friend tonight and have it out with her," I suggested. Mike didn't think that was such a good idea. "I keep telling my wife that she ought to take a trip by herself sometime, too," Mike said, "but she never does it." He professed not to be bothered, but he was clearly brooding. We let the matter drop when we reached the Pearl.

The Pearl is a two-course complex in Calabash, North Carolina, not far from Marsh Harbour. There was quite a bit of frost on the greens and fairways when we arrived, but we were allowed to tee off at our scheduled time anyway. We played Pearl East first. It's a decent layout, but at the time we played it, it was in very ragged condition. Many years had passed since the old golfing rituals of replacing divots and repairing ball marks had been observed. In the afternoon, after an unexplained sixty-minute delay, that had apparently been caused by overbooking, we played Pearl West, which was even rattier, beginning with the back nine. The group ahead of us—four hatless, beer-swilling hillbillies who had apparently taken up golf that morning—insisted on playing from the rearmost tees, from which the course measured more than seven thousand yards. One sliced his ball so dramatically that it nearly returned to his feet, like a boomerang.

When we reached the twelfth or thirteenth hole, all progress on the course ground to a halt. John said he had suspected we were in trouble when he noticed that no one in the foursome ahead of us was wearing a hat. One member of that group was playing the course twenty yards at a time: slice, duck hook, slice, duck hook, slice, duck hook. Looking off through the woods in another direction, we saw one tee that had seven or eight groups backed up on it—possibly the members of a Rotary outing, or the participants in a work-release program from some nearby penitentiary. In the woods alongside an adjoining fairway, four tubby slicers wandered aimlessly near their golf carts, waiting for the group ahead of them to advance so they could attempt to slice their balls back into play. They didn't even begin to look for their balls until the group ahead of them was out of sight. Each of them needed four or five shots just to reach the bend of the dogleg.

The most memorable hole of the day for us was a par 5 where Mike's scalded second shot traveled fifty yards at an altitude of two or three inches before striking two of my clubs, which I had left lying in the fairway near my ball. (Mike was moving so slowly by that point that the rest of us had taken to reconnoitering our own shots while he limped up to his.) Mike's ball cleanly severed the shaft of my 7-wood, while merely bending double the shaft of my 5-wood. Pieces of both clubs glinted in the sunlight as they flew three feet into the air. Mike offered to split the cost of having them reshafted—a gesture that I considered insufficiently contrite and rejected out of hand. On the next hole, Mike hit a similar shot, which missed all of my equipment but struck Jim in the left instep. After that, we adjusted our pace to Mike's.

It was quite dark when we finished. We bought two six packs of Heineken in the clubhouse, put a can in every cup holder in the Man Van, and headed for Barefoot Landing, a sort of shopping center alongside the main drag. That night, we ate our first unfried meal, at a terrific Italian restaurant called Umberto's. The restaurant was busy, and we had to wait for half an hour in the bar. The owner dropped by to chat, and he made what I interpreted as a halfhearted attempt to hire us as waiters. The man-to-woman ratio in Umberto's, as in Myrtle Beach itself, was roughly twenty-five to three, including waitresses and a couple of women who might have been off-duty strippers. The food, however, was very good.

That night, we faced the strangely sad chore of packing. I used my unworn golf shirts to wrap my sodden socks, then gave my shoes a final drying on a lamp. Our room by that point had developed a dank sort of ambience that no amount of airing seemed to affect. I gave the grooves of my irons a final cleaning and putted for a while with John. And so to bed.

The morning of our fourth and final day in Myrtle Beach dawned beautiful and clear, though still a bit chilly. There was a thirty-minute frost delay at Carolina Shores, a forgettable course that had been added to our itinerary by the proprietor of the Bates Motel. John, Jim, and I hung around the pro shop, drinking coffee and worrying in a vague way that other foursomes were somehow going to get ahead of us. Mike stayed in the Man Van, alternately reading *USA Today* and snoozing. Our van was one of eight or nine parked in a row, and more vans arrived as we waited. At last, the frost was deemed to have melted, and we were allowed to tee off.

Carolina Shores had hundreds of sand traps and thousands of rakes, but no rakers. We devised a local rule that permitted us to rake the sand under any bunkered ball before hitting it. Mike had no sand wedge, and so made frequent use of Jim's. Shoulder-deep in one bunker, he swung mightily, causing the ball to bury itself deep in the earth's core and the lower half of the sand wedge to fly high in the air, landing near the pin, while the grip and a few inches of the shaft remained in his hands. Jim laughed heartily, then realized what had actually happened and shouted, "Hey, that was my club!"

Many of the fairways at Carolina Shores are closely flanked by rows of houses. The houses were so close that I was periodically tempted to slip inside one to check out the fridge or use the bathroom. Bathrooms were in my thoughts because there weren't many likely peeing spots on the course itself; the houses were so close that the only bushes tended to be in people's yards. In a philosophical moment, my brother said, "Maybe the reason women don't like golf is that it's so hard for them to go to the bathroom while they play." I thought about this for a moment, then said, "Maybe the reason there are so few bathrooms on golf courses is that women don't like to play without them."

Hoping to cram in as much golf as possible, we ran from the eighteenth green to the Man Van, and raced to Heather Glen Golf Links for our farewell round. Our haste turned out to be unnecessary. Heather Glen had had a two-and-a-half-hour frost delay that morning, and our tee times were meaningless. In an effort to secure special treatment, I more or less claimed to be the editor of *Golf Digest*, but the starter was unimpressed. We moped around the clubhouse, ate a leisurely lunch, practiced putting, and moped around some more. When we were finally allowed to tee off, at around three-thirty, we quickly calculated that we would still be able to make our six-thirty flight if we played no more than six holes and changed our clothes in the parking lot. I had taken the precaution of wearing a pair of nice pants underneath my now grubby golf pants, so I would merely have to peel off my outer layer in order to make myself presentable to the women from Aeroflot.

As it turned out, leaving Heather Glen was heartbreakingly difficult. Of all the courses we played, we liked it the best. It consists of three separate nines, which can be played in different combinations; we played just two-thirds of the second nine, but the course made a deep impression. The holes were varied and beautiful and stunningly maintained, and the effect was heightened by the splendor of the day. As we floored our carts back to the clubhouse after holing out on the sixth, we gazed longingly at the holes we had not reached. If we hadn't had wives, children, and jobs, we might have torn up our plane tickets and stayed.

We made it to the airport by five-fifteen. John said, "You know, I think we could have played two more holes." That idea plunged us both into lousy moods. Sitting in gloomy silence as we waited to board our plane, I had thoughts of a religious nature. Never before had I been able to understand the appeal of the monastic life. What could possibly cause a man to forsake the pleasures of the world and become a monk? Now, though, I understood. "Oh, I get it," I said to myself. "Monks feel about God the way I feel about golf." The two words are even almost spelled the same. I suddenly had a vision of a sort of ideal community of golfers: a golfing monastery, or golfastery. Men who worship golf living humbly with other men who worship golf. Simple food. Lots of putting practice. A big driving range with well-spaced target greens. Excellent video-taping facilities. Careful study of the rules. Pilgrimages to the great courses of the world. Beer making in the evenings.

Who wouldn't want to live like that?

—1995

An Interview with Arnold Palmer

George Plimpton

The temptation was to pack up and leave but I had very much wanted to talk to Arnold Palmer. Perhaps that would be the climax and the purpose of my activity on the tour—a compensation for my difficulties, especially my disastrous last round. I hoped to ask him just a few specific things—perhaps about the yips or what he thought of the traveling caddies, or about the great crowds he played in—but perhaps even more hopefully to get a sure impression of the titanic player who had been such a figure in the golf world. I knew something of him from afar, having played just in front of him in the San Francisco pro-am and having had the rotten experience below the tee, and then at the Crosby I had traveled in his Army on the final day of play when my pairing with Bob Bruno had not made the cut.

I found this latter experience—being in his Army—one of the most exhilarating experiences a sports enthusiast can have: I found myself transfixed by the excitement of it, scarcely believing that it would be possible to walk around a golf course and watch a golfer—if one was lucky enough to crane over the ranks and actually see him swing—hit a golf shot and wax enthusiastic over it. Of sporting spectacles a golf stroke is surely the one least adaptable to exhilaration. And yet Palmer made it an art of such excitement. The reasons were varied: Palmer's *attack* had much to do with it, as has been said so often, and I have always admired the golfing writer Charles Price's description of Palmer walking to a tee or green quite unlike any other golfer in that he *climbs* onto them, as if clambering into a prize ring.

I asked a sportswriter acquaintance if he had any suggestions as to interviewing Palmer, any hints as to what would make him, well, unwind, so that I could catch some essence of his charisma. The answer was not encouraging. Palmer had been asked everything, I was told. Questions seemed to bore him—the obvious ones to the point of annoyance. An interviewer, unless Palmer knew and appreciated him, had to be lucky to get much out of him beyond the usual platitudes.

Well, that put me out of luck, I said, because I didn't know him, and as for being appreciated, my only credential was that I had trundled around in his Army.

My informant, however, did have one suggestion: "What makes Palmer *unwind*, to use your word," he said, "is to be asked something that really catches his fancy—a question out of the ordinary, something unexpected which he hasn't been asked before."

"For example," he said, "I asked him once, just off-hand, about the rumors of odd deportment on the ladies' golf tour. You know, things like lesbianism. Well, that really sparked him; he stayed on that subject for nearly an hour."

"Oh," I said.

"That's how you can get him going, some out-of-the-ordinary question."

"Yes, I can see," I said.

He asked: "What had you in mind to quiz him about?"

"Well, I'm not going to ask him how he *feels*," I said, "if that's what you're worried about. I wanted to ask him about the yips—unless you think that's a bad idea."

"That's tricky, of course. I mean it could be like asking a terminal case about his disease."

"Then I was going to ask him about crowds and nerves," I said, "and maybe what he thinks about when he hits a shot. You know, things like that."

"Oh, yes," he said doubtfully.

"Well," I said, casting my mind around, "perhaps I should pop him with a psychological question: is he ever struck by the *lunacy* of scraping a golf ball across the countryside and dropping it periodically into a hole. Is he playing out some internal frustration . . ."

"I wouldn't demean the game he plays—no," my informant said.

"Perhaps I could ask him about his dreams," I said, sticking to the psychological approach. "I mean, does a golfer have different dreams than, say, a dentist?"

"I'll tell you one thing," the writer said. "Palmer gets up at two A.M. every morning and without fail he goes to the icebox and drinks a Coca-Cola. Absolutely without fail. There was this one time when some of the guys he was rooming with on tour barricaded his room after he'd gone to sleep—they slid a bureau up against the door, and an armchair or two, and then they sat around and waited to see what would happen at two A.M. When the time came, they heard Palmer groan in there and stir around, and they heard the turn of the door handle behind the bureau and the creak of the door being tried. Then there was a crash and the scrape of the furniture they'd set up being moved back, the whole mass of it pushed aside as Palmer put his shoulder to the door—y'know, he's so damn strong, a bull—and he came through with hardly a glance at the golfers sitting around, on his way to the kitchen refrigerator. They said he looked half-asleep, a somnambulist, and the next morning he had forgotten it. He vaguely remember the noise of the furniture scraping back across the floor. He said, 'What were you guys doing in there last night—throwing chairs around? Hell of a racket.'"

The writer concluded: "The fact is that the hardest thing is to get Palmer aside long enough to *ask* him something, much less to think up a worthwhile question."

He turned out to be right. I called Palmer once on the phone. Someone else answered and said he was not available. I heard the murmur of voices in the background, a loud, sudden laugh, and the clink of ice in glasses. The crowds were always there—even in his private quarters. As for his presence in public, a circle of people collected and moved along with him as soon as he appeared at the locker-room door—the front runners of his Army, and they were with him at the end of his golfing day, accompanying him back to the locker room and standing around waiting once he had disappeared, as hopeful as dogs at a kitchen door, just in case he should turn up again.

One afternoon just after a round, I joined this group and leaned in among them to ask Palmer if he had a moment. He looked at me quickly. I explained I was a writer. He said he was awfully busy. I was surprised by his voice, which was very clear and loud, almost a honk, the sort many public figures seem to have, as if their interlocutors were a bit deaf. I was shoved by some people trying to get pieces of paper at him to sign.

He looked at me again, "I'm going out to the practice range to hit a few balls," he said. "You can talk to me out there if you want."

"That would be fine," I said.

I trailed him across the clubhouse lawn toward the range. His caddy, Bob Blair, moved on ahead. The crowd moved with Palmer, the hands with the slips of paper out, and he would collect the paper and cup it against one palm, bending slightly, and sign it. He signed a napkin. "What can they want with them?" he asked.

The napkin began to disintegrate under the pen. Palmer turned his body to shield the paper from the crowd.

"I'm going to send this to my son," the man said.

We reached the practice range. He stepped across a retaining rope and motioned me after him. I stood in front of him with my notebook out. The crowd pressed up against the rope, very quiet now, and respectful—craning to see. His caddy tipped a bag of balls, spilling them out, and then walked out on the range.

I was unnerved by the crowd, which had about fifty people in it. The notion of asking some of the more particular questions—the one on dreams, or perhaps, as a last resort, the one about lesbianism on the women's tour—in front of that group was unsettling, particularly if the answers were to be delivered in Palmer's strong declamatory style. I stood shifting uneasily. I began writing busily in my pad, as if my function rather than to quiz him was to sketch a word portrait of him at practice. I looked at him only sporadically while he was concentrating on a shot, so that he wouldn't catch my eye and force me to ask something. I used up a number of pages, flipping them briskly. My notes read as follows:

He takes almost a minute between each practice shot—as if each is a separate challenge. He begins with the high-loft irons. He fishes a ball out of the pile in front of him, setting it daintily with the toe of his iron on a raised lie.

When he hits, there is a rush of clothing in abrupt motion, a spray of dirt, and the ball soars. We all stare at its flight. The sun is setting behind us. Blair shades his eyes. Ball lands just beside him. He jumps. Could not have seen it. Pops ball into bag. Shades eyes. Palmer fussing around. Strips cellophane covering from new club. Hefts it. Has twenty clubs or so lying in front of him to try. Is his touch really so sensitive that he can tell one from another? Must ask. Clear throat to ask. Decide not quite right moment.

Man in crowd behind rope suddenly asks, "What do you think of the alums, Arnie?" meaning the aluminum shafts golfers are beginning to experiment with. Palmer's face lost in thought. Long pause. Palmer sets up ball. Then delivers opinion. Very clear voice. Says that aluminum shafts are an interesting development. Everybody reflects on his statement. He hits iron shot. Everyone stares at its flight fixedly. Soars out. Blair takes three, four hurried steps to left, and ball hits and bounces where he was.

"Yah, it's an interesting development," Palmer says. The same man ventures: "That an aluminum shaft you're using there?"

Everyone leans forward slightly.

"About half of these clubs are aluminum, the other half steel."

Everyone backs away, informed.

An airplane goes over, its motor very loud in the mist. Palmer looks up. Everyone looks up.

Time for another club. Strips cellophane wrapping. Hefts it. Motions Blair back.

All his practice balls are new and are marked Palmer 1. He strips glove off glove hand to get feel of club. His glove hand is dyed purple from the glove. Enormous wrists.

Another man asks: "That a four-iron you got there, Arnie?" Perceptible leaning forward again.

A pause. For dramatic effect? Palmer says: "No, got a five here."

Everyone sways back, satisfied.

I clear throat to ask about yips. Decide not quite right moment.

Airplane going over. Big noise. We all look at it.

Palmer moves to wood shots. Blair is in the distance. He hardly seems associated with what Palmer is doing. Palmer compresses lips when he hits but there is no grunt. Only sound is rush of clothing, the click of the ball, and then the tee kicks up. The pile of tees in front mounts up. Big clutter. Cellophane wrappings. Clubs. Maybe thirty clubs. Piles of tees next to balls. Kicked up tees out in front. Tees all red.

Palmer muttering to himself.

Marty Fleckman just down the line, hitting out irons. Palmer stops his routine to watch him. Fleckman had a good day, 69, 3 under. Young man, beginning career. Small man. Dark tan. White Hogan golf hat.

Palmer says: "Well, what'd you do?"

"Three."

Palmer looks at him. "Three? Sixty-three?"

"No. Three under. A nine. A sixty-nine."

"Oh, sixty-nine."

Palmer had round of 72 that day. But no doubt who is who. Crowd grins and rocks back and forth, delighted with exchange.

Palmer goes over and looks in Fleckman's bag. Hefts some irons. Fleckman's woods have fur covers. Palmer impressed by weight of Fleckman's irons. "How you swing these things?" he asks.

Fleckman makes noncommittal murmur.

Palmer: "Well, you're young and strong . . . and healthy."

Fleckman: ". . . but not wealthy."

Palmer: "Haw! Haw! Haw!"

Crowd delighted. Everyone stares at Palmer to see if he has answer for Fleckman's quip.

Palmer: "Haw! Haw! Haw!"

My notes from the practice range ended at this point. Palmer was done with his practice. He motioned Blair in and, turning, he hitched at his trousers in a quick, characteristic gesture, and stepped over the retaining rope. The crowd closed in around him immediately. I tried to keep close to him. I said I hoped he could spare me a moment or two in the locker room. I explained lamely that I hadn't really wanted to disrupt his practice with questions.

"Well, all right," he said. "I've had a lot today, though."

He kept signing papers as we walked for the clubhouse, the people calling to him, "Hey, Arnie," "Arnie," "Arnie." There was a big jam at the locker-room door, and he had difficulty getting through.

It was quiet in the locker room. "Boy, those crowds are something!" I said. "I don't suppose you ever get used to them."

He sat down on the bench and scaled off his golfing glove. The quietness was almost palpable and his voice was very loud in it. "There's one woman here in Palm Springs who embarrasses me half to death—she's always yelling these little endearments, 'darling,' 'lover-boy,' 'sweetie.' I come down the fairway thinking about my next shot and I suddenly hear her bellow out of the gallery, 'Go, lover!' It's not the best thing for your concentration."

"Are there people who follow you from tournament to tournament?"

"Yeah, yeah," he said, the honking voice somewhat mournful, I thought, and I said to myself, Oh my, this is familiar country and dull . . .

"There is a doctor from Pungsatin, Pennsylvania," he was saying. "He turns up at every tournament. He's retired, I think, getting on towards eighty years old by now, and he's always there—Japan, Argentina—and I'll be walking through the hotel in one of those places—Buenos Aires, Kyoto, I don't care where—and there he'll be, eating a steak, alone, in a corner."

Someone, a locker-room attendant, I suppose, handed him a pack of letters. He removed a rubber band and began opening them, scanning them quickly and setting the ones he wanted to keep on the bench beside him. The others, the trash mail I assumed, he crumpled and dropped on the floor.

I was going to launch the question about dreams, but I thought better of it and asked about advice—did any of his admirers, golfers or not, the people who yelled "Sweetie," with all that concern they had for him to win, did any of them come up with advice?

Palmer looked up from his mail and said that a guy once told him that he was catching his elbows on a rather loose sweater he was wearing.

"But you know it's against the rules to accept information from people on the golf course."

"I didn't know," I said.

"A guy who could afford it might have four specialists, or a dozen, out there on the course advising him. That's why they have the rule."

"Oh, yes," I said slowly, my fancy rather struck by the thought of a convocation of advisers over a difficult shot—a clutch of them sitting around on shooting sticks, the binoculars out, the pencils and the slide rules working like military people studying maps on war maneuvers.

"The only intrusions I'm aware of," Palmer was saying, "are the cameras—the whir and click of them. Of course, these have been banned from the courses recently, so it hasn't been anything of a problem."

"Hi there, Arnie!" A man looked around the corner of the locker.

"Howzitgoin'?" Palmer said pleasantly.

"Great! Great! Great!" the man said. He fussed for another sentence, but nothing was forthcoming; he backed away and disappeared around the corner.

"Superstitious?" I asked. "Do you indulge in any rituals?"

"Oh, no," Palmer said, almost in disgust it seemed, in that loud honking voice. "Oh, sure, I wear certain outfits on certain days. I use the same marker to mark the ball."

"Do you stick to a ball throughout a round if it's going O.K. for you?" I asked.

"A golf ball loosens every time you hit it; even one shot loosens it. So your professional golfer'll change his ball every three holes or so—though, of course, he'll stick to the same trademark." He spoke as if by rote, or as if reading from a training manual.

I cleared my throat and asked him about the yips and the chokes.

He ripped open a letter and dropped the contents between his toes. "Well, I'd call them pretty close cousins. Choking is a stage of the yips. Both of them have to do with being unable to study, to concentrate. It's true that a golfer can get a nerve problem that can't be helped. Those are the yips. Hogan and Nelson got them; to say that Ben Hogan or Byron Nelson *choke*, I mean that's crazy. But both of them, the choking and the yips, I say, are connected with losing the ability to concentrate, and in various degrees that happens to all of us. But you can escape it, get out of it. When I'm working well, I just don't think I'm going to miss a shot or a putt, and when I do I'm as surprised as hell. I can't believe it. A golfer must think that way. He must say to the ball, 'Go to that spot.' The best players who ever played must have thought that way, *willing* the ball there, you see. I don't mean to suggest that it's easy. In fact, the hardest thing for a great many people is to win. They get scared. And they *doubt*. Which gets them into trouble. Of course, that's not Jack Nicklaus's problem."

"I suppose one big win gets you over that problem."

"No. Because you got to want to win more, fast. The temptation if you win is to coast for a while. You begin to think that to run high in the pack is enough. Well, that's the end of you." He rubbed his chin. He snapped the rubber band from his letter packet.

"The competitive thing in golf isn't for everyone. And it hasn't got anything to do with age or horsepower."

"I see," I said.

"Well," he said.

I could see that he felt he had talked enough.

"I had this question about dreams," I said hurriedly. "I wonder if you could talk about that . . . what you dream . . ." My voice trailed off. He seemed to be staring at me, but then I noticed his eyes were fixed at a point over my left shoulder. "Hey, Albie!" he shouted. I looked around. A man wearing a small green apron, the locker-room attendant apparently, appeared around the corner of the locker. "What you done with my shoes?"

"In your locker, Mister Palmer. You think I ate 'em?"

Palmer rocked back and forth on the bench. "Haw! Haw! Haw!"

The man in the apron grinned. "You think I don't take care of you, Mr. Palmer?" He turned away.

"Albie, you're a brother. Haw, haw, haw!"

I looked back at Palmer. His face was solemn again, his jollity as swift as a wince. He was sliding off his golf shoe.

"You wanted to tell me about some dream you had," he said without looking up.

"No, not exactly," I said.

His voice sounded very tired.

I looked at my notes.

"Listen," I said. "On the PGA tour, the WPGA is it? The women's tour, that is, there is this high incidence . . ."

"It's the LPGA—the *ladies'* professional golf . . ."

"Oh, yes," I said. "Well, on the tour, I am told, there is, er, this very high incidence . . ."

"Hi, Arnie!" Another man had poked his head around the corner. This one was wearing a straw boater. "Damn good to have you here in Palm Springs."

"Howzitgoin'?" Palmer said pleasantly.

"Oh, it's just going great, Arnie," the man said. He made an abrupt motion with his fist. "You're going to take this goddamn thing, Arnie . . . you're going to have one great day tomorrow, I'm telling you."

"We're going to sure give it a try," Palmer said.

"Well, great, Arnie," the man said. His face, so full of expression and concern, froze suddenly, and then went vacant as he gazed at the golfer looking sleepily at him; his eyes popped ajar slightly. "Well, so long, Arnie," he said. He disappeared abruptly around the corner.

Palmer ripped open his last letter.

"Well, how's that for you?" he asked. "That enough?"

I looked up from my notes. I wanted to say that I had just a question or so more, if he didn't mind, but I didn't.

"Oh, sure," I said. "You've been very kind." I stood up and shuffled my notes together. "Absolutely great." I began backing away. I wanted to shake his hand in gratitude for his time, but Palmer was staring down at his feet. "Great," I said. "Thanks." I backed around the corner of the locker.

I had a quick sense of failure—that I had been accorded valuable time and had not made the best of it. I walked from the clubhouse out into the afternoon. I began singing to myself—a manifestation of embarrassment that a friend of mine refers to as "the hummings"—making loud noises in one's head to drive out discomfiting thoughts. I often have them—the hummings—waking up in the morning and thinking back on the indiscretions of word or deed the evening before. The WPGA, I thought; boy, that wasn't so hot. Why hadn't I done better with him, I wondered. The confusion over the dreams. I had been just as clumsy and ill-at-ease with him as the two men who had come around the corner of the lockers full of things to say, and whose confidence had drained like meal from a split sack at the sight of him, his proximity. Perhaps one expected too much of such superstars—that one would sit in front of them awestruck and gapejawed and no effort was necessary: one would simply bask in their presence. Of course, Palmer had not been particularly easy. Driving back to the motel I began to take it out on him. Boy, he let me down! If he knew how I strained watching him on television to help him get that putt down; or how an evening was just a little bit off if that afternoon I'd watched him charge the leaders of the tournament and just fail; or the long gloom and worry reading in the paper that he hadn't made the cut of some tournament in the West, as if some prop had been knocked out of the great order of things.

Lord, I wondered, am I going to desert him for Nicklaus, or Casper, or someone. . . .

I found out the last day of the tournament. The professionals were playing without their amateur partners. I had a chance to stick with whichever golfer I chose. I toyed with some of the others. But I found myself drawn inexorably to Palmer's Army. I joined them. I craned to see what he was up to. I agonized over his play. "Drop, drop!" I shouted, along with the others, at a long putt as it went for the hole, and when it did drop, I let out a great cry of delight. "Man, he did it!" I shouted happily at the stranger next to me. He was a man wearing a straw boater with a brim that read GO, ARNIE. His eyes were glistening with excitement. We pounded each other on the back.

"D'ja see him *will* that ball in there," I cried.

The other man nodded wildly. He seemed speechless.

"There wasn't the slightest doubt in his mind."

He shook his head vehemently.

We moved happily for the next tee.

"That fellow doesn't coast," I said. "He's got to win."

On my way my companion caught his breath. "He really *attacked* that hole," he said in a high wheeze.

"Damn right."

We were trading familiarities about Palmer.

"Guy's got a million-dollar jet," the man said. "He's got it all."

"Yes," I said. "I'll tell you something else. He has a Coke every morning at two A.M.," I said.

"Oh?"

I had him there.

—1967

Love That Golf

Rick Reilly

Rick Reilly suffered a touch of golf-kichigai—golf craziness—while exploring Japan's national obsession with the game. He also visited an oxygen bar, tried to salt his omelet with a cigarette lighter and ate a blowfish.

"No wonder we lost the war," the Japanese man said as I wore out the dimples on my ball with a 290-yard drive on the eighteenth hole. . . .

Wait. Wait. Let's start at the beginning. What is this about you trying to salt your omelet with the cigarette lighter?

You don't want to hear about the drive?

The omelet.

Well, yes, that's true. I did try to salt my omelet with the cigarette lighter. But that was only because I had taken too much oxygen.

Hold on. Where was this?

This was at Koganei in Tokyo, the most expensive country club in the world. It takes about $2.5 million to join and even that might not do it; two years ago, a businessman reportedly made an offer of $3.57 million to join and was given the big raspberry. I mean, a divot at this place might go for $63. And not only do you have to cough up the 2.5 mil, but also there are the yearly dues. Of course, tees are free.

So you were having breakfast at Koganei. . . .

Right. I'm having breakfast at Koganei, having talked my way into a big match on the Fourth of July in the most elite country club in the new money center of the universe, Tokyo. And I'm sort of on a mission. I mean, the Japanese are beating the microchip out of us these days, right? Did you know that nearly all the fax-machine makers in the world are Japanese? Did you know six of the ten richest men in the world are Japanese and only one is American?

But I don't mind that so much, and I don't mind their buying so many great American golf courses, such as Riviera and La Costa. But when I heard a rumor that the Japanese had made an offer to buy Pebble Beach lock, stock and bunker, that really fried my sand wedge. I mean, can you imagine Pebble Beach for sale? That's like selling Mount Rushmore.

Or London Bridge.

Exactly. So I just wanted to go over there and see why the Japanese were so gaga over golf and also see if I couldn't win back just a little bit of face for America, you know? Just win back a small speck of dignity in my own little way.

So you set up this match.

Exactly. U.S. versus Japan. A thousand-yen Nassau to the death. Loser eats flag and leaves town. I would pay this 6-handicapper at Koganei, owner of a textile factory. As you know, I'm an 11, and . . .

Twelve.

O.K., a 12. He agreed to give me six strokes. So I had nine days in Japan to prepare for the match. I decided to learn all I could about Japanese golf—play like a Japanese golfer would play, eat what a Japanese golfer would eat, the whole ball of wax. I set out on a course of defeating my opponent by *becoming* him.

Very Oriental thinking.

Besides, I hit the ball the way they read.

How's that?

Right to left.

Yes. And you began this face-saving mission over an omelet?

No, at the oxygen bar.

Come again?

The oxygen bar. First, what you have to understand is that there is a word in Japan for "golf crazy": *golf-kichigai*. Golf has swallowed Japan whole. People will do almost anything, and pay almost anything, if it has anything to do with golf.

For instance, weekend greens fees at clubs near Tokyo are between $150 and $300. To play Koganei as a guest on a weekend will cost you $250, including lunch. Balls are sold one at a time, at about $8 each. Getting a tee time at even the ugliest course requires a telephone call one to three months ahead. Just to hit a bucket of balls at a driving range requires a reservation.

This is a country smaller than California, with a population half that of the United States, and Japan had only about 1,500 golf courses as of December 1987. The U.S. had 12,500. Now the Japanese are building courses anyplace you can fit two phone booths. They think nothing of lopping off parts of mountains to build a course.

It's a mania, I tell you. Lawsuits have even been filed involving guys bonking people in the eye while practicing their golf swings on train platforms with their umbrellas.

One day, I played a public course called Akabane in northern Tokyo. The last guy to take a mower to this place must have been General MacArthur. It was as bad as any course in the U.S., yet it cost a hundred dollars to play on Saturdays. Doesn't matter. The golfers started lining up at two in the morning. The first foursome went off at 4:30 A.M., with 150 golfers waiting behind them. You don't know what it's like to have 150 Japanese watching you hit on the first tee.

What is it like?

I was shaking. But I managed to steer a 2-iron into the fairway only after the caddie wrestled a 7-iron out of my hands.

Understandable.

In Tokyo there's even a brothel called Hole-In-One, with a putting green in the lobby. Can't you see some guy wandering in there? "Is there anybody here who can help me with my grip?"

So get to the oxygen bars already.

Right. I started at the oxygen bar because they're all the rage now in Tokyo. Some Japanese believe breathing pure oxygen improves your golf, though I never quite found out how. Apparently they think the rush of oxygen clears your head and lets you visualize the shot more clearly and hit it more smoothly, your muscles pulsing as they are with rich, right-off-the-shelf oxygen.

You walk in—most of the bars are in department stores and spas— pony up a hundred yen (about seventy-two cents) and tell the bartender what your pleasure is: mint, coffee, orange or lemon. She flips a switch and turns over an egg timer, and you stick your face in an oxygen mask and suck for three minutes.

People sniff two or three rounds and then maybe buy a take-home can for later. The cans come in two sizes—five thousand and ten thousand milliliters—and run from five dollars to eighteen dollars. The girl at the oxygen bar in the Takashimaya department store says some customers come in once a week and take home a case.

I guess that's what's known as oxygen debt.

Right. So I ordered coffee, but the only thing I felt was woozy—and I had the overwhelming sense that I'd woken up in Juan Valdez's living room. Still, I bought a can to take with me for Koganei.

How in the world did this catch on?

There is a Japanese proverb: "The protruding nail gets hammered." Conform, or bring shame to yourself and your group. So if one person is sucking air, everybody wants to suck air. If your neighbor is bowling—as everybody in Japan was ten years ago—then you bowl. And when they stop bowling, you stop. Which explains the giant bowling pins on roofs of warehouses all over Tokyo today.

So what makes you think golf will stick?

What could be better? You not only get out of standing-room-only Tokyo—where you now must be able to prove you have a place to park before you can buy a car—but also get to be in the group at the same time. To be alone and together.

And forget weekend golf. Golf is such a national jones in Japan now, that going to the driving range has become a hobby in itself. Of course, most of the ranges are on top of buildings, surrounded by nets. There's no land for golf. You can't buy three square meters in the Ginza for a million dollars these days.

But the best and biggest range is freestanding—Shiba Golf, the world's largest practice range. When you first walk into Shiba Golf in downtown Tokyo, you notice that it's hailing. Or are those golf balls? One hundred and fifty-five golfers, stacked on three stories, turn the sky white. They hit their shots onto a 280-yard rubber-matted landing area, surrounded by nets a hundred feet high.

This place is Japan at its finest. The balls roll downhill into a trough, which is banked so that the balls then roll outwardly to gutters on either side of the range. The gutters have conveyer belts that take the five hundred thousand Shiba balls to the basement to be cleaned and dried; then they are sent to two men who sit, day and night, pulling out the scuffed and damaged balls. Next the balls are whooshed up three floors by a pneumatic system and channeled into the reservoirs at each of the hitting stations, where the customer simply pushes a button and the clean, dried, cut-free balls come tumbling out.

Of course, unless you've arranged a tee time at the range in advance, you won't be pushing any buttons for an hour and a half or two hours. That's the usual wait, without a reservation, for a first-floor spot. No problem. Shiba Golf also has a swimming pool, bowling lanes, TV lounge, three restaurants, beer garden, massage, sauna, pro shop and golf-travel bureau with a giant board telling you where you might be able to get a weekend tee time within the next two months. Right now, that's nowhere.

So when do they play?

A lot of Japanese don't. There's a story about a PGA Tour player who, while visiting one of these driving ranges, comes upon a golfer with a beautiful, fluid swing.

"What do you shoot?" the pro asks the guy.

"I don't know," he says.

"Excuse me?" the pro says.

"I've never played on a golf course," the guy says.

Whether your wallet is full of dollars or yen, golf in Japan is expensive. Only 15 percent of the people who practice the game ever play on a real course, according to the *Sunday Times* of London.

"We could have four floors and fill it up easily," says the Shiba manager, Atsushi Mitobe. Range practicing has become so popular in Japan that people carry "rangebags," minibags that hold only three clubs. You drape it over your shoulder on the way to work and then swing at Shiba by night.

The Seibu Big Box practice range—on the fifth floor of a sports and shopping complex—has an indoor sand trap, encased by glass and net on all sides. This is real sand and real golf balls. You have not lived until you've skulled a sand shot you were sure was heading for ladies' lingerie.

I'll risk it.

The Japanese are also perfecting simulated golf, in which you pick your course—they will allow you to play Pebble Beach, Augusta, St. Andrews—grab your clubs and crank it. You hit a regular golf ball into a huge canvas that has the picture of the hole you're playing projected on it.

Three cameras record how fast the ball comes off the club, with what spin, and at what trajectory. Then the canvas shows the view from what the computer says is your next shot. For instance, if you chunk one way to the right, the next thing you see on the screen might be a bunch of trees. When you hit the green, the computer tells you to putt from one of twenty-six different spots on the artificial putting green in front of you.

I understand you shot 133 on this course.

Yes, well, that was only because at the fourteenth, the computer was convinced I was hitting the ball out of bounds. I hit seventeen shots of every direction and size, and it refused to call any of them in bounds. Finally, I picked up a ball and threw it into the canvas, and the computer let me play on. I made a 38 on that hole.

I see. Now, about those salted fish chips.

Yes, I was getting to them. As I've said, in my determination to defeat my Japanese opponent, I thought Japanese, practiced Japanese, and even ate the way Japanese golfers eat. At Fuji Lakes Country Club, surely one of the most beautiful places in the world, sitting as it does on the toenail of Mount Fuji, I came off the course and was served the standard post-golf snack: dried, salted fish and green beans. That and an ice-cold beer. You know, it just doesn't get any better than that.

At Kawana, Japan's gorgeous version of Pebble Beach, only without the seals, I had the traditional "golfer's breakfast" in my room: rice, raw egg, seaweed, soybean soup, dried fish, Japanese pickles and green tea.

Seize the day.

I even ate blowfish, a sushi delicacy that kills about a hundred diners a year in Japan. I didn't eat at Steak of Steaks Holytan, however, where a steak costs $175.

You ate the blowfish but not the steak?

I figured the odds of the steak killing me were worse. I also learned how to drink beer at the twenty-eighth hole (the Japanese always try to play twenty-seven holes): Your opponent pours your beer, and you pour his, even for fill-ups. To do otherwise would be like opening his shirt pocket and sneezing in it.

Please.

Another thing. The Japanese don't flip a tee before the round to see who hits first. Instead, they draw one of four metal sticks out of a metal canister. The man whose stick has one notch in it hits first. Two notches, second, and so on. Thus, the expression, "He swings a big stick."

You made that up.

I did. However, I am not making this up: Nobody in Japan wants to make a hole in one.

Come again?

It's true. The last thing you want to do is make a hole in one. I was curious why every time somebody would hit it close to the hole in Japan, but not *in* the hole, the players would holler, "Lucky!"

It turns out that in Japan the hole-in-one maker must pop for: (1) drinks for everybody in the club; (2) nice gifts for his best friends, usually silver pens with the feat engraved on them; (3) towels or the like, with the details of the feat embroidered on them for his B list of friends, about a hundred of them; (4) a special tip for the caddie; (5) a tree to be donated to the course; and (6) a huge party within the month for all his friends, the witnesses and anybody else who knows about it. All of that can cost five thousand dollars and up.

Better luck next time.

Right. Also, for any bag that is overweight, the course charges extra. There's also an extra charge for playing on a rainy day. Not that you have a choice. There are no rain checks in Japan. We played at Kawana when it was raining miserably, yet the course was packed. "Only two groups have canceled today," the gleeful course manager told us.

In English?

Well, O.K., not in English. But what *is* weird is the English the Japanese use while playing golf. "Nishot!" they say a lot. They give it a contortionist's twist of the body and scream out, "Bunkahh!" They seem to love saying that. There's also "nisapproach" and "nistouch" and "bardie!" It's like somebody sent them the back of a cereal box with those golf expressions on it and everybody in Japan knows them.

I asked nearly every person I met on courses in Japan to tell me his favorite golf joke and nobody could tell me one. I guess they are so fascinated with the game that they have not yet gotten around to making fun of their fascination, as we do. Finally, one man said, "What do you mean, 'jokes'?"

"You know, jokes," I said. "Jokes about golf. Like the one about the guy who comes home and says to his wife, 'Boy, what a tough day on the course today.' And his wife says, 'Really? What happened?' And the guy says, 'Well, Charlie dropped dead of a heart attack on the third hole.' And his wife says, 'Oh, no, that's terrible!' And the guy says, 'You're telling me. All day long it was hit the ball, drag Charlie, hit the ball, drag Charlie.'"

The Japanese man did not laugh.

"Do you get it?" I said.

"I do not think that you showed much respect for this Charlie," said the man. "Nor for his wife."

This is what you are adding to the Japanese golf culture? Sick jokes?

Darn right! These guys need a laugh or two. Do you know how long it takes to play golf in Japan? All day and half the night is how long it takes.

The typical Sunday golf game for the average Japanese golfer goes like this: The night before, you ship your clubs off to the course, via a courier that specializes in transporting clubs, saving you the trouble of carrying them the next morning when you catch the six o'clock train, which will take you to your 9 A.M. tee time at a course far from Tokyo. Courses anywhere near Tokyo are much too costly.

You get to the course and tee off. But since the courses are so crowded, the wait is often ten minutes between shots. You play nine holes in about three hours. Now you have lunch, drink beer and sake, soak in a Japanese bath and generally just waste time until your back-nine tee time.

Back-nine tee time?

Because so many people want to play golf in Japan, clubs send foursomes off both the front and the back nines all day. After you play one nine, you have to be squeezed into the other nine. O.K., so you play the other three-hour nine, get back in the bath, have a few beers and catch the train home.

One reason golf is so slow in Japan is that most of the players practice on the rooftop driving ranges. The most their shots travel is twenty yards before they hit the net. That's why the Japanese lose so many balls when they play on a course.

It's also slow because many Japanese are just plain rotten at it. "We don't play enough," is how Japanese course designer Takeaki Kaneda explains it. "The Japanese have no time. They work so hard. Most people's club is an hour to two hours from work. Jack Nicklaus grew up five minutes from Scioto."

Another thing is that a lot of Japanese golfers don't want to be golfers in the first place. It is only *otsukiai*—"socializing for business"— that has them out there. For a Japanese businessman, the golf course has become more workplace than playing field, and his handicap more a résumé line than a hobby.

A decade ago, a businessman might have taken his client to a fine dinner in the Ginza and a few hours in Shinjuku tittering at a hostess bar; now he might take a client to a round of golf. Even if you hate golf, it would be committing career hara-kiri not to play if asked.

"If you're a businessman and you don't play golf, you're out of the promotion scene," says Toshio Aritake, an editor for McGraw-Hill in Tokyo.

The protruding nail gets hammered. So you play, but if you play lousy, you shame your group and business. "The stress is terrible," says Aritake.

Yes, I have heard about a Japanese malady—karoshi, "death from overwork." It sounds as if golf may be adding to the problem rather than solving it.

It's true. Luckily, the clubs try to make golf as relaxing as possible. At one course, Murasakizuka, north of Tokyo, a boy comes out during your bath and scrubs your back for you.

Very civilized.

Better yet, Japanese courses come equipped with the best caddies in the world, almost all of whom are women. Even on the hottest days, their uniforms never change: heavy walking shoes, long pants, matching long-sleeved smock, white gloves, hard hat with an eight-inch bill, and a tablecloth draped over the hard hat and tied loosely under the chin. The full effect is like Sister Bertrille of *The Flying Nun* pulling a double loop.

Our Holy Order of Bogey.

Right. The caddie's entire face is usually in shadow, and the only thing you hear is a voice way inside there saying, "Iz O.B."

With only one caddie per foursome, it is a mystery how she gets it all done. She marks and cleans the balls—not done in the U.S.— hands out everybody's putters, takes whatever clubs they're holding, advises everybody on the putting line, handles the pin, excuses three-putts, smooths egos and traps, takes the putters back, hands out drivers for the next hole, and makes it halfway down the fairway, ordering your clubs numerically as she goes, before you're ready to hit.

For this, she makes about nineteen thousand dollars a year—plus a tip from the entire foursome: a pair of socks or a box of chocolates from one of the on-course teahouses. At some clubs she gets free lodging in a caddie dormitory. For most golfers, though, the thought of a caddie dormitory is chilling.

Why?

Because you can imagine the conversations that go on in a place like that: "So the guy says to me, 'Two hundred thirty-five yards, what do you think it will take?' I wanted to say, 'With your swing? Two three-woods and a seven-iron.'"

Have we exhausted your store of information about caddies?

Well, there is one more thing. The caddies are seriously high-tech. At a lot of courses, when it's foggy or you can't see the hole, a caddie will whip out her walkie-talkie and check with the caddie ahead to see if it's clear to hit.

At the GMG course, west of Tokyo, the bags travel by an elaborate monorail system operated by the caddies by remote control. The four bags are loaded on a little tram—sort of a par-72 Futureland— and the caddie "walks" it along with the foursome up the side of the fairway, stopping it when she needs clubs and sending it whirring off when she doesn't. It's sort of like playing C-3PO's home course.

Japan may also be the only place on earth with escalators on the golf courses. Instead of making the players actually *walk* up hills, on many courses there are "skylators," rubberized moving sidewalks that whisk the player up the hill to the next tee.

So the players won't have to wait in order to begin waiting for their next shots.

And when you're done playing, you don't just scrape your shoes on the mat a couple of times and walk inside. You blow your shoes spotless with a high-pressure air hose.

Pardon me. This is all fine and good, but how does cleaning your shoes with a high-pressure air hose relate to your Nassau-to-the-death match on the Fourth of July at Koganei?

It's just in that I wanted to familiarize myself with the way of the Japanese golfer before I played my match on the Fourth of July, for undying respect and home-country glory.

Is that when you tried to ignite your omelet?

Yes, more or less. See, before the round I inhaled the whole can of oxygen. Then we went to have breakfast before the round. So we were having breakfast, and you must understand that things are not always as they seem at Koganei. For instance, Koganei, the most expensive course in the world, looks like a really nice muni. What makes the price so high is the prospect of the club's selling out to real estate developers. Each member would stand to make $4.4 million.

So . . .

So . . . the same goes for the table condiments. They are not all what they seem. I was looking for the salt and at first tried the little silver dish, but that was red pepper. Then I tried the gold thimble with the holes in the top, but that held toothpicks. I'm a little lightheaded from the oxygen, remember.

Certainly.

I thought I had solved it with the burnished-silver object. I held it over my omelet and tried to turn what I thought was a crank, as in, "Fresh ground pepper, sir?"

And when did you realize no salt was forthcoming?

When I saw the horror on my host's face, matched only by the ashen face of my interpreter. "No, this is not America," said my interpreter, snatching it from my hands and lighting it.

Thus you were set at a decided disadvantage to your opponent.

I was. Even though he pretended to stare out the window, he knew the humiliation I felt. So he goes out and beats me on the front side 2 up.

Of course. And did the nine-hole lunch and bath affect your timing on the back nine?

Horribly. For one thing, it is a bit disconcerting at a Japanese bath to have a *woman* handing you a towel as you get out. So, naturally, I hit my first shot out of bounds on the tenth tee. By the thirteenth tee, I was three holes down on the back-nine bet alone.

Deep shame was yours.

Yes, but then I thought of the adage: "Even a thousand-mile journey begins with a single step."

In that you took strength?

I did. I won the next three holes by parring two of them while he made three straight 6s.

Even monkeys fall from trees.

True. But we split the next two holes, and so it was that we came to the par-5 eighteenth hole all tied. And, as I said, I stepped up and absolutely hit a two-cheeker of a drive that went 290 yards and caused one man in our group to say, "No wonder they won the war."

We heard that.

Meanwhile, my Japanese opponent had hit his ball out of bounds. He was lying three, fifty yards behind where I was lying *one*. A win on the back nine was most certainly mine. I could gain a split on the man's home course, which, naturally, I would take back to America as a glorious victory.

You were gladdened.

Yes. Unfortunately, I had forgotten the Japanese proverb: "Darkness lies one inch ahead." In my excitement to save American face, I tried to reach the green in two and make an eagle.

Very symbolic.

Instead, I topped my 3-wood sideways into a trap, hit a tree coming out, bombed my approach thirty yards over the green, hit a bad chip and two-putted for a 7. During all this, he had recovered nicely and made a fifteen-foot putt for a 6 and a one-hole victory.

You choked worse than Heimlich.

This is true. But afterward, I got to thinking about the world as a global village. I remembered how George Bush wants to share our defense secrets with Japan. And I recalled seeing news of a joint microchip venture between Hitachi and Texas Instruments. And I thought about what a good time I'd had among the friendly and generous people of Japan. Suddenly, I felt proud just to have participated.

In other words, he bought the beers.

Exactly.

—1989

St. Andrews:
The Cradle of Golf

Herbert Warren Wind

The hold that St. Andrews has over the world's ten million golfers has not yet reached that point where, at five regular intervals each day, the game's devotees abruptly drop the cares of the hour, kneel, and face the old gray town on the North Sea where the game was nurtured. There is, however, little to choose between St. Andrews and Mecca in the frenetic fidelity they extract from their followers. Every pious golfer dreams of making a pilgrimage to St. Andrews, and a considerable number realize this ambition. Since the war an average of eight thousand visitors has journeyed to St. Andrews each year. For a few of them, the attraction is a tourist's sight of the house on South Street where Mary Queen of Scots slept, uneasily; the Church of the Holy Trinity, where a local boy, John Knox, cut loose with one of his most inflammatory sermons; the noble buildings of St. Andrews University, Scotland's oldest, which dates back to 1413. But, by and large, the thousands who make their way annually to St. Andrews come to worship at the Old Course, the most famous links in the world.

Considering that it is only thirty-three miles northeast of Edinburgh, St. Andrews is not an easy place to get to. The sacred town lies on the eastern tip of Fifeshire, a peninsula which noses into the North Sea between the Firth of Tay on the north and the Firth of Forth to the south. The train ride from Edinburgh, on the main line north to Aberdeen, offers a fairly spectacular crossing of the Firth of Forth via the high, gaunt railroad bridge on which Robert Donat performed his acrobatics in *The Thirty-Nine Steps*, but passengers for St. Andrews must descend at Leuchars, five miles distant, and there change to a spur line which operates on a capricious schedule. Most golfers choose to close in on the old town by auto. The road from Edinburgh, once the ferry across the Forth has been negotiated, plods through somber coastal towns, each with its links and its "golf hotel." The approach from Glasgow, on the West Coast, a drive of three hours, is far more rural and relaxing and would be altogether preferable were it not that *leaving* Glasgow necessarily presupposes *being in* Glasgow. Whatever road he travels, the pilgrim, because of the ambivalence of the route markers at all key intersections, will lose his way on the average of once every twenty miles, and he will learn from asking directions that the proper Scottish pronunciation of his goal is *Sintandrooz*.

St. Andrews makes a stirring first impression. Perched on a rocky plateau fifty feet above the Firth of Tay, not a smokestack in view, its medieval towers gleaming gray-white in the sun, it looms solemnly before the pilgrim, completely unrelated to the countryside through which he has passed. St. Andrews was named for the patron saint of Scotland, and while it is legend and not history that the relics of St. Andrew were carried there in 735 by St. Regulus, the town is old enough to have run through several full careers: Pictish stronghold, headquarters of the Roman Catholic Church in Scotland, storm center of the Reformation, prosperous trading port, plague-struck and all but deserted village—all this before the spread of golf throughout the world, beginning just about a century ago, gave the old town something new to live for.

In this town the only native who hurries to snatch the minute is the golfer. His small canvas bag over his shoulder, he strides briskly past the golf hotels lining the seaside strip called the Scores, quickening his pace as he nears the Old Course at the foot of the town in order not to be late for his assigned starting time on the first tee. The rest of the nine thousand regular inhabitants operate less by the watch than by the more luxurious chronometer of chimes and church bells. The milkman chugs his truck from house to house, resting at the wheel while his wife makes the deliveries. In the cafés the university students talk easily over coffee between classes, the girls wearing their bright-red college gowns, as they do on many occasions when they are not required, because the gown "does more" for them than any other number in their wardrobes. The slow pace and good air of St. Andrews have made it a favorite retreat of superannuated military and naval officers. It is also a fine place for thinking as well as retiring. Carlyle, Froude, Thomas Hughes, Trollope, Mrs. Oliphant, Kingsley, Millais, and Landseer are just a few of the prominent artists and writers who found they flourished in St. Andrews in summer.

It is a salutary circumstance that the town of St. Andrews is charming beyond expectation for, at first meeting, the Old Course—the shrine itself—is a majestic letdown. To an American accustomed to mounting a raised tee and squinting down a tree-lined fairway, the Old Course, a billowing sea of grass-covered dunes, doesn't even look like a golf course. Bobby Jones, who ended up thinking the Old Course the finest he had ever played, was sure it was the worst after his first round. A decade later, Gene Sarazen, on his first visit, walked off the eighteenth green indignantly demanding to know how a pasture which had traps smack in the middle of its fairways could presume to be considered a peerless test of golf. Sam Snead flew to St. Andrews expressly for the 1946 British Open, took one look at the course, asked if he were in the right town, and, finding that he was, wanted to fly right back again. Sam stayed on and proceeded to win that championship, aided in no small way by the conviction, acquired after he and the Old Course had got better acquainted, that if he honestly played better golf shots than anyone else in the field, the course would see to it that no one beat him.

It is familiarity which breeds respect and love for the Old Course. It is like no other. In the United States, for example, our courses are *constructed*—fairways blasted through hillsides, streams diverted to fit the strategy of the approach shot, greens built to order by bulldozers. The Old Course wasn't made. It was always there. Today the word *links* is used indiscriminately by most golfers as if it were simply a synonym for *course*. Actually a links, or linksland, is a stretch of sandy soil deposited by the receding ocean. Linksland fringes the eastern coast of Scotland, and it was the logical place for playing golf, a game which may have been imported in germ from Holland but which was developed by the Scots into its present sublimely contagious form.

In a strange and wonderful way, the inhabitants of St. Andrews from the earliest days sensed that nature had blessed them with the best of all links for golf. Nature alone has been permitted to alter the topography. The incredible result is that the links, in general contour, probably looks much the same today as it did in 1100, the round year that historians have fixed on as the date when the natives of St. Andrews first began to put their links to its historic use.

Until late in the nineteenth century, the Old Course, hemmed in by the Firth of Tay and the estuary of the Eden River, was the only course on the thumb-shaped spit of linksland below the town. Two other eighteen-hole courses, the New and Jubilee, laid out in 1894 and 1946 respectively, now occupy the reclaimed land between the northern boundary of the Old Course and the Firth; a fourth eighteen holes, called the Eden, was wedged in between the southern boundary of the Old Course and the Eden estuary in 1914. The ocean has receded about one hundred feet during the last seventy-five years, and assuming that this has been its customary pace of retreat over the centuries, its waters must have at one time washed up to the very edges of the Old Course and determined its singular snakelike design. It is as narrow as a course can be. The first seven holes march in an almost straight line away from the town; the eighth, ninth, tenth, and eleventh perform a small clockwise loop around the tip of the promontory; then holes twelve through eighteen march straight back to the town alongside the first seven. The adjoining fairways are not separated by rough, and there is always ample room to the left, except on the loop holes. They are tightly flanked on the right by out-of-bounds or by heavy rough composed of gorselike whins and heather, presenting the slicer with far less latitude for error than the hooker. Not only are the parallel fairways fused into one wide fairway but, save on the first, ninth, seventeenth, and eighteenth, an outgoing hole and an incoming hole share the same green, the second with the sixteenth, the third with the fifteenth, and so on. The cups for the two holes are at opposite ends of the huge double greens. The largest of these, servicing the fifth and thirteenth holes, is over an acre; putts 140 feet long are often a nerve-racking reality.

The contours of the greens are treacherous, their surface is slippery, and the earth itself so hard and resilient that a player cannot stroke his approach for the pin and hope to have the ball sit down abruptly, as it does on our soft, watered greens. Instead, he must resort to a pitch-and-run approach, landing his shot a calculated distance from his target so that the ball, after its bound and roll, will stop in the neighborhood of the pin. An equal accuracy is demanded on the tee-shots to avoid the mélange of fairway bunkers, those celebrated pits which were burrowed, long before the invention of golf, by sheep nestling behind the dunes to keep out of the bitter wind. On the direct line from tee to green on the fourteenth or Long Hole, for example, the golfer is first menaced by a formidable group of bunkers, the Beardies, lying in wait for him at the two-hundred-yard mark. A hundred yards farther down the fairway stands Benty Bunker, backed up by Kitchen, and at the four-hundred-yard mark he must deal with Hell, most feared of all the bunkers on the Old Course. To attempt the straight-line route to the green is folly on the fourteenth, and, for that matter, on nearly every hole of the eighteen. A golfer must tack back and forth among the hazards like a sailor. He must study the immediate mood of each hole each time he mounts the tee, for the slightest change in the wind requires a new strategy. It takes brains as well as technical skill to meet the challenge of St. Andrews, and therein lies its enduring greatness.

The Old Course is moderately long, measuring 6,572 yards from the regular tees, 6,883 yards from the back or "Tiger" tees, created in 1946. From both sets of tees, par is 73, and the record for the extended course, held by Dai Rees, the Welsh professional, is 67. No man has ever played a round without taking at least one 5, though Bobby Jones once got as far as the seventeenth with nothing above a 4 on his card and missed his 4 there only because he muffed a two-foot putt. This seventeenth—called the Road Hole because of the road which runs directly behind the green—is, along with the fourteenth and the eleventh (the Eden), the best known and most frequently copied of the individual holes. About 466 yards long, a most difficult par 4, the seventeenth is an easy hole to collapse on. The ideal drive involves a risky carry over the roofs of Auchterlonie's drying sheds, and the knowledge that the road lurks behind the green inflicts overcautiousness on even the seasoned golfer as he plays the long second shot. The eleventh, one of the two par 3s on the course, can be reached some days with an easy 7-iron; on other days a full spoon is not too much club, so drastically does the direction and force of the wind influence the playing character of its 164 yards. The slanting green is protected by deep, high-walled bunkers, and two finalists in one amateur championship, after frolicking in these pits, halved the hole in eighteen.

Men who have golfed on the Old Course all their lives are startled to find that they keep on uncovering new and hidden ways to play the holes. The most notable case is that of Ted Blackwell, the game's longest driver at the turn of the century, who swore up and down for thirty-five years that the sixteenth hole didn't belong on the same course with the other seventeen. No matter where you hit your drive, the contours around the green were such that you couldn't get your approach shot to sit down within birdie distance of the pin. In his thirty-sixth year of playing the Old Course, Blackwell stumbled upon the secret to the sixteenth. Left of the bunker called the Principal's Nose, Blackwell reported, there was an all but imperceptible hollow in the fairway. If you placed your drive in that hollow instead of swatting it for distance, when you looked toward the green, you saw a perfect channel down the fairway and over the apron to the pin. After this discovery, Blackwell actually was able to birdie the sixteenth on an average of once every three rounds.

The natives of St. Andrews have been reared from the cradle to regard golf as a part of living only a little less basic than eating. Seventy-five per cent of the population plays the game, and the nongolfers know the Old Course intimately from their Sunday walks when golfing is prohibited (except on the Eden) and the links becomes the village green. In the evenings there is usually a group of townsfolk gathered behind the eighteenth green, smoking pipes and chatting as they watch a pilgrim struggle home, chuckling among themselves as he lines up his putt, since they know he will fail to notice that the green slopes, almost invisibly, down from the back right-hand corner.

St. Andrews astonishes itself, and those who know it, with the wanton way it loses its characteristic dignity and turns into a Glendale of bobby-soxers when a famous pilgrim, such as General Eisenhower or General Bradley, shows up for a round of golf. The town's most fantastic performance in recent years came on Monday, May 22, 1950, when the first round of the British Amateur got under way. This was the first time since the war that St. Andrews was the scene of that tournament, and the lure of the Old Course attracted a record number of entries (324) which included a record invasion of Americans (35) which in turn included Bing Crosby. For the Scots, Crosby stands forth as the consummate American personality. When the word was released that Bing had mailed in his entry for the Amateur, St. Andrews began to seethe with an excitement it had not known since John Knox inflamed his parishioners to sack the cathedral. Crosby teed off at nine fifty-five that memorable Monday morning against his first-round opponent, a local carpenter and hillbilly singer named Wilson. A cold wind was snarling off the sea and a disagreeably wet rain was falling, but over seven thousand spectators, many of them transported by special bus from other corners of Fifeshire, were happily squashed along the roped-off perimeter of the course straining for a glimpse of the glamourous pilgrim. Bing came through magnificently. He drew spontaneous applause from his vast gallery by scoring two beautiful birdies on the first three holes. Though he ultimately lost the match, 3 and 2, he demonstrated that he was a bona fide golfer. On top of this, he did not play *too* well. He didn't avoid the Old Course's pitfalls. That would have been sacrilegious. Bing left town almost immediately after his match, and St. Andrews gradually regained its composure.

St. Andrews is extremely susceptible to love affairs with certain types of Americans and never forgets the deeds of its heroes. It is twenty-four years since Bobby Jones won the British Open on the Old Course and twenty-one years since he won the British Amateur there, but Bobby's miracles are as fresh in the minds and hearts of

St. Andrews as if they were accomplished yesterday. It is impossible
for a caddie who is toting for an American to walk down the fourth
fairway without pointing out Cottage Bunker from which Bobby
holed a full spade-mashie shot. Whenever Jones played, all of St.
Andrews streamed down to the links to admire its adopted son. On
the afternoon that Bobby opposed Cyril Tolley in the 1930 British
Amateur, the town was completely deserted, a fact that did not escape the attention of Gerald Fairlie, a novelist. In plotting his next
mystery, Fairlie selected that afternoon as the time when the villain
committed murder in downtown St. Andrews and, though covered
with the stains of his crime, was able to make his escape undetected
in broad daylight down the empty streets.

Any visitor can play the Old Course by paying a green fee of three
shillings and sixpence (about fifty cents). The Old Course is a public course, owned by the "ratepayers" of St. Andrews and regulated
by the Town Council. Until 1946, when a Provisional Order was
passed permitting the Council to charge ratepayers thirty shillings a
year for their golf privileges, a green fee had never been levied on
legitimate St. Andresans. It was their links and they could prove it
in writing, going back to the parchment covenant of January 25, 1552,
when the provost and bailies of the town, in granting to Archbishop
Hamilton permission to raise rabbits on the north part of the links,
made certain that he clearly recognized the townsfolks' right to use
the links for drying their fishing nets and bleaching their linen and
for enjoying their "golf, futball, schuting, at all gamis, with all uther
maner of pastime."

One of his successors, Archbishop Gladstanes, went a step further and issued a charter in 1614 which stated that title to the links
was vested in the town. Towards the end of the eighteenth century,
however, St. Andrews, to rescue itself from debt, sold the links to
Mr. Erskine of Cambo. No one stopped playing golf, but titularly the
town had lost possession of the links. In 1894, when the Royal and
Ancient Golf Club of St. Andrews was attempting to buy the land

back from the Cheapes of Strathyrum, into whose hands it had passed, the town was roused to action. If anyone had a right to purchase the links, the Town Council argued, it was the citizens of St. Andrews and not a private club. The issue was debated in Parliament, and two months later, in June, 1894, St. Andrews formally regained its links by paying the Cheape family five thousand pounds.

Most of the ratepayers of St. Andrews live so close to the links that a locker room is a superfluity, but for the golfer who likes to play his extra holes in sympathetic company, there are three clubs he can join. The New Club, founded in 1902, is the one to which business-men and professional men belong. It has close to eight hundred members who pay annual dues of thirty shillings if they live within the town limits or twenty-one shillings if they live in the country. The New Club's modest clubhouse fronts on Links Road beside the eighteenth fairway. Close by stands the St. Andrews Club, the trades-man's and the artisan's club, established in 1843. Since its members, who presently number about nine hundred, must cough up all of fif-teen shillings (or $2.10) a year, it is easy to understand the sudden paralysis that overtakes Scottish emigrants after they have innocently asked the cost of joining an American club. The Royal and Ancient, the third club, is an entirely different type of organization and a story in itself.

The Royal and Ancient is the most important institution in the world of golf, an eminence which its members have come to accept with equanimity. The R & A is not the world's oldest golf club— it is just about everything else—for the Honorable Company of Edinburgh Golfers had banded together a few years before the "twenty-two noblemen and gentlemen" of St. Andrews formed their club in May, 1754. At this first meeting, certain articles and laws, thirteen in number, were drafted to govern the members' play—the oldest surviving code in golf. A century later, when the R & A is-sued a revised codification of twenty-two rules, the club's prestige as a legislative authority had reached the point where all the other golf clubs in Britain willingly accepted the R & A's codification. (The most significant innovation was that eighteen holes constituted one round of golf.) Today, golf clubs throughout the world, with the exception of those in the United States and its outlying possessions, adhere to the rules promulgated by the R & A.

The prestige of membership in the club is enormous. The dues are not. Local members are charged ten guineas annually; English members, eight guineas; and foreign or "supernumerary" members, one guinea. The entrance fee for all is twenty guineas, and the total number of members is limited to one thousand, a figure that has seldom been approached. Earl Mountbatten, Field Marshal Montgomery, General Eisenhower, and the Aga Khan are a few of the front-line personalities who presently belong to the R & A. Winston Churchill was invited to become an honorary member but begged off on the grounds that he had no interest in golf. The supernumerary list includes about sixty Americans, headed by Bobby Jones and Francis Ouimet.

The R & A and the United States Golf Association, the official governing body for American golf, see eye to eye on most important issues, but there are a few interesting deviations. The official British and American golf balls, for example, weigh the same ("not more than 1.62 ounces avoirdupois"), but whereas the American ball must not be less than 1.68 inches in diameter, the R & A specifies a minimum of 1.62 inches. That .06 inch makes a surprisingly great difference, especially on gusty days when the "heavier" British ball bores through winds which blow the American ball right back into the golfer's face. The American ball putts a little better. The R & A regulation which our golfers criticize most frequently is the one barring the Schenectady putter. This ruling, which was apparently conceived in a petulance uncharacteristic of the R & A, went on the books a few years after Walter J. Travis, a choleric but skillful American golfer, had putted his way with his Schenectady model to the British Amateur title in 1904, delivering a terrific blow to British pride, since no foreigner had ever before captured that championship. In this country we define a Schenectady as a putter in which the shaft is joined to the center of the blade. In the British interpretation, however, any putter in which the minutest fraction of the heel extends beyond the intersection of the shaft and the blade is outlawed.

The home of the Royal and Ancient is a stately sandstone club-house, approximately a century old and suitably weather-stained, poised directly behind the first tee of the Old Course. Through its corridors of Canadian yellow pine have passed a succession of members whose main object in life was the advancement of their club, but it is doubtful if any single individual contributed as much as Maj. Murray Belshes of Buttergash. Up to 1834, when Major Belshes swung into action, the club was called the Society of St. Andrews Golfers. In Major Belshes' mind, that wasn't good enough. Nothing short of royal endorsement would do. In a letter to Sir Herbert Taylor, the private secretary of King William IV, Major Belshes retailed his club's glorious history and requested that the king honor the club by becoming its patron. Sir Herbert replied that he was sorry, but consent was out of the question. If the king agreed to be the patron of one golf club, every other golf club in the realm would kick up a fuss. This flat refusal did not perturb Major Murray Belshes. Perhaps he hadn't made things clear, the major wrote; St. Andrews merited a privileged rating and he couldn't see how granting it would be at all indiscreet, especially since the king happened to be Duke of St. Andrews. In 1836, King William agreed to become the club's patron and to permit the club to style itself the Royal and Ancient. In addition, the king sent along a gold medal which became the first prize at the annual autumn tournament.

Most men would have rested on their laurels, but not Maj. Murray Belshes. He next went after Queen Adelaide. She should really become the club's patroness, he argued nicely. After all, *she* was the *Duchess* of St. Andrews. Queen Adelaide gave in. In 1838 the new patroness presented the R & A with a silver medal which, since that date, has been worn by the club captain on all public appearances.

The captaincy of the R & A is held to be the highest honor a British golfer can receive. Originally, the member who turned in the lowest score at the autumn tournament automatically acceded to the captaincy, but this formula was scrapped in 1806 and a rotation set up whereby the captain for one year would be a Scot who was a prominent golfer, to be followed the next year by a distinguished member of Scottish life, to be followed in turn by a local laird, a commoner who held office—then back to a prominent Scottish golfer to start a new three-year cycle. Toward the close of the nineteenth century, after a tremendous fervor for golf had swept over England, this rotation was amended so that the captain every fourth year should be an outstanding English golfer. From time to time the sequence has been interrupted and members of the royal family have been invited to head the club that King William IV made royal as well as ancient. Edward VII accepted the captaincy in 1863, when he was Prince of Wales, and the line has been continued by Prince Leopold in 1876, the Duke of Windsor (then Prince of Wales) in 1922, King George VI (then Duke of York) in 1930, and the late Duke of Kent in 1937. The next member of the royal family slated for the captaincy is the Duke of Edinburgh. The incoming captain inherits, among other things, the locker used by Allan Robertson, the greatest golfer of the first half of the nineteenth century and the R & A's first noteworthy custodian.

One of the many traditional ceremonies which the R & A nourishes calls for the incoming captain to "drive himself into office." On the third Wednesday in September, during the autumn meeting, he steps onto the first tee, the Queen Adelaide medal around his neck. Spread down the fairway before him stand the caddies. Since the caddie who retrieves the captain's ball receives a gold sovereign, each caddie takes up the position where he thinks he has the best chance of fielding the drive. This can make for a delicate situation. When the Duke of Windsor drove himself into office, some of the caddies, in the words of Sir Guy Campbell, "stood disloyally close to the tee." Gold sovereigns are all but extinct nowadays, but rather than default on any part of this ceremony, the R & A has used its influence with the Bank of England to have a small supply of these coins struck specifically for the club. As for the captain's golf ball, it is traditional to cast a facsimile in silver (or in gold when the captain is a member of the royal house) and to fasten it to a silver golf club. All space on the original Silver Golf Club was filled before the nineteenth century had been long under way, and a replacement was then procured by subscription.

At the annual autumn dinner, the silver golf clubs, each drip-ping heavily with silver golf balls, are displayed in front of the head table where sit the former captains in their pink coats. After the toasts and speeches have been concluded and the new captain installed, the members file past and kiss the silver clubs and golf balls. These visible symbols of the club's continuity are draped in blue and white, the club's colors, and carried in front of the R & A contingent on national occasions (such as the abdication of King Edward VIII and the proclamation of the present king) when the club participates in the procession through the streets of the town. The balls and clubs are draped in black for R & A funerals, the most exotic of the club's continuing rituals. To qualify for an R & A funeral, a member must be buried within the city boundaries, for the clubs and balls cannot be taken beyond those limits.

There is at the Royal and Ancient, as in every august British club, a small but articulate coterie of members who have acquired the deep grain of stuffiness invariably produced by life in a leather chair. This ultraconservative element regards the R & A as its private preserve and is daily on the prowl to discover some new grounds for outrage. An inexhaustible subject of discussion among this set is the finan-cial beating the club has been subjected to as a reward for develop-ing the golf links. This point of view is shared by the other members. The R & A, up to 1894, voluntarily supplied the funds for keeping up the Old Course in the style it thought the old girl deserved. Then under the provisions of the Links Act and subsequent governmental ordinances, the R & A, almost as if it were being penalized for some wrongdoing, was *directed* to assume the cost of maintaining the Old Course, ordered to build the New and the Eden and the Jubilee courses and to underwrite the maintenance of the New Course. The expense of keeping the Old and the New in top-notch condition now comes to a pretty farthing, fifty-eight hundred pounds in 1949, for example. The Town Council, which is required by law only to chip in what it considers a fair amount, has seldom contributed more than five hundred pounds in any one year.

* * *

One of the best times for a golfer to make his pilgrimage to St. Andrews is in the late spring. The winters are cold and damp and it requires a native hardiness to enjoy a round without a portable fireplace. The spring is no tranquil pushover for that matter, the wind seldom somnolescent, rain not infrequent. However, it is somehow wrong to play St. Andrews when the wind is not stirring the heather and when there is no threat that a golfer may have to climb into his rainproof trousers and jacket. An excellent fortnight is the first two weeks in June, when the weather is just warm enough, just brisk enough. There are over thirty hotels in St. Andrews for the pilgrim to choose from. On his walk from his hotel to the Old Course to fill out his ballot for the next day, the pilgrim finds himself surrounded on all sides by golf. On the vast municipal putting greens by the sands, children and their mothers, having paid the fees of tuppence and thrippence, are playing the afternoon, away. The full flavor of St. Andrews cannot be savored, to be sure, until the pilgrim is actually on the Old Course, taking that wonderful examination with only his caddie to help him. The caddie fee is six shillings and a penny, but few golfers give their caddie less than a ten-shilling note.

The golfer who does not take a caddie at St. Andrews denies himself the wine of the country. They are a race apart, survivors of another age. McLaren Brown, the dean of the forty-five regulars, is seventy-eight now and not caddying too regularly. Lawrence Buddo Gourley, right behind him at seventy-seven, is almost through caddying too. Back in the nineteenth century, gentle old Gourley taught King Edward VII and the Grand Duke Michael of Russia how to play the game at Cannes. He enjoyed an Indian summer of distinction in the 1920s when he became the Prince of Wales's special caddie. The most loquacious member of the old guard is Bill Hutchison, a brother of the famous Jock. Bill Hutchison may or may not have been teaching golf to the British officers in Egypt when the Boer War broke out. He may or may not have been a boy prodigy who would bet anyone he could hole twenty-five consecutive stymies for a penny. He may or may not be the seventy-three he claims but hardly looks. You have to take Bill Hutchison with a whiff of salt air. During the busy season, starting in May, this corps of regulars is supplemented by young men in their twenties and thirties. They caddie until the slack season sets in in

October, then go up to the Labor Exchange and find odd jobs. In the old days many of these young men would have made caddying their career, but under the Labour Government it is an expensive way of earning a living. Caddies are classified as self-employed individuals and, as such, must purchase a weekly National Health and Unemployment stamp, which comes to six shillings and four pence. In another twenty years the old St. Andrews caddie will be as extinct as the mammoth.

The old St. Andrews caddies do not know every blade of grass on the course but they do know every inch of the colossal greens, each bump in the billowy fairways, the temper of each hazard on any particular morning. They also know golf. They can gauge the game of a stranger on the basis of three or four shots and his reaction to them. From the second hole on, they can tell precisely where each shot will end up simply by watching the player strike the ball—they know how each yard of the Old Course will behave and their bones fill them in on the weather. They take such intense pride in their work that to challenge their "call" on a club is, in their eyes, an attack on their personal integrity. The old regular who caddied for Johnny Bulla in the 1939 Open laid down the bag and walked off the course when Bulla persisted in thinking his next shot was a 5-iron after the caddie had counseled a 4.

The old St. Andrews caddie doesn't "butter up" his man, but no one can be more genuinely understanding of the full gamut of a golfer's feelings. When he is working with an "honest golfer," whether the player is an expert or a duffer, there is no limit to his resourcefulness in "reading the course" for his man. In the 1950 Amateur there was an unusually dramatic illustration of this quiet partnership between player and caddie which undoubtedly is the essence of St. Andrews. In one of his early matches, Willie Turnesa, the former American and British Amateur champion, hooked his tee-shot far off line on a long par 4. His ball ended up at the base of an abrupt rise which shut off all view of the fairway and the green beyond. Willie's caddie studied the situation for a brief moment. He then handed Willie his 5-iron and, pointing an old finger at the sky, said dryly, "Just hit that cloud." Willie hit that cloud and found his ball six feet from the cup.

—1950

Acknowledgements

"What It's Like to Be a Member: A Look behind the Magnolia Curtain at Golf's Secret Citadel," by Dave Anderson. Permission GOLF DIGEST Magazine. From the April 1989 issue. Copyright © 1989 The New York Times Company Magazine Group, Inc.

"The Social Aspect of Playing Through," by Peter Andrews. Permission GOLF DIGEST Magazine. From the July 1996 issue. Copyright © 1996 The New York Times Company Magazine Group, Inc.

"Lining Up a Big Future," by Sarah Pileggi (Ballard) (which appears here as "Nancy Lopez Lines Up a Big Future"). Reprinted courtesy of SPORTS ILLUSTRATED, August 13, 1977. Copyright © 1977, Time Inc. All rights reserved.

"Teravainer" and "Locomotion," by Michael Bamberger. From TO THE LINKSLAND by Michael Bamberger. Copyright © 1992 by Michael Bamberger. Used by permission of Viking Penguin, a division of Penguin Books USA, Inc.

"The Choke Factor," by Thomas Boswell. From GAME DAY by Tom Boswell. Copyright © 1990 by The Washington Post Writers Group. Used by permission of Doubleday, a division of Bantam Doubleday Dell Publishing Group, Inc.

"The Cardiac Cliffs," by Thomas Boswell. From STROKES OF GENIUS by Thomas Boswell. Copyright © 1989 by The Washington Post Writers Group. Used by permission of Doubleday, a division of Bantam Doubleday Dell Publishing Group, Inc.

"Requiem for a Milkman," by Tom Callahan. Permission GOLF DIGEST Magazine. From the September 1995 issue. Copyright © 1995 The New York Times Company Magazine Group, Inc.

"We Know Who They Are," by Tom Callahan. Permission GOLF DIGEST Magazine. From the August 1996 issue. Copyright © 1996 The New York Times Company Magazine Group, Inc.

"The Year of Getting to Know Us," from EMPEROR OF THE AIR. Copyright © 1988 by Ethan Canin. Reprinted by permission of Houghton Mifflin Company. All rights reserved.

"Westchester Keeps a Tournament and Loses an All-Male Sanctuary," by Marcia Chambers. Reprinted with the permission of Pocket Books, a division of Simon & Schuster from THE UNPLAYABLE LIE by Marcia Chambers. Copyright © 1995 by Marcia Chambers.

"A Woman's Trophy and a Men's Grill," by Marcia Chambers. Reprinted with the permission of Pocket Books, a division of Simon & Schuster from THE UNPLAYABLE LIE by Marcia Chambers. Copyright © 1995 by Marcia Chambers.

"On Diegling," by Bernard Darwin. From SECOND SHOTS by Bernard Darwin, published by Georges Newnes, Ltd., London, 1930.

"Golfing Winds," by Bernard Darwin. From A FRIENDLY ROUND by Bernard Darwin, published by Mills and Boon in 1922.

"The Once and Future Gary Player," by Jaime Diaz. From the program of the 1997 Memorial Tournament. Reprinted by permission of the author.

"The Finest Course of All," by Peter Dobereiner. Reprinted with permission from GOLF A LA CARTE by Peter Dobereiner, copyright © 1991. Lyons & Burford, Publishers.

"The Day Joe Ezar Called His Shots for a Remarkable 64," by Peter Dobereiner. Permission GOLF DIGEST Magazine. From the November 1976 issue. Copyright © 1976 The New York Times Company Magazine Group, Inc.

"Francis Ouimet—Drama at Brookline," by Will Grimsley. From the book GOLF: ITS HISTORY, PEOPLE AND EVENTS by Will Grimsley. Copyright © 1966 by Will Grimsley. Reprinted by permission of the author.

"The Layman's Ignorance," by Arnold Haultain (which appears here as "The Mystery of Golf: Chapter One") is reprinted by permission of Applewood Books/Chapman Billies from the book THE MYSTERY OF GOLF by Arnold Haultain.

"Tigermania," by John Hawkins. Permission GOLF WORLD Magazine. From the 1996 Annual Issue. Copyright © 1996 The New York Times Company Magazine Group, Inc.

"The Ride of Greg Norman's Life," by Chris Hodenfield. Permission GOLF DIGEST Magazine. From the May 1995 issue. Copyright © 1995 The New York Times Company Magazine Group, Inc.

"The Glory Game at Goat Hills," by Dan Jenkins. From FAIRWAYS AND GREENS by Dan Jenkins. Copyright © 1995 by D&J Ventures. Used by permission of Doubleday, a division of Bantam Doubleday Dell Publishing Group, Inc.

"My Semi-tough Return to Playing Golf," by Dan Jenkins. Permission GOLF DIGEST Magazine. From the March 1990 issue. Copyright © 1990 The New York Times Company Magazine Group, Inc.

"Bouncing Back from a National Bout," by Robert Jones. From the book DOWN THE FAIRWAY by Robert T. Jones, Jr., and O. B. Keller, copyright © 1927 by Minton, Balch & Company.

"Playing the Old Course with Joyce Wethered," by Robert T. Jones, Jr. From THE AMERICAN GOLFER. Copyright © 1930 (renewed 1958, 1986) by The Conde Nast Publications, Inc. Permission granted by Conde Nast Publications, Inc.

"A Zone of His Own: Tiger Woods," by Peter de Jonge. Copyright © 1995 by Peter de Jonge. First published in THE NEW YORK TIMES

MAGAZINE. Reprinted by permission of Sterling Lord Literistic Inc. as agent for the author.

"The Dogleg on Five," from JACK GANCE by Ward Just. Copyright © 1989 by Ward Just. Reprinted by permission of Houghton Mifflin Company. All rights reserved.

"The Mower," by James Kaplan. Reprinted by permission; copyright © 1981 by James Kaplan. Originally in THE NEW YORKER. All rights reserved.

"The Babe Comes Back," by Al Laney. Copyright © 1954 by Al Laney. First printed in the NEW YORK HERALD TRIBUNE, July 4, 1954.

"The Golfomaniac," from LAUGH WITH LEACOCK by Stephen Leacock. Copyright © 1930 by Dodd, Mead, & Company.

"Hidden Extras," by Henry Longhurst. From THE ESSENTIAL HENRY LONGHURST edited by Chris Plumridge. Copyright © 1962 by Henry Longhurst. Reprinted by permission of HarperCollins Publishers, Ltd.

"The Coming of the Bear," by Henry Longhurst. From THE ESSENTIAL HENRY LONGHURST edited by Chris Plumridge. Copyright © 1962 by Henry Longhurst. Reprinted by permission of Harper-Collins Publishers, Ltd.

"Swingin' in the Rain," by Charles McGrath. Reprinted by permission; copyright © 1981 Charles McGrath. Originally in THE NEW YORKER. All rights reserved.

From GOLF IN THE KINGDOM by Michael Murphy. Copyright © 1972 by Michael Murphy. Used by permission of Viking Penguin, a division of Penguin Books USA Inc.

"They Might Be Giants," by John Paul Newport from MEN'S JOURNAL, July/August 1993. By Men's Journal Company, L.P., 1993. All rights reserved. Reprinted by permission.

"Grown Men on Spring Break," by David Owen. Copyright © 1995 by David Owen. From the book MY USUAL GAME: ADVENTURES IN GOLF and reprinted by permission of the author.

"And Some of the Men in My Life," by Harvey Penick with Bud Shrake. Reprinted with the permission of Simon & Schuster from HARVEY PENICK'S LITTLE RED BOOK by Harvey Penick with Bud Shrake. Copyright © 1992 by Harvey Penick and Bud Shrake, and Helen Penick.

"Arnold Palmer," by George Plimpton (which appears here as "An Interview with Arnold Palmer"). Reprinted from BOGEYMAN, copyright © 1967. Lyons & Burford, Publishers.

"The Last Days of Bobby Jones," by Charles Price. Permission GOLF DIGEST Magazine. From the March 1990 issue. Copyright © 1990 The New York Times Company Magazine Group, Inc.

Reprinted courtesy of SPORTS ILLUSTRATED, August 21, 1989. Copyright © 1989, Time Inc. "Love That Golf," by Rick Reilly. All rights reserved.

"My Favorite Caddy," by Gene Sarazen. Reprinted with the permission of Simon & Schuster from THIRTY YEARS OF CHAMPION-SHIP GOLF: THE LIFE AND TIMES OF GENE SARAZEN by Gene Sarazen with Herbert Warren Wind. Copyright © 1950 by Prentice-Hall, Inc., renewed 1978.

"What Makes the Ideal Clubhouse—and Club?" by Jerry Tarde. Permission GOLF DIGEST Magazine. From the August 1992 issue. Copyright © 1992 The New York Times Company Magazine Group, Inc.

"Farrell's Caddie," by John Updike. From GOLF DREAMS by John Updike. Copyright © 1996 by John Updike. Reprinted by permission of Alfred A. Knopf, Inc. Originally appeared in THE NEW YORKER.

"The Pro," by John Updike. From GOLF DREAMS by John Updike. Copyright © 1996 by John Updike. Reprinted by permission of Alfred A. Knopf, Inc.

"The Camaraderie of Golf—II," by John Updike. Permission GOLF DIGEST Magazine. From the February 1986 Issue. Copyright © 1986 The New York Times Company Magazine Group, Inc.

"St. Andrews: The Cradle of Golf," by Herbert Warren Wind. From THE GUILDED AGE OF SPORT, copyright © 1961 by Herbert Warren Wind. Reprinted by permission of the author.

"Nicklaus and Watson at Turnberry," by Herbert Warren Wind. From FOLLOWING THROUGH, copyright © 1985, 1995 by Herbert Warren Wind. Reprinted with permission of the author. Originally appeared in THE NEW YORKER.

Any errors or omissions are entirely unintentional. If notified, the publisher will be pleased to make any necessary amendments at the earliest opportunity.

The editors would like to thank *Golf Digest* for their generous support in compiling this anthology.